LEGITIMACY IN THE MODERN STATE

John H. Schaar

Transaction Publishers
New Brunswick (U.S.A.) and Oxford (U.K.)

Third printing 2000
Copyright © 1981 by Transaction Publishers, New Brunswick, New Jersey.

All rights reserved under International and Pan-American Copyright Conventions. No part of this book may be reproduced or transmitted in any form or by any means, electronic or mechanical, including photocopy, recording, or any information storage and retrieval system, without prior permission in writing from the publisher. All inquiries should be addressed to Transaction Publishers, Rutgers—The State University, 35 Berrue Circle, Piscataway, New Jersey 08854-8042.

This book is printed on acid-free paper that meets the American National Standard for Permanence of Paper for Printed Library Materials.

Library of Congress Catalog Number: 79-66442
ISBN: 0-87855-337-1
ISBN: 0-88738-772-1 (paper)
Printed in the United States of America

Library of Congress Cataloging in Publication Data

Schaar, John H
   Legitimacy in the modern state.

   Includes bibliographical references.
   1. Legitimacy of governments--Addresses, essays,lectures. 2. Authority--Addresses, essays, lectures.
I. Title
JC328.2.S3   301.5'92   79-66442
ISBN 0-87855-337-1
ISBN 0-88738-772-1 (pbk.)

LEGITIMACY IN THE MODERN STATE

Contents

Acknowledgments vii
Foreword 1
1. Legitimacy in the Modern State 15
2. The Uses of Literature for the Study of Politics:
   The Case of Melville's *Benito Cereno* 53
3. Review of Diana Trilling's *We Must March My Darlings* .. 89
4. The American Amnesia 99
5. America the Homogeneous 109
6. The Circles of Watergate Hell 117
7. Reflections on Rawls' *A Theory of Justice* 145
8. Some Ways of Thinking About Equality 167
9. Equality of Opportunity, and Beyond 193
10. Equality of Opportunity and the Just Society 211
11. ... And the Pursuit of Happiness 231
12. Insiders and Outsiders 251
13. Violence in Juvenile Gangs 273
14. The Case for Patriotism 285
15. Power and Purity 313
16. Decadence and Revitalization:
    Reflections on the Present Condition 331

Acknowledgments

Most of my debts are owed to writers long dead, and one pays those debts as best one can. I try to remember the normal vanity of such casual expressions as "my idea," "my view," "my understanding," for "my idea," of course, is usually something borrowed from a lender now conveniently forgotten.

The largest of the debts I have incurred among my contemporaries are as much the debts of friendship as of particular instruction. I must hope that my service to the friendships discharged the debts even as they were incurred. I want to mention Francis Carney, Peter Euben, Marge Frantz, Norman Jacobson, Hanna Pitkin, Doug Lummis, Jeff Lustig, and Sheldon Wolin. These people have taught me something about how to think and teach. They have done their best to sweeten my mulishness, and have stood by me even at the risk of getting kicked. These people are to me, as much as I am to myself, my inner audience. Their friendship is a treasure which those who know them will appreciate.

*****

Grateful acknowledgment is made to the following publishers for granting permission to reprint previously published material:

"Legitimacy in the Modern State," in *Power and Community: Dissenting Essays in Political Science*, eds. Philip Green and Sanford Levinson. Copyright© 1970 Random House, Inc. Reprinted by permission of Pantheon Books, a division of Random House, Inc.

"The Uses of Literature for the Study of Politics: The Case of Melville's *Benito Cereno*," *Theory and Society* 7 (1979): 417-52.

"Review of Diana Trilling's *We Must March My Darlings*," *Society* 16, 4 (May/June 1979): 82-88.

"The American Amnesia," reprinted with permission from *The New York Review of Books*. Copyright© 1976 Nyrev, Inc.

"America the Homogeneous," *Worldview* (March 1974): 47-50.

"The Circles of Watergate Hell," with Francis M. Carney, *American Review* 21 (October 1974): 1-42.

"Reflections on Rawls' Theory of Justice," *Social Theory and Practice* 3, 1 (Spring 1974): 75-100.

"Some Ways of Thinking About Equality," *Journal of Politics* 26, 4 (November 1964): 867-95.

"Equality of Opportunity, and Beyond," in *Equality*, eds. J. Roland Pennock and John W. Chapman. Reprinted by permission of the publishers, Lieber-Atherton, Inc. Copyright© 1967, all rights reserved.

"Equality of Opportunity and the Just Society," in *John Rawls' Theory of Social Justice,* eds. Blocker, Smith and Trevas, Ohio University Press, 1980.

". . . And the Pursuit of Happiness," *Virginia Quarterly Review* 46, 1 (Winter 1970): 1-27.

"Insiders and Outsiders," *Steps* 2 (Fall 1966): 2-15.

"Violence in Juvenile Gangs," *American Journal of Orthopsychiatry* 33, 1 (January 1963): 29-37. Copyright© 1963 American Orthopsychiatric Association, Inc.

"The Case for Patriotism," *American Review* 17 (May 1973): 59-100.

"Power and Purity," *American Review* 19 (January 1974): 152-80.

Foreword

Where These Essays Come From

All but three of the essays collected here were first published elsewhere. Other than bringing the pieces into stylistic uniformity, I have made no, or few, and only trivial alterations in them. This is not because I love even my errors and awkwardnesses, but because so much needs improvement that silent correction would have amounted to deceit and explicit correction would have made the whole a labyrinth.

One justification for bringing together in a single place writings published in scattered places is the reader's convenience. Another is that book covers may grant a modest extension of life to work first published in sometimes obscure, specialized or now defunct journals. Whether the essays compose something like a real book, with a center and boundaries, and the parts gathering resonances from each other and the whole, is not mainly for me to judge. If they do not make a book, nothing I could write in introducing them will alter that fact.

There are overlappings and redundancies. A few themes appear time and again, sometimes in a dominant and sometimes in a minor key. This is not entirely a disadvantage, for the themes are inexhaustible, and the connections among them many and complex. But I must admit that I have sometimes enviously compared my poverty with Luther's riches: he had ninety-five theses; I have only two or three. Nor can I even say that I have treated any of my themes fully. Still, my partial treatments might help other workers toward their own fuller achievements.

The guiding themes are authority, equality, justice, and citizenship—topics mainly, though not exclusively, of political interest. Another motif, the bearing of the past on the present, runs throughout. It seems to me that one of the characteristics of our time, though of course not of our time alone, is that the bearing of the past on the present is thoroughly problem-

2 LEGITIMACY IN THE MODERN STATE

atic. I shall say a little more about that later on in these introductory remarks.

Concerning authority, I believe that genuine authority is all but lost to us today, and that perhaps we have lost even the concept of authority, so that we cannot know what honorable obedience consists in. This is no small loss, and no amount of liberation will make up for it, because if we do not know what authority is, we cannot know what liberty is either. Perhaps that is why so many people today find themselves as bewildered and unsatisfied after a succession of liberations as they were before.

On the subject of equality, Paine and Tocqueville have provided my political and moral reference points. Paine wrote, with permissible exaggeration, that "inequality of rights has been the cause of all the disturbances, insurrections, and civil wars, that ever happened. . . ." Tocqueville, looking anxiously into an equalitarian future, wrote that "to conceive of men remaining forever unequal upon a single point, yet equal on all others, is impossible; they must come in the end to be equal upon all." Paine cautions that we cannot have peace and decency without equality, and Tocqueville cautions that we may not be able to have liberty and excellence with it. I am caught between the two warnings, and clarity is the victim. Maybe the dilemma is "only" as sharp as Paine and Tocqueville posed it, and not as sharp as, say, Jesus and Nietzsche posed it, but that is still sharp enough. However, equality is on the political agenda today, and I have wanted to say something useful about it.

Concerning the third subject, participation in the shaping and sharing of the common life, I have only one thesis, and it is not new. The modern state does not want citizens, cannot recognize them when they appear, and treats them rudely when it bumps into them. Politically considered, most of us are children; and very little in our culture encourages growth towards political adulthood. This has seemed to me a lamentable condition. It is surely faithless to the premises we exchanged at the founding, and a retreat from the noble prospects we offered ourselves then.

Perhaps I have overworked the lamentation. Still, the bargain we have made—to turn public affairs over to professional politicians and administrators in exchange for private liberty—is a dangerous one. (In 1802, there was one federal public "servant" for every 1,914 citizens; in 1966, there was one for every sixty-two.) Tocqueville said that to take politics away from the American would be to take half his life. That sets a benchmark for measuring how much we have lost. And much recent experience teaches once again the old lesson that people who care only for their private liberties will lose them as well.

These essays were written to encourage, to warn, to criticize, and to recommend. They have been written by one who has a lover's quarrel with his country. Now, this does not mean that I am a patriot in the "my country right or wrong" sense. Should it ever come to the choice between betraying my country or my friends, I hope, along with E.M. Forster, that I would have the courage to stand with my friends. Nor does it mean that I think my mission in life is to do good for the Americans. I do not think of myself as a national resource. Nor do I believe that the world-historical process marches across my desk.

What it does mean is that I care a lot about the quality of the public lives we lead, and that I wish that quality was higher. I am pretty sure that we are building a future we shall not want, and one we would not choose if we knew how to choose otherwise. I am pretty sure that it is terribly difficult for young people to grow up without a country they can love and respect. That care and those two beliefs have compelled me to public questions, characteristically in an indignant and sometimes even censorious mood. I worry a lot about the effectiveness of that tone—as Lincoln said, honey draws more flies than vinegar—and about my right to assume it: who issued my commission? And I know very well that the people of this land stand much in need of comfort—though perhaps not as much comfort as, say, Norman Rockwell or candidate Carter offered them. In the big marine hospital in Danang during the Vietnam War there was a section called the "White Lie Ward." That was where the worst cases were brought, those who would survive but never be whole again. The chaplains and nurses assured the victims that they would be okay. For a generation now the people of this country have been kept in the White Lie Ward by their highest officers of state.

It is out of some such muddle of emotion and belief that these essays have been drawn. Knowing the muddle for what it is, I have been hesitant about calling other kettles black, and cautious about recommending polishes that might brighten them. Where I have offered programmatic suggestions, they are always bent toward smallness, variety, and conservation, and away from bigness, uniformity, and exploitation. I think we have learned everything there is to know about doing things in the "big" way, have experienced every advantage and disadvantage that way can offer. If I could, I would join Henry Adams' party of Conservative Christian Anarchy—with the proviso, which Adams might not have liked, that under CCA the anarchists would be required to work the factories, since the discipline would be good for them.

A number of the essays came out of and reflect back upon (sometimes directly, sometimes obliquely) a specific political milieu—the 1960s. I was in the storm center called Berkeley during those years, and watched and participated in events as a sympathetic but critical friend of the New Left: another lovers' quarrel. Sheldon Wolin and I wrote a number of pieces reporting and interpreting the events of those days while they were unfolding. Since those essays were coauthored, I have not included them here.[1]

4 LEGITIMACY IN THE MODERN STATE

The pieces included here which came out of the sixties were written after the events. They are in the nature of efforts to try to understand part of my own past and part of the country's past as well. Hence, they have the advantages and disadvantages of hindsight. I did not then, nor do I now, think it bliss to be alive in that dawn. But neither could I then, nor can I now, join the chorus of those who thought and think that either nothing or something awful happened then. A lot happened, and a lot of it was and is more hopeful than anything that has happened in domestic politics since the early days of the Populist movement. Some cracks were started in the glacier, and the recent cold spell has only temporarily glazed them over again. The great struggles of the sixties counted for much, and the silence of the seventies is not the silence of the grave but the quiet of individuals and groups rethinking their situation and re-forming their beliefs and affiliations, preparing for the uncertainties ahead.

It was soothing and satisfying for many then and now to see the struggles of the sixties as foolish and destructive. It was much easier then as now to make media sensations out of the buffooneries and excesses of a few than to look at the many thousands below who struggled intelligently and courageously to reduce the gross inequalities of dignity, power, and wealth both here and abroad. It was comforting then as now to see those thousands who taunted the powers-that-be and refused the bovine complacencies of middle-class life as themselves only children in a tantrum or animals in a zoo.

But it was and is false comfort. The sixties made a difference—in civil rights; in the unmasking of militarism and imperialism; in the revival of the women's movement; in raising the ecological question; in the development and testing of new modes of political action. Those differences remain. Their presence means that the next surge of action for political change will start from a higher theoretical and political level than was the case in the early sixties. Just as those who proclaimed the "end of ideology" in the 1950s and saw America as the good society in action were made bankrupt by the decade that followed, so will those who now seize upon the calm for comfort be surprised when the next round opens.

Those who counsel that the path of prudence is to relinquish all causes and give up hoping for good effects do more than try vainly to make the present permanent. They contribute to the rage that results when people are told their futures have been frozen.

The sixties opened on a note of hope and possibility. But action can come from anger and despair as well, and there is a lot of that now. I know no period of American history in which there has been so little joy, hope, or meaning in daily life as there is at present. What is going on in the minds of the middle-class young as they think about the world that awaits them?

Will they settle into resigned careerism, or will the gathering desperation explode into rage? Will the energies that once produced a black mass movement for change continue to fizzle into crime and into individual efforts to join the (diminishing) black bourgeoisie, or will the millions who already hold the cities and their own lives as of little value move to smash a world that has no place or need for them? As unemployment and inflation rise, as the moral absenteeism of the organized and prosperous groups grows, as we approach the end of the era of cheap energy and the private automobile, will the distresses of the poor continue to take the form of self-denial and self-disgust, or will their private hells spill over into collective nightmares that burn far more than the houses of the oppressed?

My crystal ball is as clouded as that of the Council of Economic Advisors. But it is not as clouded as that of the people who now declare noble dreams impossible and call apathy good sense. Movements can be temporarily defused, but angry and forlorn souls cannot be permanently stifled. Unless it can find hopeful political and social form, the present deceptive calm may turn into a whirlwind. It is out of that concern that I have written some essays on the sixties. I have wanted to keep the thread of hopeful memory unbroken. I have also tried to find possibilities in the present that might give encouragement to collective efforts toward a better future.

The essays have been drawn from another source as well. In my daily work I am a teacher of political theory, and I try through that work to encourage students to think about what we are doing now. These essays partly originate in that activity. Since mine may not be the typical way of doing the work (to judge from talks with colleagues, and from reading their writings) I want to say something about it.

A teacher of political theory is not a political theorist. Indeed, such a teacher may have no better notion than anyone else of what it is like to be a political theorist. Perhaps the teacher of political theory is to theory as the teacher of literature is to literature. Or, at least, one can perform many of the same operations on a theoretical text that one can perform on a literary text. And teachers of theory, like teachers of literature, are prone to develop theories of their subject—theories of writing; theories of reading; theories of interpretation; theories of theory. Among academic persons, the metatheory often comes to supplant the theory itself.

This has always seemed to me a particularly harmful move in my subject. For political theory insistently invites (solicits, begs, urges) belief and action based upon the belief. Political theory always has a didactic and practical intent. It aims to change belief, to instruct and persuade, to recommend one position or attitude over another. Some literature of course has that intent too, and so has some philosophy. But much does not.

Indeed, in philosophy, a Kierkegaard or a Nietzsche are the exceptional figures, and a Hume or a Hegel the norm.

But one surely does not teach political theory in order to persuade students to think and do as Plato or Hobbes or . . . recommends. Professional ethics frowns on that sort of thing. Besides, the effort would be largely wasted anyway, since most teachers are not masters of persuasion, and since most theorists' specific concerns and interests have no easily specified bearing on the issues we confront.

Sometimes the study of a theorist can teach much about the origins and basic character of the institutions and practices of our own day. That interest surely makes Adam Smith, or John Locke, or the authors of *The Federalist*, or Lenin, or Luther, or Aquinas worth reading. But by that criterion, many, perhaps even most, of the theorists who are usually held to be "great" would not be taught: Plato, Aristotle, Thucydides, Marsilius, Spinoza, Montesquieu, Hume, Hegel probably would not make the list. If "importance" in shaping our actual political lives were the criterion for selection, we would probably move toward those who combined an important political career with reflection and polemic on the issues of their day and place: More, Robespierre, Jefferson, Churchill, Gandhi, Mao, Castro, and Hitler.

We might study and teach political theory as part of a general course of humanistic education. Knowledge of the tradition can stock the mind with useful maxims and elegant allusions, and perhaps help shape the character toward prudence and justice. There is nothing wrong with this justification, but it does make of teacher and student little more than seller and buyer of ornamental merchandise. At least, few of us are as sure of the impact of our teaching, whether for good or ill, on the students as R.G. Collingwood was when he charged the "minute" philosophers of his day at Oxford with preparing the way for fascism.

In the heady early years of the "behavioral revolution" some writers proposed that we should approach the classics of political theory as an exploitable resource for the advancement of scientific knowledge. We could mine the great books for hypotheses, which might then be tested empirically. Those that survived the ordeal would be added to the stock of scientifically valid propositions about politics. A few actual efforts of this sort were made, Lasswell and Kaplan's *Power and Society* is a case in point, but on the whole the results proved disappointing. The testable hypotheses were either too many or too few, and it was difficult to say what they were. Science did not grow, and one does not hear much of this anymore. The scientists now proceed with their work little encumbered by "normative" theory, while continuing to advise students that there is some value in the subject, though it is hard to say just what the value might be. Most large departments of political science still have a theorist or two whom his colleagues designate as "normative." Such types usually stand off to the side of the department, and are kept on largely for reasons of habit and sentiment.

A few contemporaries, most notably Leo Strauss, Eric Voegelin, and Sheldon Wolin, have tried to say what political theory is, and even to say what correct knowledge of political theory is. However, less of that sort of thing goes on among those who teach political theory than among those who teach literature, where it is difficult to be accepted and impossible to be distinguished without a theory of literature and a theory of interpretation. There are signs of movement, however: a few years back, some teachers of theory dallied with phenomenology; now, some yearn for the embrace of structuralism, if only they could figure out what that is. But most still move within the honored tradition, founded perhaps by Hume, of being better at saying what the subject is not than at saying what it is. Hume managed, ingeniously, to lose philosophy's three primary subjects—self, substance, God—and since that loss it has been easier for philosto say what philosophy is not than to say what it is.

Following Hume's lead, it is easy to say what political theory is not. It is not ideology. Nor is it, at least essentially, a means of arousing emotion. Political theory is a cognitive enterprise of sorts, bringing knowledge of a certain kind, but it is not a scientific enterprise, at least not as we understand the term "scientific" today, and it does not bring direct and verifiable knowledge about the world. Tocqueville captured this in his aphorism that God has no need of general ideas, since He knows all the facts. Theoretical knowledge is at one and the same time a proud achievement and a confession of ignorance.

Thus, for example, it is possible to show what Socrates' thesis concerning justice is, and we might even be able to show that this thesis holds within *The Republic,* but there is no way, nor have we any obligation, to show that it holds outside that book. In the sciences that bring knowledge, on the other hand, every thesis or proposition is subject to external assessment. But in political theory, where everything that is asserted can only be debated within the text wherein the assertion is made, naturally nothing is asserted about the world. That being so, it follows that political theory has no demonstrable and direct social utility.

All these things theory is not.

This route leads to the conclusion that an interest in political theory, or a devotion to it, or a claim to see value in it, is in the end "merely" personal. There is good cause to flinch from such a sharp conclusion: academic persons feel naked outside a context of rational demonstration of the nature and value of an activity or an interest.

This may or may not be a good description of the troubled condition of teachers of political theory. It is surely no description at all of the political theorists. They had work to do in the world and it was work of the most important sort—taming tyrants, instructing kings and popes, making citizens, reforming laws, scrubbing words clean of their dirty meanings, laying the foundations of just and lasting states, defending friends and chastising enemies. We may look back and see their projects failed, but these were their projects. Seeing their projects failed, we may reflect on the vainglory of the authors, or remove ourselves even farther by developing sophisticated treatments of "theory and practice," or by fashioning elaborate theories of "interpretation." And thus our work becomes Alexandrian, our audience narrow, and our own superiority assured, if insignificant. The masters of the schools are subtle, polymath; while Sweeney stirs the water in his bath.

The world does not come to our studies seeking counsel. There is no Aristotle among us, and no Alexander either. But suppose we were asked. What then would teachers of political theory have to say to politicians and citizens? And should we not proceed in our work as if we might be asked, holding ourselves responsible for answering? Responding affirmatively to that question would alter substantially the shape and content of most teaching of political theory in universities. The strategists make plans with the generals; the planners regulate and predict; the professors of political theory sharpen their pens for—each other. Where are the counselors of the people?

For we really do have a people, a large and ready audience. Millions of young people attend colleges and universities, and tens of thousands of them take work in political theory. They will learn something, and we have something to do with that. The teacher of political theory who cannot respond seriously and substantively to the student's question, asked earnestly and ingenuously—"Why should I study political theory? Why should I devote hours to Plato's *Republic?* After all, there are so many other things to learn and do. Why this one?" has forgotten the first duty of the teacher's vocation.

So, while there remains something of the "merely personal" in the choice to teach political theory—and of what theory to teach, and how—there are also considerations of utility, and even of final value. Furthermore, even after we make all the statements (and more) that I have mentioned—statements about what theory is not and what it cannot do; statements which deny theory's practical value—this still leaves the subject on no shakier ground than many another. Pressed hard, every argument reaches some point at which statements stand (or fall) alone. It is either that or infinite regression. Bentham was just more honest than most when he acknowledged of the principle of utility that it, being used to prove everything else, could not itself be proved. Recognizing this might relieve us of some of our felt inferiorities in the face of the plainly practical subjects. It might also arm us against the temptations of metatheory and interpretation, our current forms of "bad infinity."

It now becomes possible to offer a fairly straightforward answer to the questions, why teach theory; what theory; and how?

Theory is a form or modality of thought. As such, the choice for it can be no more (and no less, either) than any choice for thinking over not thinking. The choice must rest on something like Socrates' statement that the unexamined life is not worth living. That, of course, is not wholly true, but it is a valuable half-truth. Add to that the widespread feeling that we as a people, a culture, are messing things up. A lot of our standard ways of doing and thinking, from welfare to warfare, are working badly, and we are making a lot of trouble for others and ourselves. Giving thought to what we are doing might reduce the damage and confusion. Remember that U.S. officer in Vietnam who said "We had to destroy Ben Tu in order to save it." When standard ways of thinking and acting reach such depths of bewilderment and destruction as that, then it is time for rethinking. There need be no stronger claims made for the value of thinking over blinking.

Now, taking political theory as a species of thought, what might be said for it?

Political theory invites us to think generally about matters of general or common concern. It teaches one much about the labyrinthine pathways between the seemingly most personal and the seemingly most distant and abstract things. Hence, training in this kind of thinking can help guard the mind against the egoistic fallacy—the thinker's version of what Norman O. Brown has called the *"causa sui* project." This is a beguilement, or temptation, which lures one into seeing oneself as self-caused and self-creating, while all other persons and realities are banished to the periphery. In its intellectualist version, one idea spawns another, and soon ideas, the thinker's ideas, come to seem the only reality. But the concerns and realities of others are pressingly present in good political thinking: such thinking is always what Hannah Arendt called "representative." Hence, training in political theory can provide defenses against the temptations of egoistic or solipsistic thinking. Such defenses are particularly valuable in this culture where, as many observers have noted, the narcissistic sensibility is growing.

Political theory constantly reminds us that the world we live in is a human construction, that we are creatures who to a significant degree choose and produce our own worlds. Political theory, thus, is thought in an activist mode. It implicates the thinker in the materials. It treats its materials as matters requiring judgment, choice, and action.

This activist and implicative character of political theory is fortified by two other traits of political theory as a species of thought. First, every great theorist has been intensely aware of the intricate and strong connections between personality, or "human nature," and the political regime. The polis is the individual writ large, as Plato saw it; or each type of regime rests on certain human passions and interest, as Montesquieu saw it. Secondly, unlike philosophy and science, which claim to study what is, political theory also always studies what might be other than it is. Political theoretical thinking must always seek the boundaries and draw the line between the necessary and the contingent, between that which cannot be other than it is and that which might be different. Once again, the study implicates the student, stressing engagement, responsibility, action. This is an immensely valuable feature of political theory, especially during such a time as our own when so many social forces and modes of thinking teach disengagement and passivity.

The question of theory and practice is livelier and more decisive for political theory than for any other modality of thought. Political theorists have always been concerned with reordering society, hence with action and possibility. But they have been equally concerned with the limits of the power of thought or ideas to reorder the world. Political theory is concerned with action, but it is also in part a substitute for action. Even as a substitute, however, the theorists' ideas have never been presented with a merely or even mainly "academic" intention, but always out of a yearning to realize a vision of a transformed society. Rousseau spoke for all the rest when he said in *The Social Contract,* "If I were a prince or a legislator I should not waste time in saying what wants doing; I should do it, or hold my peace." Marx's famous eleventh thesis on Feuerbach, far from overturning the traditional priority of thought over practice, as some writers have argued, echoes themes in Plato, Aristotle, Aquinas, More, Machiavelli, Hobbes, Bentham and Tocqueville. Theory and practice coexist in a wondrously fruitful tension in political theory; and that tension, once again, enlivens the student of the subject by calling attention to the world, permitting no easy compartmentalization of life into the "real" and the "ideal."

Although the passion for renewal has been very deep among the theorists, so too has been their recognition of the difficulty and complexity of the task. Out of this mixed yearning and recognition the theorists have made two things: 1) fantasies of redemption, usually personified in some potent figure (Rousseau's Legislator; Machiavelli's Founder; Plato's Philosopher-King), or located in some social formation or historical process (Hegel's *Geist;* Marx's Proletariat); and 2) profound treatments of the interconnections among the components of social order—religion, educational ideas, family institutions, law, economic practices, interstate relationships, individual and social psychology, the nature of belief both among ordinary folk and among the learned and philosophical. Hence, the great works of political theory are equally storehouses of ideas and information, and models of how to think, and how not to think about social order and change. The study of political theory can both quicken the impulse toward social reconstruction, and teach much about its dangers and complexities. This is a particularly valuable feature of the study today, when so much visionary and reformist thought is either a kind of Faustianism, or else a species of technical, administrative, or psychological gadgeteering.

The political theorists have been profoundly aware of the role of illusion (myth, superstition, opinion, religion) in individual and collective life, and have asked whether, in the interests of a just and lasting order, illusion might be replaced by true knowledge, or perhaps just a bad illusion replaced by a good one. No study known to me raises this question more sharply than the study of political theory. Must life rest on illusion? How can we know when we ourselves are laboring under one or another false belief, even while we vigorously charge our enemies with the same? We are creatures who almost "by nature" deceive ourselves, make mistakes about who we are and what we have done. The sources of self-deception are many, and it is extremely difficult to become aware of their workings. Memory is unreliable because we have a deep need for a past that is agreeable to us. The views that others take of us are important to us, and, though they are often mistaken, those views still "contaminate" our thinking. Both success and failure in our activities can produce falsification of the motives, aims, and intentions of action. Success can glorify and seem to make right any action, while failure casts the shadow of remorse over even the highest and most honorable deeds, with the result, in either case, that we may not even remember what we had intended to do and why we had intended to do it. Being able to think theoretically is no sure defense against these mistakes and self-deceptions but it is as strong as any defense we have. The great political theorists were great explorers of the empires of illusion—and architects of such empires of their own too, of course—and the student who retraces their journeys will find marvelous descriptions of real and fabulous beasts, and might eventually, with help, glimpse such beasts in himself.

Required by their subject to try to draw the line between the necessary and the contingent, impelled by the urge to reconstruct the public world, and forced to recognize the constitutive role of ideas and beliefs in the construction of "reality," the political theorists offer material that can help the student toward an understanding that the currently dominant (scientific) conception of truth, or of true knowledge, is not only not the only possible one, but in the human subjects may not even be the richest or most useful one. In the three languages (Greek, Latin, Hebrew) which have contributed the most to the formation of the Western mind the original and dominant meanings attached to the words for "truth" are radically different. The Greek *aletheia* referred to that which is made present or revealed, that which manifests itself, is not covered up or hidden. Truth is the unveiling or disclosure of the things that are, as they are. The Latin *veritas* refers not so much to things as to utterance, and indicates exact and complete statement, reporting things as they really happened, giving a strict and precise account of events. The Hebrew *emunah* concerns truth in the sense of trust and confident expectation, implying commitment and conviction: the true friend is the one on whom you can rely, whereas the false friend is of course not a nonexistent friend but a friend who fails you, who is not reliable.[2]

It is a marvelously rich resource, this concept, and one which every child understands and uses. Only in the schools, as it were, and after strict training, do we learn first to break the cluster apart, and then to argue that only one meaning of truth can be "correct." We are taught that truth is an adequate relation between the intellect and some "reality," the latter posited as univocal and "out there." Or some argue that truth applies only to utterance, and consists in coherent relationships among statements. Or the scientific conception of true knowledge (inductive, tested by an accepted method, predictive, cumulative) is offered as the only correct one. Against these narrow notions, our language reminds us that when it comes to what we need to know in order to live and act in our situation, then truth is a rich composite of varying portions of revelation and discovery, accurate statement, and commitment and conviction. The tradition of political theory provides rich resources for the study of these various possibilities of truth, and reminds us that there are other forms of knowledge and other modes of knowing which can claim equal authority with the scientific model. Given the tyranny of science today, that is no small liberation.

These are among the reasons why the study of politcal theory can be challenging and valuable work. Political theory is not a progressive or cumulative discipline, and yet it does bring valuable knowledge of a number of kinds. We do not, with each new book and theory, move a step closer to true knowledge of politics, but we do come to appreciate how theories achieve new formulations of problems and fashion new criteria of evidence and proof. Through this study, we can come to appreciate how, to a large degree, we live not in a "world"—objective, univocal, out there— but in a description of a world, where our very perceptions are shaped by our perspectives and paradigms.

All this means that for teachers of political theory the question of the relationship of the past of the subject to its present can never be definitively settled. The field has a canon of major works. Some scholars even see something like a great tradition, with classic calling and responding to classic down through the ages in unbroken line. The task of the teacher is to keep alive the truths already known, and the task of the student is to learn them. Others, myself among them, think the "great tradition" is largely an artifact of interpretation. The questions change, and so do the contexts, the logics, and the epistemologies. There is more discontinuity than development. And yet, the past in this subject does nourish the present in a way that is characteristic of few other fields. The teacher must decide what that way is. How shall we forge an attachment to the past which can nourish life in the present?

The history of thought does not declare some doctrines true and others false, some books great and others small. And yet, like all history, it makes veiled decisions. Time, change, and the shifting perspectives of teachers and students dismiss some works and doctrines as wrong or insignificant. Still others are embalmed and buried, or turned into relics and museum pieces. Others, however, stay alive, and show a marvelous capacity for regeneration. These are the classic doctrines and works. They do not stay alive because there is a close correspondence between them and some unchanging "reality," which they explain and encompass. That is why it is usually a misdirection of thought to ask of such works whether they are "still valid" or whether they have been outmoded by "the facts." As Merleau-Ponty has said, exact and disembodied truth is neither necessary nor sufficient for the greatness of a doctrine or theory.[3]

Rather, works which become classics have an expressive and suggestive, almost a generative and provocative, power which outstrips their specific statements and arguments. One does not read such works in a literalist frame of mind. Nor should the reader be basically concerned with "what Marx, or Plato, or Hobbes really meant." The classic is a work which has become part of the formulation of a problem, part of what we understand a given problem to be. One cannot know what the problem is without having read the classic works which formulated it. And one who wishes to push thought beyond the point it has reached in one's own time cannot do so without having first assimilated the classic work or works on the subject with which one is dealing. If your topic is justice, Plato's *Republic* is part of the definition of the subject, and you will accept or reject specific theses on or conceptions of justice on the basis of reasons which owe much to Plato. The same with, for example, Hobbes on obligation, or Marx on exploitation, or Mill on liberty, or More on conflict of loyalties, or Machiavelli on political greatness, or Hegel on private and public, or Rousseau on equality. No matter what the "facts" are with which you are dealing, and no matter how different those facts are from those with which the author of the classic was dealing, your facts will not be utterly outside the province of the classic, but, rather, will set up new resonances from within the classic, disclose new lights formerly hidden within it. The facts change, and the classic, far from drying up, comes alive again in new ways.

This suggests some ways the past can enrich the present in the field called political theory. It suggests too that what teachers of the subject must have if they are to keep the subject alive for themselves and for students is not so much a metatheory or a theory of interpretation, and not so much a set of "readings" of Plato, or Marx, as a certain attitude toward the materials of their subject and a set of real questions about political life in their own time. One must have genuine questions whose answers he lacks, and one must be able to approach the great writers in the spirit of humility and hope that they might help him get the questions right, and maybe even show the way toward their answers. I think Collingwood's "logic of question and answer" is the right way here, rather than the "logic of propositions" which he so vigorously assailed. One must have real questions; one must fervently desire answers to those questions; one must suppose that some of the classic books and theorists, approached in the right attitude of eagerness and respect, might give some help with the questions. If you enter the subject with no pressing questions of your own, or if you are resolved mainly to scrub the dross of illogicality and unclarity from off the works, exposing their kernels of pure, timeless truth, or deadly error, you will leave with little more than that with which you entered, or, at least, with little more that will matter to anyone other than a few academicians who have found different truths or errors in the work than you have.

What questions matter? I propose no agenda for others. For myself, the work centers on the failure of the modern, constitutionalist, centralizing, and welfare-oriented states to provide their residents with a feeling of being at home in a place they have helped make and where their voices matter. Thinking in our time must return to the simplest themes—place, vocation, fraternity, membership. We must rethink from the ground up the whole Faustian venture. It is reported of Heraclitus that one day, sitting quietly in his simple house, he heard a knock on the door and responded, "Enter. The gods are here, too."

Notes

1. They were gathered in *The Berkeley Rebellion and Beyond: Essays in Politics and Education in the Technological Society* (New York: The New York Review, 1970).
2. I have followed the discussion by Julian Marias, *Reasons and Life*, tr. by Kenneth S. Reid (New Haven, Conn.: Yale University Press, 1956), pp. 90-97.
3. Maurice Merleau-Ponty, *Signs*, tr. by Richard McCleary (Evanston, Ill.: Northwestern University Press, 1964), pp. 10-11.

Legitimacy in the Modern State

I

Authority is a word on everyone's lips today. The young attack it and the old demand respect for it. Parents have lost it and policemen enforce it. Experts claim it and artists spurn it, while scholars seek it and lawyers cite it. Philosophers reconcile it with liberty and theologians demonstrate its compatibility with conscience. Bureaucrats and politicians pretend to have it and wish they did. Everybody agrees that there is less of it than there used to be. It seems that the matter stands now as a certain Mr. Wildman thought it stood in 1648: "Authority hath been broken into pieces."[1]

About the only people left who seem little affected by the situation are the political scientists. Authority used to be a central term in learned political discourse, perhaps the governing term in philosophical treatments of politics. Except for a few renegade Catholic philosophers, that is obviously no longer the case. You can read a dozen authoritative texts on the American political system, for example, and not find the concept seriously treated. Its use is restricted to discussions of such ritual matters as "the authority of the people" or to descriptions of the "authority" of this or that institution or office. Even the recent spate of writing on the theory of democracy contains no substantial treatment of the topic.[2]

Max Weber pretty thoroughly did our work for us here. His exposition of the three types of authority, or the three grounds upon which claims to legitimate authority can be based, has the same status in social science that an older trinity has in Christian theology. Since Weber, we have been busy putting the phenomena into one or another of his three boxes and charting the progress by which charismatic authority becomes routinized into traditional authority, which, under the impact of science and secularism, gives way in turn to rational-legal authority. It all looks pretty good to the political scientists, as more and more traditional societies enter the transitional stage and gather their resources for the hopeful journey toward the modern stage, where rational-legal authority holds sway, along with

16 LEGITIMACY IN THE MODERN STATE

prosperity, moderation, and a "participant" and empathetic citizenry. It is admitted, to be sure, that there are many obstacles on the path, that some traditional folk still hold out, and that there are even one or two troublesome cases of regression. But on the whole, history is the story of the rational-legal state.[3]

But while the discipline cumulates, things outside jump. We hear of riots and rebellions, demonstrations and assassinations. Heads of state in many modern countries cannot safely go among the citizenry. Dignified ceremonies are raucously interrupted by riotous crowds chanting obscenities at the officials. Policemen have been transformed from protectors into pigs. A lot of young people are trying drugs, and a lot of older people are buying guns. A few months ago, a man entered the employment security building in Olympia, Washington, and tried to murder a computer. He failed, however, because 1401's brains were protected by a bulletproof steel plate. Some developers recently announced plans for a "maximum security subdivision" in Maryland at a minimum cost of $200,000 per house. The subdivision will be ringed by a steel fence and patrolled by armed guards, the shrubbery will hide electronic detectors, and visitors will be checked through a blockhouse. In 1968, American governmental units hired 26,000 additional policemen, an increase of seven percent over 1967; 1968 was the second year in a row during which police employment rose more steeply than any other kind of public employment.[4]

We can feel the chill of some sentences Henry Adams wrote over sixty years ago:

> The assumption of unity which was the mark of human thought in the middle-ages has yielded very slowly to the proofs of complexity.... Yet it is quite sure . . . that, at the accelerated rate of progression shown since 1600, it will not need another century or half century to tip thought upside down. Law, in that case, would disappear as theory or *a priori* principle, and give place to force. Morality would become police. Explosives would reach cosmic violence. Disintegration would overcome integration.[5]

It is the thesis of this essay that legitimate authority is declining in the modern states; that, in a real sense, "law and order" is the basic political question of our day. The seamless web of socialization described by such leading students of the subject as Easton, Greenstein, Hess, and Hyman shows rips and frays. Many of the sons are no longer sure they want the legacy of the fathers. Among young people, the peer group increasingly takes priority as the agency of socialization, and the values it sponsors are new and hostile to those of the adult world. Many people are seeking ways to live in the system without belonging to it: their hearts are elsewhere.

Others, convinced that the organized system will not in the long run permit the escape into private liberty, or feeling that such an escape is ignoble, are acting politically to transform the system. In the eyes of large and growing numbers of men, the social and political landscape of America, the most advanced of the advanced states, is no green and gentle place, where men may long abide. That landscape is, rather, a scene of wracked shapes and desert spaces. What we mainly see are the eroded forms of once authoritative institutions and ideas. What we mainly hear are the hollow winds of once compelling ideologies, and the unnerving gusts of new moods and slogans. What we mainly feel in our hearts is the granite consolidation of the technological and bureaucratic order, which may bring physical comfort and great collective power, or sterility, but not political liberty and moral autonomy. All the modern states, with the United States in the vanguard, are well advanced along a path toward a crisis of legitimacy.[6]

The essay has two subsidiary theses. First, that the crisis of legitimacy is a product of some of the basic, defining orientations of modernity itself; specifically, rationality, the cult of efficiency and power, ethical relativism, and equalitarianism. In effect, it will be argued that the modern mind, having now reached nearly full development, is turning back upon itself and undermining the very principles that once sustained order and obedience in the modern state. Secondly, it will be argued (mainly indirectly) that contemporary social science has failed to appreciate the precariousness of legitimate authority in the modern states because it is largely a product of the same phenomena it seeks to describe and therefore suffers the blindness of the eye examining itself.

What the thesis essentially asserts, then, is that the philosophical and experiential foundations of legitimacy in the modern states are gravely weakened, leaving obedience a matter of lingering habit, or expediency, or necessity, but not a matter of reason, and principle, and deepest sentiment and conviction. We are nearing the end of an era, and it is becoming clear that the decline of legitimate authority is the product of the ideal and material forces that have been the defining attributes of modern authority itself. This movement has been visible for a long time in most of the nonpolitical sectors of life—family, economy, education, religion—and it is now spreading rapidly into the political realm. The gigantic and seemingly impregnable control structures that surround and dominate men in the modern states are increasingly found to have at their centers, not a vital principle of authority, but something approaching a hollow space, a moral vacuum.

A preliminary word on the scope and perspective of the essay, and on its political and methodological orientations.

The major thesis and its subsidiaries can be expanded and elucidated in a number of ways. Its critical terms can be defined with precision, and its relevance to the contemporary political scene in the United States can be shown. Empirical evidence can be brought to bear on the propositions. But these propositions cannot be made operational, tested, and verified or falsified beyond reasonable doubt by the criteria of a rigorous behavioralism. This essay will report no opinion survey, present no input-output charts, attempt no stimulus-response or cognitive-dissonance analysis of legitimacy. It will, instead, utilize a variety of materials that help illuminate the problem, including some materials of dubious scientific quality. Perhaps it really is possible to say something about the truth without first polling a sample of one's contemporaries in order to get the facts.

The recent disturbances and novelties in the modern states have taken the political science profession largely by surprise. That is due in fair part, I think, to the very methods which now enjoy favor in the discipline and to the narrow standards set by those methods concerning the materials that qualify as worthy of professional attention. Those methods are poorly suited for dealing with change. The insistence upon rigor means that very often the methods are permitted to determine the subjects studied, rather than vice versa. The erection of the logical distinction between fact and value into a metaphysical dualism has simultaneously cut the profession off from dominant concerns of modern philosophy and rendered it vulnerable to the grossest of all logical and practical errors, the idealization of the actual. The profession has devised a whole kit of tools for dealing with the routine and predictable but is largely at a loss in the face of genuine novelty. The virtual equation of operationalism and the verifiability theory of meaning with science has meant both a narrowing of many of the most basic concepts of political life and an inability even to perceive whole ranges of empirical phenomena. But this is not the place for a discourse on method: it must suffice to say that behavioral political science has some grave debilities on subjects such as those treated in this essay.

While the essay grew out of a concern with the recent appearance of novel, radical, and sometimes violent forms of speech and action in various sectors of modern life, it does not deal directly with those matters. It is clear to nearly everybody that a limited but quite significant "deauthorization" of the dominant institutions and ideas is taking place today. The causes and consequences of this movement have been treated in a thousand books, articles, and speeches, and no literate person can be unaware of the main analyses and proposed solutions. The essay has little to say on this level of the subject. It does not discuss the generation gap or the credibility gap. It has nothing to say specifically about permissiveness and firmness. It offers no analyses of the SDS or the University of California, no judgments on Anti-Communism or Imperialism. I would like to think that the essay does, however, deal with these matters in an important way by going beneath them to the underlying sources and dimensions of the present de-authorization.

No one can pretend to full moral and political neutrality on this subject. It is easy for one of my age and vocation to be simultaneously afraid, contemptuous, and envious of much of what today goes under the labels "youth culture" and "New Left." Their language and their manners are offensive. There are good reasons for worrying about their lack of discipline, their uncertain devotion to the practices of fair play, their instant communities of dope, music, and self-indulgent rhetoric, and their readiness for extreme actions. It is no true service to keep silent about these things, let alone to take the view that the young, the black, and the radical have a monopoly of the true, the beautiful, and the good.

On the other hand, he who veils fear and envy as patriotism, and hides contempt under the slogans of tolerance, or openly urges ferocity against the young and the radical, sins against life and the future. We are members one of another. The established, the respectable, and the frightened of this land appear on the edge of an utterly nihilistic war against the future—war against their own young, who are the future; and war against the black and the poor, who once were creators of wealth, but who now are seen only as expensive and dangerous nuisances. This war must be prevented, for we are members one of another. Furthermore, at their center and at their best, the youthful, black, and radical protest movements have served America well. Their criticisms of the repressiveness, unresponsiveness, bureaucratization, and hypocrisy of the dominant institutions have been incisive and courageous. Their rejection of the "technetronic society" now being built is an effort for the common redemption, without regard to differences of age, race, or station. So, too, is their call for a more democratic and humane society and their insistence that knowledge be integrated with identity, and both tied to commitment. In a basic way, this essay is an attempt to understand the ways in which certain modern definitions of knowledge and processes of control have contributed to the weakening of legitimate authority and the dehumanization of relations among men which the radicals of our day no longer ignore or endure.

II

Start by comparing the traditional and common meanings of legitimacy with the usage of leading modern social scientists. The *Oxford English Dictionary* says the following:

> Legitimacy: (a) of a government or the title of a sovereign: the condition of being in accordance with law or principle. . . . (b)

conformity to a rule or principle; lawfulness. In logic, conformity to sound reasoning.

Legitimate: (a) etymologically, the word expresses a status, which has been conferred or ratified by some authority. (b) conformable to law or rule. Sanctioned or authorized by law or right; lawful; proper. (c) normal, regular; conformable to a recognized standard type. (d) sanctioned by the laws of reasoning; logically admissible or inferable.

The most relevant entries from Webster's *Unabridged* are: Legitimate: (1) lawfully begotten. . . . (2) real, genuine; not false, counterfeit, or spurious. (3) accordant with law or with established legal forms and requirements; lawful. (4) conforming to recognized principles, or accepted rules or standards.

Now, three current professional definitions:

1. Legitimacy involves the capacity of the system to engender and maintain the belief that the existing political institutions are the most appropriate ones for the society.[7]
2. In the tradition of Weber, legitimacy has been defined as "the degree to which institutions are valued for themselves and considered right and proper."[8]
3. We may define political legitimacy as the quality of "oughtness" that is perceived by the public to inhere in a political regime. That government is legitimate which is viewed as morally proper for a society.[9]

The contrast between the two sets of definitions, the traditional and lexical on the one side and the current scientific usage on the other, is basic and obvious. The older definitions all revolve around the element of law or right, and rest the force of a claim (whether it be a claim to political power or to the validity of a conclusion in an argument) upon foundations external to and independent of the mere assertion or opinion of the claimant (e.g., the laws of inheritance, the laws of logic). Thus, a claim to political power is legitimate only when the claimant can invoke some source of authority beyond or above himself. History shows a variety of such sources: immemorial custom, divine law, the law of nature, a constitution. As Arendt has pointed out, "In all these cases, legitimacy derives from something outside the range of human deeds; it is either not manmade at all . . . or has at least not been made by those who happen to be in power."[10]

The new definitions all dissolve legitimacy into belief or opinion. If a people hold the belief that existing institutions are "appropriate" or "morally proper," then those institutions are legitimate. That's all there is to it.

By a surgical procedure, the older concept has been trimmed of its cumbersome "normative" and "philosophical" parts, leaving the term leaner, no doubt, but now fit for scientific duty. It might turn out that Occam's Razor has cut off a part or two that will be missed later on.

A few implications of these new formulations should be articulated.

First of all, when legitimacy is defined as consisting in belief alone, then the investigator can examine nothing outside popular opinion in order to decide whether a given regime, institution or command is legitimate or illegitimate. To borrow the language of the law, there can be no independent inquiry into the title. In effect, this analysis dissolves legitimacy into acceptance or acquiescence, thereby rendering opaque whole classes of basic and recurrent political phenomena, e.g., a group or individual refuses consent and obedience to the orders of a regime or institution on the ground that the regime or institution is illegitimate; a regime or institution is acknowledged to be legitimate as such, but consent is withheld from a particular order on the ground that the regime had no legitimate right to make that order; one consents or acquiesces out of interest or necessity, although he regards a regime or an order as illegitimate. In short, legitimacy and acquiescence, and legitimacy and consensus, are not the same, and the relations between them are heterogeneous. The older formulations made these empirical situations comprehensible, while the newer usages obfuscate them. The phenomenon of legitimacy, far from being identical with consensus, is rather, as Friedrich says, "a very particular form of consensus, which revolves around the question of the right or title to rule."[11] Legitimacy is that aspect of authority which refers to entitlement.

Another important feature of these new formulations, which emerges clearly when the definitions are examined within the context of the larger works in which they appear, is that they see legitimacy as a function of a system's ability to persuade members of its own appropriateness. The flow is from leaders to followers. Leaders lay down rules, promulgate policies, and disseminate symbols which tell followers how they should feel and what they should do. Thus, Merelman explains legitimacy within the framework of stimulus-response psychology, which he rather narrowly equates with learning theory. The regime or the leaders provide the stimuli, first in the form of policies improving citizen welfare and later in the form of symbolic materials which function as secondary reinforcements, and the followers provide the responses, in the form of favorable attitudes toward the stimulators—which, to reiterate, is what Merelman means by legitimacy. The symbols become, in the minds of the followers, condensations of the practices and intentions of the rulers. Over time, if the rulers manipulate symbols skillfully, symbolic rewards alone may suffice to maintain supportive attitudes.[12] The symbols may actually conceal rather than reveal the real nature of the regime's policies and practices, as the symbols of democracy becloud the actual processes of rule in the modern states.

We should be clear about the understanding of the relationship between "community" and control that informs such a conception of legitimacy. Merelman and others in this tradition see a polity not as a people with a culture seeking together the forms of order and action that will preserve and enhance that culture, but as a mass or collective that is made into a unit of control by propaganda.[13] That is no doubt a fairly accurate conception of most modern systems of rule, but it is worth remembering that a politics of propaganda and ideology is not the only possible politics.[14]

Legitimacy, then, is almost entirely a matter of sentiment. Followers believe in a regime, or have faith in it, and that is what legitimacy is. The faith may be the product of conditioning, or it may be the fruit of symbolic bedazzlement, but in neither case is it in any significant degree the work of reason, judgment, or active participation in the processes of rule. In this analysis, people do not attribute legitimacy to authority because they recognize its claim to a foundation in some principle or source outside itself. This emerges clearly in Lipset's treatment of the specific institutional arrangements and procedures which are conducive to legitimacy: cross-pressures; widespread and multiple membership in voluntary associations; the two party system; federalism, territorial rather than proportional representation.[15] In a most confusing way, an analysis of something called legitimacy first equates legitimacy with opinion, then goes to a restatement of the standard liberal-pluralist description of the structure of power in the United States, turns next to a discussion of stability, and finally resolves stability into passivity or acquiescence caused by cognitive confusion, conflict of interest, and inability to translate one's desires into political decisions due to certain institutional arrangements. Obviously, we are no longer talking about faith or belief at all, let alone legitimacy, but about confusion and indifference, stability and efficiency. There is where the contemporary social science treatment of legitimate power rests. A fuller view is needed.

No matter where we go in space, nor how far back in time, we find power. Power is ancient and ubiquitous, a universal feature of social life. But if it is a fact, it is nonetheless a complex fact:

> Power exists . . . only through the concurrence of all [its] properties . . . it draws its inner strength and the material succour which it receives, both from the continuously helping hand of habit and also from the imagination; it must possess both a reasonable authority and a magical influence; it must operate like nature herself, both by visible means and by hidden influence.[16]

Force can bring political power into being but cannot maintain it. For that, something else is required: "Will, not force," said T. H. Green, "is the basis of the state." Once power is established and set on course, as it were, then obedience is largely a matter of habit. But there are two critical points in the life of power when habit does not suffice. The first is at its birth, when habits of obedience have not formed. The other comes when the customary ways and limits of power are altered, when subjects are presented with new and disturbing uses of power and are asked to assume new burdens and accept new claims. At those two points—and most of the states of our day, old and new, are at one or the other of the two—theory must be called in to buttress and justify obedience. There is no denying a certain pragmatic or expediential element in all theories of legitimacy. Such theories are never offered idly, they never appear accidentally. Rather, they appear when the uses of power are matters of controversy, and they are weapons in the struggles of men to enjoy the benefits and escape the burdens of power. This is not to say that all theories of legitimacy are only or merely "rationalizations"; rather, it is to say that they have an element of rationalization in them.

Theory, then, by making power legitimate, turns it into authority. All theories of legitimacy take the form of establishing a principle which, while it resides outside power and is independent of it, locates or embeds power in a realm of things beyond the wills of the holders of power: the legitimacy of power stems from its origin. In addition, most theories of legitimacy simultaneously attempt to justify power by reference to its ends. As was suggested by the earlier quotation from Arendt, the originating principles have been many and diverse. So too have the ends. But in our time this great complexity has been reduced, in virtually all states, to a gratifying simplicity: for power to become authority, it must originate in "democratic consent" and aim at the "common good" or "public interest."

I shall not rehearse here in any detail the many assaults that have been made against both these concepts. They are familiar enough. Let it suffice to say that criticism and hard events have done their work: both concepts have been reduced to rubble. Democracy is the most prostituted word of our age, and anyone who employs it in reference to any modern state should be suspect of either ignorance or bad motives.[17] The public good has not fared much better. It is widely agreed among political scientists that it is more a term of political art than of political analysis, but if it has any cognitive content at all it can mean only the sum or aggregate of individual, subjective interests.[18]

That offered little trouble for a time, because it seemed perfectly compatible with popular sovereignty and majority rule, which everyone agreed were basic principles of democratic decision making. But then Arrow showed that there was no way to produce a unique social ordering of the preferences of individuals that would be compatible with the requirements of popular sovereignty and majority rule—thereby leaving both the theory of democracy and the concept of the public interest in a shambles.[19]

There the matter stands among the sophisticated. The most benighted savage of yesterday's anthropology, sacrificing to his totemic ancestor and groveling before his sacred king, is no worse off for a theory of legitimacy that will pass the tests of reason than is the most advanced "democratic" theorist among us today.

The case is not much better among ordinary folk. Most of them really know that "the people" do not run things: a plethora of surveys and voting studies confirms that. Hence, the test of legitimacy for them is not power's origins but its ends. And from this point of view, the "public interest" means just about what it has always meant: security and material abundance. The sacred king once had to make the crops grow and provide victory in battle. The government must now defend national security and enlarge the GNP. But it is increasingly clear that the nation-state can no longer guarantee the first at all and that in the modern states the second has been accomplished to the point where it threatens the irreversible degradation of the environment and the species.

We have finally made the engine that can smash all engines, the power that can destroy all power. Security today, bought at the price of billions, means that We shall have fifteen minutes warning that They intend to annihilate us, during which time we can also annihilate them. The most powerful state today cannot provide security but only revenge. There is not a person among us who has not himself imagined the destruction of all things by nuclear holocaust. Not since civilization began has man been so totally reduced to the status of temporary occupant of his home, the earth. The dream of total security through total power has ended in the reality of total vulnerability.[20]

The case with abundance comes out about the same way. Inexcusable injustices of distribution still prevail in the modern states, but the "battle of production" is nearing total victory. Societies have always been, in part, organizations for the production of the nutrients of life, but modern civilizations are dominated as no others have ever been by the law of production.[21] Modern production is dedicated almost entirely to consumption; and since consumption is limitless, so too is production. But to produce something means to destroy something else; hence, destruction keeps pace with production. There is the deepest law of modern production: it must continue as long as there is anything left to destroy. That is not metaphor but the precise dynamic of modern economies.

Modern production has obscured the sun and stars toward which men once aspired. It pollutes the air and chews up great forests. It drinks whole lakes and rivers. It has already consumed many species of creatures, and it is making ready to consume the oceans. Its factories once ate children and more recently have been fed slaves. This civilization of production periodically devours men by heaps and piles in war, and it daily mangles the spirits of others in meaningless labor. The only aim of this civilization is to live, that is, to grow, and to grow it must consume. Ellul has shown, unanswerably I think, that the process must run until it consumes those who think they run it—until man is absorbed into technique and process. That will be the total victory in the battle of production; and as always with total victories, no atonement will avail.[22]

The modern state, then, insofar as it is provider and guarantor of increase, and insofar as its success in this task is a source of legitimacy, has succeeded too well: its success has become a threat to survival. The masses have not yet heard this message, though some hints have begun to penetrate the thicket of propaganda and inherited ideas. Most importantly, this understanding is growing among young people and among the cultural elites: even Galbraith has anxiously asked whether the impulse toward destruction might not be an inherent dynamic of the new order.[23] Once again we reach the same conclusion. The new state of production has fulfilled its promise of abundance, but only at the price of raising a new and formidable threat to freedom, and even to survival.[24]

III

I do not wish to poke about among these ruins. Rather, I shall take a backward look over the roads which have led to the modern condition, which, to say it again, is the condition of the shattering of authority. The modern condition is not "new" in the strict sense of the term. Rather, it is an intensification and a fulfillment of certain tendencies which are quite old. On the axiom that in the human sciences inquiry must begin where the subject begins, I wish to look at the basic elements, the principles or starting points, of the modern condition. The question is, what are the main routes by which modern states have reached the stage where power has lost most of the attributes of legitimate authority?

In order to be as clear as possible about the subject under discussion, it will be useful to say a few words about the nature of authority. Following Bertrand de Jouvenel, authority can be defined basically as "the faculty of gaining another man's assent."[25] The word's origins and rich associations suggest the place of authority in human life. An authority is one whose counsels we seek and trust and whose deeds we strive to imitate and enlarge. He is one who, while lacking most of the specific attributes of power as force, makes recommendations which cannot safely be ignored because they are usually right: "While power resides in the people, authority rests with the Senate [of Rome]."[26] An authority is one who starts lines of action which others complete. Hence, he is, metaphorically, the father of their actions. A person or an institution becomes a source and augmenter of others' actions in one of two ways. First, by example: he shows others the way by going there first himself. Secondly, he has the ability to assure others that the actions he recommends are rightful and will succeed. Here, then, are the two basic functions of authority: it provides counsel and justification, and it increases the confidence and sense of ability of those under it by assuring them that the actions it recommends will succeed and will enlarge the actors. Seen in this light, authority, far from confining and depleting men, liberates and enriches them by bringing to birth that which is potentially present. It is only under the impact of the liberal ideology that we came to formulate authority and liberty as opposites and enemies. In an older understanding, authority, while it defined and limited liberty, thereby also fulfilled and directed it. As Nietzsche understood, absence of horizons is not liberty but madness and impotence. Can anyone today still believe that liberty grows stronger as authority grows weaker?

If authority is to initiate actions and vouch for their rightness and success, it must have a rationale that backs its claim to assent. As Plato put it, each law must have a preamble, a statement that walks before the law, justifying and explaining it. This rationale includes an account of reality, an explanation of why some acts are preferable to others, and a vision of a worthwhile future toward which men can aspire. Put differently, the rationale consists of a more or less coherent body of shared memories, images, ideas, and ideals that gives to those who share it an orientation in and toward time and space. It links past, present, and future into a meaningful whole, and ties means and ends into a continuum that transcends a merely pragmatic or expediential calculation. Authorities at once personify or incarnate this rationale, this conception of legitimacy, and are justified by it. Without such rationales, or "stories," authority dissipates, leaving a vacuum to be filled by power. As Adams put it, morality becomes police.

This understanding of authority has concentrated so far on what R. S. Peters has called its de facto aspects or dimensions. The concept also has what might be called de jure meanings, as when Hobbes says, "the right of doing any action, is called AUTHORITY. So that by authority is always understood a right of doing any act; and *done by authority* done by commission, or license from him whose right it is."[27] Webster's clearly recognizes both usages, for while it gives, "legal or rightful power; a right to command or to act," it also gives "power derived from opinion, respect, or esteem; influence of character, office, or station, or mental or moral superiority." The de jure usage welds authority with right and connects both with office or position in a system of rules and relations. This is the usage most commonly met in traditional political philosophy and in the philosophical analysis of such concepts as institution, obligation, command, and law. The reasons for this are obvious. We live in societies, which means we regulate our relations with each other largely by systems of rules. This specifically human form of order can be maintained only if "there is general acceptance of procedural rules which lay down who is to originate rules, who is to decide about their concrete application . . . and who is entitled to introduce changes."[28] All these are functions of authority within human society.

The de facto and de jure uses of the term, while conceptually distinct at their outer margins, also have common dimensions. Both share the common root *auctor,* or originator. Furthermore, both share the idea of originator by right, though in the de facto sense the right or entitlement rests mainly upon the personal attributes of the individual who has authority, while de jure authority comes from position or office in a system of rules and practices. Finally, both stress ways of governing conduct by means other than force, manipulation, or propaganda. Authority commands, decides, recommends, and persuades, and resorts to force only when these fail. "To follow an authority is a voluntary act. Authority ends where voluntary assent ends. There is in every state a margin of obedience which is won only by the use of force or the threat of force: it is this margin which breaches liberty and demonstrates the failure of authority."[29]

In an older vocabulary, authority has both the cross and the sword; but while the former is of its essence, the latter is not.

IV

A serious account of the contemporary problem of "law and order" would be an account of the hollowing out of the theoretical and empirical foundations upon which authority (de jure and de facto) has rested in the states of the West. Weber thought that the day of charismatic and traditional structures of legitimacy was over and that both were being displaced by rational-legal authority. But he did not see far enough into the matter, for rational-legal authority has also been undermined, leaving the great institutions it brought into being gravely weakened from within. I cannot supply anything like a full map of the routes leading to this end. What follows is a sketch of the main roads on this journey into emptiness.

The Epistemological Route

This route consists in charting the connections between the status of the concept of truth on the one side, and the growing feeling of disengagement or alienation from authoritative structures of order on the other. Until recently, the concept of truth rested upon certain assumptions about the relations between the knower and the known. Two of these assumptions are of greatest importance: (1) the notion that man's cognitive apparatus did not itself basically condition the quality and nature of what was known; and (2) the notion that there existed a kingdom of order outside man and independent of him (e.g., the laws of nature, God, the laws of history). Given the first assumption, truth always meant discovery. Given the second, truth meant discovery of a pre-established order. Discoveries made by the methods of science, philosophy, and theology were not fabrications of the human mind, but faithful reflections or representations of an order independent of the discoverer. For us to increase our own harmony with the pre-established harmony outside ourselves, we had only to increase our knowledge of the world. Given the right methods and concepts, increasing knowledge brought increasing harmony between man and the world. Anthropological and mythological researches have shown that in the ages before philosophy and science, myth served this same function of bringing men into contct with the sources of order outside themselves.

Given this concept of truth, social and political life too could be seen as a harmonious association of self and society with an objective order external to man and constituted by some force independent of him. Political societies were not works of human art and will, but were embedded in and even constituted by a larger order of being. Human authority rested on bases more "solid" than individual choice and will.

That older view of knowledge and truth has now just about disappeared, and with its disappearance men have lost most of their older principles of legitimation. In the older view, a structure of order could base its claim to legitimacy on some foundation other than the choices and opinions of the members. In the newer view, order becomes dependent upon will, with no source of rewards and punishments external to the system and its members. With that, the social and political world becomes "unfrozen" as it were, moveable by skill and power, for it is seen that there is no necessity in any given arrangement of things. All things could be other than they are. It is the world of Sorel, rather than the world of Plato. It is not even a world in which change or becoming follows a necessary pattern. It is the world of Sartre, rather than the world of Hegel.[31]

Furthermore, the death of the older views also spelled death for the authoritative classes of priests and nobles who claimed a right to rule on the grounds that they possessed knowledge of the true order of things and of the methods needed for gaining further knowledge of that order. The oldest and most basic justification for hierarchy has dissolved. The only class that could conceivably make that claim today is the class of scientists. But in order to occupy this role, the scientific estate would have to transform itself into something very like a priesthood, along lines which Comte understood to perfection. The foundations for that are already present. For the masses, science is largely a matter of miracle, mystery, and authority. Translated into educational terms, the slogan that through science man has gained increasing knowledge of nature really means that a few men now know a great deal about how nature "works," while the rest of us are about as ignorant as we have always been. Translated into political terms, the slogan that through knowledge man has gained power really means that a few men have gained the means of unprecedented power over a great many other men. On the other hand, there are good reasons for thinking that the scientists and experts may not be able to perform the priestly role with enduring success. I shall indicate some of these reasons later.

When the secret that nature is no guide is finally known to all—the secret exposed by the Sophists and in our age by Nietzsche—the whole question of legitimacy will have to be reopened. Order will be seen as artificial, the result of will and choice alone, as vulnerable to change and challenge as will itself is. Structures of authority will not be able to invoke the ancient and once ubiquitous idea that each thing under the sun has its own right nature and place in the constitution of the whole. For centuries, this sense of the fitness and rightness of things set boundaries to men's pretensions to control and shaped their moral attitudes concerning the permissible limits within which they might legitimately impose their desires on the world around them. A basic piety toward the world and toward the processes that sustain it will disappear, and all things, including polities and men themselves, will come to appear artificial and malleable.[32] Whole new sets of arguments and images imposing limits on man's urge to satisfy his desires will have to be found. And until they are found, the idea and the very experience of legitimate authority cannot have anything like the bedrock importance they have heretofore had in political life.

The Moral Route

The knowledge that civilization begins when men understand that any shared custom at all is better than none is as old as Homer and as new as the researches of Lévi-Strauss. All morality is in the beginning group morality. Each tribe believes that there is no morality outside the tribe and that without its morality it is no longer a tribe. Morality is, then, both a means and the basic means for preserving a community—holding it together, marking pathways through the landscape of social relations, defending it against threats from strangers and the gods. Men everywhere are taught to fear those who violate morality and to revere its authors and upholders.

Furthermore, as Nietzsche understood, and as scientific research increasingly confirms, nations and communities are "born."[33] And birth requires a father or author, the one who, whether mythologically or actually, brought the original laws and customs, thereby making a people a people.[34] The founder of a people is usually either a god or a messenger and mediator between gods and men: The creative moment in the birth of a nation is the birth of a religion.[35] Even the Enlightened American Founding Fathers saw the Constitution as a partial embodiment of that higher order called the Laws of Nature and of Nature's God. Prophets and messengers appear not only at the original birth, but also at times after the founding when the boundaries have been altered or obscured and need to be rectified. In addition, through actions based on myth and ritual, the people themselves also reenact and reaffirm the harmony between the ontological order and their own human realm. In sum, founders and prophets create and correct, and myth and ritual recreate and restore a community identity set within a cosmology. Identity and legitimacy are thus inseparable.[36]

No one needs to be told that these ancient patterns of thought no longer prevail. The old moralities of custom and religion are husks and shells. With the growth of the special modern form of individual self-consciousness as consciousness of separation, individuals lose sight of the dependence of the group upon morality and of the dependence of morality upon the group. These paths run parallel to the one, discussed earlier, by which men have journeyed toward epistemological emptiness. Individual withdrawal from the group consciousness and individual rejection of received knowledge proceed concurrently. There is an intimate connection between the decline of custom and "nature" as the setter of boundaries in the social realm, and the Cartesian and Hobbesian rejection of received opinion as the starting point of the individual knower's search for knowledge. Each man becomes his own author and oracle, his own boundary setter and truth maker. The ego recognizes no source of truth and morality external to itself.

Bacon, Descartes, and Hobbes first decisively stated this modern perspective, and Rousseau formulated the basic political problem stemming from it. He was the first to understand fully, I think, that ours is the task of developing the theory and institutions of a community in which men can be both conscious and individual and share the moral bonds and limits of the group. Rousseau thought, and much modern experience suggests he was right, that until such a polity was built, modern men would often be, and would even more often feel like, slaves, and that no modern state would be truly legitimate.

Hobbes and just about all later writers in the liberal line—T. H. Green nearly escaped—left this problem on shaky foundations. Hobbes never conceived the possibility of a selfhood which transcended the purely individual. Hence, for him, there is no trouble so long as one self does not impinge upon another. When that happens, Leviathan puts curbs on all. In this perspective, order is a question of power, and legitimacy is reduced to prudent calculations of self-interest. That line of thought remains dominant in Sartre, though the vocabulary has shifted to "seriality," and in much contemporary behavioral science, though the Hobbesian vocabulary of "prudence" has shifted to "satisficing" and "maximizing utility."

All this might be made a little more concrete by bringing it closer to home. The United States can be seen as a great experiment in the working out of these ideas. As Lipset has pointed out, the United States is in a very real sense the "first new nation." Our founding took place at an advanced stage of the progress toward epistemological and moral individualism which was sketched above. At the time of the founding, the doctrine and sentiment were already widespread that each individual comes into this world morally complete and self-sufficient, clothed with natural rights which are his by birth, and not in need of fellowship for moral growth and fulfillment. The human material of this new republic consisted of a gathering of people each of whom sought self-sufficiency and the satisfaction of private desires. Wave after wave of immigrants replenished those urges, for to the immigrant, America largely meant freedom from inherited authorities and freedom to get rich. Community and society meant little more than the ground upon which each challenged or used others for private gain. Others were accepted insofar as they were useful to one in his search for self-sufficiency. But once that goal was reached, the less one had to put up with the others the better. Millions upon millions of Americans strive for that goal, and what is more important, base their political views upon it. The state is a convenience in a private search; and when that search seems to succeed, it is no wonder that men tend to deny the desirability of political bonds, of acting together with others for the life that is just for all. We have no political or moral teaching that tells us we must remain bound to each other even one step beyond the point where those bonds are a drag and a burden on one's personal desires. Americans have always been dedicated to "getting ahead"; and getting ahead has always meant leaving others behind. Surely a large part of the zealous repression of radical protest in America yesterday and today has its roots in the fact that millions of people who are apparently "insiders" know how vulnerable the system is because they know how ambiguous their own attachments to it are. The slightest moral challenge exposes the fragile foundations of legitimacy in the modern state.

I am aware that my argument and conclusions here stand in opposition to the standard liberal-pluralist view of American politics. In that view, Americans are enthusiastic joiners. They seek goals through associational means more readily than do citizens in other lands.[37] In addition, Americans have been found to be less cynical about politics than the citizens of some other states. And Americans early learn attitudes of trust and respect for their regime and its authority figures.

But this literature is largely beside the point; and to the degree that it has been expressed doctrinally—as evidence for the democratic and participatory character of political decision making in the United States—it is misleading.[38] What matter here are questions of quality, not quantity. The professional literature glorifies the sheer, gross quantity of associational life—though it has never quite known what to say about the majority of adults who are members of no association except a religious one. Little is said about the quality and meaning of associational life, the narrowness of the constituencies, or the intentions that bring men together.[39] The associational life praised in the literature originates in and is pervaded by the kinds of liberal intentions and feelings described above. The individual takes little part in "group life," apart from lending his quantum of power to the whole. Membership is instrumental: the association is an efficient means for the achievement of individual goals, not an expression of a way of life valued in and for itself.

Affective life centers almost exclusively in the family, and other associations are more or less useful in the pursuit of private goals. Once the goal of self-sufficiency is reached, the individual retreats from group life. Or individuals are held in formal association by the subtle arts of managerial psychology, the not-so-subtle arts of bureaucratic control, the revision upwards of personal desires and demands, and the redefinition of material goals in symbolic terms. It is, then, a question not of how many associations there are, but of what being together means.[40]

This point, however, is a minor one, even though discussion of it occupies a large place in the professional literature. The main point remains: modern man has determined to live without collective ideals and disciplines, and thus without obedience to and reliance upon the authorities that embody, defend, and replenish those ideals. The work of dissolution is almost complete, and modern man now appears ready to attempt a life built upon no other ideal than happiness: comfort and self-expression. But if this is nihilism, it is nihilism with a change of accent that makes all the difference. Gone is the terror, and gone too the dedication to self-overcoming of the greatest nihilist. All ideals are suspect, all renunciations and disciplines seen as snares and stupidities, all corporate commitments nothing but self-imprisonments. Modern prophets rise to pronounce sublimation and self-mutilation the same. We, especially the young among us, presume that an individual can live fully and freely, with no counsel or authority other than his desires, engaged completely in the development of all his capacities save two—the capacity for memory and the capacity for faith.

No one can say where this will lead, for the attempt is without illuminating precedent. But it is clear that for our time, as Rieff has written, "the question is no longer as Dostoevski put it: 'Can civilized men believe?' Rather: Can unbelieving men be civilized?"[41] Perhaps new prophets will appear; perhaps tribalism will reappear; perhaps the old faiths will be reborn; perhaps Weber's "specialists without spirit, sensualists without heart" will stalk the land; or perhaps we really shall see the new technological Garden tilled by children—simple, kind, sincere innocents, barbarians with good hearts. But however it comes out, we must be clear that already the development of the postmoral mentality places the question of authority and legitimacy on a wholly new footing.[42]

Rationality and Bureaucratic Coordination

At least one portion of the liberal impulse has reached near completion in the modern state: the urge to replace the visible with the unseen hand.[43] Personal and visible power and leadership decline, supplanted by impersonal, anonymous, and automatic mechanisms of control and coordination. Overall, we are confronted not with a situation of "power without authority," as Berle, Drucker, and others have described it, though that is part of it, but with a situation of the "autonomy of process," as Ellul and Arendt have described it. The results, as they bear on the meaning of authority and legitimacy, are mainly two: a reduction in the scope for human freedom and responsibility; and the dehumanization, in concrete ways, of leadership. We are beginning to gather the bitter harvest of these triumphs of rationality in the seemingly irrational, nihilistic, and self-indulgent violent outbursts of our day.

It was mentioned before that modern civilizations seem committed to no ideal beyond their own reproduction and growth. A man from another era might say that collectively we have sunk into mere life; the men of our era prefer to call it a celebration of life. Setting that matter of judgment aside, the point which must be understood is that this condition, combined with some of the basic characteristics of modern social systems and some of the basic components of the modern climate of opinion, decisively alters most of our inherited conceptions of authority and leadership.

Our familiar ways of thinking prepare us to imagine that a society must have "someone" in charge, that there must be somewhere a center of power and authority. Things just would not work unless someone, somewhere,

34 LEGITIMACY IN THE MODERN STATE

knew how they worked and was responsible for their working right. That image and experience of authority have almost no meaning today—as the people in power are the first to say. Modern societies have become increasingly like self-regulating machines, whose human tenders are needed only to make the minor adjustments demanded by the machine itself. As the whole system grows more and more complex, each individual is able to understand and control less and less of it. In area after area of both public and private life, no single identifiable office or individual commands either the knowledge or the authority to make decisions. A search for the responsible party leads through an endless maze of committees, bureaus, offices, and anonymous bodies.[44]

The functions of planning and control, and ultimately of decision making, are increasingly taken away from men and given over to machines and routine processes. Human participation in planning and control tends to be limited to supplying the machines with inputs of data and materials. And still the complexity grows. Modern man is haunted by the vision of a system grown so complex and so huge that it baffles human control. Perhaps the final solution to the problem of human governance will be to make a machine king. That is surely the imminent end toward which the efforts of all the linear programmers and systems analysts are headed.[45]

This is what I mean to suggest by the autonomy of process. The system works, not because recognizable human authority is in charge, but because its basic ends and its procedural assumptions are taken for granted and programmed into men and machines. Given the basic assumptions of growth as the main goal, and efficiency as the criterion of performance, human intervention is largely limited to making incremental adjustments, fundamentally of an equilibrating kind. The system is glacially resistant to genuine innovation, for it proceeds by its own momentum, imposes its own demands, and systematically screens out information of all kinds but one. The basic law of the whole is: Because we already have machines and processes and things of certain kinds, we shall get more machines and processes and things of closely related kinds, and this by the most efficient means. Ortega was profoundly right when a generation ago he described this situation as one of drift, though at that time men still thought they were in command. That delusion is no longer so widespread.[46]

The organization of the human resources needed to serve this process is done in the bureucratic mode. It would be superfluous here to describe the essential characteristics of bureaucracy: that has been done capably by a number of writers. What I want to do instead is describe briefly what can best be called the bureaucratic epistemology, the operative definition of knowledge or information which is characteristic of all highly developed modern bureaucracies, for this is the screen through which information must pass before it becomes useful knowledge. This screen is one of the basic agencies by which the autonomy of process is assured.[47]

We are taught that the three great planning and control processes of modern society—bureaucracy, technology, and science—are all value-free means or instruments, just tools, which men must decide how to use by standards drawn from some other source than the realms of science, technology, and bureaucracy. This fairy tale is widely believed among the sophisticated and the naive alike. Many things could be said about it, but here one thing is most important.[48] It is misleading to say that bureaucracy, for example—to focus on the force that matters most in a discussion of legitimacy—is a neutral means that can be used to achieve any end. Here, as in all human affairs, the means profoundly shape the ends. Bureaucracy may have no ultimate values, but it has a host of instrumental values, and among these is a conception of what counts as knowledge or useful information. This bureaucratic epistemology decisively shapes the outcomes—so decisively, in fact, that if you assign a certain task to a bureaucratic agency, you can largely say beforehand how the bureaucratic epistemology will constitute and alter the task itself. To put what follows in a phrase, if you were to assign the task of devising a religion to a bureaucracy, you could say beforehand that the product would be all law and no prophecy, all rule and no revelation.

More and more human energies are channeled through bureaucratic forms. Bureaucracy had advanced, as Weber pointed out, by virtue of its superiorities over other modes of controlling men and coordinating their energies. Hence, one can say, again with Weber, that modern bureaucracy is one of the supreme achievements of modern Western man. It is simultaneously an expression of the drive for rationality and predictability and one of the chief agencies in making the world ever more rational and predictable, for the bureaucratic mode of knowing becomes constitutive of the things known. In a way Hegel might barely recognize, the Rational does become the Real, and the Real the Rational.

Bureaucracy is rational in certain specific ways. First, it is in principle objective and impersonal, treating all cases without regard to their personal idiosyncracies: all must stand in line. The objects of bureaucratic management are depersonalized. (Though, typically, each bureaucracy has a favored clientele group: all others must stand in line.) Secondly, bureaucracy is objective in the sense that the official is expected to detach his feelings from the conduct of his office. Subjectivity is for the private life. Thirdly, since bureaucracy proceeds by fixed rules and techniques, the incumbent of an office is in principle replaceable by any other individual who knows the rules and procedures governing that office and commands the skills appropriate to it.

This form of organizing human effort has a conception of knowledge which is also rational in specifiable senses. In the bureaucratic epistemology, the only legitimate instrument of knowledge is objective, technically trained intellect, and the only acceptable mode of discourse is the cognitive mode. The quest for knowledge must follow specified rules and procedures. Thus, many other paths to knowledge are blocked. Specifically, everything thought of as "subjective" and tainted by "feeling" must be suppressed. Any bureaucrat who based his decisions upon conscience, trained prudence, intuition, dreams, empathy, or even common sense and personal experience would be ipso facto guilty of malfeasance. The bureaucrat must define whatever is to be done as a problem, which implies that there is a solution and that finding the right solution is a matter of finding the right technique. In order to solve a problem, it must be broken down into its component parts. Wholes can appear as nothing more than clusters of parts, as a whole car or watch is an ensemble of parts. In order for wholes to be broken into parts, things that are in appearance dissimilar must be made similar. This is done by extracting one or a few aspects which all the objects dealt with have in common and then treating those aspects as though they were the whole. Thus, there is in this conception of knowledge an urge toward abstraction and toward comparison and grouping by common attributes. Abstraction and comparison in turn require measuring tools that will yield comparable units: among the favored ones are units of money, time, weight, distance, and power. All such measurements and comparisons subordinate qualitative dimensions, contextual meanings, and unique and variable properties to the common, external, and quantifiable.[49]

This conception of knowledge also entails a whole conception of reality. Reality is that which is tangible, discrete, external, quantifiable, and capable of being precisely conveyed to others. Everything that is left over—and some might think that this is half of life—becomes curiously unreal or epiphenomenal. If it persists in its intrusions on the "real" world, then it must be treated as trouble; and those who act from motives embedded in the unreal world are treated as deviant cases, in need of repair or reproof. Bureaucrats still cannot quite believe that the human objects of "urban renewal" see themselves as victims.

All that remains to be added is the obvious point that he who would gain this kind of knowledge of this kind of reality must himself be a certain kind of man. The model is the knowledge seeker who is perfectly "objective" and dispassionate, detached from the objects of knowledge and manipulation, and blind to those aspects of the world that lie outside the immediate problem.

Now, when people treat themselves and their world this way, they and it increasingly become this way.[50] And somehow, this way includes consequences that an older vocabulary would have called horrible or evil. But if this is evil, it is evil of a special quality, the quality that Arendt calls banality. Bureaucracies staffed by "perfectly normal men" somehow perform horrors, but not out of ideology or love of evil. In 1576 the Duke of Alba marched into the Low Countries at the head of a uniform and thoroughly disciplined army of soldiers wholly devoted to the True Faith. When those soldiers, contrary to their disciplined and predictable appearance, began furiously burning and pillaging, the people called them "machines with devils inside." Today when we see bureaucracies perform their work of classifying, herding, expediting, and exterminating when necessary, we know they are machines without devils inside. What is inside is merely a certain conception of knowledge and the self, which has been long growing and which is widely distributed. It is a conception which means by thought only a process of rational and efficient calculation of the most efficient way to handle materials, a conception which trains men how to behave efficiently, but not how to act responsibly. When thought is so defined, the roles once filled by human leaders wither and computers can perform them better than men. Computer 1401 is worth much more to the State of Washington than the man who tried to kill it. In some remarkable way, Eichmann was no more responsible than a computer. Bureaucratic behavior is the most nearly perfect example (along with certain areas of scientific and technical experimentation) of that mode of conduct which denies responsibility for the consequences of action on the grounds that it lacks full knowledge of the reasons for action. All bureaucrats are innocent.

V

Weber's account of charismatic authority leaves one with a divided impression. On the one hand, he understood the strong bonds and powerful currents of feeling that are possible between leaders and followers, and sensed that in some way these relations were distinctively human. On the other, Weber's tone suggests that charismatic authority is for the childhood of the race and that the spread of rational-legal authority, even though it too comes at a price, is somehow progressive, more fitted to mature and independent adulthood. He frequently argues that we cannot return to that earlier condition of ignorance and innocence, for "disenchantment" has gone too far, and he recommends the Church with its music and incense for those who are too "weak" to bear the burdens of the present. "Science as a Vocation" concludes on a note of warning to those "who today tarry for new prophets and saviors" and urges all to "set to work and meet the demands of the day." Modern life is disenchanted and hollowed of meaning, but we must manfully live it anyway and not yearn for the gifts of faith and charisma. Each of us must, like Weber himself, see how much he can bear.

But Weber's formulation puts this whole question on the wrong footing. First of all, Weber "romanticized" charismatic authority, making it seem much more mysterious than it really is. He also dealt mainly with very "strong" figures, thereby skewing perception away from charismalike phenomena on a smaller scale and even in everyday life. He emphasized its dark aspects and saw it nearly always as the ravishing of the weak and gullable by the strong and hypnotic, almost as Mann described it in "Mario and the Magician." But more importantly, the basic opposition is not betweeen charismatic and rational authority, but between what can only be called personal and human authority on the one side and bureaucratic-rational manipulation and coordination on the other. It is obviously not charismatic leadership that has been driven out by rational-legal authority, for our age abounds in charismatic figures and putative prophets: Rome of the second century of the Christian Era was no richer. Such men have set the destinies of states, and they can be met on every street corner and in every rock band. The proliferation of these figures is plainly the dialectical fruit of technological and bureaucratic coordination.

Rather, what is missing is humanly meaningful authority and leadership. For this, the age shows a large incapacity. Establishment officials and hippies alike share the conviction that the only alternatives to the present system of coordination are repression or the riot of passion and anarchy. Both groups, the high and the low, are unable to escape the crushing opposites that the world presents to us and that Weber taught us to believe are the only possible choices. Both groups conceive of authority almost exclusively in terms of repression and denial and can hardly imagine obedience based on mutual respect and affection. Confronted with the structures of bureaucratic and technological coordination, the young fear all authority and flee into the unreason of drugs, music, astrology, and the *Book of Changes,* justifying the flight by the doctrine of "do your own thing"—something that has never appeared on a large scale among any populace outside Bedlam and the nursery, where it can be indulged because there is a keeper who holds ultimate power over the inmates. No doctrine was ever better designed to provide its holders with the illusion of autonomy while delivering real power to the custodians. When those in high positions are confronted with challenges, their first response is to isolate themselves from the challengers by tightening the old rules and imposing tougher new rules. When the managers do attempt reforms in a "humanistic" direction, the result is nearly always a deformity: to humanize leadership, institute coffee hours, fabricate human-interest stories to show that the powerful one is human after all, and bring in the makeup artists when he has to go on television; to humanize bureaucracy, appoint T-groups and ombudsmen; to humanize the law, introduce the indeterminate sentence, special procedures and officials for juvenile offenders, and psychiatrists who will put a technical name on any state of mind for a fee. It is always an alliance between "democratic" ideology and expert manipulation, in a hopeless attempt to reconstruct something now almost forgotten—the idea and the experience of genuine authority.

To escape this trap, we must reject Weber's false opposites, and with it his test of manliness. It is not a question of either retreating to charisma or advancing bravely to the rational-legal destiny, but of developing something different from both. It is perfectly possible that the march toward the rationally integrated world is not progessive at all, but a wrong turning, a mistake, whose baneful consequences need not be supinely accepted as inevitable or slavishly rationalized as developmental.[51]

It is certainly necessary to understand that natural human authority has been overwhelmed by the combined impact of the very forces, structures, and intellectual and moral orientations that we identify with modernity. A mere partial listing must suffice. Huge populations have made us strangers to each other and have made it necessary to develop efficient means of mass measurement and control. Centrally controlled communications systems can reach into all corners of the society, encroaching upon small human units of unique experience and outlook. Furthermore, the communications revolution makes possible the elaborate feedback circuitry necessary to the processes of automatic control. Intricate division of labor reduces common experience, producing both pluralistic ignorance and fragmentation of the process of work. The data explosion has produced microspecialization of the mind and the narrowing of perspectives on human problems. The relativization, materialization, and secularization of values makes it impossible for men to relate to one another on the basis of shared commitments to transcendent and demanding purposes and values. The sheer quantity and variety of artifacts and material needs and desires requires a vast system of administrative regulation and control, and thoroughly blurs the distinction between public and private, with the result that authorities cannot pretend to speak for public and objective goods but must accept the popular equation of private desire with public right.[52] The decline of tradition removes another rich source of shared meanings and limits, while rapid technological change proceeds by its own imperatives and enslaves its human attendants. All these add up to a scope and complexity so vast that humanly meaningful authority and leadership are baffled. Control must be accomplished either by bureaucratic coordination and self-regulating devices that govern the technical system by standards generated by the system itself, or by deliberately fabricated ideologies and images.

All these structures and processes will have to be confronted—and radically revised, in ways that no one can clearly foresee—before humanly meaningful authority and leadership can reappear.[53] But before that confrontation can begin—or begin in ways that offer some prospect of a worthy and merciful outcome—there must be an even more basic shift in our understanding of the kind of knowledge that can properly be accepted as constituting a claim to authority in the human realm. I presented the administrative and scientific conception of knowledge as a specimen of what such knowledge must not be. It remains to sketch what it must be.

All leaders perform the same functions. They interpret events, explore possible responses to problematic situations, recommend courses of action, and vouch for the rightness and success of actions taken. They advise, recommend, warn, reprove, and command.[54] All this is so manifest in common experience that the large social science literature which attempted to "explain" leadership by distinguishing between "functional" and "trait" theories should have been seen from the outset as superficial and unimportant, doomed to trivial answers because it asked trivial questions. The fact that it has been taken seriously supports the suggestion made earlier that certain experiences of leadership and authority really have become rare among men in the modern states. The question is not whether leaders hold their positions by performing certain functions or possessing certain traits. The question is, rather, precisely how those functions are construed and what kind of knowledge is understood to be appropriate to their performance.

Each person is born, lives among others, and dies. Hence, each one's life has three great underpinnings, which no matter how far he travels must always be returned to and can never be escaped for long. The three underpinnings present themselves to each one as problems and as mysteries: the problem and mystery of becoming a unique self: but still a self living among and sharing much with others in family and society: and finally a unique self among some significant others, but still sharing with all humanity the condition of being human and mortal. Who am I as an individual? Who am I as a member of this society? Who am I as a mortal member of humanity? Each of the three questions contains within itself a host of questions, and the way one formulates and responds to them composes the center and the structure of one's life.

Given this, it can be said quite simply that humanly significant authorities are those who help us answer these questions in terms that we ourselves implicitly understand. The leader offers interpretations and recommendations which set off resonances in the minds and spirits of other men. When leaders and followers interact on levels of mutual, subjective comprehension and sharing of meaning, then we can say that there exists humanly significant leadership. The relationship is one of mutuality, identification, and co-performance. The leader finds himself in the followers, and they find themselves in the leader. I am aware that to the rational and objective men of our day, this is mysticism. But it is those same rational men who cannot understand why the rational, objective, and expert administrators are losing authority, if not yet power, in all the modern states. The answer is mysteriously simple: to the degree that the rational, expert administrative leader achieves the objectivity and expertise which are the badges of his competence, he loses the ability to enter a relationship of mutual understanding with those who rely on him for counsel and encouragement.

Humanly significant leadership bases its claim to authority on a kind of knowledge which includes intuition, insight, and vision as indispensable elements. The leader strives to grasp and to communicate the essence of a situation in one organic and comprehensive conception. He conjoins elements which the analytical mind prissily separates, unites the normative with the empirical, and promiscuously mixes both with the moral and the aesthetic. The radical distinction between subjective and objective is unknown in this kind of knowledge, for everything is personal and comes from within the prepared consciousness of the knower, who is simultaneously believer and actor. When it is about men, this kind of knowledge is again personal. It strives to see within the self, and along with other selves. It is knowledge of character and destiny. Most of the facts which social scientists collect about peoples are in this epistemology superficial: information about external attributes, rather than knowledge of human identities and possibilities.

One who possesses and values this kind of knowledge bases his claims to its validity on grounds which are quicksand to the objective and rational man. One of the foundations is strength of conviction. A belief is true, or can be made true, when it is believed in strongly enough to serve as a basis for action, in precisely the way James described in his essay on "The Will to Believe." The other ground is the resonance set going between leader and followers when communications "make sense." When leader and followers begin to understand and respond to each other on a profound, personal level, each gains confidence that what is being communicated is true. All authority must believe that its knowledge is true. Rational, scientific authorities enjoy this confidence when they have followed the prescribed methods of inquiry and when their professional colleagues also share the belief. Personal authorities mean by verification the sympathetic vibrations set going by communications between leaders and followers who share a common background and outlook.

The language in which the knowledge appropriate to humanly significant leadership is expressed is also very different from the language of rational and objective discourse. It is a language profuse in illustration and anecdote, and rich in metaphor whose sources are the human body and the dramas of action and responsibility. This language is suggestive and alluring, pregnant, evocative. It is in all ways the opposite of the linear, constricted, jargonized discourse which is the ideal of objective communication. Decisions and recommendations are often expressed in parables and visions whose meanings are hidden to outsiders but translucent to those who have eyes to see. Teaching in this language is done mainly by story, example, and metaphor—modes of discourse which can probe depths of personal being inaccessible to objective and managerial discourse. Compare the Sermon on the Mount with the latest communiqué from the Office of Economic Opportunity in the War on Poverty; or Lincoln's Second Inaugural with Nixon's First.

The final distinctive characteristic of the knowledge appropriate to humanly meaningful authority is that it is dynamic and transactional. Currents of meaning and influence flow back and forth during the process of transmission, so that both the content of the message and the parties to the transaction are caught up and transformed in the flow. The contrast between this and objective discourse is decisive, for the goal of the latter is to send information economically from transmitter to receiver, altering neither the instruments nor the message in the process. Most of what modern information theory calls noise is of the essence of human communication between human authorities and their followers. Scientific students of language do not like to study pragmatics.

VI

Very little of this—especially the material on leadership and authority— is new; and up until a short time ago it would have been unnecessary to say it. The tradition of political theory has always included leadership and authority among its central themes, and in that tradition the languages of discursive reason and of metaphor and myth were not permitted to fall apart and oppose each other either in the analysis of action or in the education of actors. As examples, consider Plato's theory of learning as remembrance, his emphasis on the right music and poetry in the education of statesmen, and his dialogues on justice and power. Artistotle said in the *Politics* that "the same education and the same habits will be found to make a good man and a good statesman and king." In the *Rhetoric* he tried to construct the emphymeme as a tool specifically appropriate to practical discourse just as the syllogism was appropriate to theoretical discourse. Logic and rhetoric were important subjects in the education of citizens because both taught ways of thinking and speaking which would make actors intelligible to each other. Or consider the incomparable treatment of prudence, which is excellence in action, formulated by Aristotle and perfected by Aquinas.[55] This treatment ascends from custom and circumstance, through the psychology of motivation, to ethics and philosophy organized for the sake of action. Or take the literature of counsel, ranging from the profound and subtle works of More and Machiavelli through the more limited works of Bacon and the "Mirror for Princes" literature. All these branches of the tradition are rich in precise observation of men and manners, historical allusion, story, myth, and metaphor, and also in scientific and philosophical argument and analysis. The tradition starts with men where it finds them—located in a community, tied by custom and memory, full of prejudices, vices, and fears, but also possessed of natural virtues—and strives by a language appropriate to the subject to refine and enlarge character and knowledge so that men will be fit for action and the exercise of authority.

In the modern world, and in the social science spawned by that world, the "two sides" of this language have fallen apart. We take it to be almost natural that the political world, and the language and methods appropriate both to understanding and to acting in that world, should be divided, as it were, between Sorel and McNamara. While I have concentrated on the moral and material conditions producing the crisis of legitimate authority, it should be clear that that crisis also extends to our dominant ways of studying these matters, which in turn conditions our ways of transmitting a political culture and preparing men to participate in it. Political Science has become a political problem.

In conclusion, there are senses, which I have tried to specify, in which de facto, humanly meaningful leadership does carry its own principle of legitimacy. But there are other senses in which it does not, or may not. There obviously can be illegitimate, albeit humanly meaningful authority. Without the setting and limits imposed by tradition, shared values and experience, institutions, and philosophical reason, humanly meaningful leadership can be as pathological and dangerous, and as illegitimate, as the processes of power-without-authority characteristic of modern states. Hence, one way to describe the crisis of legitimacy is to say that the basic features and tendencies of modernity have produced a situation in which the established processes and formal structures of control are at war with the conditions necessary for authority. In this battle, legitimacy is destroyed.

Events, institutions, and moral and epistemological ideas which, taken together, constitute modernity have virtually driven humanly meaningful authority and leadership from the field, replacing it with bureaucratic coordination and automatic control processes, supplemented when necessary by ideology and phony charisma. Furthermore, our methods of study have blocked us from seeing that such mechanisms of control are inherently vulnerable and in the long run unworkable, incapable of responding to our needs for understanding and counsel on the basic, inescapable questions of human existence. So long as men remain what we have hitherto called human, they will require of power which strives to become authority that it respond to those questions in ways that have personal meaning. The current epidemic of revolts and uprisings, the current challenging of established institutions and processes, the thickening atmosphere of resentment and hostility, the dropout cultures of the young—these are something other than the romantic, reactionary, or nihilistic spasms which they are taken to be as in some quarters of the academy and the state. They are the cries of people who feel that the processes and powers which control their lives are inhuman and destructive. They are the desperate questionings of people who fear that their institutions and officials have no answers. They are outward and visible signs of the underlying crisis of legitimacy in the modern state.

Notes

1. From "The Whitehall Debates," in A. S. P. Wodehouse, ed., *Puritanism and Liberty* (London, England: J. M. Dent, 1938), p. 127.
2. The only important exception is Yves R. Simon, *Philosophy of Democratic Government* (Chicago, Ill.: University of Chicago Press, 1951), pp. 1-72. Simon's book lies within the Aristotelian-Thomist tradition.
3. For a recent specimen, see the sections by Lerner in Daniel Lerner and Wilbur Schramm, eds., *Communication and Change in the Developing Countries* (Honolulu, Hawaii: East-West Center Press, 1967).
4. *San Francisco Chronicle*, June 5, 1969, p. 42.
5. Letter to Henry Osborne Taylor, January 17, 1905. In Harold Dean Cater, ed., *Henry Adams and His Friends*. Quoted here from William H. Jordy, *Henry Adams: Scientific Historian* (New Haven, Conn.: Yale University Press, 1963), p. xi.
6. When I refer to a crisis of legitimacy, I mean more than an intensification of controversy about various public issues and policies—the kind of thing Dahl discusses in his analysis of the periodicity of opposition in the United States; or the kind of thing treated by the Michigan group under the category of critical or realigning elections. For a study of American voting patterns and electorial behavior that is important to an understanding of legitimacy in the United States, see Walter Dean Burnham, "The Changing Shape of the American Political Universe," *American Political Science Review*, LIX, No. 1 (March 1965), 7-28. What I mean by legitimacy will become clear as the essay proceeds.
7. Seymour Martin Lipset, *Political Man* (Garden City, N.Y.: Doubleday, 1960), p. 77.
8. Robert Bierstedt, "Legitimacy," in *Dictionary of the Social Sciences* (New York, N.Y.: The Free Press, 1964), p. 386. Bierstedt is here paraphrasing Lipset, *Political Man*, op. cit.
9. Richard M. Merelman, "Learning and Legitimacy," *American Political Science Review*, LX, No. 3 (September 1966), 548.
10. Hannah Arendt, "What Was Authority?" in Carl J. Friedrich, ed., *Authority* (Cambridge, Mass.: Harvard University Press, 1958), p. 83.
11. Carl Joachim Friedrich, *Man and His Government: An Empirical Theory of Politics* (New York, N.Y.: McGraw-Hill Book Company, 1963), p. 233.

12. There is evidence that in the United States symbolic rewards alone do largely suffice. See Herbert McClosky, "Consensus and Ideology in American Politics," *American Political Science Review*, LVIII, No. 2 (June 1964), 361-82. A study of the tables on cynicism and futility shows that on item after item members of the general electorate express a strong sense of their own political powerlessness. Yet, ninety percent of the respondents say that they "usually have confidence that the government will do what is right."
13. David Easton's treatment, in *A Systems Analysis of Political Life* (New York, N.Y.: John Wiley & Sons, 1965), esp. Ch. 18, also remains within this perspective, although his reification of "the system" and his employment of the term as a noun of agency becloud what actually goes on. But consider: "Under the usual conception of legitimacy as a belief in the right of authorities to rule and members to obey . . . the major stimulus for the input of diffuse support would arise from efforts to reinforce such ideological convictions among the membership" (p. 288).
14. Lipset also sees legitimacy largely in terms of symbol manipulation. Thus, he says that "a major test of legitimacy is the extent to which given nations have developed a common secular political culture, mainly national rituals and holidays." The United States has passed the test, for it possesses "a common homogeneous culture in the veneration accorded the Founding Fathers, Abraham Lincoln, Theodore Roosevelt, and their principles" (Lipset, *Political Man*, p. 80). I refrain from comment on this pantheon.
15. Ibid., pp. 88-92.
16. In Necker, *Du Pouvoir executif dans les Grands États*, 1792, p. 22. Quoted here from Bertrand de Jouvenel, *Power*, trans. by J. F. Huntington (London: Barchworth Press, 1948), p. 30.
17. Put less polemically: the looseness of the term is indicated by the fact that virtually every new or modern political ideology or system has been identified somewhere in the literature as democratic. See, for example, C. B. MacPherson, *The Real World of Democracy* (Oxford: Oxford University Press, 1966).
18. I think this contemporary professional understanding of the public interest is a superficial one. It fails, for example, to consider Rousseau's effort to distinguish qualitatively between aggregated private interests and genuine common concerns. It fails also to come to terms with Burke's distinction between interest and opinion—an important distinction which appears in many everyday expressions, as when we say a man is "mistaken as to his interest." It excludes J. S. Mill's attempt to make qualitative distinctions between types of subjective interests and values. It is blind to Madison's distinctions between types of groups and publics: reasonable and long-range, versus passionate and temporary. Above all, the contemporary understanding restricts and debases the function of discussion in political life, reducing all speech to the lowest common denominator of "rationalization" or deception, or, at best, bargaining. American political parties and legislatures are not the whole of the political experience relevant to an understanding of the concept of public interest.

The whole question of the status and function of the notion of the public interest within the framework of democratic theory is complex and problematic. Historically, the notion has often play about the same role in

46   LEGITIMACY IN THE MODERN STATE

domestic politics as "reason of state" or "national interest": it releases officials from restrictions imposed by the democratic principle of popular sovereignty. But if officials can claim authority, usually on grounds of superior knowledge, to determine the public good, then democracy, or democratic consent, is nothing more than a method for selecting rulers. Richard E. Flathman, *The Public Interest* (New York, N.Y.: John Wiley & Sons, 1966) has tried to restore the concept to a status of philosophic dignity, with results that are, for me, murky. Brian Barry, *Political Argument* (London: Routledge and Kegan Paul, 1965), esp. Chs. 11-13, has laid solid foundations for further analytic work on the topic.

19. Kenneth Arrow, *Social Choice and Individual Values* (New York, N.Y.: John Wiley & Sons, 1963). Lindblom has argued that Arrow's conditions are not the preconditions of popular sovereignty. Lindblom's formulation, however, rests upon a very special understanding of democracy. He asks what process can produce the right ordering of preferences, answers that it is "partisan mutual adjustment," and concludes that this process is "democratic" *because* it produces the public good. See Charles E. Lindblom, *The Intelligence of Democracy* (New York, N.Y.: The Free Press, 1965).

20. I am aware that the typical, explicit popular response to this radical insecurity is: "Well, what can I do? Besides, we've all got to die sometime, anyway, and when you're dead, you're dead." That is now, as it has always been, the response of fools, though for ages wise men and saints had enough authority to persuade men to our impose upon them a belief in responsibility and immortality, so that fools were ashamed or afraid to speak their foolishness aloud. I am also aware that the typical, explicit professional response to this radical insecurity is something like: total vulnerability is equal to security so long as the vulnerability is both mutual and really total. This is the strategy of deterrence. This theory redefines security to mean, not freedom from fear, but the ability to believe that fears will not be realized. Such a notion of security requires endless and accelerating technological advance, increasing military power, and permanent inequalities of distribution. But all this is really beside the point. What matters here is that the "strongest" nation-states have failed the test of legitimacy through the provision of security. See Georges Bernanos, *Last Essays,* trans. Joan and Barry Ulanov (Chicago, Ill.: Henry Regnery, 1955), esp. pp. 195-97.

21. Some perspective is provided by Walt Whitman's assessment, made over a century ago, that America had already overdeveloped the economic sector of life and should now turn to other efforts.

22. Jacques Ellul, *The Technological Society,* trans. John Wilkinson (New York, N.Y.: Vintage Books, 1967).

23. He, of course, did not put the point as bluntly as it is put here. Rather, he argued that high and ever-increasing military expenditures are an organic feature of the new industrial state, and concluded that "modern military and related procurement and policy are, in fact, extensively adapted to the needs of the industrial system." John Kenneth Galbraith, *The New Industrial State* (New York, N.Y.: New American Library, 1967), p. 241. See also Chs. 20 and 29.

24. Galbraith again: "If we continue to believe that the goals of the industrial system . . . are coordinate with life, then all of our lives will be in the service of these goals. . . . What will eventuate . . . will be the benign servitude of the household retainer who is taught to love her mistress and see her interests as

her own, and not the compelled service of the field hand. But it will not be freedom." Ibid., p. 405.
25. Bertrand de Jouvenel, *Sovereignty: An Inquiry into the Political Good*, trans. J. F. Huntington (Chicago, Ill.: Chicago University Press, 1957), pp. 203-204.
26. Cicero, *De Legibus*, 3, 12, 38. Quoted here from Hannah Arendt, "What Is Authority?" in *Between Past and Future* (New York, N.Y.: Meridian Books, 1963), p. 122.
27. *Leviathan*, ed. Michael Oakeshott (Oxford, Blackwell, n.d.), p. 106. I have borrowed the de jure-de facto distinction for this discussion from R. S. Peters, "Authority," in Anthony Quinton, ed., *Political Philosophy* (Oxford: Oxford University Press, 1967), pp. 83-96, at p. 84.
28. Peters, ibid., p. 94.
29. De Jouvenel, *Sovereignty*, p. 33.
30. Even Hume's thought reflects these patterns. Hume is, of course, famous for shattering the two-thousand-year-old concept of natural law—the idea that man could, by rational processes alone, discover universal norms of moral and political conduct. But while Hume, through his skeptical analysis of the character and functions of reason, undermined the ancient rationalist and transcendental conception of natural law, he replaced it by still another, more empirical, conception of natural law whose norms were as certain as those they replaced. He tried to show that the empirical existence of universal norms could be established by observation and that these norms were necessary products of social life. His logic was similar to that of the ancient theorists of the *jus gentium* and remarkably like that of modern linguistic philosophers, who argue that certain broad and necessary truths can be derived from the prerequisite conditions essential for the existence of a language. See Hume, *Treatise of Human Nature,* Book III, Part II, Sections I-VI; Part III, Section VI. See also his essay "That Politics May Be Reduced to a Science."
31. The scientific, objective, manipulative epistemology presupposes that the knower stands outside nature and takes it by assault. Thus: "A long time ago, we developed modern science as veritable outsiders of nature. In order to become scientific observers, we had to denature ourselves. We have succeeded. When we say, now, that we are reasonable we mean that we are engaged in calculations. When we hold something to be irrational we are merely indignant that our predictions have not been borne out, or perhaps, we are amused, for we make rash distinctions between the irrational and the stupid. When we say 'naturally,' we are hardly ever right." Hans Speier, "Shakespeare's 'The Tempest,' " reprinted in Speier, *Social Order and the Risks of War* (Cambridge, Mass.: M.I.T. Press, 1969), p. 132.
32. For the impact of this upon the scope and nature of violence in the modern world, see Sheldon S. Wolin, "Violence and the Western Political Tradition," *American Journal of Orthopsychiatry*, XXXIII, No. 1 (January 1963), 15-29.
33. The words *nature* and *nation* come from the same root, the word for birth. Etymologically, a nation is a birth, hence a group of persons made kindred by common origin. Nations are also continually reborn, through the death of old customs and institutions and the generation of new ones. A nation has a unique birth and is also a continuous rebirth.
34. Law means limit or boundary. In Greek, the words for law, boundary line, and shepherd had the same root.

48 LEGITIMACY IN THE MODERN STATE

35. Vico expressed the point perfectly in his assertion that there were as many Joves, with as many names, as there are nations. *The New Science of Giambattista Vico*, trans. Thomas Goddard Bergin and Max Harold Fisch (Garden City, N.Y.: Doubleday Anchor Books, 1961), pp. xxix, 31.
36. Machiavelli, obviously not under the spell of mythological thought, gave great attention to this problem of how to keep alive and intact the guiding spirit of a polity and in the end saw it as almost synonymous with popular remembrance of the founding premises: order and action perpetually recreated and renewed through remembrance of origins.
37. Tocqueville is frequently cited at this point in the standard exposition. But Tocqueville has been abused. He hoped and thought that, through voluntary associations, Americans could break out of the cell of individualism and learn the art of politics. But for this to happen, the associations themselves would have to be democratic and political in their internal character. That is rarely the case; but in its absence, Tocqueville's argument simply does not support the uses to which it has been put by contemporary pluralists.
38. Hopefully, Grant McConnell's work *Private Power and American Democracy* (New York, N.Y.: Alfred A. Knopf, 1966) will put an end to the idealization of the interest-group system as a process of partisan mutual adjustment which assures rationality and secures the public interest, thereby meeting the criteria of democracy. McConnell shows that "to a very considerable degree the system of private power makes a mockery of the vision by which one interest opposes another and ambition checks ambition. The large element of autonomy accorded to various fragments of government has gone far to isolate important matters of public policy from supposedly countervailing influences" (ibid, p. 164).
39. I am, of course, speaking here of American writers, not of the European pluralist tradition of Von Gierke, Maitland, Duguit, Figgis, et al. Mary Parker Follett's *The New State: Group Organization the Solution of Popular Government* escapes these restrictions.
40. At the least, it is a question of authorities here. Against the professional view of the seamless web of political socialization stand Malcolm X's *Autobiography* and, say, the two major studies by Kenneth Keniston. Against the voluminous professional accounts of the American as joiner stands the literature of the great American novels, which, from Melville to Faulkner, is an exploration of metaphysical and social isolation, a literature which sees the American as the outsider, the one who does not belong.
41. Philip Rieff, *The Triumph of the Therapeutic: Uses of Faith After Freud* (New York, N.Y.: Harper & Row, Publishers, 1966), p. 4. Rieff's book is an important attempt to come to an understanding of the meanings of "postcommunal culture."
42. The spread of this new, postmoral mentality is bound to have corrosive consequences for the liberal doctrine of contract—the doctrine which bases government on consent of the governed and postulates an original contract by which the people who voluntarily set themselves under authority reserve the right to resist government when it abuses the agreement. The doctrine has always been a quicksand for logicians, a despair for sociologists and historians, and an invitation to resistance for men of conscience and just plain egotists. Historically, obedience has rarely been founded on contract; and as Hume said, "in the few cases where consent may seem to have taken place, it

was commonly so irregular, so confined, or so much intermixed either with fraud or violence, that it cannot have any great authority." ("Of the Original Contract," in Frederick Watkins, ed., *Hume: Theory of Politics* [Edinburgh: Nelson, 1951], p. 201). Few men really consent to government, whether openly or tacitly. And as Jefferson understood, the logic of contract is incapable of binding men to the promises made by their predecessors. These logical shortcomings all become otiose in the face of the simple sociological fact that "obedience or subjugation becomes so familiar that most men never make any enquiry about its origin or cause, more than about the principle of gravity" (ibid., p. 197). But all such habits are weakening in the modern states. As they weaken, the doctrine of consent becomes explosive. Every society rests upon a fiction, which usually encompasses both the society's origins and its ends, thereby helping make life and the world intelligible and endurable. Most of these fictions have failed. The fiction of contract and consent was never one of the best (strongest). To take it seriously now would mean the dissolution of the modern state.

43. Ironic evidence is provided by the "Who Governs?" literature. After prodigious professional labors we still have no authoritative answer. Apparently, everybody governs. Or nobody.

44. Admittedly, there are more sanguine vocabularies for describing the situation: "The fundamental axiom in the theory and practice of American pluralism is, I believe, this: Instead of a single center of sovereign power there must be multiple centers of power, none of which is or can be wholly sovereign. . . . Why this axiom? The theory and practice of American pluralism tends to assume, as I see it, that the existence of multiple centers of power, none of which is wholly sovereign, will help (may indeed by necessary) to tame power, to secure the consent of all, and to settle conflicts peacefully." Robert Dahl, *Pluralist Democracy in the United States* (Chicago, Ill.: Rand McNally & Co., 1967), p. 24.

This description, I believe, misses three central features of the situation: (1) it fails to point out that with all this dispersion there is still a powerful central tendency of policy, a pattern of movement; (2) it fails to point out that some persons and groups in the right positions and possessed of the right resources benefit much more from the system than do others—"noncumulative inequalities" is a dangerous euphemism; and (3) it fails to point out both the real nature of what is lost by the losers—identity, self-respect, and faith in others, as well as wealth and power—and the reparations those losers might someday demand. Thus: The chief of an Indian tribe, seeking redress for a grievance felt by his people, was advised to present his case to the government. He went from this office to that, was sent from one official to another and back again and again. He met no one who looked like himself, though everybody seemed to listen politely enough in the special way that bureaucrats listen. But much time passed, and nothing happened. The chief sadly concluded that the fault was his, because, despite his many interviews and diligent searchings, he had apparently failed to find the "government." Here indeed power was tamed, consent obtained, and conflict settled, but that Indian may not always conclude that the fault was his.

45. See Robert Boguslaw, *The New Utopians* (Englewood Cliffs, N.J.: Prentice-Hall, 1965).

46. The description is not limited to control processes on the nongovernmental sector. In fact, any distinction between public and private, in both process

and substance (except for the military power) would be very hard to draw in the United States. In 1908, Henry Adams wrote: "The assimilation of our forms of government to the form of an industrial corporation... seems to me steady though slow." (W.C. Ford, ed., *Letters of Henry Adams* [Boston, Mass.: Houghton Mifflin Company, 1930], Vol. II, p. 482). Public, governmental bureaucracy grows apace: in 1947, there were about 5.8 million people in government civilian employment, and in 1963 there were 9.7 million; government expenditures, exclusive of "defense," space, veteran, and debt outlays, grew eightfold between 1938 and 1973. The main impulse of large organizations, as most students of the subject agree, is toward the maintenance and growth of the organization itself, which requires increasing control over all aspects of the organizational environment.

47. The following draws heavily on Weber's classic analysis and on the equally incisive work of Kenneth Keniston. *The Uncommitted: Alienated Youth in American Society* (New York, N.Y.: Dell Publishing Co., 1967), esp. pp. 253-72.

48. Though I cannot resist adding a brief appeal to those who still believe that science—especially social science—acquires "objective" knowledge and that any such knowledge that can be acquired is worthy of being acquired. Nietzsche exposed the fallacies here. The number of things one might want to know is, in principle, infinite. Therefore, every act of knowing requires a prior act of choosing and desiring. The knowledge sought and gained necessarily reflects, in many ways, the impulses (values, intentions, urges) which launched the search. Since it is a manifestation of desire and choice, knowledge is subject to moral judgment; and its "worth" is partly a function of the motives that led to its acquisition. Our age, for example, has chosen to know how to command power over nature and other men. Since Nietzsche, we must recognize both the psychology and the morality of knowledge.

49. As a measure of the bureaucratization of American higher education, consider Clark Kerr's incisive definition of the multiversity as "a mechanism held together by administrative rules and powered by money." *The Uses of the University* (Cambridge, Mass.: Harvard University Press, 1963), p. 20. He is talking about what used to be called the community of scholars.

50. Reread W.H. Auden's "The Unknown Citizen," dedicated to JS/07/M/378, in *Another Time* (New York, N.Y.: Random House, 1940). Or C. Virgil Gheorghiu, *The Twenty-Fifth Hour* (New York, N.Y.: Alfred A. Knopf, 1950).

51. I wish to make it explicit here that while I have often treated Weber critically, the "real" Weber was a far more powerful man than the Weber canonized by social science. Social scientists have borrowed Weber's discussion of the ideal-typical characteristics of bureaucracy, but without his passionate concern to defend politics against bureaucracy. They have enthroned his fact-value distinction but have not even begun to come to terms with his profound criticism of the social science model of cumulative knowledge. They cite his dedication to science and rationality, but they ignore his acceptance of Nietzsche's view of contemporary conceptions of science and rationality as potentially dehumanizing forces. What was not "operational" in Weber has been largely ignored.

52. Perhaps this is excessive. Perhaps it is not yet a "popular equation." Most adult Americans do limit private desire by public right. But among the young the equation is surely growing: either private desire is equated with public

right, or the existence of anything like public right is simply denied, leaving only private desire.
53. In the earlier ages of man, leaders were made by art to appear as more than human: as divine or semidivine personages. Today the ones who stand at the command posts and switching points are made by art to appear as more than mechanical: as human beings.
54. This formulation cuts accross Jouvenel's distinction between *dux* and *rex*, though that distinction is very useful for locating the performance of leadership roles within a social setting. Jouvenel, *Sovereignty,* esp. pp. 40-70.
55. Aristotle, *Ethics* 6; Aquinas, *Summa Theologia,* i-ii 57.4-6; 58.4, 5; ii-ii 47-56.

The Uses of Literature for the Study of Politics:
The Case of Melville's *Benito Cereno*

The mainstream tradition of American political thought flows from the twin fountains of Enlightenment Liberalism and laissez faire capitalism.[1] From these two sources we have inherited a set of political terms and attitudes which have a public and authoritative, an almost-official, status. They are the terms we use for mapping and moving about in the political world. Among the leading members of this official family of political words, one would surely include the following: contract, right, law, due process, liberty, individual, representative, opportunity, competition, private, property, majority, justice, corruption, interest, progress and power. As laissez faire capitalism developed into corporate capitalism, and as the small state grew into the big state, other terms joined the family: corporation, market, organization, regulate, administer, bureaucracy, production, growth, pluralism, union, welfare, statistics, depression, technology, export, profit and centralization.

The list is meant only to be suggestive, and what it is meant to suggest is a certain tone or qualilty in our public words themselves. The words are latinate. They are abstract, cool, distancing. This is a lexicon of surfaces and structures. It directs our view toward large-scale phenomena, big and tangible things, and routine and complex processes, while it veils interiors and mutes emotions. It teaches us to see the political world as existing "out there"—external to ourselves, given, somehow objective and constituted by its own laws. It is also a language of utility and control, teaching us that our ends are mainly material and our means mainly mechanical—as though the polity were a factory and ourselves consumers and workers. About the most colorful member of the family is "corruption," while the warmest is "welfare"—which, we are learning, leaves both donors and recipients cold.

Such a language leaves out half of life, and renders much of our real politics inaccessible to ourselves. This parched public language gives no nourishment to citizen life—no words for saying in public most of the important things about who and what we are and need, and fear and love and hate.

That his condition is dangerous one should need no saying or proving. And yet, even the 1960s, when most of what was happening in American politics could not be said or heard through the official vocabulary, have not moved us to enrich our public vocabulary. Our shared language, as it is heard in politics, the newspapers, magazines, and television is hollow and vapid where it is not evasive and mendacious. It is a simple fact that among us public discourse is largely designed to conceal the truth, to distort and trivialize reality, and to sell shoddy goods under false claims in the satisfaction of manufactured appetites. We have made a desert of the rich possibilities of language, and turned our public spaces into Saharas where gusts of nineteenth century editorial bombast and streams of advertising sloganeering substitute for air and water. About the only place we think and feel and try to tell the truth is in private.[2]

The results are anger and confusion, estrangement from public concerns, and the growing sense that nobody is listening to anybody. Dozens of opinion surveys report that most people no longer even expect the politicians to listen to them. The women have been saying with rising anger that the men are not listening to them. The whites and the blacks cannot hear each other, and the young and the adult are out of touch. The students are not listening very carefully to the teachers. Much of our real politics, which is increasingly a politics of estrangement and despair, is left out of what passes officially for politics. Much of what Americans seem to be wanting to say about their collective lives cannot rise to expression through the baffles of our public rhetoric. We need to find new terms and recover old ones, terms that can help us name and map a different political reality than the one available to us through the official vocabulary.

This situation is not new, nor are efforts to alter it. Underneath the authoritative and official voice there have existed from the beginning of the Republic other voices speaking in different tones and using different words. These are the voices of the losers and the outsiders. These include both actual groups—native Americans, the blacks, displaced farmers and craftsmen, among others—and the greatest of the great American writers. From the anti-Federalists to the New Left, from Cooper to Faulkner, many have tried to show us a politics other than the one that is official.

Speaking as they must against the chorus of liberalism and capitalism, patriotism and progress, these voices are hard to hear, for one of our firmest convictions is that failure has nothing to say. Among us, getting ahead means leaving others behind, and falling behind is its own condemnation. Our history has been a succession of accelerating waves of change, and that means that somebody's past and future are always being washed away. But that, we say, is the price of progress; and, had we been too sensitive to the cries of the drowning, we would have reduced our resources for the great work of getting on with the work of getting on.

Successful Americans might be more ready now than in the past to learn from these failures, for we are no longer so sure as we once were of the meanings of winning and losing. Some are now saying straight out what Henry Adams said obliquely: success on American terms is failure. Even so, the learning will not be easy, for the losers speak strangely. Their meanings are often expressed in unfamiliar words. Their gestures and accents can seem uncouth, or wild, or crazy, making listeners nervous and defensive. Besides, what good is it now to be reminded of the roads not taken? That reminder might evoke nothing more salutary than guilt and remorse in the listener, or anger toward the reminder. No need to add to the nervousness.

Still, the losers and the outsiders are the best source for terms that might revitalize our political discourse and return our politics to ourselves. At the least, the losers and the outsiders might help us strike a different balance sheet of gains and losses, report a different national product, describe another politics than those presented to us in the official vocabulary.

This is so because the losers and outsiders necessarily stress values which are neglected or subverted by the dominant culture. So tight is the dialectical encounter that the minor voice might almost be said to form an alternative tradition to the dominant one. Of course, there are large differences of tone and accent among the outsiders—so large that one might more accurately speak of alternative traditions, rather than an alternative tradition. Still, a very few themes dominate the efforts of the outsiders to instruct, or warn, or defend themselves against the insiders. Against the prevailing ethos of individualism and formal equality, the losers and outsiders stress community and dependence. Against the abstract theories of natural rights and individual liberties forwarded in mainstream thought, the alternative voices stress loyalty, commitment, and obligation. Against the ethos of progress, the outsiders call for limit and proportion, and assert the claims of place and past. Against the formal and legal conceptions of contract and consent, the alternative tradition affirms the need for humanly meaningful authority. Community, limit, loyalty, tradition, dependence, authority: these are the main members of the family of terms which the outsiders would set against the official family. "What life have you if you have not life together? There is no life that is not in community...." Those words, in their content and in their source (T. S. Eliot), might stand as a condensation of the concerns that the dissenters have held foremost.[3]

This is not the place to try to describe fully the content of the alternative tradition. Rather, in what follows I want to take one document from one writer and examine it as a case study in how certain kinds of materials might be used to enrich the meager resources of the mainstream political vocabulary. Melville's *Benito Cereno* is the text: "authority" the term that needs enrichment. Put in one way—an academic way—my intention is to enlarge the canon of authoritative works in the syllabus for "American Political Thought." My larger intention, of course, is to try to recover and make accessible to ourselves aspects of our politics that are now remote and obscured. I want to read Melville's story as a meditation on authority and rebellion.

Authority is a minor and worrisome term in American political discourse. It is one of those topics we would rather not talk about. And when we do talk about it, we do so with and through an impoverished set of sources and concepts, and within a constricted set of attitudes. "Conservatives" argue its utility and lament its decline; "libertarians" challenge its claims and applaud its passing.[4] Our standard sources of thought on the topic are such works as the Constitution, *The Federalist,* Mill's *On Liberty,* a few law cases, and some scraps from Max Weber on the three types of authority. The concepts are perfectly familiar: consent, liberty, law, obligation. Nearly every political-theoretical treatment of the topic builds on these terms, together with a few close relatives (e.g., limit, jurisdiction, office, illegal, disobedience). These ingredients are mixed together to form two standard theoretical products, which have the status of liturgy within the tradition: (1) legitimate authority rests on consent; and (2) authority and liberty are always in tension, and the political trick is to keep the two in balance. There, with but a few unimportant elaborations, thought and feeling end. The discussion is legalistic, abstract and formal, and moralistic throughout.

Let's admit Herman Melville into the conversation, for, after all, the subject preoccupied him from *Typee* to *Billy Budd*. And he must be admitted in the only way he could find congenial—as a storyteller. We might take one of Melville's fictions as a symbolic event, to use Kenneth Burke's term, and look at it almost as we might look at an actual event—a nominating convention, say, or a court trial, or a debate in the Senate. And, at the outset at least, let us approach his story as though it might be true. Let us respect Melville's claims that great literature is the "Art of Telling the Truth," even though it be covertly and by snatches,[5] that he himself was one of the "divers," and that his own stories provided "more reality than reality itself can show."

Now, to approach one of Melville's stories as an event, albeit, of course, a symbolic event, is only one way, and not the usual one, of importing literature into the study of politics. To avoid confusion, let me mention some of the ways that will not be followed here.

First, I shall not try to extract a specific political doctrine from Melville. Nor shall I try to show Melville's own views on the political questions of his day. Nor shall I examine his religious and philosophical beliefs. It is useful to know, for example, that Melville greatly admired Lincoln, and thought his assassination a national tragedy.[6] It might be useful to argue, say, that he was neither an abolitionist nor an antiabolitionist, but one who could condemn the injustice of slavery and fear its evils could be expiated only by blood, while refusing to condemn the slaveholders.[7] You might even argue that his metaphysical views qualify him as an early and undiscovered Pluralist, albeit one who yearned to be a Monist, and who was always threatened by Dualism.[8] All these things have been done, and no doubt there is gain in the doing. How much gain is uncertain. Labels have their uses, but they do not help much in learning from or about a great writer. As Sartre has put it, Flaubert was indeed a bourgeois, and *Madame Bovary* is in some sense a bourgeois novel. But not every bourgeois is a Flaubert, and not every bourgeois novel is a *Madame Bovary*. In any case, approaching a story as a symbolic event providing food for thought is a different enterprise than expounding a writer's social doctrines, or putting a label on his literary style, or examining his metaphysics.

Another way to use literature in the study of politics is to examine the publication and reception of a book as a political event, to assess the book's impact on opinion and action. Certainly, many books have had important effects on our political life, from Paine's *Rights of Man* to Marcuse's *One-Dimensional Man,* and including along the way *The Federalist, Uncle Tom's Cabin,* Thoreau's essay on *Civil Disobedience,* George's *Progress and Poverty*, Alger's tales of pluck and luck, Heller's *Catch 22*, and Goodman's *Growing Up Absurd*. Even the complex works of Reinhold Niebuhr are about to have their day, if we may believe President Carter. The study of such "influences" is certainly worthwhile, but it is not what I shall do.

Next, approaching a work of fiction as a symbolic event, seeing the story as an episode around which thought might move and imagination play, is not the same thing as applying some metalanguage of interpretation to the author's own language, and arguing that the metalanguage provides the key to the right reading of the author's meanings. Thus, you might bring Marxian categories to the reading of Melville, as Bruce Franklin has done, or Freudian categories, as Henry Murray did, and sift Melville's meanings through those screens. In that way, both Melville and his fictional characters can become victims and heroes of the class struggle, or figures driven by unresolved oedipal conflicts and incestuous desires. Such reductions are sometimes illuminating, and sometimes not. They are not what I shall do. I shall try to listen to Melville the way one listens to a wise and compelling storyteller, rather than the way a psychologist listens to a patient, an anthropologist to a native informant, or a jury to a witness. There is, I think, no method which can guarantee right reading. And the prevalence of such methods among academic readers today is not so much a proof of growing sophistication, as a measure of the spread of the Baconian conviction that rare and difficult results can be obtained by common and easy techniques. One who would learn from a great storyteller needs not so much the right method as the right attitude. That attitude is a compound of ardor, humility, and openness to surprise. I mean: one must have real questions whose answers he does not have but fervently seeks; a humble and grateful acknowledgement that the storyteller is wiser than oneself; and a readiness to be surprised by novel and disconcerting truths.[9]

Finally, there is a difficulty in the way of using literature in the study of politics. That difficulty must be admitted, for it cannot be avoided. Put it this way. Great literature is most easily made out of dramatic encounters and "strong" events, and those are not the stuff of ordinary politics. Politicians normally spend most of their time in mundane and wearying activities. They encourage, explain, administer, advise, assure, and organize. They try to persuade reluctant and uncertain persons to stick together in a common enterprise despite differences of opinion and interest. They compromise, bargain, and negotiate. They cajole and plead and promise. They spend their days puffing up the egos of others, salving injured vanities, repairing broken connections. They have little enough opportunity for the display of either great virtue or great vice, towering strength or supine weakness. Their labors rarely issue in tangible and enduring results—which is why politicians are so often mad for concrete monuments. It is hard to make great literature, or even moderately interesting stories, out of such stuff as this—though surely Stendahl in *The Charterhouse of Parma* accomplished the former, and C. P. Snow the latter. The point is, literature is likely to look to politics mainly for "excessive," strong, even pathological material: war, rebellion, assassination, personal and public corruption, desperate plots and schemes, chaos and turmoil, occasions when all may be won or lost on a roll of the dice. Politicians just do not spend most of their time doing or thinking about such things. Hence, when one looks to literature for the illumination of political things, one sees there what appears only infrequently in "reality."

Perhaps this is why specifically political novels so often fail to satisfy, either as politics or as novels: too unrepresentative of the real world of politics; too schematic and histrionic as literature. Political novels typically draw stock characters—the schemer, the fanatic, the idealist, the boss, the lackey—and then plunk them down in stock dramatic situations, letting the violence of the situation substitute for the exploration of character and relationship. Too close to sensational journalism; too far from psychology. *Benito Cereno* is not a political novel in the usual sense; and yet, it has important things to say about some perennial political relationships. The fictional works that teach most about politics are those that explore character, perception, and role behavior under the conditions of inequality and imperfect knowledge.

New World-Old World

As Robert Penn Warren has noted, Melville's mind could be deeply stirred, his imagination fully engaged, only by the "right subject."[10] His right subject was characteristically some powerful event of real life, whether come upon in his own experience, or found in his reading: episodes gravid with the irrefutable validation of actual life. He found one such subject in the chronicle of the bloody uprising of a lot of slaves aboard a Spanish ship, and the subsequent repression of the rebellion by the captain and crew of an American merchantman. From that seed grew *Benito Cereno*.

Melville wrote his story around 1855. The events on which the story is based occurred in 1799. Both of those years were critical ones, years when an old order was falling apart. In the United States, the Kansas-Nebraska Act had recently been passed, foreshadowing the dissolution of the Federal Union and the struggle between North and South. All Europe in 1799 was being convulsed by the arms and ideas of the French Revolution.[11] Santo Domingo was still bleeding from the huge slave revolt there, and power still rested in the hands of Toussaint l'Ouverture, despite the strenuous and ultimately successful efforts of both England and France to dislodge him and restore the blacks to subjection. Both Europe and the American Federal Union (though Melville never explicitly mentions this) were strained to the breaking point by the same questions of liberty, equality, and authority. The story, then, emerges from a world in convulsion, and is presented to another world on the edge of disintegration.

Melville evokes this mood of calamity, actual and impending, in the opening images of his story. A gray, wracked ship looms out of the haze, and drifts across a dead sea under a leaden sky into a silent and remote harbor. She is the San Dominick, her name itself evocative of Santo Domingo, scene of the slave revolt.[12]

The ship's name also evokes the memory of the Dominicans, who had been among the most zealous of the Catholic monastic orders in the suppression of heterodoxy and the maintenance of the true faith. The ship's rigging is in tatters, and the figurehead at the prow is shrouded in weathered canvas. We learn later that the original figurehead has been replaced by a new one. Alejandro Aranda, owner of the slaves, was taken into the bowels of the ship and murdered, along with twelve other whites. Aranda's flesh was stripped from his bones, and three days after the murder his skeleton was brought up from below and fixed at the ship's bows—a gruesome re-enactment of the Resurrection of Christ. The ship's original figurehead was an image of Columbus—discoverer of the New World; founder of the first European town in the New World on Hispaniola, later called Santo Domingo; conquerer and enslaver of the native population of the island. The ship's motto is "follow your leader." The leader, of course, is the murdered Aranda.

Are we in the Old World or the New? Our history does not begin with the "discovery of America," as we like to say, but with conquest and enslavement. At the very moment of initial contact the Old World transmitted to the New the deadliest of its old diseases—conquest, murder and slavery, religious oppression, political power based on force and fear. Or, perhaps there never was a New World. Certainly, those who were already here did not think of their world as "new," or of themselves as now "discovered" by the strangers from the ships. Furthermore, the latter men were not even looking for a new world, but for a shórt route to an old one. For nearly a century after the "discovery" they saw the new world as an obstacle to be gotten around or through on their way to India. Perhaps the New World is only a pretty story we inheritors have told ourselves, needing greatly to believe it. "New World." "Discovery." Comforting labels for blindness and violence.[13]

In any case, large themes are suggested in these opening pages. First, the incapacity of the masters and discoverers to "see" what lies before their eyes. From the beginning, and for centuries, the Spanish, the English, and the new Americans really saw neither the land they had taken, nor the native peoples who lived in it, nor the blacks who were brought as slaves. The land was a thing to be possessed; the natives enemies who must be exterminated or dominated. There was no "touching," as William Carlos Williams put it in *In the American Grain*. Wherever they looked, the conquerors saw only distorted images of themselves—their own beliefs, desires, and fears. They surrounded themselves with palisades of doctrine and stereotype, and grounded their claim to rule in nothing but their own locked hearts. Within the story of *Benito Cereno* itself, this solipsism of perception is one of the dominant motifs. Delano emerges as a man nearly incapable of seeing the world from another's point of view. Proud of his own commonness, encased in the conviction of his own rectitude, which is really little more than a lack of either fulfilled virtues or vices, Delano soothes himself with comforting phrases about his own pleasantness, competence, and fairness. He sees nothing outside himself for what it is. The immediate result of that in the story is near-catastrophe; the final result is continuing failure to learn from experience. On such blindness does authority make its decisions in this story. It is as though the masters were seeing a silent movie, in which the movements of the actors have only the meanings projected onto them by the audience.[14]

Next, the storyteller strongly insinuates in the opening scenes that the Old World is reborn in the New. All the old bad seeds were replanted in the discovery and first plantations, and their bitter fruits will be the same. We are still following our leader, Columbus-Aranda. Later in the tale, Delano muses whether it is he who is lightly leading Cereno's fate, or whether it is really Cereno who is darkly foreshadowing his own. The thought is disturbing, and he shakes it off.

It is significant that the morality of slavery is not even put in issue in the story.[15] The institution is only occasionally referred to, usually by Delano, and never debated. Delano's musings reveal no interest in the question of the rights and wrongs of slavery itself. He assumes throughout that whites shall be masters and blacks shall serve them. That is the order of nature, which the law and practices of slavery only reflect. What is at issue in the story, rather, is the nature of authority, and the purposes which power may serve. There has been a rebellion on ship, made possible by the negligence of the Spanish masters and the presence of the desperate Babo. The ship has recently been the scene of murder and chaos, now concealed under the sinister puppet show arranged by Babo. Established authority has been shattered, and disguised terror has replaced it.

Into this ruined world comes a new man, Captain Amasa Delano of the Bachelor's Delight. He must first size up the situation, grasp the true state of affairs, and then adjust principles to perceptions so as to permit a judgment which can launch a valid and effective course of action. He must understand the nature of the collapse, and then shape measures for reconstructing order and authority on the ship. Delano's eyes are now ours.

He suspects trouble, of course. The whole look of the San Dominick is suspicious. But he is not suspicious by nature and does not like to trouble himself with things beneath the surface.[16] Even when he feels the twitch of danger in the calves of his legs, even when the charged atmosphere condenses and the currents run along his spine, he suppresses the messages. His conscience is clean, and God is good. Who would want to harm Amasa Delano? When his suspicions can no longer be quelled, he makes Don Benito their target. Those vain and coddled aristocrats, he muses, live lives too soft. They grow weak and fretful under adversities which a hearty and self-sufficient man would take in stride. He looks on Cereno with a mixture of pity and mild contempt.

His contempt for the blacks is so thoroughgoing that he cannot credit them with the capacity to act for themselves at all. They are a simple race, more animal than human, and cannot move without masters. At one level, his contempt is benign. Seeing a black woman lying on deck calmly nursing her baby, oblivious to the surrounding disorder, he admires her handsome and nurturing body, and enjoys thinking how admirably suited black women are for procreation and mothering. Later he learns that the ferocity of the black women during the uprising exceeded that of the men. At another level, his contempt takes him blandly, unconsciously, to the depths of moral perversion. Observing how solicitous Babo is for the comfort of his master, Delano remarks that Babo seems more "friend" than servant. Then, thinking how helpful such a friend could be to himself, he offers to buy Babo from his master. Bland corruption, seeing itself as benevolence, can go no deeper than to offer to buy a friend.

This is racism—to use today's word—of the most refractory sort, for it does not know itself for what it is. Delano is not unwilling to change his attitudes, but unable.

At its most benign, paternal authority, which is how Delano sees his own role, finds sufficient justification in the natural needs of those under it, and in its own superior experience, knowledge, and strength. Children need adults if they are to grow up. That is paternal authority's sole justification and obligation: it must recognize and encourage the capacity for autonomy in its subjects. But when a whole race is put under paternal authority, that race is reduced to permanent childhood, denied the capacity for maturation. And when one assumes that others are by nature incapable of acting for themselves—including acting evilly—then one has excluded those others from humanity. So, Delano reflects that the best policy for slaveowners is to treat their charges as good masters treat their faithful dogs. Contempt here sees itself as affection and moderation. Thus, Delano never shows indignation toward the blacks, not even after their atrocities are revealed. Indignation is a democratic emotion. It implies that you share with another a common standard, which the other has failed to meet but is capable of meeting. Contempt looks down from a height, judging others from a pure and lofty place which they can never reach. Here is exactly the difference between moral and moralizing discourse. Authority is prone to the latter by virtue of its very distance from its subjects. Probably the best safeguard against the abuse is frequent and unexpected humiliation.

Delano, then, surveys this shattered world from the high ground of unconscious pride, which he sees as benevolence. He is unable to see that his own legacy includes violence and conquest, and when the time arrives for action, he perpetuates that legacy, never doubting that the blacks must be restored to slavery and the whites to mastery. Others have done the dirty work of slavery—if dirty work it was—and he remains innocent. At bottom, his own experience, accepted unreflectively, is his own worst enemy.

He shows, even while priding himself on his competence, that much experience alone does not add up to a moral quality.

Furthermore, his superficiality is not just a form of obtuseness, but a quality of his civilization, which cares little for memory, and teaches that each is the sole maker of his own fate—even while assuming that for others their race is their fate. In assuming superiority over both the blacks and Don Benito, Delano fails to understand that he is as much a product of his circumstances as they are of theirs. He sees his circumstances as though they were choices freely made by himself, testifying to his own superiority. Delano refuses kinship with others, while still claiming authority to govern them. That refusal means that his moral and political education ends where it began.[17]

Delano, then, the inheritor, is a good American of the enterprising kind. He thinks his inheritance will do as well for everyone as it does for himself. He is no jingoist, certainly, but no curdled critic either. His country is pretty good, on the whole. No doubt it has its faults, but they are surely fewer than the faults of other countries. On the question of slavery, for example, we cannot see him as exactly supporting the institution, but neither does he condemn it. On the whole, he equates character with independence, with the capacity to stand alone, needing no others. And yet, he is ambivalent. Perhaps he does not believe in slavery, but on the other hand, there are those who by nature cannot be their own masters. Besides, he could use a slave. In some moods, with part of himself, he thinks it would be comforting to have a Babo to lean on. In sum, his attitudes toward slavery and servitude are just not thought through; and, along with many of his countrymen, he equates this superficiality with goodness.[18]

Don Benito, however, has experienced the full horror of the rebellion, and what he has learned destroys him. After the rebellion has been crushed, and the ship brought safely to port, he musters the resources needed to make the required deposition for the legal inquest. His deposition is sufficient for the purposes of the law, but otherwise shows no deep understanding of the events. The blacks seized the advantage provided by Aranda's kindness, returning evil for good. Hence, their punishment is just, and Cereno willingly aids the law in its work of retribution. But he knows that that only touches the surface of the matter, leaving everything underneath unchanged. When Delano, regarding the affair as happily ended, asks the still gloomy Cereno what it is that burdens him so heavily even clear skies and the balmy trade winds bring no relief, Don Benito replies, "the negro."

That answer, given in Spanish, refers not just to the blacks, but to blackness—that is, to the capacity for evil in human beings. Slavery is a wrong. But wrong too are the enormities worked by the blacks in their revolt. Nor do the two sets of wrongs cancel each other, leaving the slate clean. Turning the world upside down still leaves a world of masters and slaves. Nothing has happened here to change that. If anything, the case is more desperate at the end of the story than at the beginning, for now each race knows even more acutely what it has to expect from the other.

How to break the cycle? Keeping order always requires a measure of repression. When the order kept is a slave order, the measure of repression must be large. The work can be done only by masters who have the will and the means to strike when need requires. Of course Aranda's kindness was a weakness, and all, black and white alike, pay for it. Violence is the response of those who have had their futures taken from them and delivered over to others. No amount of kindness can erase that theft, or forgive it. Authority and privilege nearly always give up too late what they can no longer keep. "Gifts" so given will be seen by their recipients as confessions of weakness, providing fuel for more demands. Perhaps the only way the cycle can be broken is for the masters, freely, out of strength and not weakness, and from the conviction that justice demands it, to relinquish their power.

Neither Delano nor Cereno comes close to that possibility. Delano will reap his bitter harvest later. Cereno's comes sooner. He no longer has the faith and the will to do the hard work of power. His scabbard is empty, and the church whose doctrines justified the use of the sword in converting and governing the underlings is no longer militant. Don Benito goes off to a monastery in the hills outside town to die, thereby truly following his leader Aranda, whose bones already lie buried there. The church, while it can no longer furnish the faith which arms men for the work of conquest and domination, can at least still offer Don Benito the last consolations of religion.

He is an affecting figure, Don Benito: a trembling wreck of former dignity and grace, in tattered finery. We must see him as late in that succession of heroic explorers and conquerors in the New World. He is no Cortes or Pizarro, able to wreck and kill without tiring, driven by dreams of gold and glory, licensed by mandates from church and state. He is from Lima, that endlessly fascinating white city, rotten with corruption and decadence, where Spaniards beat gold out of slaves, and keep observances as elegant and grave as those followed at the Court of Castile itself. In Lima, the energy of empire has dissipated into bureaucratic lethargy and aristocratic vanity. The masters live in a closed world, and prefer to hear no word from those they have violated. But Cereno, after the revolt, can no longer ignore those voices. "Memory," as he puts it, overwhelms him. He is the ruined figure of a civilized mind overcome by its encounter with the primitive darkness within his own self, his own past, and his own civilization. He is the brother of Conrad's Kurtz. Or, perhaps better, he lives and dies on a smaller and later stage the life and death of the great Emperor Charles V, King Charles I of Spain—the figure fascinated Melville—who after a life spent in zealous service of unity in church and state, abdicated all power, and died a recluse in the monastery of Yuste.

Domination—Rebellion—Revenge

On the other side of the gulf stands Babo, the one who initiated the uprising and orchestrated the puppet show that followed it. The story says two things about Babo. The more important he speaks himself, when, in response to Delano's question, he says that he is twice a slave—in Africa, a black man's slave; in America, a white man's slave. The second thing about Babo is told us by the narrator late in the story: Babo's brain is a "hive of subtlety."[19]

Twice a slave. Babo has no home or people anywhere. His wound is so grievous that nothing can heal it, and only revenge can give relief. His fellow slaves are as much the tools of his rage as the whites are its target. Atufal, the true king, is Babo's pawn. His real aim is destruction, as shown by his unwillingness to follow Atufal's prudent counsel and avoid close encounter with the Bachelor's Delight. Rather, he mounts his desperate scheme to take the ship, and when it fails, makes his last free act the effort to take Cereno's life, even at the cost of abandoning his fellows on the San Dominick, even at the peril of his own life. It seems plain that he has no real hope or intention of returning to Africa, where he had been a slave, and where he would surely become a slave again, or a tyrant. Babo's real strength is his despair. To use Nietzsche's words, he would "will the void, rather than be void of will." When the masters are mediocre and without vigor, as Delano and Cereno are each in his own way, then despair and madness are a force.

The storyteller, I think, is insinuating some disquieting thoughts here. Slavemasters, or the masters of any population sharply divided into rulers and subjects, are not the leaders of a political nation. Their power can in the end rest only on force and fear. Given that, no matter how such power meets its end, by whatever kind of upheaval, it cannot meet its end by a political process hopeful of good moral consequences. A rising of slaves is nothing but a rising of slaves, and the roots of the rising, which are hatred and lust for revenge, will appear in its fruits, which are violent efforts to make slaves of the former masters. Rebellion does not imply transvaluation.

In such upheavals, not the best but the worst come to the front. Victims are not morally elevated by their victimization, and it is sheerest fantasy to expect the best from the most violated. Babo, twice a slave, is the total victim. Most violated, he is also most violent. In him, total violation has produced the deepest rage for revenge.[20] Babo is the natural child of wildly unjust power; but, once such a child appears, there may be no way to redeem or to restore it. Authority then must, for the general safety, stand ready to check such actors, even though they are authority's own creations. And that standing ready is immanent in the very constitution of authority, even the most benign. All order is built on one or another kind and degree of prohibition and repression. A social order *is* a formation in which not all things are permitted, in which some desires are forbidden, some needs not fulfilled, some personalities thwarted. Being built on some measure and kind of repression, each social order necessarily produces encripplements and perversions that are the fruit of repression, and authority must check their expression, even though they are authority's own children. In short, at the base of even the best and most benign social order there is a measure of ultimate injustice and disharmony. Perhaps humans can never fashion a wholly just social order that is also stable and efficient, and that is so not because we are evil by nature, but because we are social and yet diverse. Slavery is only the extreme case of the general situation.

Just as power and authority in part create the specific characteristics of their subjects, so too are power and authority in part creations of their subjects. Cereno, for example, is Babo's creature. The storyteller here expresses in that image once again the interdependence of leader and led, of master and servant—an interdependence so close that an external observer can hardly untangle appearance from reality. But Babo is also both the blacks' creature and creator. Part of what he is comes from his former situation as a black's black, who now, by nerve and cunning, has made the other blacks his pawns. As the blacks' own crippled child, now become their master, he reflects the most ferocious possibilities in them. The leaders thrown up by the powerless and oppressed are likely to magnify the worst possibilities in those who have made them their leaders, for the leader has the will to do in fact what they have wanted in fantasy. He licenses their lusts. The world such rebels make is likely to be as horrid as the one they unmake. An outsider may see no radical difference between the two nightmares.

The storyteller suggests that such is the case. The story opens aboard a ship whose shrouded figurehead is the skeleton of a murdered white man, and closes with the image of a prison atop whose walls stands the piked head of a murdered black man. The black rebellion is crushed and white power restored. But neither power can claim in the backing of a moral standard, whether in the form of a civilization, a mission or a personal moral ideal. From a moral point of view, there is little to choose between the two killings, and neither can break the cycle of domination—rebellion—revenge.[21]

The Country of the Blind

The story makes us think about perception. The storyteller's characteristic way of treating this matter is by playing on, moving back and forth between, surface appearances and underlying realities. That tension or dynamic furnishes the energy which moves the action to its conclusion. When Delano first boards the San Dominick everything that matters lies wrapped and hidden from his eyes. The surface does not look right, but many "theories" could account for the appearances. Occasional flashes of illumination arc between the surfaces and the depths, and these provide the sinister and unnerving movements of the action. But at the end neither Delano nor Don Benito (and probably not the blacks either) really understands the full meaning of the events.

The reason for that becomes clear if we examine the surface-depth dynamic in political terms. Then we can approach the story as a meditation on perception under the conditions of harsh inequality and domination. Under such conditions, when the world is sharply divided into masters and subjects, everything is instantly doubled into two realities, the world of the masters and the world of the slaves. No object or activity or event, not even the most ordinary, such as food or costume, or the conventional forms of greeting and address, appears or means the same to both classes. Then, each of those two worlds is doubled again. There is the world of the masters and the world of the slaves, but there is also the world of the masters as it appears to the masters and as it appears to the slaves, and the world of the slaves as it appears to the slaves and as it appears to the masters. But each of these worlds is doubled still again, first into the world of the masters as they think the slaves see it, then into the world of the slaves as they think the masters see it. Finally, both the masters and the slaves will have introjected something of the "others" into themselves, and projected something of themselves into the others.

The world of domination, then, is a world doubled four times over. There are no fixed or common points in it, no genuinely shared world at all. The light is nowhere steady and clear, objects and events have no or few shared meanings. The participants in such a world are doomed to struggle in abysmal confusion and ignorance over prizes and goals whose value no one can establish. Such a world is impenetrable. Surfaces give no reliable clues to depths, and the basic realities do not disclose themselves through steady manifestations. And this is not a matter merely of the conscious deceits and maskings practiced by the participants. Of course, both underlings and masters hide from each other, wear masks and practice deceit, but that is the smallest part of it. Neither party knows what is "real" about itself and the other, for each has taken into itself part of the other, and may be most like the other just when it thinks itself autonomous. Even as Babo runs the puppet show, for example, and thinks himself leader, he is only doing what the whites did when they ruled. So he too "follows the leader." This world is impenetrable not mainly because the participants deliberately conceal themselves, but because it is a world without center. There is no way "in" to this world, because its basic structure is difference or separation riddled with introjection and projection. There is no getting to the bottom because there is no bottom. There is no way out because there is no way in. Everything is not what it seems, but it is not what it does not seem either.[22]

Such doubleness and bewilderment make us dizzy and anxious. Like Delano, we too retreat into the haven of stereotype and slogan, blame and accusation. The story is brilliant on these themes, more illuminating on the dialectic of perception and identity under the conditions of domination than the Hegelian text on master and slave which has become fashionable in our time. Melville is more honest, too. He denies us the Hegelian happy ending, the fairytale hope that through struggle the real and the rational become one, and all are liberated from illusion and come into full knowledge of self and other. In fact, of course, it rarely works that way. And the price of the misperceptions that come from separation and domination are greater today than they used to be. The gods of the ancient world could sometimes be satisfied with the sacrifice of a single hero. But the god of modern politics, which is a politics of masses, huge technological powers, and entrenched elites, is hungrier than that, and more inclined to take its victims from among those far removed from the centers of command.[23]

Moral Man—Political Man

These beginning reflections on the complexities of perception open a new line of thought, and also help place the story and the storyteller in an old line of thought. Delano, as I and many other readers have pointed out, is self-centered and sure of his own rectitude. He knows he is a good-hearted man, and he knows his actions spring from that goodness. Most readers of the story locate Delano's shortcomings in the banal quality of his goodness. I too have commented on that. But in the end, it is not so much the content of Delano's goodness that blinds him, as his conviction of his own goodness as such. Knowing himself as good; knowing he acts toward others out of that goodness—exactly those traits make him unfit to govern others. Those traits cause him to act as a "moral" rather than a "political" man. He acts largely with reference to the private requirements of his own moral character, but he does so in a situation where he must act in relation to others who are also acting. Hence, their needs, values, and interests must be regarded as of equal importance and validity with his own. It is not just the content of his moral ideas that nearly produces disaster and which leaves him as ignorant at the end as at the beginning of the action, but the very fact that he acts as a moral man in a situation which calls for a political man. Thoreau would have done no better than Delano, and for much the same reason.

It will help to set the distinction within a certain context of political thought, and to call Melville's orientation Machiavellian rather than Aristotelian or Ciceronian.[24] I use "Aristotelian" here as a shorthand reference to that long and rich tradition of thought which centers on an analysis of the moral qualities rulers should possess. This body of thought is conventionally called political, because it is addressed to political persons, but it is really a species of ethical thought. The main idea is that the good man and the good ruler have the same moral qualities. The ruler's personal moral constitution—the way he governs his passions and shapes his desires—is not only a matter of private life, but is also mirrored in the way he governs others in the public realm. Thus, the virtues which Aristotle assigns to the good man in the *Ethics* are also and altogether the virtues assigned to the good ruler in the *Politics*. This germinal idea flowered into an entire genre during the Middle Ages and the Renaissance in the "Mirror of Princes" literature—works of moral advice and exhortation to those in power. The tradition survives in our own day in discussions of "ethics and politics." Most such discussions are less works of political theory than they are a species of casuistry, the application of general moral principles to particular conditions.

But with Machiavelli, a very different line is started, a line, I think, which brings us closer to Melville's thought. In this new line, the governor's care for his personal moral condition is made secondary to his care for the state and his awareness of the dimensions and problematics of action in a political situation. Of all those dimensions, the moral is only one, and often not the most important. Other persons are present. They are acting too. And they are looking at the leading actor or actors. Need, interest, opinion, and power matter as much as morality, and the final question is always the question of who will rule and who will be ruled. To make the contrast clear, consider that if the main question in *Benito Cereno* were a moral question then the case would be very simple: the slave revolt is fully justified, and it is Delano's duty if not to aid it, at least not to obstruct or crush it.[25]

Discussion of the morality of slavery has no part in Melville's story at all. Cereno never mentions it, and Delano mentions it only to muse, when Don Benito (apparently) cuts Babo with a razor after Babo (apparently) accidentally cut him, how slavery can make some masters willful and cruel.

Machiavelli opens this new theme in deliberate opposition to the Christian teachings and to the literature of advice to princes. Before he has done with it, he has turned the whole "moral" tradition inside out, reversing both Aristotle and the Christians. Here is Machiavelli's famous opening.

> Many have fancied for themselves republics and principalities that have never been seen or known to exist in reality. For there is such a difference between how men live and how they ought to live that he who abandons what is done for what ought to be done learns his destruction rather than his preservation, because any man who under all conditions insists on making it his business to be good will surely be destroyed among so many who are not good. Hence a prince, in order to hold his position, must acquire the power to be not good, and understand when to use it and when not to use it, in accord with necessity.[26]

Thus, political actors must learn how not to be good in the conventional and Christian sense. They must learn to act as circumstances require.

Now, circumstances are infinite in their variety, of course, but every political situation has certain features which may be said to make it a political situation. First, a variety of persons with a variety of points of view are present and involved: a political situation is characterized by plurality, as Hannah Arendt calls it. Next, the specifically political question is, what shall we do? Political questions have no single, determinate answer, no solution which all who are in command of the evidence and capable of rational argument will accept as the necessary or correct solution. But all who are included within the "we" and affected by the decision will be expected to obey it, or suffer the penalties of disobedience. Finally, in any political situation, some persons—call them leaders or notables—are more visible than others. They are prominent. They stand out. Others look at them. What they say and do matters more than what ordinary people say and do. Such persons must not only attend to the policy question at hand, but must also and equally give care to the matter of maintaining their own prominence.

This means that the ones who are highly visible must always be aware of how their actions appear to others. Their characteristics, insofar as they are politically relevant, are not their own so much as they are those which the others ascribe to them. Hence, leaders must take greatest care for the attributes, including the moral attributes, that will be ascribed to them by others. The leader lives in the minds and imaginations of others. Public image and appearance to others—politically speaking, these are, in large part, what a ruler is. How the notables appear to the others is the largest portion of the political reality shared by the two groups.

In sum, political leaders and authorities must always pay the greatest attention to their appearance to others. This means they must be in touch with those others, must know accurately how the others are thinking and feeling. Above all, political authorities must be able to see themselves and the world through the eyes of others.

This is the supreme, and supremely moral, political ability. And it is precisely that ability which Delano lacks, and which, firm in the conviction of his own goodness, he prides himself in lacking.[27] His is a pride shared in common with many good people, and perhaps particularly good Americans. Like Delano, many of us justify our apolitical lives on the argument that we are morally superior to the others—especially to the others who are political—and that our moral superiority both requires and justifies staying apart from those others. The argument and the stance were matured already in Roger Williams.[28] It appears also in Delano, where it is harder to see it for what it is, because the "goodness" he cherishes is so thoroughly common. But at its center is the same self-satisfaction, now hardened into the individualism of the self-made man, which takes competence as its theology, and whose secret fear is the fear of being touched by and dependent on others. It is an attitude which denies moral equality and cuts off its holders not only from their contemporaries but also from those who came before and those who will follow after. I think the final teaching of the storyteller is the danger and sterility of those who do not much try to enter, because they do not much respect, the worlds of other people. The final teaching is a teaching of democracy and fraternity, across all barriers. We return to the marriage of Ishmael and Queequeg. Against the long tradition of the "mirror of princes" literature, Melville, perhaps, offers us a "mirror of democrats."

No prophet, let alone an unarmed one, can redeem his own age. He can perhaps only tell it what it has already lost. Melville surely did that. The work of his middle and late years is filled with images of remoteness and isolation, and with descriptions of unredemptive authority. *Bartleby* is only the most desolate of the lot. As American civilization advanced, Melville found less and less genuine human association in it, and no truly legitimate authority at all. He offered such warning as he could, though there were few to listen. The *Confidence-Man*, which appeared in 1857, the last work of his fiction to be published during his lifetime, is a dark comedy of people victimized by their own self-deceptions. Perhaps during this period, Melville himself, harried by poor health and poverty, and burdened by the knowledge that while no one is innocent, human action nearly always brings most harm to the most nearly innnocent, fell into a kind of lethargy and cynicism. Closer to the point of *Benito Cereno* is his collection of Civil War verses, *Battle-Pieces*, published in 1866, after nearly ten years of silence. Shortly after the work appeared, Melville went into the Custom House.

Melville says he was moved to write *Battle-Pieces* by "an impulse imparted by the fall of Richmond." The work opens with a poem called "The Portent" whose commanding image is that of John Brown, "the meteor of the war,"

> Hanging from the beam,
>
> Slowly swaying (such the law),

The law had its way, as it did in *Benito Cereno*, and made "weird John Brown" the first of the million sacrifices in the great war for the Union and the Constitution. The Union also prevailed. But, as poem after poem insists (and for readers who might miss the point in verse Melville made a straight-out appeal in his prose "Supplement") unless the nation north and south, black and white, made a genuine turning toward fraternity and equal liberty that Union would be soulless and heartless, fit only for the uses of the masters of the impending utilitarian age. Lincoln called for the same turning in his remarkable "Speech in Independence Hall," of February 22, 1861, where he as much as said the Union would not be worth preserving were it not the ark of the covenant of liberty and equality.[29] That turning has yet to be made. The same shadow which haunted Benito Cereno darkens our lives as well.

The Puritan Dilemma

Let us go back and look once again at the storyteller. Can we, without prying or pushing, get him to disclose a little more of himself to us? We should not expect, or even want, the storyteller to open himself to us as yieldingly as Ishmael gave himself to Queequeg, or as longingly as Melville opened himself to Hawthorne, but perhaps we can get some glimpses of his deeper intentions and orientations.

In *The Encantadas*, following the opening passages of melancholy and sinister description there appears this line: "In no world but a fallen one could such lands exist."[30] In *Hawthorne and His Mosses*, published in August of 1850 (Melville started *Moby-Dick* that same summer), and offered by "a Virginian spending July in Vermont," there appear some more suggestive lines. *Hawthorne and His Mosses* is a richly mixed piece. Among other things, it is partly a tribute and a love letter to Hawthorne, together with an insisitence that "the world" has not even begun to understand him; partly a bouyantly patriotic affirmation of the future of literature in America; partly an essay on the oblique and crafty methods by which great artists go about their work of telling the truth; and partly a conjecture about the source from which such artists draw the power to tell truths "so terrifically true that it were all but madness for any good man, in his own proper character, to utter, or even hint of them." It is that conjecture which is of interest here. Writing about Hawthorne, but obviously about himself as well, the "Virginian" says:

> "The Christmas Banquet" and "The Bosom Serpent" would be fine subjects for a curious and elaborate analysis, touching the conjectural parts of the mind that produced them. For spite of all the Indian-summer sunlight on the hither side of Hawthorne's soul, the other side—like the dark half of the physical sphere—is shrouded in a blackness, ten times black. But this darkness but gives more effect to the ever-moving dawn, that forever advances through it, and circumnavigates his world. Whether Hawthorne has simply availed himself of this mystical blackness as a means to the wondrous effects he makes it to produce in his lights and shades; or whether there really lurks in him, perhaps unknown to himself, a touch of Puritanic gloom,—this, I cannot altogether tell. Certain it is, however, that this great power of blackness in him derives its force from its appeals to that Calvinistic sense of Innate Depravity and Original Sin, from whose visitations, in some shape or other, no deeply thinking mind is always and wholly free. For, in certain moods, no man can weigh this world without throwing in something, somehow like Original Sin, to strike the uneven balance.[31]

A "fallen world"; a world whose inmost core, despite the "Indian-summer sunlight" of its surfaces, is "shrouded in a blackness, ten times black"; a world in which those who face the truth must recognize the force, "in some shape or other," of "Innate Depravity" and "Original Sin." This is surely something very like the world John Calvin envisaged, but with some differences: Calvin's God is dead; so too is the theology that made some sense of the ways of that God; so too is the human community devoted to that God and made understandable to itself in terms of that theology. We might say that nothing remains of Calvin and Calvinism except their mood and the problem they tried to solve.

That may be too cryptic, or too condensed, for a time in which, while the Puritan dilemma still exists, the language and the institutions for describing and enduring it have largely disappeared. In his great essay on "The Augustinian Strain of Piety," Perry Miller perhaps found words that can translate into our own time this timeless sense of the gravity of the human condition. The passage must be quoted extensively:

> It is obvious that man dwells in a splendid universe, a magnificent expanse of earth and sky and heavens, which manifestly is built upon a majestic plan, maintains some mighty design, though man himself cannot grasp it. Yet for him it is not a pleasant or satisfying world. In his few moments of respite from labor or from his enemies, he dreams

that this very universe might indeed be perfect, its laws operating just as now they seem to do, and yet he and it somehow be in full accord. The very ease with which he can frame this image to himself makes reality all the more mocking. . . . It is only too clear that man is not at home within this universe, and yet that he is not good enough to deserve a better; he is out of touch with the grand harmony, he is an incongruous being amid the creatures, a blemish and a blot upon the face of nature. . . . There are moments of vision when the living spirit seems to circulate in his veins, when man is in accord with the totality of all things, when his life ceases to be a burden to him and separateness is ecstatically overcome by mysterious participation in the whole. . . . When these moments have passed he endeavors to live by their fading light, struggling against imperfection in the memory of their perfection, or else he falls back, wearied and rebellious, into cynicism and acrimony. All about him he sees men without this illumination, exemplifying the horrors of their detached and forlorn condition. They murder, malign, and betray each other, they are not to be relied upon, they wear themselves out in the chains of lust, their lives have no meaning, their virtues are pretenses and their vices unprofitable. . . . Mortals pursue illusions, and success inspires only disgust or despair. They seek forgetfulness in idolatries and narcotics, or delude themselves in sophistical reasonings, and they die at last cursing the day they were born or clutching at the clay feet of their superstitions.[32]

And, adds Miller, lest we exempt ourselves too easily, the "Puritans did not believe that they saw things in these terms merely because they were victims of melancholia, but because they were there to be seen." The facts and teachings that confirmed this vision of existence were of course in the *Bible,* and the *Bible* was of course the word of God. But the facts are also there in the experience of all ages and every life, and no clear-eyed or "deeply thinking" man will deny what is everywhere about him.

I think something like this vision of existence came down through the ages to settle in with Herman Melville, and to cast over his mind (or, he says, over Hawthorne's mind) that "Puritanic gloom" which simultaneously darkens and lightens his work. But for him, as for many others in his time, the God that gave ultimate reason to everything had died. Other deaths followed that one: the system of explanation that gave believers some bearings for their journey through this broken world; the institutions of church, righteous state, and school that embodied and gave shape to the restless, chaotic strivings of the natural self; and, above all, the possibility of a gracious illumination that could give men the strength and balance needed for finding some harmony in the midst of ubiquitous disharmony. Grace of course comes as the free gift of God; and just as God is harmoniously possessed of attributes which in nature jar against each other, so the gift of grace makes natural men in some degree capable of maintaining this same supernatural balance among jarring qualities. "Natural men alternate between joy at one moment and sorrow at another; gracious persons are filled simultaneously with exultation and grief."[33] It is they, in Melville's terms, who can "strike the uneven balance" in this world-battlefield where good and evil, joy and despair, constantly struggle, and where men and women, haunted by memories of the first lost Eden, tormented by their yearnings to make a second and better Eden, characteristically choose for themselves a dismal halfway condition between the bounteous will to live and build on the one side, and the guilty urge to expiate by suffering and destruction on the other—thereby perpetuating the hopeless cycle of sin and atonement.[34]

So, I think, the storyteller did live in a fallen world, and yearned for a redeemed one, but with little faith in its advent. In such a world, on what ground can authority stand? Such a world is without any stopping point (such as God) to limit thought and challenge. There is no theology or teleology to redeem the present or hold out the possibility for a better future and a different history. There is always the likelihood that the strongest and most passionate will give themselves over to the demonic Ahab-urge to "strike through the pasteboard mask," and wholly embrace the "blackness ten times black" as ultimate reality, taking the weaker along as their victims.[35]

Lesser, more ordinary spirits, like lost children in this shattered world, will make their lesser and more ordinary pacts, settling for security and easy absolution. Cardinal Newman wrote that deep and glowing faith was no longer the mark and gift of his times, and that all that could be expected and required of the believer was to resist doubt. Since Newman's time, most observers agree that the power of faith has diminished further, and that the privilege of faith is given even less frequently. In a sense, that is correct. Faith in and commitment to the established religious traditions have obviously declined. But in another sense it is inaccurate. It is not so much that people in our times lack the capacity for faith, as that they lack the capacity for faith in anything great, steady, and demanding. The age abounds in small and easy faiths, crawls with instant saviors. By comparison, religious life in Rome of the second century A.D. was steady. There is a prophet on every street corner and a messiah in every rock band. Millions go in passionately for mind-cures, and hundreds get rich from them. People find salvation in everything from deep mulch to transcendental meditation. What is characteristic of these faiths is that they are so trivial and privatistic. It is not that the age lacks spiritual values; rather, it teems with so many that all become cheap. There is a Gresham's law of spiritual currency too, whereby the cheap coin drives out the good.

In all these senses, our times are truly Machiavellian and democratic. Ours is a time, of course, of great and growing concentrations of power, but that power lacks foundation in legitimate authority. No God; no theology; no teleology. On the one side, there is concentrated power, which can only continue the tendencies of the present but can start nothing new. On the other side are deepening confusion and despair, which also can start nothing new. That is what it means to still have the Puritan dilemma, but to lack the Calvinist possibility of resolution.

How can authority be reconstituted in such a world? That is surely one of the questions Melville pondered, and one his readers cannot evade. And we cannot stop by saying that all he had to say on the matter was that discipline on board a man-of-war cannot easily be reconciled with democratic doctrine. Everybody knows that, and if Melville knew no more he would no longer be read. His own claims were much larger.[36]

I think Melville did start from something close to a theological view of the problem, but he knew no theological solution was possible. His own doubts precluded that; and, if they were not enough, the realities of a secular and increasingly dogmatically atheistical age were. The writer alone could not resacralize history, no matter how desperately that was needed. But, although the writer could not perform the priestly function, he could be a storyteller.[37] And, if he were a great storyteller, his fictions, while "only" fictions, could still have more reality in them than reality itself. Through art, one might create a new mythos more real and truer than reality itself, for reality is always diverse and inchoate, and will answer to numerous interpretations. In this way, while authority could not be given an ultimate ground in some realm beyond the human, it could be grounded in a compelling fiction—an imaging of the human condition so imperious, so close to the primitive and archetypal in human experience—that men would yield to it. With that, the old cycle of sin and atonement might be broken and a new history begun.

This, I think, is what Melville yearned to do, and it is what he attempted in those regions of his work where his eschatological appetites got the better of him.[38] *Benito Cereno,* however, is entirely humanistic. It admits no values or authority from another realm into our own, but it does allow for the possibility that we can create our own values, and in them find self-definition and some degree of moral peace. Granted that, perhaps it is not stretching too far to say we can find some authoritative, albeit contingent, values in Melville, together with an ethic of action in a fallen or relative world.

For a glimpse of those values, let me present one image and three quotations. The image is that of the interracial, intercultural union of Ishmael and Queequeg. The quotations are: (1) "Heaven have mercy on us all—Presbyterians and Pagans alike—for we are all somehow dreadfully cracked about the head, and sadly need mending" (*Moby Dick,* Ch. 17); (2) "No American writer should write like an Englishman or a Frenchman; let him write like a man, for then he will be sure to write like an American" (*Hawthorne and his Mosses*); and (3) "The Declaration of Independence makes a difference" (Letter to Evert Duyckink). I am aware that different beads could be strung together to form the loop of Melville's central values, but these, I think, can make as good a claim as any others. In a fatherless world, the writer affirms a vision, a fiction, and a mythos of universal fraternity. But it is a fraternity more earthly than the unchastened boast of the Declaration, with its vain declaration that all men are born free and equal, morally complete, and thus not dependent on others for nurture and fulfillment. Rather, Melville sees that we all "sadly need mending." Still, the Declaration makes a difference: the commitment to equality is the American promise to the future. Or, as he put it in the Supplement to *Battle-Pieces,* in what amounts to a prayer for rededication: "Let us pray that the terrible historic tragedy of our time may not have been enacted without instructing our whole beloved country through terror and pity; and may fulfillment verify in the end those expectations which kindle the bards of Progress and Humanity."

An Ethic of Action

Can we find in Melville suggestions toward an ethic of action? To start, let us return to that "theological" description of the human condition which I outlined earlier to see whether it offers any guides for right action in an equivocal world.

"Original Sin," with its accompanying idea of "Innate Depravity," is not some event that happened in some remote place some long time ago, whose burdens we (unjustly) inherit. Rather, the ideas take their force from our innate and frequently used capacity for disruption. It is as though, to use a language faithful to Puritan belief, God gave us a good home, but he also gave us the ability to disrupt that home, which we continuously do, thereby making ourselves no longer at home. The universe, since it is the creation of a good and harmonious God, must itself be good and harmonious at its center, but that center is something we only occasionally glimpse, or see through a glass, darkly.[39]

Disharmony (sin, in an older vocabulary), however, is the pervasive and palpable reality of everyday life. It is what we feel in ourselves and see in the world most of the time. And most of our actions, despite our soundest judgment and best intention, add to it. Nor need one be of a gloomy temperament to see the world this way: due attention to the nightmarish spectacle of history should bring the lesson home even to the cheerful.

Nor can we refuse to play the game. Human beings, unlike the cattle, must choose what they will do and be. We are not governed by our instincts or totally dominated by our keepers. Rather, we are free; and our freedom puts us under an imperative of decision and action. And each action is in time. It is taken on the knife-edge of the present, and thus both completes a life to that point, and projects it into the future. Stories such as *Benito Cereno* only dramatize and sharpen this quality of the human condition.[40]

We can see the story, then, as a concentrated description of our general condition as beings who are under an imperative of decision and action. It offers us a sharpened account of the features of all action. A number of those features stand out.

First, knowledge is always imperfect, insufficient to the occasion. And this, while obviously an imperfection is also a condition of our freedom. Ignorance makes action perilous, but it also makes it possible. One who had perfect knowledge could not really be said to choose; he only does what is necessary. Hence, we require theories, attempts to explain and cope with the unknown in the light of the known.[41] With that, the complexities begin, stemming from two sources: the situation will nearly always answer to more than one explanation; and, we meet ourselves in our explanations. Our theories are in some part more or less accurate reflections of "reality," but they are also in some part reflections of ourselves—compositions built out of our values, needs, interests, and intentions. An actor's theory or explanation reveals—is—his character. Consider how Delano's explanations tell us everything about the sort of man he is.[42]

Secondly, the moral complexities of action are unfathomable. We hardly know our own real motives and intentions, though we like to think we do. We frequently mistake the motives and intentions of others, characteristically judging them less generous or noble than our own. As the great Puritan divine Thomas Hooker put it, we are quick to see the sins of others, but a true sight of one's own sin is hard to come by. Social institutions of criticism and exposure are needed for that, and such institutions are in disrepair in our time. It is all too easy for us, as it were, to make an unknowing pact with the devil. In general, what matters here is that, given the moral complexities of action, we cannot act without great danger of bringing damage to ourselves, our companions, and the world itself—often unknowingly.

Thirdly, acting changes the situation or conditions in which the acting is done, and those changes occur in unpredictable ways. This has a number of consequences. It means, obviously, that the outcomes of action are unpredictable. Hence, the question of what the actor is responsible for, and what not, can almost never be answered in a thoroughly satisfactory way, but must be the subject of endless discussion and meditation. That is in large part what accounts of action are all about, and the story form is as competent a form of discourse for the discussion of this question as any of the other forms we have devised (such as law, abstract ethical philosophy, the social sciences, ideology). It means also that the premises or explanations upon which the action was initiated, and which seemed sufficient then, may later become hopelessly inadequate. But, characteristically, that awareness comes late. And even when it does come, actors find it difficult to discard the old premises and adopt new ones. To do so often seems a confession of incompetence: pride is involved; so is reputation; and changes of direction easily confuse one's companions, making them anxious and mistrustful.[43]

Finally, since acting changes the conditions of action, and since action has unpredictable consequences, the knowledge that seemed sufficient for the original action, may be insufficient for an understanding of the (known) consequences of the action. It follows that one cannot know with certainty either before, during, or after action the full nature and scope of the good and evil one's actions have brought into the world. It is in recognition of this that we vaguely say: we cannot know; history must decide. But of course history, which means historians, never "decides" unequivocally. There can never be a definitive, exhaustive assessment of the nature or consequences of action. We who come after the action and are its heirs, can only choose one or another more-or-less ignorant version of the legacy, and live it through as our own.[44]

Given the dynamic and inherently limitless quality of action, we are always trying to fence it in. We try to limit its scope and consequences, provide rationales for acting, and set bounds to responsibility. The oldest of all fencing materials are law, custom, and religion. Newer ones are ideology, whose tutelary genius is Karl Marx, and rational choice theory, presided over by Jeremy Bentham. The older forms are in disarray in our times, and the newer ones have fallen short of expectations: the "revolution" always gets out of hand and runs off in unanticipated and usually undesirable directions; "reality" is always messing up the tidy world of rational planning. The real forces restricting the scope of action in our day are bureaucratic coordination of mass populations, and the dominance of routine, automatic processes of economic production and distribution. Both constrict the space in which action or liberty can appear, pushing it into the private realm, and squeezing it even there. Melville was well aware of this tendency, and warned against it as strongly as he knew how.[45]

80 LEGITIMACY IN THE MODERN STATE

Given the nature of action, are there some kinds of characters and moral orientations which, if they cannot assure success, can at least reduce the likelihood of disaster? Can we find in Melville, can we draw from *Benito Cereno* some suggestions toward an ethic of action? I think there are such suggestions. They are few, and valuable.

First of all, it is clear from all his writing that Melville thought it impossible to separate character from belief. He was an explorer and mapper of the hidden connections between character and ideas, personality and opinion. One might say that he, like Nietzsche, was a student of the genealogy of morals, seeing a person's beliefs as a function of that person's whole constitution and lifeway. In the human realm, then, ideas are not to be judged abstractly true or false, good or evil, because the tone and temper of the person, the depth of experience, the person's awareness and understanding of self and others, are part of the truth or falsity of the ideas themselves. In assessing the quality of a belief or value one must always ask not just whether the belief is right, but also whether the believer is the right kind of person, who holds the belief in the right way. Two people, sharing the same "value," can act very differently in the world. "Love" makes one a coward, and another brave. Obviously, love is as the lover is—not a fixed quality, but a function or expression of self.

It follows that one cannot, without pernicious results, set an ideology or abstract doctrine of any kind above human character and the values, interests, sufferings and strengths that go with different types of characters. Delano judges Cereno's "aristocracy" by his own "democracy," and finds it wanting, thereby never seeing the man and his situation at all. Blacks are inferior by nature, and could not possibly command. Like Delano, we too retreat into absolutes, but the storyteller warns that we must endure the painful relativity of experience and character, denying ourselves the false refuge of doctrinal and formulaic solutions.

Like Delano too, most of us are hopeful creatures, and think that without hope we would not have the will to push forward against the obstacles set by external conditions and our own weaknesses and remembered failures. Yet, Delano's optimism, while it brings him strength, is also his greatest weakness. He is spared disaster not by his own cheerfulness and skill but by Cereno's desperate courage in jumping into the small boat, and by Babo's rage for revenge, which sends him after Cereno and into the hands of his enemies.

Hope seems necessary to life, yet the storyteller warns against hope. I think he leaned toward a reading of the story of Pandora's box other than the one we are usually taught: hope is not the sweet gift which leaves the box last, giving us strength to bear the ills that precede it, but is itself the worst affliction, betraying us into the delusion that we can escape the ills. As

Melville put it elsewhere, ". . . that mortal man who hath more of joy than sorrow in him, that mortal man cannot be true—not true, or undeveloped."[46]

"More of joy than sorrow." That is what is warned against. This is a warning against optimism, but it is not a recommendation of pessimism. Rather, it seems to be a teaching of balance and tension. "There is a wisdom that is woe; but there is a woe that is madness."[47]

What does that balanced character and outlook look like: earlier (note 16), I suggested the formulation, "pessimism of intelligence, optimism of will." It is something like the temperament of the person touched by grace, as the Puritans understood that: the one who has the almost divine or supernatural ability to hold incompatible qualities in harmony; the one who lives in the world fully and caringly, and yet with "weaned affections," neither wildly raised up nor woefully cast down by victory or defeat but hewing to the middle line. To try another formula, perhaps the right temperament for action is a stoicism blended of equal parts of self-assertiveness and self-denial: an assertiveness which gives one the resoluteness to act and accept responsibility; a self-denial which enables one to subdue one's personal pain in a compassionate awareness of the general human lot, which is mainly a condition of shortage and failure. If I read Melville correctly here, his real hero Jack Chase and his fictional hero Captain Vere most closely meet this standard of the whole man and actor. Delano and Cereno represent crippled halves of the whole.

All who act must do so, if they are "developed," out of readiness to face defeat and in recognition of the impossibility of knowing the truth. The pursuit of failure in ignorance, but still the pursuit—that, it seems to me, is Melville's understanding of our lot. Furthermore, he insists in *Benito Cereno* and elsewhere that the search for meaning can lead to the awful discovery of the inevitability of evil, or to the vision of a terrible equivocality amounting to blankness beneath the solid surface.[48]

But the defeat need not end in rout, as it does for Benito Cereno. Stripped of his pleasing illusion of just dominion, he loses the will to live. Delano, on the other hand, has hardly lived at all in any distinctively human sense, for he comes out as he went in, "undeveloped." The storyteller is suggesting that we become fully human only if we can open ourselves to the full complexities of both our inward selves and our outer circumstances, risking fire and blankness, and still return, tempered and enlightened, to the world of action. The saving chastening comes when we recognize our self in the other, and acknowledge kinship in the common plight of right in wrong and wrong in right.

With that, the ethic of action, the right character of the whole actor, and the final aims of action become one, or as nearly one as they can become. I proposed earlier that a case could be made for Melville as an equalitarian—not equality as uniformity, but equality as giving proper consideration to all of those with whom we share an interdependent life, and, ultimately, as acknowledging our kinship with all of humanity, with whom we share the common condition of "fatherlessness." No one of us can claim a higher authority for our values than any other can claim for his. Thus, in situations of struggle and conflict, that side is to be preferred which, if it were victorious, would be able to give the largest, most sympathetic consideration to the ideals of the defeated. And that will usually be the side whose members best recognize themselves in the other, and understand that beneath all differences they and their opponents share a common humanity. In that way, the right actor, the right ethic of action, and the right aims of action become nearly one. Perhaps we can claim no solider ground for our values than that, but surely we should not settle for less.

Notes

1. The Puritan founding has had little significance, save as a negative benchmark—the place we want to get away from. Neither has the moment of radical republican thought of the pre-Revolutionary and early Revolutionary periods contributed more than a trickle to the mainstream, though it endures as the source of an alternative rhetoric and as a potential force for political renewal.
2. And even there the problem appears, for the public words increasingly fill our horizons. We hardly notice how they have spilled over our whole lives.
   Compare: ". . . our words are our calls or claims upon the objects and contexts of our world; they show how we count phenomena, what counts for us. . . . Our faithlessness to our language repeats our faithlessness to all our shared commitments." Stanley Cavell, *The Senses of Walden* (New York, N.Y.: Viking Press, 1974), p. 65.
3. Characteristically, the writers explore the consequences of the absence of community and authority in American lives. Positive efforts to show what community and benign authority might look and feel like, and how they might be nurtured, are relatively rare. For every *Looking Backward* or *The Country of the Pointed Firs,* one might say there are a dozen *Caesar's Column(s)* or *Winesburg, Ohio(s).* But that should occasion no surprise, because the mainstream tradition has been so overwhelmingly and mindlessly expansionist and individualistic: for every Josiah Royce there have been a dozen William Graham Sumner(s); for every Lincoln a dozen Jackson(s). The dissenters have been a small and ignored minority always close to the edge of despair and pessimism and thus inclined to the language of rebuke and warning, revenge and punishment.
4. Two recent works, one by a conservative, the other by a libertarian, both widely noticed, fit comfortably within the archetypal framework of American thought and feeling on this subject. Robert Nisbet's *Twilight of Authority* (Oxford: Oxford University Press, 1975), laments the passing of legitimate authority, and blames the murder on "the intellectuals." Robert Paul Wolff's

In Defense of Anarchism (New York, N.Y.: Harper & Row, 1970), which sets out to solve the problem of "how the moral autonomy of the individual can be made compatible with the legitimate authority of the state," concludes that the problem cannot be solved, and that, therefore, the state is without legitimate authority. Wolff, I think, assumes a (Kantian) theory of ethics which on its own terms forecloses a "solution" to the "problem." And, sociologically speaking, all Wolff omits from the discussion is the actual fabric of how people live together and make a shared world.

5. From Melville's "Hawthorne and his Mosses" (1850).
6. See, e.g., his poem "The Martyr," in *Battle-Pieces* (1866).
7. "These South Savannahs may yet prove battlefields" (*Mardi*, 1849).
8. Or as Hawthorne put it in his *English Notebooks*, "He can neither believe, nor be comfortable in his unbelief, and he is too honest and courageous not to try to do one or the other."
9. Closely related to this is the problem of the author's own intentions: What did the author mean? What did he believe? Readers have tormented themselves with this question from the beginning, and must forever do so, until the library shelves can bear no more. Those greatest of all interpreters, the Jews, accumulated in the *Talmud* the greatest of all interpretations of the greatest of all Authors, only to see the interpretations spin out more interpretations hopelessly into infinity—despite the efforts of zealous medieval Christians to bring relief by burning whatever copies of the *Talmud* they could lay hands on. Borges has given us wonderful parables on the subject. The fruit is in the quest, not the conclusion.

I make no claims to an authoritative understanding of Melville's own meanings. Melville said quite a lot about his meanings, but he also left a lot unsaid. No doubt, as D. H. Lawrence argued, he sometimes revealed in his art meanings he hid in his explicit words. No doubt, too, he sometimes said more than he meant, and sometimes less. And Melville told a lot about his own "theory" of writing, and of how he should be read, in his review of Hawthorne's *Mosses*.

I have consulted the leading sources, and tried to listen to Melville. But in the end, one can only submit one's reading to the jury of knowledgeable readers, and accept their verdict—which will not be unanimous—with such grace as one can.

10. Robert Penn Warren, ed., *Selected Poems of Herman Melville: A Reader's Edition* (New York, N.Y.: Random House, 1967), p. 11.
11. Melville gave much thought to the challenge to order posed by the French Revolution. The mutiny on board the English ship *Noire* during the Revolution sets the background for *Billy Budd*.
12. The revolt in Santo Domingo was so unsettling to the leaders of the American South that they censored reports of it and tried to block the importation of slaves from the island.
13. One of Nietzsche's epigrams condenses the profound and unconscious perversity at work in the European discoveries of and relations with other civilizations: "'I have done that,' says my memory. 'I cannot have done that'—says my pride, and remains adamant. At last—memory yields." *Beyond Good and Evil*, tr. by R. J. Hollingdale (Baltimore, Md.: Penguin Books, 1972), Maxim 68, p. 72.
14. The story reminds one of the bewilderment expressed by many good whites when the blacks burned the cities in the late 1960s: "Why are they doing that? What do they want?"

84 LEGITIMACY IN THE MODERN STATE

15. This has troubled many readers, including F. O. Matthiessen, who saw Melville's failure to reckon with the fact that the slaves were slaves, "and that evil had thus originally been done to them," as responsible for making the story, "for all its prolonged suspense, comparatively superficial." *American Renaissance* (New York, N.Y.: Oxford University Press, 1941), p. 508. John Howard Lawson is even harsher. He calls the story "propaganda for slavery," and sees it as a "cheap melodrama, a distortion of human and moral values . . . a pitiful attempt to accomplish the task which Shelley rejected—to reconcile 'the Champion with the Oppressor of Mankind.' " *The Hidden Heritage* (New York, N.Y.: Citadel Press, 1968), pp. 430-31. More on this later.

16. The storyteller comments: "Whether in view of what humanity is capable, such a trait implies, along with a benevolent heart, more than ordinary quickness and accuracy of intellectual perception, may be left to the wise to determine." Melville's protagonists characteristically—unlike Hawthorne's, incidentally—come to ruin more through lack of intelligence than for want of a "benevolent heart." An acute pessimism of intelligence, balanced by a vigorous optimism of will—that might be Melville's (and Machiavelli's) formula for mature authority.

17. The storyteller suggests as much in the episode of the "Gordian Knot." An old sailor tosses Delano a large and wondrously contrived knot, like no knot ever seen before, yet which, Delano notices, is built up of real and familiar knots. One of those knots is the "Three Crowns," which in the work of the story suggests the three worlds of the Spaniards, or Old World, the Americans, or New World, and the blacks, or Hidden World. Delano must find the secret reality behind appearances before he can hope to build a better order. (Much of the world is always hidden to authority, for the underlying realities of authority realationships are never as settled as appearances suggest.) He fails. The knot is seized by a watchful black, who pokes about in it for something that might be hidden, and, finding nothing, tosses it over the side.

18. Robert Lowell, in his marvelous dramatization of the story, sees Delano under a harsher light. At one point, Perkins, the young bosun, asks, "Do you believe in slavery, Captain Delano?" Delano replies:

> In a civilized country, Perkins, everyone disbelieves in slavery, everyone disbelieves in slavery and wants slaves. We have the perfect uneasy answer; in the North, we don't have them and want them; Mr. Jefferson has them and fears them.

And, in the play's climax, after Babo has surrendered, Delano shoots him. Robert Lowell, "Benito Cereno," third play of *The Old Glory* cycle (New York, N.Y.: Farrar, Straus and Giroux, 1965), pp. 124-94.

19. Perhaps there is a third item of information. It is probable that Babo's name means "no" in one of the West African languages. Babo: Bartleby's violent brother.

20. It is plausible to say, when we trace the motif through Melville's works, that in his view the original sin is to strike back against wicked or inexplicable injustice, or dire provocation. The original sin is the passion for revenge. Ahab is an avenger. The Indian Hater in *The Confidence Man* is an avenger. So too are Babo and the blacks. And so too is Billy Budd, that "upright barbarian," that one "who in the nude might have posed for a statue of young

Adam before the fall." No matter what mode of retaliation he might choose, the avenger cannot keep his own goodness intact. Striking back against the world's evil implicates one in that evil, and adds to it. The "heart," or "nature" may be on the victim's side, but Melville seems to suggest that following the heart only adds to nature's flaws.

I am not sure I am right in proposing that this is Melville's view. Nor, if it is his view, am I sure it is the correct view. Most modern, and all radical, thought would deny it. Does Melville stand with Socrates, who taught that it is always better to suffer than to do injustice?

21. Political philosophers, with very few exceptions, have not looked to the wretched and broken as the agents of a better political order. The tradition teaches that the best cannot come from the worst, and looks to one or another superior group for renewal. The great religions, on the other hand, have characteristically sought the seeds of the new spiritual kingdom amongst the wretched and ruined of the earthly kingdoms. Among political theorists, Marx stands as the great exception to the pattern; and it is this which gives his thought an unmistakeably religious and chiliastic flavor.

22. Kings used to have fools and jesters to help them cut through these bewilderments. The ruling classes in modern states, since they may not announce themselves as ruling classes, are denied such help.

23. Consider this report from a modern battlefield: "According to these 'rules of engagement,' it was morally right to shoot an unarmed Vietnamese who was running, but wrong to shoot one who was standing or walking; it was wrong to shoot an enemy prisoner at close range, but right for a sniper at long range to kill an enemy soldier who was no more able than a prisoner to defend himself; it was wrong for infantrymen to destroy a village with white phosphorous grenades, but right for a fighter pilot to drop napalm on it. Ethics seemed to be a matter of distance and technology. You could never go wrong if you killed people at long range with sophisticated weapons." Philip Caputo, *A Rumor of War* (New York, N.Y.: Holt, Rinehart and Winston, 1977), pp. 229-30.

24. Or, perhaps better, in an American setting, to call the orientation Lincolnian rather than Wilsonian. See Lincoln's "Temperance Address" of February 22, 1842. Roy P. Basler, ed., *Collected Works of Abraham Lincoln* (New Brunswick, N.J.: Rutgers University Press, 1953), Vol. I, pp. 271-79.

25. This is the view most moderns would take. It is the view which many commentators have brought to the story. But it is not the only possible view, and not the obviously correct view. I remind the reader of Socrates' teaching, mentioned earlier.

26. *The Prince*, Ch. 15. Tr. by Allan Gilbert, *Machiavelli: The Chief Works and Others*, 3 vols. (Durham, N.C.: Duke University Press, 1965), Vol. I, pp. 57-58.

27. Lowell's dramatization includes a scene which expresses perfectly the inability of the moral Delano to see how his morality looks to others. Babo shows Delano a black Virgin and Child which the blacks have set up as part of their puppet show. Then, this dialogue:
Babo: Do you want to shake hands with the Queen of Heaven, Yankee Master?
Delano: No, I'm not used to royalty. Tell her I believe in freedom of religion, if people don't take liberties. Let's move on.
Babo: [*kneeling to the Virgin Mary*] I present something Your Majesty has

never seen, a white man who doesn't believe in taking liberties, Your Majesty. Of course, to the blacks, white men are exactly those who live by "taking liberties."
28. For Williams, see Perry Miller's *Roger Williams: His Contribution to the American Tradition* (New York, N.Y.: Bobbs-Merrill, 1953). Miller corrects the conventional portrait of Williams as the "irresponsible democrat."
29. Roy F. Basler, ed., *The Collected Works of Abraham Lincoln*, 8 vols. (New Brunswick, N.J.: Rutgers University Press, 1953), Vol. 4, pp. 240-41. See also Lincoln's (unpublished) "Fragment on the Constitution and the Union," ibid., pp. 168-69.
30. The line appears in "Sketch First" of the work. *The Encantadas* was first published (over the signature of "Salvator R. Tarnmoor") in early 1854, a little over a year before the first publication of *Benito Cereno* (which appeared anonymously). Both were republished in *The Piazza Tales*, 1856.
31. I have quoted the text from Edmund Wilson's *The Shock of Recognition*, 1943 (New York, N.Y.: Grosset and Dunlap, 1955), p. 192.
32. Perry Miller, *The New England Mind: The Seventeenth Century*, 1939 (Boston, Mass.: Beacon Press, 1961), pp. 7-8.
33. Ibid., p. 29.
34. This is Augustinian throughout, of course. Augustine's description of the divided soul and world (Augustine was a Manichaean for nine years of his early manhood) fits no one better than it fits Herman Melville. Melville's wild swings of mood and belief show that he himself was never able to "strike the uneven balance," though he gave his life to the task. Is *Billy Budd* reconciliation or submission?
35. Calvinists, in their quaint langauge, called that solution making a pact with the devil. Everyone knows the secret motto of *Moby-Dick*. I have read somewhere that T. E. Lawrence had a shelf of "diabolic" books in his library. The section contained three works: *The Brothers Karamazov, Thus Spake Zarathustra*, and *Moby-Dick*. The other Lawrence, D. H., whose *Studies in Classic American Literature* (1922) has shaped my way of reading the great nineteenth-century American writers, calls Ahab "atheist," and identifies the Pequod as the "ship of the American soul" (Doubleday, 1953, p. 161). With that identification, the sinking of the Pequod becomes an Americn event: after it goes down, what are left are flotsam and jetsam, the "orphan" Ishmael—or, as Lawrence puts it, "post-mortem effects" (p. 174). I suppose that what this means is that in Lawrence's view a great American writer had already in 1851 laid bare the inmost secret of the American mission of conquest and mastery.
36. "I seek for truth. . . ." "I am Posterity speaking by proxy. . . ." (*Hawthorne and His Mosses*, op. cit., pp. 200, 204). The first is quoted from Hawthorne. Both refer to Hawthorne. But Melville nearly assimilates himself to the older writer in this piece. Moreover, he announces that an American writer as great as Shakespeare may already be here, unknown to his countrymen. "It is of a piece with the Jews, who, while their Shiloh was meekly walking in their streets, were still praying for his magnificent coming. . . ." (p. 195). Melville, by the way, reads the obscure use of "Shiloh" in *Genesis* 49:10 to refer to the Messiah.
37. Melville puts Emerson in the priestly role, and flenses both the priest and the creed.
38. Say, in long stretches of *Moby-Dick*. *Billy Budd* ("God bless Captain Vere!") resolves the question formally, though we are excluded from that last

conversation between Vere and Budd. *Clarel,* published in the centennial year of the Republic, ends in a draw.
39. Melville offers a few visions of this ultimate harmony, most wondrously in Chapter 87 of *Moby-Dick,* "The Grand Armada," and most sensuously in Chapter 94, "A Squeeze of the Hand."
40. Bartleby's "I would prefer not to" is of course also an action. Its negativity spares it none of the complex equivocality of all action.
41. As Tocqueville put the point, God has no need of theory, for he knows all the facts. Theory is in one sense the highest form of knowledge, and in another sense the confession of ignorance.
42. The two times when even the most superficial are likely to think are before action, and after defeat. Delano declines the latter invitation. Cereno accepts it, and cannot endure what he learns.
43. Delano is only a little slower than average to discard his initial ideas. I have found that most students reading the story for the first time solve the riddle no sooner than he did. Then, they are distressed to see how much of Delano is in themselves.
44. When an action is public and of enduring significance, our interpretation of it can shape our whole conception of membership and obligation. Consider how interpretations of the American founding have shaped our politics and political thought. Was the Consititution the work of public-spirited statesmen building a home for liberty and justice, or was it the self-interested creation of the moneyed classes, designed largely to protect their class position? What kind of union did the Framers intend? Did the Constitution complete the Declaration of Independence, or was it a betrayal of the revolutionary promise? And what is the status of the Framers' intentions anyway?
45. In "Bartleby," of course. See also "The Bell-Tower" and "The Paradise of Bachelors, The Tartarus of Maids."
46. *Moby-Dick,* Ch. 96, "The Try-Works."
47. Ibid.
48. His renderings of this are many. Here are a few of the most familiar: cannibalism in *Typee;* the practices of the "cities of the plain" carried on below decks in a man-of-war; the river boat *Fidèle,* her decks a crowded congress "of all kinds of that multiform pilgrim species, man"; the fire-worshipping Parsees; the whiteness of the whale; Bartleby's service in the Dead Letter Office, where "on errands of life, letters speed to death"; Pierre's "Pierre is neuter now"; Cereno's "the negro."

Review of Diana Trilling's
We Must March My Darlings

Diana Trilling has collected and republished a dozen of her reports on the battle scenes of the last decade. The pieces range from a eulogy to President Kennedy to a homily on the antics of Timothy Leary. There are a number of reports from the sexual front: two pieces on women's liberation and the female fate in America, an essay comparing Roth's *Portnoy's Complaint* with J. R. Ackerley's *My Father and Myself,* a review of Nigel Nicolson's *Portrait of a Marriage,* and an essay on the varied reactions to D. H. Lawrence's views on sex and marriage—not to mention Mrs. Trilling's snappish response to the sexual and pedagogical snarls at the new Radcliffe. The film critics are rebuked for their lax treatment of the ethics of *Easy Rider.* Two long essays on higher education—one on the mishmash at Radcliffe, the other on the 1968 disaster at Columbia—make up over half the book. Finally, some old political scores are settled in a piece on "Liberal Anti-Communism Revisited" and another on "What's Happening to America?" The anti-Communism essay was first published in 1967 and amended in 1976 in order to respond to Lillian Hellman's *Scoundrel Time.* Notwithstanding prepublication rumors that Mrs. Trilling had some scorching things to say about Miss Hellman, her remarks are tepid.

Surveying the scene from her redoubt atop Morningside Heights, the author finds little that cheers and much that dismays. The Introduction strikes a somber note. The pace of history has so accelerated that there is no longer space for the "orderly growth" of the "life of culture." Protean man has been "replaced by man in solution; indeed, by man dissolved...." The assassination of President Kennedy left us a nation of Ancient Mariners. "It altered our sense of ourselves as a people; it deprives us of the promise of a future." The book's title comes from Whitman's "Pioneers! O Pioneers!" and Mrs. Trilling uses the reference to suggest that, contrary to the poet's high hope, it is now the young and not the old who "droop and end their lesson," shirking the responsibilities of the present, evading the challenge of the future.

All that is in the Introduction. As the book unfolds, the author's dismay deepens, darkening toward gloom, lightened only by sporadic flashes of temper. Rebuke follows upon rebuke. What is not ridiculous is despicable or deadly. Deaths by drugs are laid at the doors of Leary and Alpert. (Strangely, even knowledge of "seven LSD casualties within my own small circle of acquaintances" does not move the writer to reflect that perhaps Leary and Alpert were more symptom than cause of serious social dislocations.) The anti-anti-communists are found guilty of grave disservices to America, to freedom and candor, and to the reputation of George Orwell. The insurrectionary students at Columbia had no political ideas but only "adversary postures in life and particularly in relation to life in America. . . ." Besides that, they pissed in the wastebaskets in President Kirk's office. Still, we perhaps should have expected nothing better from such darlings, cossets of adoring parents.

The Vietnam war demonstrators lost all claim to the sympathy of decent people because "anti-Americanism" was the "overarching principle" of their protest, and because they sometimes even marched "under the flag of the Viet Cong." The political left at the moment is so absorbed in criticizing the CIA, that "the greater part of the hard work of dealing with our difficult public problems is today being done not on the Left but at the Center or often on the Right." That fact fills the author "with dismay about the present relation of our enlightened classes to politics." The students at Radcliffe, male and female, are upbraided for their mindless self-satisfaction, their lack of spine, and their general slovenliness of manner and dress. While encounters with a few students did provide at least occasional touching moments amid the general squalor and boredom ("How they do bore me much of the time!"), the author's response to the College authorities was "hard, unitary, and only unhappy." It was impossible to learn from them what the College thought it was up to, other than "what-ever is certified as most forward-looking in contemporary culture. . . ." President Bunting cheerfully presided over the death of Radcliffe as though that death were "yet another of its landmark achievements," as though "something awesome and beautiful had been accomplished for our sex."

It is hard to take so unrelievedly ponderous a book entirely seriously. Mrs. Trilling, apparently, never needs a moral holiday. But most of us, made of ordinary stuff, do. I managed a few myself, though not without some guilt. The most refreshing was provided by the writer's withering reply to Robert Lowell's good-spirited effort to suggest a certain lack of proportion in her response to the Columbia affair as compared to her response to the Vietnam war. "She seems more preoccupied," he wrote, in a letter Mrs. Trilling reprints, "with the little violence of the unarmed student uprisings than with the great violence of the nation at war. She implies that we who are horrified by napalm on human flesh are somehow indifferent to the piss on President Kirk's carpet." And Lowell asks: "On the great day when she meets her Maker, John Stuart Mill on his right hand and Diderot on his left, they will say, 'Liberalism gave you a standard; what have you done for liberalism?'"

Mrs. Trilling, in reply, sees "nothing in the conduct of the SDS to persuade me that today's piss won't be tomorrow's lethal weapon...." Nor will she be "as much at a loss for words as Mr. Lowell suggests" at that conversation in heaven. "To Mill I shall say that I did my best to see the truth, and to Diderot I shall say that I did my best to look beneath the appearance of things, especially the things which announce themselves as virtue. And surely it is not impossible that I'll get by." There is a certain dash in that vignette of the writer weighing-in at the Last Assizes, and finding herself up to the mark.

Proportion and measure, however, an earnest effort to see the world from another's point of view, some hesitancy about judging as wrong or dangerous what may not conform to one's own standards—these qualities are in generous supply nowhere in this book. Diana Trilling, as best I can tell, is a critic who hates evil more than she loves good.

The guiding intention of the work is didactic. One can have no quarrel with didactic intention as such, but in these essays that intention is characteristically expressed in a tone of censure. Seriousness gives way to harshness. Moral discourse gives way to moralizing. Indignation, an emotion which implies that the judge shares with the judged a value or standard which the latter has dishonored, gives way to contempt, an emotion which suggests the judge pronounces from on high, from a pure and lofty place which the judged can never reach.

More troublesome even than the ungenerous and hard tone of the "liberalism" which this book claims as its own is the way that liberalism turns into an ideology which clouds memory, substitutes denunciation for thoughtful argument, and blunts perception of complex fact. Mrs. Trilling's political and moral outlook was forged in the 1930s and tempered in the anticommunist Cold War combats of the 1940s and 1950s. That Manichaean mapping of the world was simplistic enough in its own time. It leaves those who still cling to it defensive and judgmental in our time, immobilized by their own armor.

Perhaps the psychological center of these essays is found in a passage about the blacks who participated in the Columbia disturbances of 1968. "They were frightening—all demonstrated power not of one's own election is frightening—but they were serious even in their menace.... They were not cosseted middle-class boys playing violent games whose consequences they felt no necessity to assess." If "all demonstrated power not of one's own election is frightening," what chance is there of understanding what the demonstrators were up to? And indeed, we get no sense that Mrs.

Trilling's "middle-class boys" had important differences of intent, style, and belief among themselves, or that they had any personal qualities at all other than ignorance and rudeness. Furthermore, the most "violent games" of all at Columbia were not played by the demonstrators—black or white, middle-class or any-other-class—but by the police. And surely, of all the participants, those who felt the least "necessity to assess" the consequences of violence were the University administrators who called in those police.

While the social and economic content of the liberalism offered in this book is not defined, one can gather from scattered passages that Mrs. Trilling's liberalism in 1976 is about where John Stuart Mill's was in 1848, before he had made such additions as the chapter on "The Probable Futurity of the Labouring Classes" to *The Principles of Political Economy*. She recognizes, as Mill had a century and a quarter earlier, that liberalism must "be rigorously reassessed to see how it can be made to apply to the social and technological circumstances of contemporary life . . ." The direction that reassessment might take is hinted at when we are told that, in case after case, liberal accomplishments have produced grave problems: "the right of labor to bargain collectively has . . . spurred inflation and unemployment; the gains of feminism have been lost in the nuclear family; [what does that mean?], programs of public welfare issue in corruption and bankruptcy; universal compulsory education has produced mass subliteracy." But that parade of familiar horribles is accompanied by no serious analysis of actual social power or responsibility. There is no recognition, for example, that the tax structure hugely favors large corporate enterprise, or that industrial methods have so debased work that high wages are virtually the only reason left for working, or that companies can pick up and move where they will in search of higher profits, mindless of the waste and hardship they leave behind. One would not suspect from this list of horribles that perhaps the single largest inflation-inducing factor today is the price of energy, and that that price is decided by alliances of states on the one side, and huge international corporations on the other. There is simply no recognition that this society is ruled by elites of power, largely based in the giant industrial and financial institutions, and that major political and economic decisions are practically inaccessible to democratic processes.

Mrs Trilling's liberalism finds its sharpest definition in a negative: "I am, was, and always shall be an anti-Communist." "Not all anti-Communists are liberals, but . . . no one can call himself a liberal who is not an anti-Communist." Trilling righteously, and accurately, reminds us that during the fifties she resolutely refused both communism and McCarthyism. But her heaviest charges are brought against the anti-anticommunists.

By the time she finishes with them, they are found guilty of perpetrating or abetting the greatest political crimes of our era.

In her account, anti-anticommunism, while it did not receive its name until the 1950s, was born in the 1930s, when new radicalized intellectuals, abandoning the ancient liberal faith, began to identify the good with whatever furthered the Soviet cause. These people, many in number and strong in influence, corrupted our highest political counsels during World War II, making us unsuspicious of our Soviet ally, and thereby smoothing the road for the delivery of millions of East Europeans and Germans into the hands of Stalin at Yalta.

This sweeping conclusion is announced without any serious historical argument, or even any effort to confront alternative explanations of events. Such diplomats as Averell Harriman and George Kennan, staunch anticommunists both, deeply mistrusted the Russians. Both were important actors in the events Mrs. Trilling alludes to, and both have given careful accounts of the period which cast much doubt on her easy conclusion. Nor has Mrs. Trilling the slightest suggestion to make on how, and at what cost, the Red Army could have been kept out of Eastern Europe at the time. Here as elsewhere idelogy and indignation substitute for analysis.

By the late forties, Mrs. Trilling continues, the progressives were "well-prepared . . . to mount battle against President Truman's foreign policy. . . ." Mrs. Trilling manages to make criticism of Truman's foreign policy sound like some vicious or misguided un-American, pro-Stalinist plot. Yet, one might, and still without accepting the extreme allegations of the Cold War revisionist historians, find plenty that was troublesome in American policy during those years. That was the time when the "pitiful, helpless giant" who later came crashing in Vietnam was being born. That Truman's foreign policy resulted in a vast buildup of American military power, fueled by a volatile and repressive anti-communist consensus, and backed by practically every powerful politician, business leader, and newspaper in the United States, is of no interest to Mrs. Trilling. To confront this historical reality would interrupt the righteous flow. Therefore, she cannot take the first step in a serious analysis, distinguishing between Stalinists on the one hand, and, on the other, those who in different and often complex ways argued that the military and ideological excesses of the Cold War were dangerous, whether in violating rights and repressing dissent at home, or in supporting dictatorships and narrowing the possibilities for more just and peaceable arrangements abroad. Neither Walter Lippmann nor George Kennan, say, could escape Mrs. Trilling's anti-anticommunist net, for both criticized the anticommunist monomania of the policies of Truman, Acheson, and Dulles.

As the charges broaden, the anti-anticommunists are found guilty even of the war in Southeast Asia: "had our opinion-forming class not for so many years blindly played the Soviet Union's game, Russia would not only not have achieved her present strength in Europe; she might not have been able to back North Vietnam as she did and there would have been no Vietnam War for us to have become engaged in as unwisely as we did." That is surely the flimsiest causal chain forged in recent American historical writing. Such power in the hands of scribblers! Such a disastrous *trahison des clercs*! But just who are in that "opinion-forming"class? The establishment press, most of which encouraged American involvement from early on, and supported the war almost to the bitter end? The Senators who gave us the Tonkin Gulf Resolution founded on trumped-up evidence fabricated by the Defense Department? For Diana Trilling, neither French colonialism (which the U.S. supported right up to the collapse at Dienbienphu), nor the long indigenous struggle against it seems ever to have existed.

That covers only the international front. Here at home, according to Mrs. Trilling, the anti-anticommunists prepared the way for McCarthyism. By neglecting or evading "their own principled job of intellectual housecleaning," the anti-anticommunists did much to create "a climate of opinion favorable to the existence of the House Un-American Activities Committee and McCarthy." For, "had the left-wing intellectuals . . . confronted the truth of Stalinist oppression and murder instead of measuring their liberalism by their sympathy with, or at least silence about, Soviet dictatorship, HUAC and McCarthy would never have had the field they had for their incursions upon democratic freedom."

But Mrs. Trilling seems to forget that Senator McCarthy had the greatest difficulty finding communists in the government. His long "lists" shortened under inspection, and he had to invent people to play the role of villain, often by "exposing" and defaming such liberal anticommunists as James Wechsler. Mrs. Trilling also ignores the extensive investigations and purges of the federal bureaucracy under President Truman's loyalty-security program, and she has nothing to say about the purges of the national labor unions conducted by the AFL and CIO leaders. The Henry Wallace Progressives mustered 2.4 percent of the vote in 1948. The Americans for Democratic Action (ADA), impeccably anticommunist, commanded far more prestige and support among liberal and left intellectuals than any procommunist group.

All of that happened well before Senator McCarthy made his first phony and sensational charges in the spring of 1950. He only captured, accelerated, and symbolized forces in motion. But Mrs. Trilling does not attend to the actual events of the period, events which included some of the most thorough "housecleaning" in our history—none of it discouraging to McCarthy or to HUAC.

As one studies Mrs. Trilling's pages on these episodes, a pattern of thought emerges. It goes like this. Someone (say, McCarthy) accuses another of some evil (say, communist affiliations or sympathies). On the basis of this accusation, he claims to be justified in harming the accused, and proceeds to try to do so. Others (say, liberal anticommunists who criticize McCarthy's methods, or perhaps "Progressives" who sometimes take policy positions similar to those of the communists) are also harmed in the process. These victims, whether because they fear the accuser or because they share his aims while deploring his methods, partly blame the original accused for the harm worked by the accuser. After all, had it not been for the Communists, there would have been no need or rationale for McCarthy. Later on, an observer (say, Diana Trilling) concludes that while the original accused is responsible for what befell him and the others, those others are even more responsible, for had they done to each other and to the original accused what McCarthy tried to do, he would have had no platform and no power. It is thus the anti-anticommunists who are most to blame for McCarthyism.

At bottom, this is a version of "the victims have themselves to blame, for they are incorrigible." That can sound like a justification of McCarthy. It is surely the logic of what passes for explanation in this book. As such, it is not very different from the tried and true method of first giving the dog a bad name, then hanging him.

Mrs. Trilling's fullest statement on the kind of liberalism she admires can be found in her eulogy to President Kennedy, written a year after his death. His assassination, she writes, was the great tragedy of our time, for in him America and the Free World had found the leader worthy of their devotion and adequate to their needs. He held realism and idealism in balance. In him, modesty, dignity, and pride were perfectly fused. He allied "unimpeachable modernity" with "a developed regard for tradition," holding past and present together, thus giving us hope of "a continuing life in civilization—which is to say, a future." It is true that, victimized by bad counsel, he erred grievously in the Bay of Pigs invasion, but that error was redeemed in his magnificent handling of the Cuban Missile Crisis, his "major achievement in international affairs." There, America gained a desperately needed "triumph of forceful principle," and invested "the symbol of Kennedy, the heroic son, . . . with something of the importance of Franklin Roosevelt as symbol of the wise and benevolent father." In sum, we found in Kennedy the true "champion of freedom," a "national leader whose personal aura is one of heroism, romance, gaiety, and even a certain rakishness . . . but who has the stern substantiality of mind and character to guide his country in international crisis and to propose new paths of domestic enlightenment. . . ."

Well, not all of us await the return of the paladins of Camelot. Some may even think that President Kennedy's major advance in international politics over the policies of John Foster Dulles was that while Dulles only orated about going to the nuclear brink, Kennedy twice took us there, once in Cuba and once in Berlin. President Kennedy's rhetoric even exceeded Dulles's in its vision of apocalypse. Remember the first Kennedy "State of the Union" address: "Each day the crises multiply. Each day their solution grows more difficult. Each day we draw nearer the hour of maximum danger." Following that, Kennedy began the largest and fastest military build-up in our peacetime history.[1] Have we forgotten that it was Kennedy who deepened our involvement in Vietnam right up to and possibly past the point of no return? And how can Mrs. Trilling describe his handling of the Cuban Missile Crisis as a masterpiece of "purposiveness and control" when, in simplest fact, his strategy there left the ultimate decision entirely in the hands of Khrushchev?

And what were those "new paths of domestic enlightenment" which Diana Trilling says President Kennedy proposed to us? The great domestic crisis of his time was the civil rights struggle, which Kennedy ignored right up until Birmingham, when it could no longer be wished away. The moral leadership of the nation in that struggle was to be found not within the White House, but outside it, in the person of Martin Luther King. Indeed, as we now know, the chief response of the Administration to that moral leadership was to unleash the FBI against it.

In economic policy, the New Frontier set growth as its major priority ("not how to divide the economic pie, but how to enlarge it," as President Kennedy told the U.S. Chamber of Commerce in 1962). This was to be achieved by a "full-fledged alliance" between government and business (Kennedy's speech to the National Industrial Conference Board, February 13, 1961), one that would enhance the safety of the "Free World." Hence, business needed tax incentives and labor needed restraint. Both got what they needed: during the Kennedy years, corporate power and profit boomed, as did the national security bureaucracy, while pressing social needs went begging. In their major outlines, the economic policies of the New Frontier were as old as the Republicanism of William McKinley. The goals, and the consequences, were the same. All that was really new was the "practical management," as Kennedy called it, of the economy by experts skilled in a modified Keynesianism.

Confrontation abroad with a world communism mythicized as monolithic in structure and wholly malign in intent; the absence of any serious vision of a better America at home—such is the liberalism lauded in this book. As such, it is a liberalism obsessed with visions of apocalypse and of worlds in decay. Yes, we must march my darlings, but under brighter banners than those waved here. Without the certainties of doctrinal anticommunism and inviolable self-rectitude to blind us, we might even discover a hopeful path.

Note

1. See Theodore Sorensen, *Kennedy* (New York, N.Y.: Bantam, 1966), p. 686.

The American Amnesia

A Review of
Nightmare: The Underside of the Nixon Years,
by J. Anthony Lucas
The Time of Illusion, by Jonathan Schell

According to St. Augustine—no better name to invoke when one is discussing political sin—"the seat of mind is in memory." If Augustine was right, the nation is now mindless, and we shall have to find such comfort as we can in the hope that when mind goes, habit and instinct may still remain, assuring life if not direction.

Surely the most striking aspect of the present political scene is the absence of the recent past from it. There seems to be something like a tacit agreement among the presidential contenders, and between them and the public, that the record of recent events has no bearing on our present condition and future prospects. The closest Gerald Ford comes to touching the past is in vague allusions to some dragon called detente, against which he will guard us just as he will preserve our ethnic treasures here at home. Those fronts secured, we can move forward into the third century, which is to be the century of American Individualism. Ronald Reagan sounds like Teddy Roosevelt, all teeth and bluster, about to lead the Rough Riders in another charge, this time into the Panama Canal. Jimmy Carter overleaps the recent past by centuries, and assures us that America still stands in a covenant of nations with God. The people and their leaders agree: let's forget the recent past and get on with the business of building a brighter future. That, of course, is exactly the advice Richard Nixon gave the nation at the height of Watergate.

This silence is all the more remarkable when one remembers that among the unspoken events are a constitutional crisis greater than any since the

Civil War, absolute proof that for years national law enforcement and intelligence agencies violated law and elementary decency here and abroad, and a desolating war in Southeast Asia. The constitutional crisis has been reduced to an exciting film entertainment about the thrills and triumphs of investigative reporting, and to something like court scandal based on dubious research methods and ethics. Behind the scenes, the war continues to exist in the same basic doctrines and inflated military budgets that produced and sustained it in the first place. Out front, it exists only in occasional stories about the affairs of Lieutenant Calley and the difficulties of adjustment experienced by the Vietnamese refugees.

As the *Mayaguez* incident showed, not even the most obvious "lessons" of Vietnam have been accepted. In that episode, President Ford replayed Vietnam in miniature. He unleashed force against a small Asian country without consultation outside the Executive. The force was vastly greater than any sensible appraisal of the situation would have recommended. The affair was misrepresented to the public and casualty lists were falsified. The President crowed that the encounter was a victory for America, proving once again that we would stand behind our word and use our arms to back our interests.

Not one of the major contenders in the presidential primaries was an outspoken opponent of the war in Vietnam. The meaning of the war is not discussed. The military budget booms. The Trident program has been launched (ten submarines planned, each capable of virtually destroying a continent). President Ford has proposed a plan for reorganizing the "intelligence community" which amounts to a method for making it easier for that community to do what it has always done. The same kind of double-think that characterized foreign policy during Vietnam still prevails: then, we withdrew ground troops while secretly bombing Cambodia, and mined Haiphong harbor against Soviet ships while secretly arranging grain deals with the Soviet Union; now, we pour money into the hands of rightist foreign politicians and make huge arms sales to a dozen despots while mouthing the slogans of peace and democracy.

Apparently, nothing has changed and nothing is remembered. Public discussion in this presidential year has virtually nothing to do with recent public reality. It appears that the political parties and electoral coalitions are no longer a force for memory, even as they long ago ceased being a force for change. They have joined Congress as vestigial organs—likely to flare up and cause a little trouble now and then, but with no vital functions to perform in the body politic, save the production of bombast and the distribution of spoils.

Given this decay of public life, is it possible now to write about Watergate-And-All-That and hope to have some good effect on national politics? Has that whole convulsive decade which produced and culminated in the abuses of the Nixon presidency been so thoroughly repressed as to be inaccessible to ordinary methods of public recollection? That is an interesting problem in political psychology, and a question of some significance for the future.

Woodward and Bernstein's book *The Final Days* solves the problem neatly, albeit in the most likely way. They have shown, with the help of a national news magazine, that there is still a lot of interest in politics as a spectator sport, and a lot of money to be made in selling tickets to the game. Their book has presented the image of the Nixon presidency that is most likely to remain fixed in the public mind: a befuddled and desperate Nixon beseeching a frightened Kissinger to kneel with him in prayer, all else having failed. Let us hope that this vignette will be enough for Nixon haters and Nixon lovers alike: no more need either to bury or to praise that Caesar. And *The Final Days*, in reducing Watergate to personality and entertainment, will relieve many of having to think more deeply about the special brand of elective Caesarism that is now the dominant feature of national politics in this country.

Woodward and Bernstein's melodrama will also reduce the impact of Anthony Lukas's *Nightmare*. That is regrettable, for Lukas has written a solid, comprehensive, and excellent contemporary history not just of the Watergate events but of the systematic abuse of power during the Nixon presidency which Watergate exposed and typified.

The problem with writing a contemporary history of Watergate is not the scarcity of facts but their abundance. Congress and the press got off to a late start in exposing the crimes and abuses of the Nixon presidency, but what they lost in time they made up for in zeal. There are now carloads of data—much of them contradictory, based on obscure sources, and issued for selfish motives by persons of doubtful reliability. The problem is not one of discovering, but one of sifting, assessing, and connecting the available evidence. On the whole, Lukas has done a workmanlike job. He has not added much to our knowledge of the abuse of power in the Nixon presidency but he has brought a great many facts together and strung them on a lively narrative line.

In Lukas' version—and he is surely correct—the Watergate story began long before the bungled break-in of June 17, 1972. It began in the earliest days of Nixon's first term, with the small, tentative, first steps toward the building of a secret and illegal spy apparatus: "investigative support for the White House," John Ehrlichman called it. That small seed, planted in the soil of hate and weakness, cultivated by the self-righteous lackeys of a president who needed assurance the way an aging actor needs applause, soon blossomed into the "enemies list" and wiretaps of May 1969. By the midterm election season of 1970-71, the blossom was in full flower. Watergate and the coverup were of a piece with all that had gone before. Lukas covers all this familiar ground thoroughly. In addition, he explores with particular care some of the darker regions of the terrain: the Howard Hughes-CIA White House links; the sale of influence and office for money; the full sweep of the Plumbers' activities; the misuse of federal agencies and money to reward friends and punish enemies.

The book is as long on facts as it is short on analysis. *Nightmare* is all foreground: personality, event, episode. In so far as Lukas offers an explanation of the forces that pushed these men, he centers on their fear of losing and their resentment of those for whom winning seemed easy. Not really tough, but just mean, resentful, and opportunistic, these men were driven by their fear of losing to the point where they became the sleaziest, clumsiest pack of losers in American history. Nixon swept into office by a huge margin, and still saw himself weak, hated, standing virtually alone in a world of enemies. H. R. (Bob) Haldeman, all righteousness and rectitude, wheedled and cajoled Nixon for a pardon on Nixon's last day in office, and suggested the deed might be sweetened by issuing at the same time a blanket pardon to all draft resisters and evaders.

John Dean, who saw politics as "just like selling Wheaties," ended up selling out his own boss. Tom Huston, that Jeffersonian Democrat, reduces Dostoevsky to banality, in his maxim that "everything is valid, everything is permitted" if one's object is the defense of liberty. Charles Colson, whose heroes were John Wayne and General Lewis B. "Chesty" Puller, and whose personal motto was the Green Berets' "When you've got 'em by the balls, their hearts and minds will follow," lied and bullied as long as he could, and then turned tail and ran as fast as the rest of them. Of the whole pack, only John Mitchell emerged with any personal dignity.

Well, it's all there in the 626 pages of *Nightmare*. If you need it, read it.

The last ten years or so have surely been the most bewildering in American history. During that time the nation seemed to become a stranger to itself—unsure of its own purposes, divided and angry, its projects and hopes reduced to confusion. Nothing seemed to come out right, and nobody really knew why, though lots of people had lots of theories, ranging from the terminal crisis of capitalism to the hair styles of the young. Disaster followed upon disaster, each adding to the confusion of the one before it. The movement for racial justice ended in bitterness. The program to end poverty ended with the poor still poor. The New Left fell apart and the "cultural revolution" dissipated. The parties splintered. Lyndon Johnson left office bewildered and saddened. Thousands of people met violence and jail in protests against a war that the nation did not want but could not end. Nixon swept into office promising peace and unity, and immediately expanded the war abroad and opened hostilities against the opponents of the war at home. Congress lost all ability to shape events while more and more power was concentrated in the small circle of men around the president.

The Watergate disclosures revealed that for years the Executive had systematically deceived the public and had carried on a secret war against the other branches of government. The true thoughts and the spoken words of the men in power seemed to have nothing to do with each other. Nor did their words make sense of their deeds. Nor were the words and deeds of one "point in time" intelligibly connected with the words and deeds of other points in time. As one phase of the crisis opened onto the next—without warning, without apparent connection—the bewilderment deepened. We seemed to be the victims of a senseless fate, carried along by forces we could not name toward an end we could not see.

Even now, when much is known that was then obscure, the feeling is widespread that the events of those years still defy understanding. In fair part, that is due to the fact that the information necessary to an understanding has appeared in bits and pieces, often long separated in time from the relevant events, and frequently couched in obscure phrasings. This, added to deliberate deception, concealment, and manipulation, has made it supremely difficult to assemble the fragments into a coherent whole.

That is the first job of interpretation—to make the fragmentary record whole, so that memory and mind might have a coherent experience to work on. After that, one can move forward to the second task of interpretation—to compose a theory, or at least some systematic thoughts, on the nature and causes of the basic enduring crisis of our time, of which the Nixon administration was a part.

These are the tasks Jonathan Schell takes up in *The Time of Illusion*. He completes both admirably. Schell's book offers the most coherent reading we have of the Nixon years. The "record" of those years actually consists of four parts. First, the administration's own presentation of itself to the public. This part of the record was systematically manipulated to show the administration in the best light—defender of peace, protector of law and liberty—and its enemies in the worst light. In had little to do with truth. Second, there was the record as presented on television and in the press. This record was fuller than the first one, but it was largely reflexive—dependent upon the first record—for the administration has enormous power to set the agenda of the mass media. Next, there were the events themselves—troop withdrawals, judicial nominations, legislative proposals, and the like. But events do not come to us bearing their own meanings. They must be interpreted, and this is done largely by the first two records, with all their distortions and partialities. Finally, there is the record of the administration's secret thoughts and covert activities, which became public only as the administration itself was coming to an end.

Schell has assembled these disparate records into a coherent composition—a thing that was impossible during the life of the regime itself. He has brought together the underground and the surface streams of American history during the Nixon years, connected discrete particles of information from a variety of sources and times, and established the chronology of words and deeds. The result is a work of great force. Reading this book is like "seeing" for the first time events which, when they happened, struck one as absurd and bizarre. This book brings order to whirl.

But to find a pattern is still not necessarily to have a meaning. What is the key to the pattern? What are the causes and origins of the political disorders of the recent period? In addressing this question, Schell makes his boldest and most thoughtful proposals.

By the end of 1968, when Nixon was elected to the presidency, the war in Vietnam was already dominating American political life. Whatever it touched—and it touched nearly everything—withered. But if the war was at the bottom of our disorders and defeats, what was at the root of the war? Certainly the North Vietnamese did not want to fight us. No Vietnamese force, north or south, posed any threat to the United States. Nor was the American public screaming for war. On the contrary, public support for the war was already so weak in 1964 that Goldwater, who called for "victory" in Vietnam, was smashingly defeated by Johnson, who promised to send no troops abroad. By 1968, uncertain support had turned into resolute opposition. Both Nixon and Humphrey promised withdrawal and peace. And still the war grew. American policymakers decided to continue and to enlarge that war, even if doing so meant warring against its own citizenry. Why?

The war was fought, Schell answers, in order to show that America was willing and able to fight. Its importance, according to a memo prepared by the Joint Chiefs of Staff in 1962, lay in "the psychological impact that a firm position by the United States will have on the countries of the world...." The United States was in Vietnam, said President Johnson in 1965, because we have "a promise to keep," and because to withdraw would shake "confidence in the value of an American commitment and in the value of America's word." "We are involved," said Secretary of State Rusk in 1967, "because the nation's word has been given that we would be involved." The war had to be fought to show the countries of the world that the United States has power and that Americans have the "will and character," as President Nixon put it, to use that power. Vietnam was a test case of our will to use our power in world affairs and to stand behind our word when the going got tough. If we failed that test, we would lose "credibility."

The doctrine of credibility, for which American policymakers were willing to commit horrors, was in its turn a deduction from a strategic theory designed to deal with the ultimate horrors—nuclear destruction and domination of the world by totalitarian communism. The theory, whose principal architects were Professor Henry Kissinger (*Nuclear Weapons and Foreign Policy*, 1957) and General Maxwell Taylor (*The Uncertain Trumpet*, 1960), was an effort to deal with the central paradox of strategy in the nuclear age: the possession of great power—enough power to annihilate mankind—tended to weaken rather than strengthen the capacity for action. As Kissinger put it, "the dilemma of the nuclear period can... be defined as follows: the enormity of modern weapons makes the thought of war repugnant, but the refusal to run any risks would amount to giving the Soviet rulers a blank check." Great power produced great impotence.

The strategy of "massive retaliation," which prevailed throughout the 1950s, required the U.S. to rush to the brink of nuclear war at each occasion of perceived threat to its interests, and then hope that the foe would be sufficiently frightened to draw back and comply with our wishes. Exactly that strategy was employed in the Cuban Missile Crisis. But, Kissinger argued, in the end that strategy not only entailed the possibility of a miscalculation at the brink, but it also lacked "credibility" for the communists were not likely to believe that we would be "willing to commit suicide to prevent encroachments, which do not, each in itself, seem to threaten our existence directly but which may be steps on the road to our ultimate destruction." We needed a policy that would steer a middle course between death by nuclear suicide and death by "creeping aggression," As Taylor called it.

That policy was found, of course, in the "strategy of limited war." This new strategy would free us from the twin threats of paralysis and holocaust. It would give us room to maneuver and provide the means to stop communism from taking over the world. Above all, action in limited wars would give us opportunities, in Taylor's words, to demonstrate to friend and foe alike "that we have the will and determination to use our retaliatory power without compunction if we are attacked." In other words, willingness to fight limited wars would demonstrate our credibility.

With that, the circle of theory was complete, and ready for testing in Vietnam.

I opened this review by noting that we have largely agreed to forget the recent past. Now, obviously, not all the past is helpful in finding a path through the present. Some even argue that our conditions are so new that the past offers no counsel at all. Surely, we are still thinking politically in categories drawn largely from the eighteenth and nineteenth centuries—to our endless confusion. In any case, memory is always selective.

But the peril of blocking out the recent past—Vietnam, and the Johnson-Kissinger-Nixon years—is exactly that that past is our present and our most probable future. The burden of nuclear weapons is ours. The shadow of nuclear destruction falls over our world. The dilemma which the theory of deterrence, limited warfare, and credibility attempted to cope with remains our dilemma. What we saw in Vietnam and in recent American political life, as Schell points out, is the failure of our most serious and intellectually coherent effort to come to terms with the realities of world politics in the nuclear age. Whatever might be said about the shortcomings of the Kissinger-Taylor conceptions, they are surely less reckless and more intelligent than the Dulles strategy of brinksmanship and massive retaliation which they replaced. Indeed, one of the current dangers is that we might conclude after Vietnam (just as we concluded after that earlier protracted, unpopular, and costly war in Korea) that the simplest way is the best way: better a terrible end than endless terror.

Hence, it is important that we try to salvage from the recent past whatever can be learned from it. Jonathan Schell turns to that task in the superb concluding section of his book. Drawing largely on him, and accepting the risks of brevity and oversimplification, I want to suggest what some of those lessons might be.

- We did not stumble into the war in Vietnam. On the contrary, that war was, as Schell says, "a theorists' war *par excellence.*" The quagmire metaphor, still popular as a way of talking about our involvement there, blurs the amount of forethought, planning, and theoretical reasoning that lay behind the war. In Vietnam, abstractions from the books of professors and generals came to life.
- The conception of the war's origins and nature most popular on the left—that it was a racist and imperialist war—also obfuscates more than it clarifies.
- Foreign policy in the nuclear age has to be, to an unprecedented degree, theory-guided. The basic fact is that our condition is unprecedented, and the accumulated experience and lore of centuries of statecraft is of little help in that condition. Even Metternich (*pace* Kissinger) would be as much at sea now as Lyndon Johnson was.
- Still, theories are implemented by individuals, so the variables of intelligence, virtue, and basic commitments matter as much as they always did. Johnson, for example, believed in the deterrence-limited war-credibility theory as much as Nixon did, and left office convinced that he was right and the nation wrong. But, given his political faith, there were limits beyond which he would not go in pursuit of the "right," and those limits stopped short of the corruption of democratic processes and the ruin of the constitutional system.
- While action now must be guided by theories to an unprecedented degree, theories are always implemented under local, particular conditions and within a specific atmosphere of assumptions and convictions. The limited war theory was formulated in very abstract and general terms, almost global ones. But it was applied in Vietnam—a particular

place, with particular ways and conditions. The particularities turned out to be far more important than the theorists had ever imagined they could be.

Similarly, the atmosphere of opinion at the time in the United States made it easy to assimilate Vietnam to a general category of event important in the theory, namely, an aggressive move under the direction of the monolithic force called World Communism. But the war in Vietnam was really at bottom a local event, rather than an instance of the global encounter between the "forces of freedom" and the "forces of totalitarianism." Hence, it was an utterly wrong place to test the theory. We fought the wrong war in the wrong place for the wrong reasons, because we made a disastrous mistake in moving from general categories to particular situations. Given the increasing number and prominence of "scientifically" trained persons in high policy posts, such mistakes are likely to grow in frequency, for social scientists are trained to reason generally and abstractly. They reason about the "logic" of action, the "laws" of human behavior, the "structures" of situations, the "typology" of motivation, and lose the feel for local textures.

- Under the strategic theory of the Vietnam years, the main purpose of policy was to achieve an image or reputation—to appear so formidable or resolute that we would never be required to prove our willingness to use all the power at our command, for the actual use of that power could mean extinction of both ourselves and our opponent. Policy making became image making. But images are inherently obscure and fleeting. It is difficult to ascertain a state of mind (such as resoluteness, or willingness to sacrifice). In addition, the image one is trying to project concerns a future time: one tries to show by actions in the present what one will be willing to do in the future, under certain conditions. But those conditions can never be precisely stated. And present conduct is no sure indicator, either to yourself or to others, of future conduct. Hence, it is almost impossible to be sure that you are projecting the image you really want to project, or that your viewer is perceiving the image you want to project.

  There is, then, an inherent expansiveness or dynamism in action taken for psychological objectives that is not present in action taken for tangible, almost material objectives. What this suggests is that "limited wars" fought for the purpose of establishing credibility are hard to keep limited. Consider the "escalation" of the war in Vietnam. This dynamism was not thought through by the architects of the theory of limited war.

- Action taken for psychological objectives (e.g., credibility) inherently contains an element of theatricality, and can easily slide into pure theater. Policymakers come to think of action—even military action—

in theatrical terms, and lose their feeling for the real costs. Policymakers' and spectators' senses of reality become attenuated. Even death seems unreal. Image and substance become independent of each other. Public policy becomes public relations.

A war fought for symbolic ends is very difficult to explain and justify to the citizenry. Officials easily employ concealment and evasion, and retreat into isolation. Government and public get out of touch with each other. Furthermore, when the symbolic end sought is an image of national toughness or determination, then any domestic opposition or criticism threatens that image, thereby threatening—in the eyes of the government—the national defense. Under these conditions, opponents at home seem even more deadly than the enemy abroad. Feeling beleaguered on all fronts, seeing enemies everywhere, officials fear loss of authority and strive for more and more power, even at the expense of constitutional processes. The government becomes enclosed in a private reality, and wrapped in a mood of paranoia and impotence. That was exactly the mentality of the Nixon administration. And that mentality drove it to the near destruction of the Indochinese peninsula and the American constitutional order.

It is clear now that the strategic doctrine which has guided our policies during recent years is a catastrophic failure. It is equally clear that this nation is not facing up to that failure. The costs of that evasion might well exceed even the costs of the recent catastrophe, for every one of the realities—and, above all, the reality of nuclear weapons—underlying the ruinous experiences of the Vietnam years is still present. As Schell says in the final lines of his excellent book, the questions raised by those realities are unprecendented, boundless, unanswered, and "wholly and lastingly ours." Seen in that light, the mindlessness and triviality of public discussion in this presidential year appear as a sin against humanity.

America the Homogeneous

With his latest volume Daniel Boorstin brings to completion a work begun some twenty-five years ago. In earlier volumes he interpreted *The Colonial Experience* (1958) and *The National Experience* (1965). Now, in 717 pages of text and seventy-eight pages of bibliography, he offers *The Americans: The Democratic Experience.* The journey which began with the landfall of the *Arabella* on June 6, 1630, comes to a temporary resting place on July 20, 1969, when an American sets foot on the moon.

Three large volumes are none too many for the telling of the story; from Massachusetts to the moon is a longer journey than the seventeenth-century geographer Hakluyt ever heard of. Furthermore, Professor Boorstin is telling the story of a whole people, a nation, not just the bold deeds of small bands of adventurers. Measured by any standard—variety and sweep of subject, size, author's intention, significance for the conception of the historian's vocation—Boorstin has completed a big work.

The sheer number of facts, many of them interesting or entertaining in their own right, is impressive (My favorite is the account of a "great Mimical Dramatic Ballet" celebrating Edison's victory over darkness presented in Noblo's Garden in 1883. The Wizard of Menlo Park himself devised the special lighting effects. "Moving about among the girls and adjusting their corsets so the lights would work, he inserted a little battery in the bosom of each dancer, so that lights would actually glow from their foreheads.")

Many and motley though the facts are, however, they are no mere magpie collection. Nor are the data given specious coherence by stringing them together on a thread of chronology. Boorstin is little concerned with strict chronology. He moves freely back and forth through time, juxtaposing events and developments from different times and places, with an insouciance that might trouble his more punctilious colleagues in the historical guild.

This work takes its form and meaning from two qualities: Boorstin has guided his researches by a question; and he has sought to make generalizations about the dynamics, quality and meanings of "the American experience." Boorstin's sovereign question is the one posed most famously by Crevecoeur: "What is an American? What, then, is the American, this new man?" The entire trilogy is in response to this question, an effort to describe a distinctively American national culture and character and to describe the forces and principles of action that made that culture and character what they are. It is this search for generalizations that distinguishes this as a work of history and not just a marvelous collection of historical facts.

The American who emerges from these pages will be no stranger to anyone familiar with Tocqueville and Turner, or with Professor Boorstin's own *The Genius of American Politics*. The American is a democrat and a pragmatist; his characteristic motives, values and rhythms of life have been shaped less by theory than by response to the American landscape. Our great theoretical achievement is to have no theory. The American is, as it were, a natural naturalist in philosophy. Dewey might be the national philosopher, but the Americans already know without the aid of his teaching that facts are only values seen from another angle of vision, and that the facts-values are already "there," given in activity and environment.

Boorstin admires this American and has little but contempt for his opposite. Already in the first volume of the trilogy, *The Colonial Experience*, the Pennsylvania Quakers and the Georgia philanthropists were sentenced to failure because of their rigid adherence to Old World theories in the face of New World realities. The practical men of Massachusetts and Virginia, on the other hand, succeeded brilliantly because they knew when to set aside their theology and philosophy and attend to the tasks of the moment. In volume two, *The National Experience*, the South meets its deserved defeat because it tried to build a "static society" according to a theoretical blueprint. In Boorstin's view, the surest symptom of the South's disease was John C. Calhoun, the only systematic political theorist of stature America has ever produced. Boorstin has little sympathy for losers of any kind, and none at all for those who let their love of theory blind them to the challenges of the American environment.

The same tale is told again in the present volume, *The Democratic Experience*. The heroes of the story now are the go-getters, the grabbers, the inventors and developers—those who saw what was there and took it; those who sensed what was needed and supplied it; those who searched and found what others had never even imagined might be there. Boorstin tells the stories of dozens of such figures, many of whom will be unknown to most readers.

The book opens on the Great Plains, where most of the land was "ownerless and governmentless," and both cattle and range were "there for the taking." It practically closes on July 20, 1969, at 4:17 p.m., Eastern daylight time, when an American landed on the moon. "The most ambitious goal of human technology had been achieved by Americans, and on time." And just as the conquest of the Great American Desert—making beef grow where before there had been nothing but savages and buffalo—was a tribute to the democratic and practical genius of the people, so too was the moon reached "precisely because the United States had been so democratized ... [that] ... the Old World barriers ... which traditionally separated the men who *thought* from the men who *did*, were broken down."

The volume is divided into four books, ten parts, and sixty-one chapters. Book One, "Everywhere Communities," tells how the "new civilization found new ways of holding men together—less and less by creed or belief, by tradition or by place, more and more by common effort and common experience, by the apparatus of daily life, by their ways of thinking about themselves." Here Boorstin sketches the development of important products, activities and ways of thinking that bound Americans into categorical collectives (e.g., suburbanities, those with average I.Q.) and loose "communities" of consumption (Ford owners, beef eaters). Book Two, "The Decline of the Miraculous," continues the same story, but with an emphasis on the overcoming of the obstacles to comfort presented by nature (space, weather, the irreversibility of time, the perishability of foods). The result is further homogenization of life and attenuation of experience. Book Three relates various chapters and trends in the development of "A Popular Culture." Here Boorstin discusses, *inter alia*, new forms of property control and ownership, the art of packaging commodities and stimulating the desire for goods and services, the triumph of vulgar over learned language in dictionary and school and the development of mass education. Book Four, "The Future on Schedule," relates some characteristic episodes in the deliberate invention of the future motivated by "the need to keep people buying."

A number of leitmotifs recur, but the dominant one is democratization. America is "the most democratized nation on earth." All the old barriers fall before the logic of equality and growth. Life for more and more people becomes more and more homogeneous. Experiences that are unique, intense and unpredictable are replaced by those that are similar, bland and repeatable. The uniqueness of America is its ability to erase uniqueness. Everywhere you go the clothes, food, cars, houses, and speech are about the same. So too are the very rhythms and texture of life and the fabric of human relationships. Even nature and time have been smoothed out, the power of the seasons and the elements to delight and hurt subdued. It's all pretty pleasant and pretty much the same for just about everybody everywhere. America has turned life into Kansas-without-twisters: level, regular and safe.

There is no way to recount in brief form either the rich detail with which Boorstin tells the story or the persistence with which he develops its main themes. Despite a thousand variations, the story always ends the same way. Like the Mississippi, democracy gathers up the thousand minor streams of the national life into one channel. There is a relentlessness about it all, a mindlessness, almost an inevitability. Nobody really wills the overall direction of affairs, and certainly nobody is in charge, but everything contributes to the main flow. The "system" itself seems to rule, directed by its own inner logic and moving at an ever accelerating pace.

Perhaps one way to suggest the character and mood of this work as a work of history is to specify some of the many things it is not. It is not history-as-important-event, not an account of those decisive moments when much is at stake: war, grand diplomacy, the rise and fall of states and empires. Boorstin, I think, would regard that kind of history as old-fashioned, Old World history. Nor is this history as an account of the intersection between biography and collective event. There are many individual men (no women) in Boorstin's history, but they are not presidents, generals, diplomats and such. Rather, they are food processors, oil developers and cash-register inventors. This is not political history in any recognizable sense of that loose rubric. Boorstin discusses politics in a very few places. He places the usual blame on the Irish for the invention of the urban political machine, briefly describes the development of foreign aid policies, mentions President Kennedy's decision to launch the moon landing program and discusses FDR's use of radio as a means of mass communication (why not Huey P. Long, who was earlier and better at this than Roosevelt?). This is in no way a history of struggles for the American future, or even of struggles within the American soul. There is no treatment of Populism, nor of the battles between labor and capital, nor of the civil rights and peace movements. Neither the Old nor the New Left is to be found here. There is a rather detailed account of the Johnson County War, in which three people died, and nothing on World Wars I and II, or the Spanish-American War, or Korea or Vietnam. No Negroes are lynched in this book, no presidents assassinated, no workers shot down. There is no discussion of significant regional differences.

Nor is this social history in the usual sense of that term. There is, for example, almost no attention given to matters of social-economic class, or work, or religion. Marriage and divorce are discussed only within the context of a brief treatment of the Nevada divorce industry. Child-raising practices are ignored, save for a brief exposition of a few of the ideas of

Arnold Gessell. Youth culture is not mentioned at all. Nor, as a final example, is this a history of the American as thinker. There is no account of American philosophy or literature. John Dewey gets a few pages, as the philosopher who stressed activity and blurred distinctions, but that is about all for the life of the mind. Even the American-thinking-about-America appears only in the form of the developers of the craft of recording and influencing public opinion. All the others who think in this book think in order to invent a tool, exploit a resource, develop a market, or devise a more efficient process of production. Boorstin's book seems to confirm the most supercilious of European opinions about the banality of the life of the mind in America.

The reader is not told that there might be some losers in American life, some human and natural wreckage, and a fair measure of violence too. There are no Indians in Boorstin's book and no old people, no serious labor troubles or inflation, no Appalachia or urban slums. Americans fight no wars, other than an attractive little range war. Political corruption appears only in the form of the urban machine. Senator Joseph McCarthy does not even make the index, though the CIA does get one entry. The Pentagon Papers are mentioned once, where Boorstin cites James Reston's opinion that the real source of the many leaks of government secrets to the press is Chester Carlson, the inventor of the Xerox machine. There is nothing on police beyond a mention that when radio station WGN began to do police broadcasts the crooks got the news about as quickly as the cops. There is nothing on prisons.

Racism, race riots, civil rights, the Klan, Martin Luther King, Jr. and Black Power are all dispatched in one page—and a fair portion of that page is devoted to a warning that some of the efforts of black people to secure justice "threatened to postpone the day when the Negro would be undistinguished from all other Americans and so frustrated their proper purpose." In fact, black people appear here mainly as participants in the "Harlem Renaissance" and as protagonists in a rather superficial telling of the origins of jazz. Huge modern corporations are described as "democratizers of property." We are told how many millions of people own stock, but not how few thousands own most of it. Women as a group are given less than a page, where they figure as beneficiaries of the movement for coeducation. On another page, two wealthy women are mentioned as art collectors. Puerto Ricans are mentioned at least once in the book, though not in the index.

Now Boorstin surely is not ignorant of these matters. We must conclude that, in his conception, they are not a significant part of America or of "the democratic experience." You just will not learn from this book that a lot of Americans have done a lot of serious and troubled thinking about the democratic experience, that a lot of others have never shared in it, and that still others have been victims of it. In Boorstin's reckoning, those people don't count.

What kind of history is this, then? I am still not sure. I think Boorstin intended to write an account of the persons, products and processes that have been most significant in shaping the quality of everyday life in modern America. Seen this way, it makes perfect sense to give a lot of care to cattle brands, refrigeration, the automobile, sewing machines, glass manufacture, food packaging and the like. It also makes sense to relate the stories of inventors and inventions.

But if the book is viewed this way, then it must be said that Boorstin has omitted some of the most important aspects of the subject and distorted others. For example, we are given thirty-six rather conventional pages on the familiar story of the development of the cattle culture, and nothing on plastics. There is no treatment of the processes and institutions of bureaucratic and centralized control, and surely no processes and institutions have flourished as these have in democratic America. There is no discussion of the shaping impact of war, including technological war, on modern America. We are given a schematic and rather glossy account of the importance of organized "Research and Development," but no mention of those branches of R & D suggested by the names Rand Corporation and Hudson Institute. The treatment of popular culture includes no serious discussion of the motion picture as art form or taste-maker. There is a sketchy account of the origins of jazz, but nothing on the powerful and distinctive music of the youth of the 1960s. Given Boorstin's emphasis on community, this last omission is remarkable, for music was then perhaps the most significant force in both shaping and expressing the culture of the young.

If we view the book as primarily an exploration of certain themes in American life, other troubles appear. Boorstin has not defined some of his central concepts carefully enough; others he has defined in ways that are morally and intellectually questionable. The results are twofold: the criteria for deciding what to include and what to exclude become uncertain; the treatment of some subjects becomes superficial, or morally repellent. Numerous examples of these vices are provided by Boorstin's treatments of "community" and "democracy," two of the most important themes in this book.

This book on "the democratic experience" provides no specific definition of the term democracy. The index refers to "American democracy," where two entries are provided: "frontier origins of"; "life's enrichment and." But it is clear enough that Boorstin's idea of democracy has nothing to do with the central meaning of the term: rule by the many; widespread, popular participation in the conduct of affairs and the shaping and sharing of the common life. By democracy Boorstin really means the growing uniformity or homogenization of experience over the past hundred years. The principal agent of this social change is technology, and its principal form is mass production and distribution of uniform products. An accurate title for this book would be "the homogeneous experience."

More is at stake here than a quibble over words and titles. Boorstin's idea of democracy relieves him of any need to examine most of the important matters one would treat in a book on democracy properly defined. He need not inquire into the actual structure of power in the United States. It is sufficient to characterize the corporation as a "democratizer of property"; no need to ask who makes the decisions in those corporations, or what it is like to work in them, or who controls access to the major means of production. Politics—every significant political question—simply disappears. Everything becomes part of the great flow called democratization.

I think this is what accounts for Boorstin's composure, or at least lack of apparent dismay, in face of the processes he describes. When you relinquish or forget the moral imperatives contained in such a term as democracy, you give up the footing necessary for a genuinely critical stance toward the regime. The book itself becomes, in the end, almost as bland as the life it describes and purports to understand. The sharpness of experience is blunted by the fuzziness of the major concepts. Compare Tocqueville and Boorstin on democracy; or Mumford and Boorstin on the city; or Giedion and Boorstin on mechanization; or Henry Adams and Boorstin on the accelerating and mindless momentum of technological culture.

A final word: My sense of duty and my respect for the author require me to attempt an overall assessment of this work, though I am not confident of my ability to make one. The book is well written, vigorous and lucid. The information presented is remarkable for its range, interest and accuracy: portraits of inventors and developers, descriptions of dozens of industrial products and processes, informative reports on the origins of words and on customs and states of mind. The bibliography alone is a delightful and instructive account of what is known and not known about the American social landscape; it should provide a battalion of needy graduate students with dissertation subjects. The rich and disparate material is gathered around a few major themes and organizing concepts. None of the themes is new, and some of the central concepts are too loosely defined. This produces a certain critical blandness in the work and permits Boorstin to ignore a lot of the harder questions and more troublesome realities of American life.

These major shortcomings stem, I think, from the presence in Boorstin's own thought of the very "presentism" and "naturalism" which he so tellingly criticized in an earlier work on the thought of Thomas Jefferson (*The*

Lost World of Thomas Jefferson). The major, though surely unintended, lesson of the book is that America's citizens, leaders and teachers need more of that "theoretical" and "speculative" vision which Boorstin has told us we do best without.

The Circles Of Watergate Hell

Watergate has dragged on so long and been called a crisis so often that both the events and the word have lost their power to disturb. Still, Watergate is a crisis; and right now, part of the crisis is our very weariness of it, our wish that it would go away. But in politics, memory matters: when citizens' memories are short, their governors' leashes are long.

Hence, we must not yield to weariness. If we do no more than drive out a wicked president named Nixon, we shall have removed a painful symptom without reaching the source of the malady.

This is so because Watergate differs in important ways from earlier episodes of scandal and corruption in American political history. First of all, the crimes and allegations of crimes are more numerous and more sweeping than those charged or proved against any earlier administration. They also involve more high officials of state, including the president and his closest associates. Secondly, the events are more sinister than the characteristic American ways of corruption. Most of our notorious political scandals have stopped at peculation and graft. Our politicians sell the public interest for money. The Nixon way is un-American. Power, a passion to cleanse America of dirty elements, subservience to the president and hatred for his enemies—these, and not love of lucre, moved the president and his men. Their wrongdoings were distinctly political. The thing smacks of the Dreyfus affair.

Next, the Watergate events have brought us face to face with a constitutional and political monster of our own making: a derangement of powers among the branches of government; and a deadly imbalance between the powers of the government on the one side and the resources of the citizenry on the other. Watergate is a story of the abuse of power, but the power was there to be abused. Finally, Watergate is a symptom of a deep disorder in the national spirit and character. Richard Nixon is no stranger to us, and Nixonism is not a political style forced upon us by an alien power. Both are ours, fashioned out of the materials of our own lives.

These things, then, distinguish Watergate and make of it a genuine crisis, a turning point. They are the sickness we must try to understand.

Four Circles of Watergate

Watergate is a tale of four worlds. Imagine these worlds as a series of concentric circles: the one closest to the center is inhabited by the man named Nixon; next, a set of individuals and offices we shall call the presidential entourage; beyond that, a circle of nonpresidential national elite institutions—Congress, courts, the media, political parties; and finally, the millions of us who make up the electorate.

You can tell part of the story from within any of these regions, and you can begin the whole story from any point within the system. If you begin with the innermost circle, for example, Watergate is a tale of a president who went too far, so that he must now be impeached. Starting from the outermost circle, Watergate becomes a tale of a citizenry debased and disheartened, betrayed, but powerless to strike at its tormentors.

Telling the whole story, however, means charting the system of connections among the four circles of Watergate Hell. That is what we shall try to do. Moreover, the system itself can be viewed from more than one vantage point. We shall move back and forth between two perspectives. Call the one institutionalist and the other republican. The former is quite familiar, the other less so.

In the institutionalist view, American society is an aggregate of individuals and groups, each seeking a private good, using others when possible, submitting to them when necessary. Politics in this view is nothing more than competition among groups and individuals for limited, usually material, goods. Liberty is the absence of external restraints on the pursuit of desire. The whole system is held together by a government with sufficient might to overawe private concentrations of power and adjudicate the conflicts among them. Government in its turn must be controlled. As Madison wrote in *The Federalist,* the great problem is that you must first enable the government to control the governed, and then oblige it to control itself. The solution: give government power sufficient to its tasks, but distribute that power among various agencies so that no one of them can dominate the others. Ambition checks ambition, interest counteracts interest, within both government and society. The governors are no more and no less virtuous than the governed. The secret of the whole system is that it does not require virtue for success. The raw materials of interest, envy, and ambition, processed through the machinery of checks and balances and separation of powers, emerge in finished form as justice, liberty, and order.

The system requires two master obligations of both governors and governed: pursue your interest diligently; abide by the general rules of the game. Beyond that, there are only functions. The functions of the governing classes are to take special care for the rules themselves and, within the rules, to forge the competing claims and interests of private parties into public policy. The main function of the electorate is to provide raw materials—desires, opinions, demands—which the decision makers can process into policy. The electorate should also have realistic and moderate expectations about what and how much government can provide in the way of goods and services, and it should have at least enough political savvy so that it is not easily duped by demagogues and liars.

Set within this Madisonian framework, the Watergate events will appear as a drama among the elites, with the citizenry as spectators. A drama, but not a morality play: in this view, Nixon and his men did not commit and then conceal the Watergate atrocities because they are bad men and bad citizens; rather, they are bad men and bad citizens because they violated the rules of the game and threatened the balance among the system of competing power centers. Actors' motives and intentions are secondary; institutional roles and relationships are primary.

Seen from the institutionalists' vantage point, the implications of Watergate are not all bad. The electorate has leanred a lesson, and it will be a little harder for the next political hustler to manipulate and dupe them with dirty tricks and glossy promises. Watergate also means returning to the real world after the fantasies of Camelot and the Great Society. Moreover, the citizens are competently performing their function of providing input to the decision makers. Hence, the elites in Congress, courts, and the media can proceed to their task of bringing down the ones who broke the rules and upset the balance. Watergate shows that the Constitution still works.

But there is another way to look at Watergate. In the republican perspective the members—citizens—are held together by a political bond and vision, a vision of diverse people living together under one rule, united by ties of civic friendship, and sharing the vocations of ruling and being ruled. A republic so conceived is a community of citizens gathered for the purpose of shaping and sharing a common conception of the good life. Liberty and politics are virtually synonymous: the process of acting together, in public, to define and to strive for a good which is good for all. Such a community can never be merely a collection of individuals arbitrarily held together by administrative regulations, a majority, a religion, or even by the national ties of blood or soil, and certainly not by the economic advantages of the division of labor. What matters is the political bond.

The spirit of the republic is shaped by the conviction that the open life, the life lived among, through, and with others, is the natural life for man. The rock on which the polity is built is a virtuous, that is, public-spirited, citizenry—a citizenry that cares for public liberty and that understands, as Hannah Arendt said of Nazi Germany, that nothing is easier "to destroy than the privacy and private morality of people who think of nothing but safeguarding their private lives."

To call the public life the natural life for man is not to say that all live it all of the time, but only that man is most fully human when living that way. We are more likely to marvel at that old idea, or mock it, than we are to believe in or even to feel it. We think that the important decisions are private and personal, and because we think so, they are. For us, the primacy of the personal and the private is both natural attitude and sacred right Both are grounded on the rock-bottom conviction that each lives and dies alone. The citizen, in contrast, starts from the conviction that we naturally live and die together.

So, the citizen really is Aristotle's man—the being who, caught between the gods and the beasts, the high and the low, stuggles to live rightly and decently and thinks it natural that the struggle should take place in a polity. From John Locke to R. D. Laing, individualist thinkers and societies have denied that. Laing even teaches that living in a modern state necessarily makes us sick. Put so starkly, this teaching at first shocks us, but in the end it is easier for us to accept than to believe that the natural life is the life of the citizen.

If we look at the system of Watergate from the republican perspective, we shall see most clerly the innermost circle called Nixon and the outermost called the people. And we will not be optimistic about what we see. Watergate becomes the story of a man who would be tyrant and of a people who first acquiesced to him and then were helpless to resist him. Much of our language will be moral and political, not functional and institutional. We shall talk about corruption not in the sense of peculation or the purchase of influence or the violation of law in the interests of power. Corruption takes on a deeper and older meaning. It means the triumph of privatism, the loss of public spiritedness, among a people and its leaders, a pathology in the whole political culture rather than an imbalance among decision-making agencies.

Both the institutionalist and the republican perspectives are needed to understand our crisis. Hence, we shall shift perspective from time to time.

The First Circle: Nixon

There he crouches at the center of the first circle of Watergate Hell, glaring at us, ready to strike or dodge. For twenty-eight years now he has both fascinated and repelled us. No movie star or sports hero, no Kennedy even, is more familiar. His face, his voice, his choice of friends, his spiritual counselor, his personal finances, the decisive episodes of his political career, even his dogs and his wife's plain cloth coat are all familiar to us. His stiff postures and jerky movements, his shovel nose and shifty eyes, and sweating upper lip, his flashes of rage and self-pity—we know them all.

Similarly, his uncanny ability to reduce public events and issues into episodes of the Dick Nixon Story is one of the most familiar yet most remarkable things about him. From his first campaign against Jerry Voorhis in 1946, right down to the latest imbroglio over doctored tapes and censored transcripts, wherever Nixon goes he is the issue: his motives, his troubles, his failures to be understood, his pleas and excuses, his appeals for sympathy and understanding. When Nixon is involved, there is little debate over matters of public policy. Rather, there are charges and countercharges, talk of treachery and treason, accusations and denials. It is astonishing. And Nixon has made it perfectly clear that he intends to hold us in his desperate embrace right to the end.

One of Nixon's most marked traits is his almost total indifference to the substance of public policy. To be sure, it is easy to locate him on the right wing of the Republican Party—against labor, against welfare policies, for the military and the corporations. But he has never been a leader or shaper of conservative policy. He is no Taft, say, or Goldwater or Thurmond: he follows where they lead, consulting only his own expediencies. The manager of the first secret Nixon campaign fund said that the rich businessmen who supplied the money never had to tell Dick how to vote because they knew he would vote right.

Nixon has always been passionate about policies only when they catch his own compulsions—enemies to be fought, guilty secrets to be exposed, wrongdoers to be punished, supporters to be accommodated, votes to be gained. The public life of the nation has no autonomous meaning for him, no claims and needs of its own. It is but a stage for his performance. In domestic politics, he won his fame as an anti-Communist, a hunter and slayer of America's internal enemies. And he personalized that struggle to a degree even greater than that to which Joseph McCarthy did—although, certainly he was more careful than McCarthy: as Adlai Stevenson put it, "Nixon was McCarthy in a white collar."

The same is true in foreign policy. Nixon was a fierce cold-warrior. His rhetorical stock-in-trade consisted of vituperation against the "soft" policies of Truman and Acheson—no reluctant cold-warriors themselves. But he displayed no interest in the complexities of the containment strategy which was the high-level doctrine of those years. For him, containment was appeasement; and his task was to expose the appeasers. A vintage specimen of Nixon's way of personalizing policies is his charge against Stevenson that "Adlai received his Ph.D. in Dean Acheson's College of Cowardly Communist Containment." Nixon never could see anything wrong with such canards, just as he still cannot understand why people continue to "wallow in Watergate." That same obsessive interest in himself, that same inability to distinguish between the nation's needs and his own was put on display in his famous "Kitchen Debate" with Khrushchev: he actually presented that exchange as an historic moment in the life of this country.

It is just these inner voices of egotism and self-interest that make Nixon deaf to the voice of common decency, contemptuous of the responsibilities of civic life and office. That is also why the onetime cold-warrior could so easily become the bringer of detente with Communist China and the USSR—he had made personal contact with Brezhnev and Chou En-lai; they were no longer his enemies. And finally, this is also why Nixon can turn the methods of the cold war against his domestic opponents. Nixon always has "enemies." His interest in policy is largely an interest in getting at his enemies as well as rewarding his allies. He cannot distinguish between the nation's benefactors and adversaries and his own.

What demon is it in Nixon that makes him run to such extremes? The standard explantion of the Nixon performance has three main propositions. First, Nixon is by nature tenacious. It was dogged resolve that pushed him from the last place on the fourth string of the Whittier College football team to the first place on the big team in Washington. Secondly, Nixon believes he is right and righteous, and that most others are wrong and unrighteous. Thirdly, his enemies never quit trying to bring him down, and he must fight back. Driven by party spirit, or hating him for his assault on such liberal darlings as Hiss and Stevenson, or maybe just fearing him for his tough political style, Nixon's enemies give him no peace. In this light, the furor over Watergate, the unwillingness of others to "put Watergate behind us" and get on with the public business, is only the latest and culminating battle in the unending campaign to "get Nixon." Nixon keeps on fighting because the others will not let him stop.

But this standard account misses something. It does not quite explain certain characteristic ways of the man, his personal style. We believe that the key to a better understanding is this: Nixon knows he is right, but he also knows he is wrong.

Consider the traits of character and conduct that are commonly ascribed to him. He is foul-mouthed in private, prissily clean-spoken in public. Similarly, as the presidential transcripts reveal, he connives and dissimulates outrageously behind the scenes, but is excessively sincere and sanctimonious in public.

Nixon mouths the old pieties and wields them as weapons against his enemies, while his own conduct mocks and defies those pieties. He claims all the high moral symbols for his cause, but stoops to low indecencies in his conduct. The man shamelessly violates the limits of custom and propriety, while calling for decorum and a return to the old values.

Nixon is secretive, while forever protesting his readiness to reveal all. He fumes over White House leaks, and obstructs publication of the tapes. He inflates a normal need for confidentiality of conversations and documents in the executive branch into a principle bigger than the Constitution itself. He prefers his windowless room deep within the maze of the Executive Office Building to the airy and gracious Oval Office. Each "full and voluntary" disclosure only raises more questions than it answers. That began with the Checkers speech and has continued for more than a year of the Watergate affair. And through it all, Nixon has relentlessly ferreted out the secrets of others, for he assumes that we all have terrible things to hide. He came to national prominence through his investigation of Alger Hiss. He ordered taps on the telephones of newsmen. The Watergate burglars sought evidence of secret links between the Democrats and Castro. The "Huston Plan" would have made his search for secrets nationwide.

The Nixon political style can tell us still more about the man and about the relations between him and the electorate. Nixon is a technician and a tactician, a political engineer. Politics is a business of identifying targets and designing missiles to hit them. Everything is turned into an instrument. The self that is shown to others is a fabricated self. Policies can be shifted at will, for they are instruments too. Images and slogans are counters in the battle. Leadership is a problem in image control. Nixon's speeches do not employ our oldest and richest symbols to illuminate new terrain and beckon people across it. Rather, he manipulates hackneyed phrases and slogans like "law and order" to manage emotions and to lull listeners into the illusion that they are safe in his hands. The difference is as real as that between Martin Luther King's "I have a dream" and Nixon's "America must remain number one," as real as the difference between Lincoln's "government of the people, by the people, and for the people," and Nixon's "executive privilege."

All of these familiar Nixon traits bespeak a man who needs to control others, for they are threatening, and who also needs to keep iron control over the self, for the forces within are explosive. They also bespeak a man who, having much to hide, is sure that others do too. They tell us of a man who is so utterly private and so empty in so many ways that he needs to incorporate the whole external world into himself, or to demand that it become only an extension of himself, without autonomous existence. In an older vocabulary, these are precisely the defining qualities of the tyrannical soul.

These traits make Nixon unlovely and unlovable. There are some people—a John Kennedy, say—who can go from foolishness to failure and not only be forgiven all, but loved into the bargain. There are others whom we never forgive, and Nixon is one of them. That alone is enough to make him bitter. And yet, there are good reasons why we pick certain people whom we will not forgive. One of them is that we sense that the sin they were caught committing is as nothing to the sins they burn to commit.

Nixon's unlovely ways provoke antipathy, but what we suspect is that those ways hide others even more hateful. The hateful one knows that too. He knows what we suspect, for he suspects it in himself. He knows that people hate him because he is hateful. Once again, we return to the starting point: what drives Nixon is not only that he knows he is right, but that he knows he is wrong too.

There is another factor which suggests that Nixon knows he is wrong. He has to recognize that while the public believes that all politicians are more or less crooked, only he is known the nation over as "Tricky Dick." The public has held up a mirror to him, and the face in it is the face in the Herblock cartoons—scowling, furtive, vengeful.

Such self-knowledge can drive one in two directions. First, one will conceal, but conceal so clumsily that one will be suspected or caught—and Nixon is always suspected and often nearly caught. That pattern, present in all his campaigns, is present in Watergate too. At the same time, such a man can be driven by a terminal passion for revenge, and give himself over to doing in his enemies. Others compiled the White House enemies list, but the impulse clearly came from Nixon.

The projective cast of Nixon's thinking also helps explain the deep punitive streak in his character. He is a punisher. The code words for this were "law and order," but they mainly meant punishment. The public knows this about him and readily turns to him when it needs some punishing done. His whole career has been spent punishing America's enemies. He is still doing that. John Dean said that Nixon told him to follow up the case of a man who had darted toward the presidential limousine during the inaugural parade and see that he was punished. He wanted the *Washington Post* punished. He wanted Edward Bennett Williams punished. He wanted a lone picket outside the White House punished. The work goes on and on. The Watergate affair is of a piece with his whole career. He must punish, in part because he suspects the same motives in others that he sees in himself, in part because the sight of the lawlessness in others reminds him of the lawlessness in himself.

Nixon has few gifts and little natural grace. What he wins he wins by sheer will and technique, despite rather ordinary abilities and a very difficult and irksome temperament. Given that temperament, winning does not come easily, and it nearly always requires of him that he must appear to be what he is not. But in the end, whatever Nixon wins he loses because those suppressed aspects of his character break through and steal the victory. It is as though Nixon were a loser by nature and a winner only by the art. And in the end nature prevails.

In a society dedicated to winning, losers easily become resentful and angry, desirous of pulling down the winners. That is manifest in Nixon as an individual, but more importantly, he has converted his own resentfulness into a mastery of the politics of resentment. Hence his resentment has important political resonances, especially in his role as punisher. His targets are characteristically two: the most favored and successful—Hiss, Stevenson, liberal intellectuals; and various pariah groups who mock or violate the hard-won victories of middle-class life—"student bums," "welfare chiselers," "draft dodgers." He is at his best when he subtly links the successful ones to the despised ones. Much of Nixon's punitiveness stems from resentment, while his mastery of the politics of resentment puts him in touch with whole large class and status groups in the population. And it is no accident that Nixon's psychology of envy and resentment is also reflected, as we shall see, in his entourage of advisers and henchmen.

Projectiveness also helps explain one of the more puzzling aspects of the Watergate affair—namely Nixon's prolonged paralysis from April to August of 1973. Both Nixon and his daughter Julie have said that his low point came when he had to get rid of Haldeman and Ehrlichman. Following their departure he drifted closer and closer to ruin. Naturally any leader would miss two close and trusted subordinates and be hampered for a time by their absence. But clearly, Haldeman and Ehrlichman were not simply more or less able and trusted counselors. They were all but irreplaceable because to Nixon they were extensions of himself. He could get a new chief of staff and a new head of the Domestic Council, but it would not be easy to get new parts of himself. Their removal was an amputation rather than a changing of the guard. In their appearances bvefore the Ervin committee, Haldeman and Ehrlichman astonishingly suggested the two sides of Nixon's character: Haldeman, the pious, upright, cooperative public servant; Ehrlichman, the scowling, mean, political gut fighter.

All of these manifest traits of Nixon's personality brought him inexorably to Watergate and make of the Watergate story a characteristic chapter of the Dick Nixon Story. Once again, law and the responsibilities of public life were contemptuously ignored in the service of his needs and ambitions. His enemies were treated as public enemies. His secrets had to be guarded and the secrets of others exposed. Punishment had to be dealt to as many as possible. His plight had to be seen as the defense of the presidency.

The style was perfect, too. It was all so familiar: Plumbers, Water-buggers, cover-up artists—all of them bunglers. They were caught, and the torrent of denials, explanations, and clarifications of the explanations had to follow. We were right back again in Whittaker Chambers's pumpkin patch. We witnessed again slander, perjury, accusations of treachery, and strange, night-crawling people skulking about on Nixon errands. From the Voorhis campaign to Watergate, Nixon's career inscribes a circle from which there is no exit. And we must add: whatever pathos and pain might lie at the center of that circle, from a republican or civic perspective it must be seen as a circle of corruption, a nearly total subordination of the public realm to the ambitions and fears of a very private man.

The Second Circle: The Entourage

"To one who was in the White Houe and became somewhat familiar with its interworkings, the Watergate matter was an inevitable outgrowth of a climate of excessive concern over the political impact of demonstrators, excessive concern over leaks, an insatiable appetite for political intelligence, all coupled with a do-it-yourself White House staff, regardless of the law." Thus did John Dean, in the standard syntax of the Nixon staff, open his memorable performance before the Ervin committee. During that week in June 1973, not only did Dean plant the heaviest charges in the sapping of the Nixon presidency, but he also gave an astonished nation a close look into the Nixon White House. The view was appalling. Even senators were shocked as Dean heaped up the horrors at the White House door.

The men who were named as the perpetrators had impressive titles and were very close to the president, but they were not familiar figures to the millions who watched the hearings on TV. Tough John Mitchell was the best known. The others had previously been almost faceless. Inside the Washington community, it was different. There, the Palace Guard had been seen as an important part of the story of the first Nixon Administration, just as Dean was now revealing that they had been the authors of the Watergate story. Haldeman and Ehrlichman, "The Prussians," were at once the most prominent and the most detested for their arrogance. They were also the builders of the "Berlin Wall," the guardians of access to the president.

The main thing the Nixon men had in common is that they were his men. Without him, they were insignificant. They did not come to Washington from political careers. (Though Haldeman had been politically associated with Nixon for a long time: way back in 1962 he had helped Nixon try to cheat his way into the governorship of California.) Not one of them had ever been a candidate for elective office. None of them was a recognized leader of an important constituency in the nation or in their localities. None emerged from a movement or cause. Not one of them spoke as a stand-in for some significant figure behind him, a powerful senator or governor, say, or a big contributor from the corporate world. None of them was associated with any idea about public policy more specific than law and order. No one came from the academic world. No one spoke for farmers or workers or young people or an ethnic constituency.

They were Nixon's creatures, his to command. It was chief of staff Haldeman's goal to make of them an extension of Nixon's will and personality. Nixon set the tone; they harmonized. None of them sounded a dissonant note. Many things were so well understood among them that they did not have to be said. Thus, Mitchell sensed that the pressure to approve Liddy's spy schemes came from "the top." Or again, when the Watergate burglars were caught, the top hands knew instantly, with no need to consult Nixon, that a cover-up was the only way to go. They were right: when Nixon later learned that Hunt was demanding hush money, his first question was, "How much?"

We said earlier that Nixon has always been a technician of politics. The leader set the style for the entourage, though neither he nor they had any patent on it. For it is a familiar style in the big corporations and strategic think tanks. Call it CORPSTRAT. A few key terms suggest the style: "game plan," "scenario," "time frame," "option," "risk," "target," "operative." It is a language of combat and technique. It is not the language of an older American politics. In this new style, means are never bad or good, they either "pay off" or are "counterproductive." If the means for achieving an end are available, they become a "capability"; and to have a capability is virtually to argue that it should be implemented. Thus, if political intelligence is wanted and the means of achieving it—burglary and bugging—are available, they should be employed. Winning is everything. It is even the basis of loyalty in this Nixonized version of the corporate style. Loyalty is fine if there is a payoff, but if it is counterproductive one must look to one's options and, perhaps, cut and run or cop a plea. Were Nixon given to irony, the sight of his young men reexamining their options when the game plan failed might have given him some wry amusement.

Although the Nixon men, like their leader, were primarily technicians, they were not Eichmanns. They had no grand schemes or visions of the good society, to be sure, but they did have a sense of the ends for which power was desired and by which power was justified. Mitchell and Ehrlichman, whose faces hint of a baleful power one would not expect in the ordinary municipal bond specialist or provincial lawyer, show this most clearly. There came a passage in Mitchell's scornful appearance before the Ervin committee when Senator Talmadge asked him whether he thought a Nixon victory was more important than his personal and legal obligation to tell Nixon about the Watergate break-in. Mitchell replied: "Senator, I think you have put it exactly correct. In my mind, the reelection of Richard Nixon, compared with what was available on the other side, was so much more important that I put it in just that context." Ehrlichman, at the end of his week of truculent testimony, said that he hoped that young people with "high ideals" would still seek careers in government, but he warned them that "if you come here . . . you will encounter a local culture which scoffs at patriotism and family life and morality just as it adulates the opposite, and you will find some people who have fallen for that line." Never mind that Ehrlichman had just finished saying that he knew no limit of any kind which the president might not overstep when he deemed the national security to be involved. In sum, their ends were two: the advancement of Nixon's power; and through him, the purification of America.

Their style was American Gothic, joyless and stern. They entered Washington not like Texans swarming to a barbecue, nor like political intellectuals all polished and shining with sheer brilliance, but like a band of earnest missionaries entering Sin City, knowing that nothing lay before them but hard and dirty work. Their statements to the Ervin committee, and to the media before that, were full of talk about duty and hard work, sacrifice, endless labor in the public interest with little expectation of any reward save the chastening of their enemies. The political style of the Nixon men was the fruit of a union between an Anti-Saloon League lady and a Pinkerton Detective agent.

Many commentators have characterized the style of the Nixon men as pragmatic. They were no more pragmatists than the Politburo, say, or De Gaulle. What is striking about them is that they did not choose just any means that would gain their ends. On the contrary; they were astonishingly rigid and narrow in their choice of means. Like their chief, they showed a positive preference for sordid means and for maneuvers that strained decency and legality. They routinely favored surreptitious, devious, risky methods of action. Putting such men in charge of the national morality is, as Khrushchev said when he heard that Eisenhower had entrusted Nixon with disarmament duties, like setting the goat to guard the cabbage patch.

The means chosen were fitted to the ends pursued. So far as one can learn from the public record, these men had one big vision of America. America had grown slack and dirty. Hippies, radicals, war protestors, longhairs, blacks, welfare chiselers, drug addicts had raged across the land in the 1960s, desecrating the shrines and vilifying the priests. There was a big cleanup job to be done; and when you have a dirty job to do you are likely to get a little dirty yourself. The vile means to which these men so easily resorted were determined by the wretched ends they pursued. They are punishers and purgers.

Mitchell, Ehrlichman, Colson, and Haldeman set the example. The younger men were not made of such stern stuff. Freebooting careers and "political hardball" were what they were into. Most of them were quick enough to toss in their gloves when the game started going the wrong way. They weren't up to Ervin's questions or Sirica's sentences. Among the young ones, only the crafty Dean looked capable of moving up to the big leagues. But the top Nixon players really wanted to cleanse the country of the filth of the 1960s and restore the old pieties. They did not understand at all that the world of the corporations, the military, and the advertising agencies, whose language and values they had thoroughly assimilated, had damaged those pieties more severely than all the demonstrators and dissidents ever could.

Nothing illustrates the punitive lust of the Nixon men better than the trial of Philip Berrigan and his companions—the Harrisburg Eight. Poor Sister Elizabeth, after a spiritous evening with Berrigan's friends, wrote to her imprisoned lover about some of the talk that night. They might kidnap Henry Kissinger, and maybe also some prominent people "of the liberal ilk," and make the latter serve as Henry's judges in a kind of Stockholm War Crimes trial. Berrigan let her down gently by replying that she should seek "to weave some elements of modesty into the plan." Wham! Mitchell hit this deadly pack with a conspiracy charge. That is the same vindictive Mitchell who thought the four students killed by the National Guard at Kent State had got no more than they deserved, or who watched with satisfaction as the Washington police broke up the Cambodian antiwar demonstration and illegally arrested hundreds of people: the apotheosis of his law and order campaign. In their appearances before the Ervin committee, the chief White House men returned again and again to their obsession with protests, disruption, obscenity, and general lawlessness in the land. Jeb Magruder claimed that the Administration's lawlessness was prompted by the general lawlessness. Haldeman was more revealing. In the famous memo from an aide suggesting that demonstrators might direct violence and obscenity toward the president and Billy Graham in Charlotte, North Carolina, Haldeman had underscored the words "violence" and "obscenity," and written "good!" and "great!" in the margins. Ehrlichman worked himself into a transport of indignation over the low state of public morality, pointing to the spectacle of senators and representatives "tottering to the floor" in an alcoholic stupor to cast their votes on public bills. These spasms of anger and punitiveness jumped easily from Nixon to his henchmen. As the tape transcripts reveal, Nixon thought the whole land befouled. His curses spared nobody.

These men saw abominations everywhere they looked—except in themselves, and in the world of corporate business. The world inside the White House and inside the corporations was different from the rest of America. It was clean, quiet, efficient, and private rather than public. These men ran the White House on the corporate model; their goal, in Haldeman's words, was a "zero defect system." They built the Berlin Wall to block the ugly sights and sounds that they hated and knew their chief hated. The world beyond that wall was hostile and dirty. To Nixon, these men were ideal instruments in his work of revenge, purification, and the aggrandizement of his power. To them, he was the ideal leader, the chief avenger. They were made for each other. None of them could understand that what was abominable about America was not the disorder they loathed but the order they loved.

The Third Circle: Court and Constitution

Nixon and his men resembled nothing so much as a royal court. Watergate was done in the style of palace intrigue. When Nixon dolled up the White House guards in those Graustarkian costumes back in 1969, we all guffawed. We should have been instructed. Similarly, most commentators thought that George Reedy, in his *The Twilight of the Presidency*, had exaggerated the courtlike atmosphere of the modern presidency. The Nixon regime has confirmed the truth of Reedy's account.

Kennedy's glamour, Johnson's arrogance, and Nixon's passion for control and secrecy were not the forces that transformed a modest, constitutional chief executive into a near monarch. The outcome has deeper sources than that. First, there is a monarchical strand in the fabric of the Constitution. But, secondly, there is a subtle, strong strain toward monarchy in our whole conception of political order. The two influences are closely connected, but the second is the more worrisome and important. If we can understand these strains toward monarchy, we shall recognize that it is superficial to say that Watergate may help us reduce presidential power and restore a healthier balance among the parts of the constitutional system.

The framers of the Constitution, of course, did not foresee that the United States would become enmeshed in foreign politics on a world scale, but they certainly knew that we would have some measure of international involvement, and therefore some need for military forces. They also understood that the conduct of foreign and military affairs, in the very nature of things, had to be concentrated. Lodging authority for those affairs with the president gave the office a monarchical element from the beginning. That seemed safe enough in 1789, but our recent history has been one of large and ever-growing involvement in foreign and military affairs. And that has necessarily meant growth of presidential power. It is obvious that we cannot tame the presidency without first scaling down our international and military involvements and undertakings. Getting rid of Nixon will not even touch this aspect of our constitutional and political disorders. Nixon knows this: "national security" is his justification for everything.

What we have called the strain toward monarchy results partly from the character of the American people and partly from a flaw in the institutionalist, or mechanistic, conception of order itself. In 1787 the framers viewed the American people as fragmented into many factions and imprisoned in private concerns. The constitutional theory rested on the beliefs that fragmentation and privatization were the natural conditions for Americans and at the same time the best guarantee of their liberty. Thus, division of powers within the government was designed both to reflect and to nourish factionalism among the people. But the framers also located sovereignty in the people. Indeed, their ideology was such that they could locate it nowhere else. Absorbed in their private concerns, however, the people could not effectively exercise sovereignty, could not speak decisively, could not discover and pronounce the common good. So, the mechanistic system never did work. From the outset, it required a central, commanding figure who personified the highest hopes and aspirations of the nation, and who could give constant care to the public good. That is why George Washington is called, in that ancient monarchical metaphor, the Father of his Country. Jefferson knew that too: when he was elected to the presidency, he said, in words that flew in the face of his professed agrarianism and decentralism, that now, with his ascension, the American Revolution could begin. John Adams said it from the beginning and suffered much ridicule for his efforts to attach to the president the grandiloquent style and titles of kingship.

A kind of constitutional monarch, again, seemed safe enough when government had little to do. But as more and more was demanded of government, we turned more to the president as our one symbol and guardian of the general interest. We drained power out of the localities, the states, the parties, courts, and Congress, and channeled it into the presidency. Above all, we surrendered our own power, for by insisting that only the president could guard the national interest we deepened our own helplessness. We lost the habit of acting for ourselves. If living in a republic meant putting public things first and private things second, then we would suffer a king and console ourselves by calling him a president. But we have loaded so much power in the office that the man has escaped the confines of the Constitution.

That is why the impeachment of Nixon costs so much travail. Impeachment is a constitutional process. It was designed as a remedy for *ministerial* abuse. You do not remove a king by impeaching him. You remove him by revolution or by regicide. Our president is a chief minister and we would like to remove him by impeaching him, but we cannot get the minister without striking at the king. And this causes subjects great anguish.

As a measure of how far we have traveled, consider the impeachment of Andrew Johnson. That process was wholly ministerial; there was no whiff of regicide in it. It was undertaken by a strongly led political party which had just won a two-thirds majority in each of the houses, and whose policies were opposed to the president's. The congressional Republicans feared that Johnson would obstruct their plans for reconstruction of the defeated South. They thought it proper to move against him by impeachment. The whole process took only three months. The House actually adopted a resolution of impeachment before it received the charges against him. The trial in the Senate took three weeks and fell one vote short of conviction. Johnson did not escape impeachment because of any aura or mystique about "the presidency." He was tried and nearly convicted because he favored policies a strong party thought were wrong and dangerous.

Today, the national political parties scarcely exist. They are largely vestiges, mere instruments of presidential elections and a convenience of local elections. They do not govern or legislate. They do not mobilize the citizens or even aggregate the interests. They are on the way to extinction. Congress has not governed the nation in this century. In every new "crisis," it confesses its inadequacy by turning to the president for leadership. Congress cannot even legislate unless it is led by a strong president. Now, in the nation's and Nixon's agony, the Congress still wishes he would make the decision to abdicate.

What is left of checks and balances? In this season we all talk consolingly of the media and the courts, saying that it was these elements of the constitutional system that uncovered Watergate and set the other forces in long-delayed motion. The machinery still works. But, more precisely, it was a pair of police reporters on the *Washington Post* and a stern judge who did the work. The mighty Washington press corps would have missed the story but for them. The press "never laid a glove" on Nixon all during the campaign of 1972, as McGovern bitterly reminded us. The media can act as effective checks on power only if there is a citizenry which cares about such matters. Otherwise, the media play a role all too familiar in societies ruled by a king. They purvey the gossip of the court circles.

We are left with the judges, then. Perhaps we have found our Lord Coke in Judge Sirica, and perhaps not. Perhaps Nixon will obey a "definitive decision" of the Supreme Court, and perhaps not. In either case, if the judges do save us, what they will have saved could not be called a republic. For that, citizens are needed.

The framers of our Constitution were greatly impressed by some of the ideas of Montesquieu—"the celebrated Montesquieu," as Madison called him. They drew their whole notion of separation of powers from him. But they, and we, failed to heed the deeper warnings of Montesquieu's political philosophy. Montesquieu taught that there are only three basic forms of government—republic, monarchy, tyranny—and that each form has its own generative force or principle: in the republic, the spring of action is public spiritedness; in monarchy, honor; in tyrannies, fear.

Public spiritedness has never been in abundant supply among us, nor did the framers think it needed to be. In their view, popular suffrage plus a balanced constitutional machinery were all that was needed and all that was possible. The records of the Constitutional Convention and *The Federalist Papers* crackle with derisive remarks about the foolish dreamers who have thought that republican liberty rested on civic virtue and that citizens could be encouraged to public spiritedness by the right kind of political education and association.

Honor of and obedience to the laws also did not need to be actively taught and inculcated, for, once again, the constitutional machine would automatically compel good and obstruct bad behavior. The motives and intentions of rulers and citizens could be largely disregarded.

But when the constitutional machinery becomes unbalanced under the impact of events and the need of a people for a symbolic center, the full force of Montesquieu's teaching begins to appear. This country does seem to be headed toward a kind of despotism, and fear and suspicion have become the reigning principles of action among us. That fear pervades both subjects and rulers. Among the subjects, the races and ethnic groups fear and suspect each other; so do the old and the young; so do the rich and the poor. We all fear the future. Watergate has revealed for all to see that fear and suspicion are rampant among the rulers and between rulers and subjects. This nation of strangers looks at Watergate and sees itself.

The Fourth Circle: The Citizenry

The commanding institutions are in disarray, but there is a malaise in the land: institutional crisis and civic inertness. How account for this remarkable phenomenon of apoplexy at the center and paralysis in the members?

It is not that the citizenry does not know or care about the crisis in Washington. The polls, the by-elections, the letters-to-the-editor columns, the countless conversations show that the people do know and that what they know saddens and angers them. What is significant, however, is that the sadness and anger (since the tape transcripts, revulsion too) are taking no decisive political shape. No movements of protest and reform have appeared. A large majority believe that Nixon should resign or be impeached, but impeachment rallies draw only a few hundred people. No new leaders have sprung up, offering new banners for the dingy old ones. There are few visible signs of important change even within the established parties. The Democrats keep a low profile, praying that Nixon's disaster may become their victory. The prizes they seek are more Democrats in Congress and another in the White House. The Republicans hope to limit their losses, put Watergate behind them, and head into 1976 weakened but united, perhaps behind good old Gerry Ford. The only substantial popular movement is a continuation of the trend away from party loyalty: the largest single bloc of the electorate, forty-one percent, now identify themselves as independent. There are millions of detached electoral particles loose in the land, but no political magnet to attract them. The citizenry is apparently resigned to the conclusion that whatever is to be done will not be done by them. The prevailing attitude seems to be: someone else is in charge, I just live here. This response to Watergate measures how far we have fallen from the ideal of a participant citizenry and how close we are to the reality of a privatized mass.

It has been a long journey. Tocqueville saw the Americans of the 1830s as a highly political people, but he also warned that the deepest tendencies of the culture were against their remaining that way. Unless vigilantly guarded against, individualism, self-interest, and the passion for material comfort and security would drain the springs of public virtue and open the way to "democratic despotism." Thus Tocqueville:

> I seek to trace the novel features under which despotism may appear in the world. The first thing that strikes the observation is an innumerable multitude of men all equal and alike, incessantly endeavouring to procure the petty and paltry pleasures with which they glut their lives. Each of them, living apart, is as a stranger to the fate of all the rest—his children and his private friends constitute to him the whole of mankind; as for the rest of his fellow-citizens, he is close to them, but he sees them not;—he touches them, but he feels them not; he exists but in himself and for himself alone; and if his kindred still remain to him, he may be said at any rate to have lost his country.
>
> Above this race of men stands an immense and tutelary power, which takes upon itself alone to secure their gratifications, and to watch over their fate. That power is absolute, minute, regular, provident, and mild. It would be like the authority of a parent if . . . its object was to prepare men for manhood; but it seeks . . . to keep them in perpetual childhood. . . . For their happiness such a government willingly labors . . . : it provides for their security, foresees and supplies their necessities, facilitates their pleasures . . . , directs their industry . . . —what remains, but to spare them all the care of thinking and all the trouble of living? . . .
>
> After having thus . . . taken each member . . . in its powerful grasp . . . the supreme power then . . . covers the surface of society with a network of small complicated rules, minute and uniform, through which the . . . most energetic characters cannot penetrate. . . . The will of man is not shattered, but softened, bent, and guided: men are seldom forced by it to act, but they are constantly restrained from acting: such a power does not destroy, but it prevents existence; it does not tyrannize, but it compresses, enervates, extinguishes, and stupefies a people, till each nation is reduced to be nothing better than a flock of timid and industrious animals, of which the government is the shepherd.[1]

This, the standard form of democratic despotism, "degrades men without tormenting them." One possible variant of the form would be worse: "one which, after having concentrated all the powers of government, should vest them in the hands of an irresponsible person or body of persons." This species both degrades and torments. That, of course, is the condition we have reached in the Nixon Era.

We cannot blame others for foisting this government on us. Nixon only completed what we had been long preparing. America is the home of the private individual. Citizenship itself is understood to be not the vocation of joining with others in the activity of shaping and sharing the common life, but a formal status conferred on all as a shield against encroachments on private rights and a tool for the advancement of private interests. The democratic ballot, along with the familiar rights of free speech and assembly, were supposed to make the government ours, and secure the citadel of liberty against the aggressions of power. The American land itself completed this circle of our felicities, for its great size and richness gave scope for each of us to go as far as his talents and virtues would take him, without bumping into the wall of scarcity. Private liberty was the tool, America herself the resource, and material abundance the product. Politics, public liberty, hardly mattered. Americans could solve the ages-old problem of living together by living apart.

From the very beginning, this soothing myth covered up a host of harsh realities: it left a lot of people out; it put a lot of others down. But at least through much of the nineteenth century, it was not totally misleading to call ours a government of the people. By the end of that century, however, the myth and the reality had grown so far apart that millions of people felt the strain. Our way of bridging the gap was to cling to the myth while tinkering with the reality. That process has continued at an accelerating pace ever since, so that now anyone who calls our political and economic system democratic must be suspected either of bad faith or of invincible ignorance. The ideology of private rights and formal democracy functions today mainly to mystify and justify vast and irresponsible concentrations of power in both economy and government, and to persuade the population that the life of endless consumption is the life most worth living.

The trouble appeared first in the economic sector. The ideology of liberal individualism provided fertile soil for the growth of corporate capitalism, and giant economic concentrations sprang up everywhere, reducing the power and liberty of individuals. As popular sentiment against corporate power and piracy grew, the government had to do something. The solution: enact economic regulatory laws and establish administrative agencies to enforce them. Then the individual would be safe once again to return to private pursuits. We did not save capitalism, but we did save the corporation. In this land of the private citizen, no truly political solution was ever seriously contemplated. Such a solution was and still is feasible: smash the legal form called the limited liability corporation by making members of boards of directors individually and personally liable for the damages and injuries caused by corporate activities; give every stockholder one vote—no more, no less—in the affairs of the corporation. This would be a truly political solution to the "problem" of size and irresponsibility, a solution that would begin to return the world to the producers, that would use liberty for the purpose of expanding liberty.

Instead of that, our basic wish has always been to get as much as we can for ourselves, and we have been happy to let experts and officials manage the whole system and repair the worst damages. Herbert Croly, in *The Promise of American Life* (1909), found the perfect formula for this ethos and method: the pursuit of Jeffersonian ends by Hamiltonian means. Big, centralized government can exact responsibility from big, centralized corporations. The individual would remain free.

The result, of course, is that both public and private, both governmental and economic, organizations have grown beyond the power of the citizenry to control them. More than that, the electoral campaign of 1972 showed conclusively that big business is perfectly capable of buying big government: the regulated regulate the regulators. We are dwarfed by our own productions, made powerless by the very instruments that were supposed to expand our power. As this process has matured, the ideology of formal democracy touches reality at fewer and fewer points. As a legitimating myth, it is losing its power to persuade. The result is a growing crisis of legitimacy.

That crisis is tempered and postponed by a number of other social processes and doctrines. Chief among the doctrines is the complex of ideas extolling the joys and enlarging the rights of the happy consumer. We are taught that the life of bounteous consumption is the fullest life, and that the system is ours because it is dedicated to providing the goods of that life. "Consumer sovereignty" compensates for the loss of control over work and over public policy. Government and business are partners in this enterprise: both engage in the production and distribution of ideology.

No one can say whether the consumer ideology will succeed where the ideology of formal democracy has failed. We have doubts. For one thing, the restless dynamic of production for consumption and waste is pushing against ecological limits. For another, more and more people have filled themselves to bursting, and still feel empty. The conviction is growing that the really desperate shortage in our society is a shortage of human dignity and significance, of meaning and purpose, of worthy aims and vocations. That shortage can never be met by material goods and administrative directives. But, by a fatal dialectic, as once hallowed cultural aims and disciplines continue to erode, we must rely increasingly on administrative means and material rewards for maintaining economic efficiency and social order. The result is that regulatory agencies and methods grow apace in every sector of life, while public respect for any regulation at all declines: as Henry Adams put it, "morality becomes police." Watergate showed that Adams's prophecy is our reality.

In a closely connected process, public agencies must pick up the huge bill for goods and services that the society needs but that the private economy finds unprofitable to provide. The public must also repair damages that the corporate economy does not wish to pay for—social welfare, unemployment, blighted cities and countrysides. The results are pauperization of public services, increasing bureaucratization, permanent inflation, and a growing tax burden which people are increasingly reluctant to carry.

Finally, as people become estranged from the huge structures that dominate economy, government, and society, they respond in ways that are troublesome or disruptive from a systemic point of view: personal breakdown; absenteeism and malingering; the formation of drop-out and retreatist cultures; escalation of material demands, which stimulates inflation and throws the burden of rising costs on the unorganized and the unemployable. Most disruptive of all are the large and growing numbers who are making psychological and political demands (e.g., for dignity, autonomy, and participation) that cannot be met without changing the structure of the existing order.

For all these reasons, the modern bureaucratic-corporatist states stand on shaky foundations of legitimacy. Perhaps those foundations can be repaired without transforming the whole structure of state and economy, but it is more probable that they cannot. Be that as it may, political passivity and the decline of legitimacy are the underlying conditions of political life in the United States today.

These conditions were intensified by the course of American politics during the 1960s, which prepared the way for Nixon and the Watergate events. To that story we now turn. It is a story of a nation deceived and disheartened by lies and false promises, but powerless to do much about it; of citizens who have learned that the great centralized government that promised to do everything for them can do almost anything to them; of a people that now stands face-to-face with the tyrant within itself.

The 1960s opened with Kennedy on the road to the New Frontier and ended with Nixon on the road to Watergate. At first view, that looks like a ninety-degree turn to the right: from young to old America; from progress to reaction; from generosity and hope to selfishness and despair. The turn is real, and yet the two roads are connected. Three large developments in the politics of the 1960s paved the way to Watergate.

The first was the collapse of Kennedy-Johnson liberalism. Kennedy awakened the nation from the lethargy of the Eisenhower years with his personal dash and his promise to "get America moving again." The promise was twofold: a real effort to confront some grievous and long-neglected domestic ills; and a rekindling of the spirit of citizenship, a rebirth of civic life.

The Kennedy Democrats could deliver on neither promise. Kennedy searched for grand projects that could catch the national imagination, and he came up with two: the Peace Corps and the conquest of space. The New Frontier turned out to be the moon, and the big thing was to get there before the Russians. Beyond a few warmed-over proposals remaining from the Truman days, he found no program for getting America moving again. He followed, rather than led, the civil rights movements. He made no effort to halt the mushroom growth of corporate and military power, despite Eisenhower's belated warning. He did not even do much to reshape his own political party into a vehicle for participation. Beyond finding places for a few thousand volunteers in the Peace Corps, he offered no outlets for the rebirth of idealism he had called for. Although millions of Americans really were ready to ask not what their country could do for them, but what they could do for their country, the answer turned out to be little more than tune into the Apollo trips on your television and admire the élan and grace of the princes and paladins of Camelot. The call to action turned out to be a call to attend a few symbolic spectaculars. The spectator's role was already familiar to most of us, but it became particularly frustrating when a dashing leader kept telling us to lead lives of vigor and service. The result was a deepening of the sense of powerlessness and cynicism.

Johnson's vision was clearer than Kennedy's and his energy as great. He proposed to lift up those who had fallen by the way in the race for prosperity by completing the work of the New Deal in the Great Society. He was a much more skillful and energetic legislative leader than Kennedy. So there were lots of programs, many fanfares, much motion. But, again, there wasn't much for the citizenry to do except watch. No significant assaults were made against the great structures of public and private power. The most generous and innovative of the Johnson programs soon lost momentum and bogged down in the sands of the bureaucratic wasteland.

This was partly the result of the administration's preoccupation with a hateful war, which Johnson had first promised to contain and then escalated. That war cost tens of thousands of lives and billions of dollars. It also drained the trust and patriotism of millions of citizens, particularly those who served in Vietnam, and it tarnished our reputation among the nations.

But the desolation of the Great Society programs had another source. The reports began to come back: things were not working. The methods of welfare liberalism seemed to have lost their force. Even the goals were not very exciting. Politics as we were practicing it in America could not rebuild the cities, end poverty, overcome racial injustice, penetrate the strongholds of public and private power. We began to expect less and less from politics, and to tell ourselves that nothing basic could be changed. Might as well stay home. We were getting ready for Nixon.

The second crucial development that carried us toward Watergate was the near disapperance of checks on the presidency, and the willingness of the presidents to employ high-handed and deceitful means to gain their ends. This pattern is best illustrated in foreign and military policy. Kennedy committed us to the Bay of Pigs adventure and to a game of diplomatic Russian roulette in the Cuban Missile Crisis. Both acts were taken with virtually no consultation beyond the president's immediate circle of advisers. Kennedy also made both war and a shaky peace in Laos, and took fateful steps toward a military commitment in Vietnam, which led to the disaster there. Again, these courses were pursued without any public discussion save futile postmortems in the press and in Congress.

Johnson conducted a major, undeclared war from the White House. He lied to Congress and to the public. He turned a deaf ear to all objections to his policies. Believing that Congress and the public could not be relied upon to understand and do what had to be done in Vietnam, Johnson and his crisis managers resorted to concealment, deception, and manipulation.

Deceit, bad faith, and contempt for the opinions of those outside the inner circle thus became normal practice in the White House of the 1960s. Believing that the nation was not worthy of trust, the executive branch, in effect, conducted a coup against its own people. The Pentagon and the CIA were secretly granted hugh increments of power and vitually escaped from civil control. The FBI was turned loose to spy upon and wreck dissident and antiwar organizations until the Huston Plan went so far that even J. Edgar Hoover had had enough.

Those are the ways of a despotism, not of a constitutional republic. A lot of people abroad came to hate and fear America for its technological cruelty in Vietnam. A lot of Americans began to hate and fear their own government for the irresponsible power it wielded and for the wicked means it employed in its campaigns against both its own and other peoples.

Against such a background, Nixon appeared to be a horse of the same color. Consequently, many of the old reservations about his character and career seemed irrelevant. Judged by current White House standards, his sins were unexceptional. At the same time, the precedents of the Johnson years must have encouraged Nixon to believe that the old limits no longer stood. Certainly the citizenry and Congress had lost the ability to enforce them. It is ironical that Nixon created the Plumbers out of his anger over the publication of *The Pentagon Papers*—which had exposed the duplicity of his predecessor.

By the end of the decade, the third of the major developments overwhelmed the nation. It was, quite simply, the demand for order. All through that decade another politics had been growing outside of and in opposition to the official politics. This new movement arose in response to the failures of Kennedy-Johnson liberalism, the accelerated growth of uncontrollable power in both the government and the economy, and the inability of the electorate, the Congress, and the media to stop the war in Vietnam. Its tone was moralistic, and its methods were direct and disruptive. Its members were mainly young, and their life-styles and attitudes were disconcerting to the majority. A whole generation had turned radical and gone on a cultural and political binge—so it seemed on television. Another America seemed to be forming in the streets and on the campuses, and most of the old nation feared it. This new nation showed little regard for the old pieties, little regard even for the rest of the populace. While demanding the right to educate and lead, many of the spokesmen of the new politics daily committed the unpardonable sin of the teacher: contempt for the students.

Nixon and the Republicans knew they could never reach this new constituency and did not even try. What Nixon could do, however, was isolate the new forces from the rest of the country and associate them exclusively with public turbulence and disorder. With his mastery of the rhetoric of American piety, he was able to capitalize on the resentment many felt toward the dissidents, and to offer himself as the defender of peace and patriotism. No one could match him at that game.

Nixon's "Vietnamization" policy defused the war as an issue for most Americans, leaving the peace movement in disarray and depriving the left of its chief moral issue. Without the glue of dissent against the war, the left fragmented and became ever more isolated from the rest of America.

But then Nixon nearly threw it all away. He invaded Cambodia, and the campuses erupted in their greatest explosion of all. The massacre at Kent State University was the symbol of this brief renewal of the radical impulse and of the administration's reaction to it. Though the surge of dissent ebbed swiftly, letting Nixon carry forward his policy of reducing the ground forces in Vietnam while escalating the bombing, he never recovered his balance. He and his administration became obsessed by lawbreakers, slackers, deserters, and draft dodgers. Nixon, Agnew, and Mitchell became the symbols of a flinty and repressive policy at home.

As time went on, the left lost all coherence. Social justice became transmuted into the baser coin of personal liberation; and personal liberation looked to the average American like little more than the repudiation of any authority outside the self, coupled with a demand that the state pay the bills. Stunned by assassinations, frustrated by the futility of Kennedy's calls to idealistic service, betrayed by Johnson's unleashing of the war, disillusioned by the new programs in welfare and education, many of them badly conceived and administered, the electorate had lost most of its impulse for humane and generous reforms and innovations. What little remained was turned off by the mocking of its deepest beliefs and values, to say nothing of its manners, by the liberationist left.

By 1972, the great majority of American simply wanted the new nation silenced. Reform, change, social justice—all those things that had seemed possible at the beginning of the 1960s—fell before the demand for order. It was a perfect time for Nixon. He had always insisted that his enemies were America's enemies and that he knew how to deal with them. To protect his secrets and the nation's, he had turned his agents loose in 1971. In 1972 he felt confident enough to turn them loose on the political opposition. He was finally in the position to screw his enemies.

Though his hour had come round at last, Nixon was still no welcomed hero. The prolonged decline of citizenship, accelerated by the events of the 1960s, had prepared the nation to submit to him, but not to love or even trust him. We knew him too well for that, and our knowledge of him was a disquieting intimation of our knowledge of ourselves.

The relationship between Richard Nixon and the people now caught in his embrace has been disturbing and twisted, crackling with fretful vibrations. It is hard to give a name to this foreboding many share when they ask, having chosen Nixon, what have *we* come to? Perhaps the best formulation is this: when we look at Nixon what we see is the American Dream gone wrong, the American character curdled, and ourselves implicated in the disaster.

We still believe that we ought to be public spirited and that our public life ought to be generous and good. Yet, our founding theory and our formative experiences have always stressed the values of individualism and privatism: let someone else care for the public good, I've got other things to do. This mood, which from a republican or civic perspective is exactly what is meant by corruption, is now taking new and perverse forms. Our individualism has become an ever-narrower love affair with the self. When we used to think of individualism, we thought also of work and responsibility and discipline. Now we mean by it mainly self-love and the right to do as we please. That is largely what the demand for "liberation" means today. To what is left of the public realm we bring only the demands of the self—that the commodities we stuff ourselves with should flow without interruption; that whatever we want should be ours; that whatever we do should be called good.

Nixon obliterates the public realm by defining it as himself and denying its autonomous existence. The American people overload the public realm with demands for private gratification and then cheat the government that must meet those demands. With his one hand in the public till to maintain his lavish estates and life-style and build up his net worth, while with his other hand he withholds his taxes, Nixon is the mottled image of what we ourselves have become but know we cannot respect ourselves for being. Hence, we can never respect or trust him. But at the same time, he relieves some of our guilt because his conduct affirms the worthlessness of that very public sphere we have been killing with our neglect. That draws millions to him, though with reluctance and even mortification.

Nixon also disturbs us because we sense that he respects no limits, that he is shameless. Yet we, too, seek lives without limits and form. We have hollowed out the institutions and codes that once disciplined our individual desires and made us willing to temper private impulse by public ends. Family, church, neighborhood, work, the moral law—all are in shambles. Nixon knows this, and the knowledge releases him from the duties of civic responsibility and piety other than to pay them lip-service. Seeing that in him, we also recognize it in ourselves. But once again the ambivalence enters. There is the secret suspicion and fear that Nietzsche's formulation is right, that "absence of horizons is not freedom, but madness."

Hence, millions of us yearn for ordered and disciplined lives. Nixon offers the image of the man of discipline and control. *Six Crises* reverberates with that theme. His public speech is full of it. He also endlessly intones the rhetoric of responsibility and propriety. But then there are those flashes of rage and self-pity, those intimations of an imperious egotism, and we see the man who teeters on the edge of loss of control and who respects nothing. Seeing that, few can believe that image and inner reality are the same, and that is part of the reason why we call him Tricky Dick. But many, perhaps most, of us want to believe him; or, at least, we are grateful to him for affirming the old pieties even while he and we violate them in our acts. Again, his hypocrisy disgusts us, but we recognize its similarity to our own. Perhaps if we forgive it in him we absolve ourselves too. Or, following him, we can turn in fury against those who openly scorn the pieties. We know he can punish, and we give him our grudging respect for that because we are not really sure we have the right to punish. His vengefulness is disturbing, but that's part of the package.

And so it goes on and on, this baleful dance between the man and the people. It is too much to say that we wholly deserve Nixon, but there are so many ways in which we have earned him. This helps account for the torment it costs us to remove him: we need him, but we must get rid of him. Still, we know that purging Nixon will not remove our kinship with him. To do that, we must become a nation of citizens, and few among us believe in that possibility. We as a nation have arrived at the point of believing in too little, and that is a condition in politics more dangerous than believing in too much.

Note

1. Quotations from Alexis de Tocqueville, *Democracy in America* (New York, N.Y.: Schocken, 1961), Vol. II, Bk. 4, Ch. 6.

Reflections on Rawls' *A Theory of Justice*

I shall have some critical things to say about *A Theory of Justice*, but everything I say takes its tone from my great respect for the book. This is a powerful book, the noblest in its line of moral and political philosophy since Kant. Rawls' work should be seen as a contribution to one of the perennial quests of Western philosophy and politics: to provide stable foundations for a political order that will encourage freedom and welcome a diversity of conceptions of the good life, but still escape the worst possibilities of relativism. His book is a search for principles of right or justice which, by virtue of their philosophic cogency, can provide the foundation of a stable order that will advance human autonomy and secure the conditions necessary for individual self-respect.

In that quest, Rawls has relied for help mainly on the thinkers of the liberal-social contract tradition.[1] This help is both logical and substantive. Rawls has brought the contract tradition to a culmination; and, by doing so, has simultaneously renewed its vigor and sharpened our appreciation of the weaknesses that were in it from the beginning.

Measured by the standard of its possible significance for political practice, *A Theory of Justice* is potentially one of the most important books of our time. Rawls has strengthened the philosophical bases of that passion for equality which Tocqueville saw as the deepest desire of the modern age. This book could give the liberal democratic and welfare oriented states renewed confidence in their rectitude and a broadened agenda for practical action.[2]

Measured by the standard of its significance for a political study and discourse, this book is one of the most important works of the past fifty years. From its beginnings right up until our own century, political theory was understood to be inextricably connected with moral philosophy. That marriage was broken early in this century by the positivists, and contemporary political science is the orphaned child of the divorce. Contemporary political science is built upon the belief that most past ethical and political theory started from the mistaken idea that value judgments could be given rational grounds and could claim to be, in an important cognitive sense, true. According to the modern persuasion, that mistake so permeated past political philosophy that there was little reason at all to study it, save, perhaps, in order to arm oneself against error, or, perhaps, because a little such knowledge ornamented the mind and provided a stock of elegant allusions. At best, we could divide past political theories into normative and empirical components and search among the latter for testable propositions that might take their place in a science of politics. But, certainly, the mistake meant that political scientists must deny scientific status to the very subject matter of past political theory: inquiry into the nature and possibility of the just polity.

Contemporary ethical theorists, both Anglo-American and continental, have largely freed themselves from this positivist prison. Very few moral philosophers today hold the view that ethical theory is really elaborate and obfuscating talk about tastes in cake or music. Unfortunately, many political scientists seem not to have heard the good news. For most members of our guild, ethical theory and "normative" political philosophy are still really about noncongnitive tastes, feelings, and preferences.

Given that background, we are in a position to assess the significance of *A Theory of Justice* for political study and discourse. Rawls holds, and shows, that ethical theory is not only an important but a rational, even scientific, activity.[3] Also, he has restored the old but recently interrupted view that the subject of political theory is the just state, and that the proper study of political life permits no radical dichotomy between "normative" and "scientific" discourse. Rawls' book is an invitation to contemporary political scientists to reunite what should never have been torn asunder. If we accept that invitation, we might return to the work which Plato called the first duty of those who teach the young: to see that the main themes of conversation among citizens are public rather than private things—justice, not flute-playing.

The Basic Argument

Rawls starts where a theory of justice must start: with the recognition that there are a variety of principles and theories of justice, and that philosophy has so far been unable to reduce that diversity to unity. He proposes to bring order to this jumble by the logic of the "original position." The original position is that hypothetical set of conditions in which people like ourselves, if we were to undertake the task of developing principles of justice, would in fact arrive at principles which all would consider fair and reasonable, and would accept as governing all future disputes over distribution (21, 587).

The description of the original position is reached by a process of thinking "back and forth, sometimes altering the conditions of the contractual circumstances, at others withdrawing our judgments and conforming them to principle . . ." until we reach a "description of the initial situation that both expresses reasonable conditions and yields principles which match our considered judgments duly pruned and adjusted. This state of affairs I refer to as reflective equilibrium" (20).

The principles of justice reached by this process make no appeal to self-evident premises. Also, the principles chosen by persons choosing in the original position are fairer than any others that have been advanced. They also conform well enough to our considered opinions about justice, and they do not clash with our basic knowledge of human nature and social processes. Furthermore, persons who act from these principles "express their nature as free and equal rational beings" (252). Thus, in the conception of the original position we have found that "Archimedean point" beyond relativism from which "we are able to derive a conception of a just basic structure, and an ideal of the person compatible with it, that can serve as a standard for appraising institutions and for guiding the overall direction of social change" (263). Pure or ideal theory can do no more. The rest is for nonideal theory or practice.

This, in outline, is my understanding of Rawls' basic argument. The specific features of the original position, the content of the two principles of justice and of the priority rules for applying the principles are familiar to many of us. I shall not repeat them here, but refer to them when necessary in the pages that follow.

The Original Position and Justification

The basic question we must ask concerns the use of the contractualist logic itself. Does this logic give us that "Archimedean point" from which we can derive principles of justice that "can be affirmed by everyone"? Have we found here the vantage point which enables us "to regard the human situation not only from all social but also from all temporal points of view" (587)?

Rawls describes actors in the original position as rational (capable of knowing what their interests are) and self-interested (each cares more for his own interest than for others'). Furthermore, they choose their principles behind a "veil of ignorance" (they are ignorant of their natural gifts and abilities and of the social positions they will occupy in the future).

Each is aware that it is advantageous to himself to live in a social collectivity, but none has anything like a nonegoistic attachment to the social group.

Could persons so described reach any agreements that we would comfortably call moral? We can easily imagine such persons adopting Rawls' principles in a situation of complete uncertainty or ignorance about the future, but it is hard to imagine them keeping those agreements once they begin to acquire some knowledge. Rational egoists who are required to choose without knowledge might agree that "social and economic inequalities are to be arranged so that they are . . . to the greatest benefit of the least advantaged" (302), because such persons could understand that they might find themselves among the least advantaged. In that sense, concern for self would be the same as concern for justice. But, lift the veil of ignorance even a little and the two concerns split apart. The principles of justice are accepted precisely because they can be shown to be advantageous to everyone, and that showing simply cannot be made in the postcontractual situation, where persons know their real condition and can adopt strategies and principles appropriate to it. Put differently, if "advantage" is accepted as the guiding criterion in the original position, it must also be given sovereignty in postcontractual situations. It will be instantly clear to any rational egoist that the two principles are not advantageous to him in every concrete social situation. Hence, on Rawls' own argument, which makes advantage sovereign, he would not be bound by the two principles in cases where they damaged his interests. Rawls has not escaped the curse of all egoistic arguments for moral principles: "One can neither draw blood from a stone nor extract moral principles from the decisions of rational egoists."[4]

We might, on various occasions and by various criteria, describe the decisions of such actors as prudent or reasonable, but it strains language to call them moral. Rawls does strain language in exactly this way when he subsumes ethical choices under the theory of rational choice. There are connections, of course, but not identity: the theory of justice is part of, but also something more than, the theory of rational choice.

Rawls is aware of this, but that awareness is something that escapes the logic of the social contract. In chapter eight, Rawls lays the groundwork for a discussion of principles of justice that not only owes nothing to the contract logic, but is a superior alternative to it. Rawls intends in this chapter to flesh in the "Kantian interpretation" of the original position—the idea that by acting in the manner of persons in the original situation and on the principles chosen in that situation we express our nature as "free and equal rational beings" (252). But calling principles right because they are freely chosen is a different matter from choosing principles because they are right. In the first (Lockean) case, consent is the basis of right; in the second (Kantian) case, consent is based on a priori principles of right—on the idea that some ways of life express better than others our nature as moral beings, and should be chosen for that reason.

This second argument is strongly reminiscent of T.H. Green's conception of man as a social being whose moral perfection requires interdependence, and who ought, therefore, to base society on principles which nurture interdependence. Such a conception, as Parekh says, makes "the fact that certain decisions are taken in the original condition . . . morally irrelevant and superfluous."[5] If you argue on that basis, then the logic of the original position is merely a cumbersome distraction. If you describe the actors in that position as Rawls does, then it is doubtful whether you can derive moral principles at all.

Even if one grants the utility of Rawls' logic, I am not sure his account of the original position as such is coherent and convincing. That account is intended to exclude from discussions concerning justice "the accidents of natural endowment and the contingencies of social circumstance. . . ." (15). But his account is not without ambiguities. Sometimes he says the choosers have a conception of morality and religion but of no specific morality or religion. That is impossible. We cannot have a conception of morality that is not "contaminated" by a specific morality.[6] It is as though Rawls invites, or requires, us to think about something without knowing anything of that thing. We cannot imagine human beings without culture, morality, or religions: human beings are creatures who have those things; they do not think detached from those things. Rawls seems to be saying that we can arrive at general conceptions prior to, or perhaps apart from, concrete experience. I doubt that very much. I doubt whether it is possible to gain knowledge of our basic condition as moral creatures prior to or apart from our actual experiences as social creatures. In sum, Rawls has offered a confused account of mind, an account that wavers between Locke and Hegel, as it were, without the simplicity of the former or the depth of the latter.

Another way to see the problematic character of Rawls' account of mind is to look at the characteristics he assigns to actors in the original position. They are mainly two: persons "are not considered as taking an interest in one another's interests" (13); and they are rational "in the narrow sense, standard in economic theory, of taking the most effective means to given ends" (14). Later on, Rawls adds the "special assumption" that "a rational individual does not suffer from envy" (143). This assumption is needed in order to avoid Hobbesian conclusions.

Marx wrote that Bentham went in search of human nature and found the English shopkeeper. Rawls has done about the same: he has mistaken a specific social character type for human nature. That character type, of course, is the one described in liberal theory and classical political economy, and recently revived in the work of Arrow, Sen, Simon and others. It is distressing to see a thinker of Rawls' power commit once again the philosopher's sin of idealizing and universalizing the actual. About all one can say is that "rationality" is a word of many meanings. There are many possible and plausible conceptions of rationality other than the one enshrined in our economic theory. The meaning of rationality is culturally and historically variable. On some understandings, our conception of rationality is profoundly irrational in the precise sense that its implementation has deranged the spheres of life by permitting the passion for profit and power to run unchecked by customary, religious, social, and esthetic considerations.[7]

Rawls has, in sum, poured a good bit of liberal, economically oriented psychology and morality into the "state of nature." Having done that, he has little trouble pouring it back out again. The debilitating results can be seen in Part Two of the work, on institutions. This is the thinnest part of the book. The world presented there looks distressingly like the one we have, with a little more equalization of income and welfare. But now, since that world came out of the original position, Rawls can time and time again characterize it as "nearly just" or "well ordered for the most part" (363).[8]

Theory and Practice

After completing his discussion of the original position, Rawls turns to the task of deriving the specific principles of justice. He starts by mentioning "a few misunderstandings" which the reader must try to avoid:

> First of all, we must keep in mind that the parties in the original position are theoretically defined individuals. . . . Of course, when we try to simulate the original position in everyday life . . . we will presumably find that our deliberations and judgments are influenced by our special inclinations and attitudes. Surely it will prove difficult to correct for our various propensities and aversions in striving to adhere to the conditions of this idealized situation. But none of this affects the contention that in the original position rational persons . . . would make a certain decision. This proposition belongs to the theory of justice. It is another question how well human beings can assume this role in regulating their practical reasoning (147).

My points here will be two: the logic of the hypothetical or contract method ineluctably produces a gap between theory and practice; Rawls' effort to bridge that gap fails. Starting, as Marx might put it, from the heaven of the original position, Rawls is unable to descend to the earth of practice. Or, to use Rawls' own terms, ideal and nonideal theory never come together.

Rawls' effort to bridge theory and practice is to be found mainly in his discussion of reflective equilibrium and his treatments of various economic and political problems in chapters five and six. I shall try to show that Rawls must treat both matters more thoroughly than he does.

The concept of reflective equilibrium is designed to elucidate the process of thought by which we simultaneously purify our considered opinions concerning principles of justice and move closer toward an understanding of the situation within which we are most likely to reach correct judgments. Rawls says that by following this hypothetical course of reflection "eventually we shall find a description of the initial situation that both expresses reasonable conditions and yields principles which match our considered judgments duly pruned and adjusted" (19). Thus, this process provides the crucial link between received or inherited notions of justice, and Rawls' primary contention that the best possible concept of justice is the concept of justice as fairness derived from the original position. Since it occupies such an important place in the whole theory, the process and concept of reflective equilibrium must be examined fully. My simple contention is that Rawls does not make that examination. Rather, he excuses himself from the work of close examination with the (curious) remark that "a theory of justice is precisely that, namely, a theory" (50-51). But reflective equilibrium is a crucial part of that theory.

Rawls himself provides a list of the topics that must be treated here, and it is worthwhile reminding ourselves of how important they are:

> For example, does a reflective equilibrium (in the sense of the philosophical ideal) exist? If so, is it unique? Even if it is unique, can it be reached? Perhaps the judgments from which we begin, or the course of reflection itself (or both), affect the resting point, if any, that we eventually achieve. It would be useless, however, to speculate about these matters here. They are far beyond our reach (50).

To put these questions beyond reach is to introduce a dichotomy between theory and practice into the very foundation of the system—the derivation of the original position. Again, we are confronted with the basic question of what is the right way to think about justice. For example, it might make sense to a man highly trained in hypothetical reasoning to think that the "veil of ignorance" is a reasonable condition to impose on discussions of justice, but a lesser man might consider such a restriction bizarre. It is doubtful that we can, or should, set aside what we know and who we are when we come to choose the basic principles of distributive justice. Probably most human beings do have a conception of justice, a conception derived from tradition and education, and experienced in living together. I doubt whether the sense of justice, or specific principles of justice, can be derived, described, or purified by abstracting to a hypothetical condition where all are considered equally free and rational—that is, uniform.

Plato's *Republic* provides another model of how thought on these subjects might proceed. Socrates talks with different men who hold different ideas about justice, and those ideas are integrally connected with the character and circumstances of the men themselves. The very tone and expression of the speakers tells us much about them, and provides us with information important to an assessment of their ideas. Some speakers are so enraged by philosophic discourse that the conversation cannot proceed in their presence. Examples and illustrations are drawn from everyday life. Character, mood, and circumstance affect the conversation. Each can speak only what he knows, or thinks he knows, and it takes a variety of speakers, each with his own peculiar experience and outlook, to clarify the issues and advance the argument. We get a sense of reality that is absent from Rawls' geometric method. A reading of *The Republic* might teach us that Rawls' hypothetical method in fact reflects the very contingencies of temperament, training, and circumstance which he so earnestly wants to eliminate from the argument.

Even if we set these difficulties aside, there is still no assurance that the process of reflection, as Rawls describes it, can lead to a unique first theorem, or "philosophically most favored" (122) description of the original situation. Rawls acknowledges that there are "many possible interpretations of the initial situation," and he conjectures "that for each traditional conception of justice there exists an interpretation of the initial situation in which its principles are the preferred solution" (121). This suggests that the process of thinking "back and forth" between our conceptions of justice and the original position will produce different interpretations of the original position depending upon the conceptions of justice we start with. Hence, our interpretation of the original position is already loaded with, or contaminated by, our initial conception of justice, and vice versa. We must ask Rawls whether the two principles were really derived — in any fairly strict sense—from the original position, or whether their sources are elsewhere, perhaps in Rawls' own "special inclinations and attitudes" (147). At the very least, it matters a lot what conceptions of justice one starts with, or as Rawls puts it, what alternatives are presented to the persons in the original position. "Ideally of course one would like to say that they are to choose among all possible conceptions of justice" (122).

Practical and theoretical difficulties prohibit that, however, so Rawls presents the parties with "a short list of traditional conceptions of justice ... together with a few other possibilities suggested by the two principles of justice" (122). This reader noted that the conceptions of Plato, Aristotle, and Aquinas are missing from the list. But these writers are surely among the most powerful on the subject. The first two are the very source of the subject itself. Does their exclusion suggest that what Rawls is really doing is providing a justification for current (liberal democratic and welfare oriented) tendencies of thought?

In any case, if the idea of reflective equilibrium is to be anything more than a myth which spares us the terrors of relativism, it must be explored more thoroughly and grounded more solidly than Rawls has done so far.

Let me turn next to the other side of Rawls' effort to unite theory and practice, his treatment of nonideal theory and his discussion of various policy problems in chapters five and six. Here again I shall only suggest some difficulties Rawls faces in building a bridge between theory and practice.

Rawls specifies that "the primary subject of justice is the basic structure of society, or more exactly, the way in which the major social institutions distribute fundamental rights and duties and determine the division of advantages from social cooperation" (7). The theory of justice, in turn, has two parts:

> The first or ideal part ... develops the conception of a perfectly just basic structure and the corresponding duties and obligations of persons under the fixed constraints of human life.... Nonideal theory, the second part, is worked out after an ideal conception of justice has been chosen; only then do the parties ask which principles to adopt under less happy conditions (245-46).

Ideal theory, then, is intended to provide a standard by which we may assess the justice or injustice of whole systems and of particular practices and policies. Rawls readily admits that the measure of departures from the ideal is "extremely rough" and "left importantly to intuition" (246). Still, he asserts, the two principles and the priority rules provide a fair guide to practice. I am not so sure.

My doubt is rooted in the fact that when Rawls works through a number of concrete attempts to apply the priority rules to problems of distribution, his examples are drawn from and discussed within the context of a system that already has the right basic institutions and is basically just and well-ordered. Without that background, it seems, distributive justice is simply not possible. With that background, distributive justice becomes an interesting technical problem in computation, in fiddling with various possible, slightly different, distributions to determine which fits the criteria most precisely. Justice then is a matter of charts and graphs, of more or less sophisticated mathematics.[9]

In a similar way, the whole topic of obligation is rather summarily dispatched with the observation that "clearly unjust institutions" give rise to no obligations, not even if we consent to them, because parties in the original position would so insist (343). It seems to follow that the ideal theory of justice denies, or cannot explain, the experience of millions of people who in fact do feel bound under much less than ideal conditions in the real world. Rawls' hypothetical method, once again, draws us away from an inquiry into how human beings do in fact concretely experience, think about, and act upon justice and injustice in the real world.[10]

Even if we restrict the discussion of the theory-practice question to the application of the ideal principles under reasonably just conditions, the same abstractness vitiates our efforts. Consider, for example, the problem of applying the first principle and the first priority rule, which tell us that "each person is to have an equal right to the most extensive total system of equal basic liberties compatible with a similar system of liberty for all," and that "liberty can be restricted only for the sake of liberty" (302). That teaching is a familiar and attractive fruit of the liberal democratic tradition, but it offers little guidance when we must make decisions. It is obvious that no society can regard all possible plans of life as equally desirable, and it will restrict some plans even when they do not impair other persons' liberties. There are different kinds of liberties, and we are always deciding which to prefer and which to deny. Liberties must always be weighed and evaluated, and the formal principle of "equal liberty" is of little help in that (political and moral) activity.

Or take the second principle, which provides that "social and economic inequalities are to be arranged so that they are . . . to the greatest benefit of the least advantaged . . . (302)" and try to apply it to a concrete question of social policy—equality in public education, for example, including the specific question of racial integration in the schools.

Since at least 1954, liberal opinion has held that all should have equal access to schooling of approximately equal quality because education is a crucial factor in the development of cognitive abilities and a necessary resource for upward social mobility. In Rawls' terms, education is a social primary good. Hence, where educational opportunity is not equal it must be made equal. That might require busing, compensatory programs, changes in teacher employment policies, and a host of other practices to improve the quality of education offered to the least advantaged. As nearly as I can tell, Rawls' second principle would counsel and recommend this course of policy.

Meanwhile, of course, the evidence has been accumulating that differentials in educational attainment are products of more factors than unequal educational resources. Jencks argues that none of the things that have been done to equalize education—racial desegregation, compensatory education, preschool enrichment programs—has significantly affected inequalities in cognitive skills.[11] It appears that the schools, despite vigorous efforts to the contrary, largely solidify cognitive inequalities that the children bring to school. Furthermore, cognitive skills themselves are only loosely related to later income and status: luck and personality are far more powerful. And finally, while quantity of schooling is related to income, attempts to equalize educational opportunity have had virtually no impact on the overall distribution of income. In other words, schooling affects earning power but does not equalize the distribution of income.

In summary, equal access to the social primary good called education does little to equalize income, status, or cognitive ability. It seems that education just is not a divisible social good in any simple sense: too much depends upon motivation, genetic endowment, accident, personal habits, family background, and so forth. I suspect that this might be true of other social primary goods which Rawls would advise us, in principle, to distribute equally. This suggests that the second principle could easily lead us to a series of policy choices trying to assure equal opportunity that will have no significant impact on the overall distribution of wealth and power. Jencks concludes, for example, that if we want to diminish economic inequality we must straightforwardly redistribute the wealth, and quit fooling around with ingenious manipulations of such institutions as schools. But such a direct redistribution of income will raise profound questions of desert, questions that Rawls has deliberately purged from his theory of distributive justice.[12] I conclude that the two principles, and especially the second, could easily lead us into confused and disheartening policy efforts because the principles seem to assume that many social primary goods are easily and simply divisible when they really are not. In addition, if we abandon the ingenious manipulation of opportunity and access, then we face questions of desert, and those questions Rawls excludes.

The difficulties here are as old as Aristotle, whose discussion in the *Ethics* and the *Politics* is the *locus classicus* of all work on distributive justice. Distributive justice is concerned with the distribution of divisible goods—such as honors, offices, payments of money for public service, or in a share-out of surplus funds or of prizes taken in war. The problem is to determine the correct principle or formula by which such divisions should be made. But since justice is a relation among members of a political community, the problem of distributive justice can be solved only after we have first determined the true or proper end of the polis itself. That end is the good life, or good actions. Hence, the basic principle of distribution is that each should receive rewards according to his contribution to the specific end of the state. As one gives to the state, in the way of personal virtue and contributions to its essential end, so one should receive from the state, in the way of office, honors, and payments. It follows that distributive justice consists not in treating unequals equally, but in distributing benefits in proportion to the merit and public service of each citizen.[13]

Aristotle was convinced that men's sense of fairness and equality is not offended by the idea that rewards should be proportionate to merit and contribution. All will agree to this. Disagreement enters when we ask which merits should count, and what we mean by merit: "All men agree that just distribution consists in distribution according to merit; but all men do not mean the same thing when they speak of merit."[14] An element of interest and ideology inescapably enters into the answer to that question: democrats mean one thing by merit, aristocrats mean another. Furthermore, when the discussion concerns contributions to the whole social order or polis, as distinguished from contributions to limited enterprises and associations, then many different sorts of merits have to be considered and somehow compared. This, in turn, requires a metric that can reduce dissimilar things to a system of equivalences without undue distortion.

In our day these problems are multiplied because when we discuss the social products that must be distributed according to some rule of justice, we include many more things than Aristotle ever thought of. To his offices and honors, we add education, housing, social and physical mobility, health, working conditions, leisure, and even freedom from fear. All these, and more, we think must be treated in a discussion of distributive justice. Each presents its own complex problems. We simply do not know how and in what ways these things are comparable, and thus we do not know how to divide and distribute them—or, indeed, in what senses they can usefully be regarded as divisible.

I suspect that had Rawls discussed some of these substantive policy areas in detail, he would have concluded that the practical power of the two principles and the priority rules is quite small. Lacking that discussion, each reader might try a few practical exercises on his own, as I did, for example, in the sketchy discussion of education presented above.

Justice and Equality

Rawls acknowledges the exteme difficulty of implementing the priority rules, and he further admits that "at some point the priority of rules for nonideal cases will fail; and indeed, we may be able to find no satisfactory answer at all. But we must try to postpone the day of reckoning as long as possible, and try to arrange society so that it never comes" (303). I have argued, in effect, that the day of reckoning is here now.

When that day is reached—whether on Rawls' calendar or on mine—then we must fall back upon what Rawls calls a "general conception" of justice to guide our practice. The general conception "lacks the definite structure of the two principles in serial order," but "in more extreme and tangled cases of nonideal theory there may be no alternative to it" (303). I have argued in effect that most cases of nonideal theory are extreme and tangled. Hence, we must examine the general conception. It reads as follows:

> All social primary goods—liberty and opportunity, income and wealth, and the bases of self-respect—are to be distributed equally unless an unequal distibution of any or all of these goods is to the advantage of the least favored (303).

Now, that formulation appears to commit us to a virtually unlimited form of equalitarianism. Rawls, I think, goes farther in the direction of equality than even Marx proposed in his principles of distribution for communist society, for while Marx recommended that each receive according to need, he also required that each contribute according to ability. That requirement is no part of Rawls' general conception.

In effect, Rawls has collapsed justice into equality. Part of the cost of doing that is suggested by Blake's aphorism that "one law for the lion and for the ox is tyranny" and by Plato's argument that democratic regimes are unjust and contemptible because they treat equals and unequals alike. The experiences of daily life simply will not let us believe that all persons are equally capable and good. Every person, I expect, has a settled conviction that those inequalities will remain, unless we undertake an enormous effort to alter the conditions that produce them. To many, it will seem the height of arrogance and peril to undertake that effort. We might, for a variety of good reasons, only some of which concern justice, wish to see more equality in the distribution of social primary goods than we see now, both within our own country and between our people and other peoples.[15] We might, again for a variety of reasons, want to fix a minimum below which no person would fall, and which would be provided to all as a matter of right. We might also want to keep the ceiling rather low, so that the floor could be comfortably high. But all of that stops far short of the destination demanded by Rawls' general conception.

Another way to assess the cost of collapsing justice into equality is by pointing to a striking feature of Rawls' argument, namely, his vigorous effort to exclude the categories of "desert" and "deserving" from the discussion of justice (103-04, 310-15). In our ordinary thoughtful talk about justice, we proceed as though those categories were germane to the discussion. When we talk about distributive justice, we usually consider such categories as desert, merit, contribution, and reciprocity. We ask who deserves what, and why. We want to know whether rewards should be based on effort, or contribution, or need, or on some combination of these and other factors. We ask whether some needs take priority over others, and whether some contributions are more worthy than others. Altogether, we proceed as though some people, on a number of grounds, deserve or need more than others, and that any concept of distributive justice must take those differences into account. It does violence to our settled traditions and considered opinions to exclude such considerations and turn the whole field over to equality. Those traditions and considered opinions teach that at a certain point liberty and equality really are in conflict, that merit and need are too, and that the just society tries not to deny this but to work out a shifting balance. In his urge to set aside the "accidents of natural endowment" and the "contingencies of social circumstances" as "arbitrary from a moral point of view" (15), Rawls proposes a course or direction of policy which is full of perils to human excellence and diversity.[16] Certainly the "general conception" of justice offered by Rawls cuts through the questions of practice raised in the previous section, but it does so at the cost of violating some of our strongest conventions about the matters that are appropriate to a discussion of justice. Perhaps those conventions are in need of correction; perhaps the theory of justice that excludes them is in need of correction. My point is that this matter is not persuasively treated in Rawls' book.

The Right and the Good

One of the fundamental propositions of the entire theory is the idea that "in justice as fairness the concept of right is prior to that of the good" (31). By making right prior to good, and by assimilating the theory of right to the theory of rational choice, Rawls escapes the rock that has wrecked all intuitionist theories: how to reduce or reconcile the multiplicity of competing first principles. With these propositions established, Rawls hopes to have gained the "Archimedean point" from which persons can derive principles of right that are "general in form and universal in application" (135). With this grounding, the principles of right overcome ethical relativism and yet ensure political stability, for we shall have found precepts for the guidance of policy that are both theoretically unimpeachable and effective in practice.

The principles of right are generated by abstract actors in an abstract situation. Those abstractions are required "if one is to have any theory at all" (139). As I have argued above, there is much that is problematic about this procedure in general, and about the descriptions of the actors and the original position in particular. But if this part of the theory is problematic, then the crucial proposition of the priority of the right to the good also becomes problematic, and we are thrown back into the chaos of competing goods, or warring gods, with no principles to adjudicate among them. I argued above that this is indeed what happens. A fuller examination of Rawls' conception of the good and its relation to the right will lead to the same conclusion.

Essential to Rawls' argument is the idea that an individual will agree only to that which he can see to be in his own interest or to his own advantage. This is as true of conceptions of good as of conceptions of right. Now, this requirement of the theory means that some conception of good must be already implicit in the original position. This is necessary because in order to reach principles of right one must make some assumptions about actors' motives, and you cannot do that without discussing what persons desire. What people desire they usually call good.

And so indeed it turns out. "Rational individualists, whatever else they want, desire certain things as prerequisites for carrying out their plans of life. Other things equal, they prefer a wider to a narrower liberty and opportunity, and a greater rather than a smaller share of wealth and income" (396).[17] In order not to jeopardize the priority of right (that is, in order not to jeopardize the universality and objectivity of the principles of right) this conception of good is reduced to the bare essentials. It is what Rawls calls the "thin theory of the good" (Sec. 15, and 395-99). The purpose of the thin theory is "to secure the premises about primary goods required to arrive at the principles of justice" (395).

Hence, a conception of the good, albeit a thin one, is required in the very foundation of the theory of justice. How is that conception derived? What are its sources?

Primarily, the thin theory of the good is derived from certain assumptions about human nature and about the original position: rational actors choose principles of right and good behind a "veil of ignorance." Being rational, they will prefer more rather than less of the social primary goods and of the bases for self-respect.

Once again, then, Rawls engages in the process of stripping away all the many diverse things that human beings actually say and do about the good, in order to come to a universal good. Men are torn out of their actual contexts and reduced to a plane of abstract equality and rationality.

Human complexity falls away, and abstract, calculating man stands forth as a chooser of the good. The content of the thin theory of the good, in sum, has no other foundation than the argument that abstract men under abstract conditions would choose that content. But if the theory of mind and the understanding of rationality ascribed to the actors are questionable, then the thin theory of the good stands on shaky foundations.

There are further troubles in Rawls' understanding of the relations between the thin theory and the full theory of the good. Two points matter here. Rawls writes that "the characteristic feature of this full theory ... is that it takes the principles of justice as already secured, and then uses these principles in defining the other moral concepts in which the notion of goodness is involved. Once the principles of right are on hand, we may appeal to them in explaining the concept of moral worth and the good of the moral virtues" (396). Now, this supposes that human beings build their conceptions of the good life on top of, or out of, a few abstract principles of right which are chosen in ignorance of the concrete, actual conditions of life. We germinate our basic principles under artificial conditions, and then transplant them in the soil of life, where they flower into a full conception of the good.

In "real life" we usually proceed exactly the other way around. Rather than starting from an abstract depiction of the human condition and proceeding toward a conception of the good, we occasionally, in quiet moments, stand back from the confused flow of life and, if we are blessed and thoughtful, reach a few, tentative, general statements about the basic human condition. Once again, Rawls abolishes human complexity in the interests of quasi-mathematical theory. Put differently, Rawls employs a propositional logic rather than a logic of question and answer to reach practical truths in the human subjects. I have found R.G. Collingwood's criticism of the propositional method persuasive.

The second point concerns the fit or linkage between the thin and full theories of the good. The thin conception of the good is chosen behind the veil of ignorance, while the full conception of the good is chosen in conditions where our knowledge of self and world is very extensive. The more extensive our knowledge, the better are our chances for reaching a fully rational conception of the good: "Our good is determined by the plan of life that we would adopt with full deliberative rationality if the future were accurately foreseen and adequately realized in the imagination" (421). So, "a rational plan is one that would be selected if certain conditions were fulfilled" (421). Those conditions are mainly two: extensive information; and a clear understanding of the criteria of rationality in making life-plans. It is clear, then, that the criterion of the good is hypothetical in the same way as the criterion of justice: the good, like the just, is that which is chosen when certain conditions are met. But now, the conditions are radically different—full knowledge, rather than complete ignorance.

This puts the theorist, along with the rest of us, in a strange position. We are asked to choose, out of our full knowledge, a good plan for life that is congruent with principles of right chosen under hypothetical conditions of ignorance. More than that, what we chose in ignorance takes priority over what we choose in knowledge: good must not violate right. We must judge actions and choices made in the midst of life by criteria chosen in abstraction from life. Knowledge must be judged by ignorance.

Much is at stake here. If rational choosers are not capable of this abstraction, if they cannot judge the good by the right, then they have no criteria for adjudicating their conflicting claims. Political stability and the escape from relativism rest on the priority of right, which includes the supremacy of the thin theory of the good over full conceptions of good chosen in the midst of life.

Although I have looked hard, I have not found either in Rawls' book or in my own experience an unbreakable theoretical link between the thin and the full theories. We often let our specific ethical choices, taken under the imperatives of action and based on the fullest possible knowledge of context, override our abstract conceptions of right. Moreover, we are often convinced that it is moral and reasonable to do so—even as diseases caused by law must sometimes be cured by equity.[18]

The Return of Cephalus

If the theoretical link between the just and the good is weak, is there another link of some different kind that can replace it? There is, and Rawls uses it, though at considerable cost in theoretical cogency.

That link is habit, settled disposition, sentiment—a set of attitudes that check and restrain us from following our interests when they bump up against the interests of others or the principles of right. Such sentiments build fences around desire, confining it within socially approved limits, moderating its intensity. These habits and sentiments are not the fruit of reason and abstract argument, but the product of custom and education. They amount to a kind of piety toward the collective order; and modern social science has pretty largely returned, after the intoxication of the Enlightenment, to the ancient understanding that society cannot endure without them. Without something like a founding myth, settled customs, and attitudes of care toward the whole, transmitted through the institutions of family, church, and school, there is no way to bridge the theoretical gap between individual desires and interests on the one side, and collective need and good on the other.

While Rawls fails to provide a coherent theory of justice, he has perhaps shown the way to a new myth, or noble lie, that can give the welfare-oriented regimes of our day a firmer foundation for political stability and a surer confidence in their own rectitude. That the myth he fashions contains large elements of calculative reason does not make it any the less a myth. Rather, those elements only make the myth appropriate to our time, for the language of science now enjoys great authority. And obviously, the equalitarian tone of the doctrine makes it far more congenial to us than Plato's myth of the metals, for our moral and sentimental propensity is toward equality. About the only hierarchies we will permit are those based on technical skill. The task of political education becomes the task of assuring the devotion of the populace to the regime, and this is accomplished by teaching the winners in the social race to show some care for the losers, and teaching the losers to moderate their demands on the winners. Rawls' principles of justice, taught as a civic religion, can be a powerful aid in this task. That is the importance, in my judgment, of the banishment of the categories of merit and desert from this book.

Seen politically and morally, I think this is the significance of *A Theory of Justice*. It may seem a strange way to put it, but I think we have in this book the ideology that the "end of ideology" theorists of the 1950s were seeking. We have here a justification for the social welfare policies that came to their culmination in Lyndon B. Johnson's vision of "The Great Society." And it is worthwhile remembering that Rawls' version of that vision requires little in the way of citizenly care and activity. As Rawls puts it, "in a well-governed state only a small fraction of persons may devote much of their time to politics. . . . But this fraction . . . will most likely be drawn more or less equally from all sectors of society. The many communities of interests and centers of political life will have their active members who look after their concerns" (228). Sounds a lot like interest-group politics *cum* professional bureaucracy equipped with the two principles, lexical ordering, and counting methods. And while Rawls sees no hint of tyranny or despotism in this, others might see it as the shortest road to that "democratic despotism" which Tocqueville presents at the end of *Democracy in America*.[19]

Seen in a broader historical perspective, Rawls' book appears as an effort to fulfill the promise of the liberal contractarian and Enlightenment philosophers to ground social order on truths rationally apprehended rather than on lies authoritatively propagated. The great thinkers of the Enlightenment yearned to replace the mythical foundations of states with rational foundations. They knew, and modern social science continues to affirm, that social orders are built on myths or ideologies which justify the idea of justice and the distribution of power established in the regime.

Myths are unacceptable to rational men, and the Enlightenment thinkers held that all were capable of becoming rational. Hence, those thinkers attempted to base legitimacy on the foundation of consent expressed in the original contract. Today we can see that that was a myth like the others, and every bit as full of deceits and as vulnerable to abuses as any of the older (typically religious) myths it replaced.

The liberal thinkers tried to construct the foundations of political order out of the myth of the contract. Furthermore, they thought that men could be made loyal to the regime out of rational calculation of self-interest. They thought it possible to fashion a civil order which did not require men to overcome their selfish desires and devote themselves to the common good or general welfare. Indeed, such a requirement is utopian; only fools would attempt it.[20] Nor did selfish desire itself have to be chastened or tempered. Rather, it could be kept in bounds by well-fashioned institutions which could arbitrate and subdue the clash of desire against desire. And finally, the development of new techniques for forcing nature to yield its riches gave promise of almost infinite satisfaction of desire. The problems of political allegiance and of social justice were thus solved on new grounds. As Allan Bloom has put it, "A civil society which provided security and some prospect of each man's acquiring those possessions he most wishes would be both a more simple and more sure solution than any utopian attempt to make men abandon their selfish wishes. Such a civil society could count on men's rational adhesion, for it would be an instrument in procuring their own good as they see it."[21]

John Rawls' book is the latest chapter in this history. The social contract is renewed. Calculative reason is refurbished as the origin and arbiter of the good and the right. Citizens can remain largely indifferent to the good of others. Conflicting desires and visions of the good can be channeled by institutions equipped with the sophisticated techniques needed to arrange a just distribution of the social product. Allegiance is given the firmest possible ground in interest. Self-love meets no challenge.

Rawls has improved and strengthened this legacy by bringing it in line with the equalitarian impulse. As the liberal societies developed, great inequalities of power and wealth appeared within them, inequalities so great as to threaten the very stability of the social order. If the principles of this book were applied, they would do something to alleviate the growing dissatisfaction of the losers. Whether they would do enough, I cannot say. For a very long time now, men in the liberal states have been conditioned to want More and to regard More as their right. And even though the whole social product is gigantic and increasing, great differences among the classes remain in the distribution of that product. Men are less and less patient with those differences. Even while the total product increases, each wants both more of it in absolute terms and a greater share of it in relative terms. The Hobbesian skeleton of envy, which has always been there in the liberal closet, may yet disrupt the enterprise.[22] Besides, nature itself is showing signs of fatigue: the mine of More is running out. If the ethos of equality, or envy, prevails while the promise of growth and abundance is threatened, the liberal states will come to a day of reckoning when other principles of justice than those presented in this book will be needed. We may have to readmit Cephalus to the conversation about justice.

Notes

1. He sees Locke's *Second Treatise,* Rousseau's *Social Contract,* and Kant's ethical works "as definitive of the contract tradition," and says that "for all of its greatness, Hobbes' *Leviathan* raises special problems." John Rawls, *A Theory of Justice* (Cambridge, Mass.: Harvard University Press, 1971), 11n. Hereinafter, Rawls will be cited in the text by page number.
2. I doubt whether Rawls' work will have much appeal in those countries where the urgent political task is "development." Rawls' preference for liberty over efficiency or growth and his treatment of the problem of justice between generations are sufficient to make his book seem a luxury, irrelevant to the needs of poor and weak states. Does this suggest a flaw in the logic of the "original position"? Rawls assumes throughout a condition of "moderate scarcity."
3. "The theory of justice is a part, perhaps the most significant part, of the theory of rational choice" (16). This proposition permits Rawls to assimilate the recent work on rational choice theory and welfare economics into the contract tradition.
4. Leonard Choptiany, "A Critique of John Rawls's Principles of Justice," *Ethics,* 83 (January 1973), 150.
5. B. Parekh, "Reflections on Rawls' *Theory of Justice," Political Studies* 20 (December 1972), 478-83. The next couple of paragraphs owe much to Parekh.
6. Parekh, 480, makes the same point.
7. The basic idea is as old as Aristotle's distinction between economics and chrematistics, between the "natural" activity of producing goods for use, and the "unnatural" activity of producing goods for the purpose of making money. (*Politics,,* Bk. I, Chs. 8-11). The latter activity is unnatural because it has no limit. Marx, of course, is the modern master of the subject. See *The Communist Manifesto.* It is worth remembering that *Capital* opens by calling upon Aristotle's distinction. Karl Polanyi, *The Great Transformation,* offers a splendid account, based largely on Malinowski's work among the Trobriand Islanders, of the social destructiveness of the liberal concept of rationality.
8. I chose these specific passages because they appear at the opening of the discussion of civil disobedience, but similar phrases appear throughout Part Two.
9. Rawls himself is tempted to more than a little of this, but his commentators have outdone him by far. The secondary literature contains a large and growing number of such precisionist efforts. One might remember Aristot-

le's maxim that it is a mark of the educated man to require no more precision of a subject than the nature of the subject permits.

10. For an example of the contrast I am trying to make, compare Rawls on obligation with the richly historical, sociological, and philosophical discussions in Michael Walzer's *Obligations: Essays on Disobedience, War, and Citizenship* (Cambridge, Mass.: Harvard University Press, 1970).
11. Christopher Jencks, *Inequality: A Reassessment of the Effect of Family and Schooling in America* (New York, N.Y.: Basic Books, 1972), examines and interprets much of the evidence. A good many liberal idols are rudely challenged.
12. The question of desert is considered more fully below.
13. For the whole argument, see *Ethics*, Bk. V, and *Politics*, esp Bk. III, 9-13.
14. *Ethics*, V, Sec. 7.
15. This touches on an important point. Rawls assumes that the actors in the original position all come from the same already existing society. That assumption seems to me arbitrary. Above all, it permits Rawls to ignore the whole question of distribution of goods between different (say, rich and poor) societies. Rawls' brief discussion of international relations (377-82) is silent on the question of economic inequality among nations.
16. For an excellent discussion of this question, see Ralf Dahrendorf, *Essays in the Theory of Society* (Stanford, Cal.: Stanford University Press, 1968), 151-215. At one point, Dahrendorf offers an idea which might alert us to some of the dangers Rawls neglects: "In the vast domain between the ceiling and floor of the status hierarchy, the domain in which equality of citizenship can be taken for granted, equality of social status is an enemy of liberty. As a stimulus, a medium, and a reward of personal self-development, social stratification is essential to human freedom. . . . The more pluralistic and differentiated a system of social stratification is, the more easily can it do justice to the citizens' multifarious individual needs and talents. Once equality of citizenship is assured, inequality of social status is necessary to the chance of liberty." Ibid., 202.
17. There is a flaw in the reasoning here. Rawls seems to be saying that if something is a good for an individual, it is good for the whole social order that all individuals have that good. But the collective good is not always the sum of private goods. It might be a good for some individuals to have a car, but a social disaster if everyone had one. Rawls here makes the mistake that has vitiated most liberal individualist thinking about the "public good."
18. The point I want to make here can be formulated in a narrower way, one that exposes a basic confusion in Rawls' reasoning. Rawls describes the original position as though the people in it were choosing what kind of society to enter [see 164.] This permits him to postulate the features of the original position. Most important among these postulated features is the "veil of ignorance"—nearly total ignorance and uncertainty. But the people in the original position are not choosing among societies. Rather, they are choosing criteria for distributing goods in their society. When applying criteria, the degree of ignorance is a question of fact, not a matter of postulation. And that degree will rarely approach the nearly total ignorance and uncertainty that are postulated as features of the original position. This confusion, I think, totally vitiates Rawls' derivation of the maximin criterion.
19. Rawls is sanguine throughout, and obviously has the interests of the many at

heart. And yet, he should have seen the troublesome political possibilities contained in his own recognition of the need for considerable mathematical sophistication in applying the principles of justice. It is not likely that the masses will develop this sophistication. The just society built on Rawlsian principles will require a technically trained elite managing the agencies of distribution, and there is nothing in Rawls' book that persuades one that such an elite will remain any more "just" and responsible than other previous priestly classes known to history.

20. The supreme expression of this teaching is found in Locke and in Madison's powerful essays in *The Federalist*.
21. Allan Bloom, *The Republic of Plato* (New York, N.Y.: Basic Books, 1968), 368.
22. Does this suggest the "special problems" which Rawls finds in Hobbes? See notes 1 and 10.

Some Ways Of Thinking About Equality

I

Nature spreads its gifts unequally, so that inequalities among men on virtually any trait or characteristic one might mention are obvious and probably ineradicable. In this sense, it is manifestly silly to say that all men are equal. Furthermore, think how stupefyingly dull the world would be if all really were equal, as similar to each other as one brick to another. Inequality, while it may be the root of much that is cruel and hateful in human life, is also the root of just about everything that is admirable and interesting.

In the face of these plain facts, we have set equality as our moral and political ideal. Justice demands equality before the law; all should receive equal treatment in the public realm; each to count for one and nobody to count for more than one—these formulas are at the core of what it means to be liberal and democratic.

Nature, then, shouts "inequality." We reply, "nonetheless, equality." It is as though the liberal democrat said with Rousseau, "let us set the facts aside, as they do not affect the matter."

This situation has seemed to many writers a theoretical embarrassment. When the outer eye, the eye of sense, reports so many manifest inequalities, how can the inner eye, the theoretical vision, still claim to see equality? But the case here is really no different in kind from that which the political theorist typically faces. Theorists are forever flying in the face of facts. All theory, all artifice, civilization itself, is an "embarrassment"—if not an outrage against the facts of nature, then at least a thorough reworking of them. Nature urges us to procreate. Civilization replies, control yourself; rape and incest are not allowed. Nature tells the hungry man to eat. Civilization replies, do not take these apples for they belong to another. In sum, the large discrepancy between the observed facts of inequality and claims for equality presents the political theorist with a case no different in kind from that which one typically faces when dealing with a large and complex subject: to point to the discrepancy here is merely to specify a particular example of the theorist's general problem.

There is only one way to completely abolish the embarrassment. If we are willing to draw a sharp line between fact and value, and say, in effect, that equality is a preference which one may freely choose regardless of facts, then we are no longer faced with a difficult theoretical task. This essay assumes that we are not willing to draw that sharp line. It is of course correct to say that no conclusion in the imperative mood can be derived logically from statements cast in the indicative mood, and in this sense there is a logical gap between fact and value. Still, we shall persist in asking for more than logic can give on these matters. Most people want to feel that there is a reasonable fit, a fair measure of harmony and appropriateness, between what they think they know about the world and what they think should be done in the world. Certainly that feeling, rather than the prissy satisfaction one gets from being logically impeccable, is the fountain of moral and political theory. Indeed, a rigorous adherence to the "fact-value dichotomy" renders intelligence cautious just where it must be bold, dumb where it should be articulate. I shall take the large discrepancy between the observed facts of inequality and the policy or value of equality as a serious intellectual embarrassment.

Although it is not different in kind from any other complex and serious issue of theory, the case of equality may be different in degree. The discrepancy here is so large, the outrage which the policy of equality works on the facts of inequality is so gross, that theorists seem to have found it especially difficult to make sense of the problem, and have been severely pressed for persuasive solutions of it. This essay will discuss some of those solutions.

It is worthwhile to remember at the outset that the pursuit of equality as an ideal of justice is a rather recent political fashion, one belonging distinctively to modern constitutional and democratic thought. The classical writers who invented political theory were profoundly, almost instinctively, inequalitarian. Our modern notion of justice as equal treatment of all under a uniform rule would have seemed a monstrous error to Plato and Aristotle. To be sure, they held that equals should be treated equally, but this really meant that *only* equals should be treated equally. Both thought that the differences among men should be reflected in all social and political arrangements. Plato thought that justice consisted in a system wherein each person performed the function for which nature suited him, and in which each large natural and social grouping was under a law specifically appropriate to it alone. Justice for the guardians was one thing, and for the artisans another, because guardians were one kind of person fitted for one kind of work, and artisans were a different kind of person fitted for a different kind of work. Aristotle argued that each man should be under the law most appropriate to himself and to the natural group of which he was a member. There should be one law for citizens, and another for those who were slaves by nature. Artistotle was prepared to follow this argument out to its conclusion: if one man in the polity showed himself greatly superior in virtue and wisdom to all others he should be a law unto himself. In short, both writers held that justice required that only similars should be treated as though they were similars.

Medieval political organization also followed the rule of inequality. The medieval polity was a regime of privilege—that is, of private law—a regime in which the notions of public law and equal citizenship hardly existed. Persons' legal rights and duties were defined by virtue of their membership in a given status and corporate body. These, in turn, were governed by laws appropriate to their special needs and circumstancses. This system endured throughout the West until very recent times, and it still endures in scattered places.

Past learning and practice, then, do not overwhelmingly indicate the manifest rationality and good sense of our modern notion of justice as treating all alike despite their differences. Nor is the notion confirmed by the ordinary experiences and the commonsense conclusions of everyday life. The premises of private "justice" are opposite from those of public justice. In our personal and private relations with those who matter most to us the rule of inequality prevails. We treat them according to their differences from all others, and not according to some trait or characteristic they presumably share with all others. If you want to lose your friend, treat him by an equal rule which applies to all. Tell him that you're sorry, but he will have to wait in line like everyone else, and he should please not ask for special treatment. One's personal relations with others stand or fall on the clarity of one's understanding that each of those other persons is unique and irreplaceable, and that this uniqueness raises a just claim for unequal treatment. What is justice for all others is injustice for your friend. To treat those closest to us by a rule applicable to everyone would amount to an insane cruelty. One must look at the friend, and guide a course with him according to the special things he is. That is why the maxim has it that there is no justice among friends.

There is no justice among friends because justice is blind. In the public realm we proceed on the theory that justice cannot be achieved if the judge and the law actually look at the object before them as a person. Public justice looks not at persons nor does it listen to them. In our higher courts this ideal becomes literal reality: the concrete individual for whom justice must be done does not even appear before the judges. The judges see only lawyers, craftsmen trained in what Blackstone called "the mysterious science of the law." Any intrusion of the human and personal violates the whole process and threatens its validity.

We believe, then, that the very blindness and indifference to personality which we recognize as the grossest violations in relations among familiars become somehow transformed on the public stage into the conditions necessary for achieving justice itself. The soundness of that belief is not self-evident. Once again we meet a situation in which our commitment to equality offers as many questions as answers.

II

How can we reduce the discrepancy between the facts of inequality presented by nature, wisdom, and personal experience, and the democratic commitment to equality? Perhaps the most popular way to do this today is by revising the commitment to equality to read "equality of opportunity." We are fully aware, say those who propose this formula, that people are not equal in any empirical sense: this one is strong, that one weak; this one has a keen ear for music, that one is tone-deaf; this one has high intelligence, that one only average. But the commitment to equality as equality of opportunity does not mean a commitment to some uniform way of life based on the preposterous idea that all are equal in their possession of the various talents and virtues. What it does mean is that each shall have equal opportunity to develop those talents and virtues which are his, and that there shall be equal rewards for equal talents. The understanding of equality not only achieves justice, say its proponents, but it also unlocks the energies necessary to social and economic progress, and surely that is in its favor.

This is almost the official theory today. We seem to think it answers the objections which have been made against the equalitarian policy, and simultaneously lets us keep everything that is good in the idea of equality. It is as though, over the decades during which the idea of equality has beckoned, we had finally purged the original formulations of their dross and achieved a pure and sympathetic understanding of the matter. I want to suggest that the doctrine of equality of opportunity compounds the confusion.

First of all, not all talents can be developed equally in any given society. Every group has a set of values, and these values are arranged in a more-or-less tidy hierarchy: each group evaluates talents and virtues differently from every other group. Out of the (practically) infinite human resources given by nature, each society elects to use and reward some capacities and not others. Hence the formula, equality of opportunity for all to develop their talents, is radically misleading. To be accurate, it must read, equality of opportunity for all to develop the talents which are highly regarded in a given group. When cast in this way, it becomes clear that a commitment to this formula requires a prior commitment to an already established social-moral order. The commitment to equality of opportunity is implicitly or indirectly a thoroughly conservative doctrine enjoining support for that which a society already is and is obviously coming to be. We should think seriously about the implications of this. The tone and content of very much of our recent serious literature and social thought warn that we are well on the way toward building a culture which the best among us will not honor. The facile formula of equal opportunity quickens that trend, for what it really means is more and more opportunities for more and more people to contribute more and more energies toward the achievement of a mass, technological, privatized, bored and thrill-seeking, consumption-oriented society.

Secondly, it is clear that the doctrine of equality of opportunity will increase the inequalities among men. In previous ages, when opportunities were largely restricted to those of the right birth and station, it is quite probable, given the fact that nature seems to delight in distributing many traits in the pattern of a normal distribution, that a large proportion of those who enjoyed superior opportunities to develop their talents lacked the native ability to benefit from the opportunity. It is reasonable to suppose, therefore, that many members of ascribed elites, while they appeared far superior to the ruck, really were not that superior in actual attainment. But under the regime of equal opportunity, only those who genuinely are superior in the desired qualities will have the opportunity to develop those qualities. The consequence, over time, must be a situation where the members of the elite really are immensely superior in ability and attainment to the masses. We shall approach a condition where the natural and social aristocracies coincide—a meritocracy, as Michael Young has called it. Furthermore, as we approach this condition, the gap in attainment between the highest and the lowest will widen. This will happen because in so many fields there are such prodigious quantities of things to know in order to be certified as competent in the field that only the highest talents plus the most dedicated work and study will enable one to make the grade. We call ours a scientific age. What that really means is that a small handful of men have a tremendous scientific knowledge, while the rest of us are about as ignorant of science as we have always been. So the gap widens: the distance between an Einstein or a Bohr and the ordinary men of our day is far greater than the distance between a Newton or a Kepler and the ordinary men of their day. In addition, the growth of large and powerful organizations provides positions from which those who have been favorably endowed by nature and society can command far more power over the unendowed than was the case in the past. The doctrine of equality of opportunity, which in its origins was a rather embarrassed attempt to overlook the great natural differences among men, ironically now magnifies those differences. The doctrine itself, social institutions made in pursuit of it, and advancements in knowledge all conspire with nature to produce more and more inequality.

Finally, we have told ourselves that the doctrine of equality of opportunity is a generous one. It imposes no artificial limits on the individual; on the contrary, it so arranges social conditions that each individual can go as high as his natural reach will permit. Surely, nothing could be fairer or more generous.

But the generosity dissolves under analysis. The whole point is, that this doctrine, seriously followed, takes the question out of the realm of human control and responsibility and returns it entirely to nature. Where is the generosity in telling a person he can go as far as his talents will take him when his talents are paltry? Imagine a footrace of one mile in which ten men are to compete. All must start at the same time and abide by the same rules. Three of them are forty years old, three are overweight, three have weak ankles, and one is Roger Bannister. What sense can it make to say that all ten had an equal opportunity to win the race? The outcome is foreordained by nature, and the nine will think it a mockery when they are told that they have all been given the same opportunity to win. The cruelty of the jest, incidentally, is intensified with each increase in our ability to measure various traits and talents at an early age. Some day our testing devices may be so keen that we can tell, with high accuracy, how well a child of seven or nine will do in the social race. The canon of efficiency would then dictate that we use these measuring tools to separate the superior from the inferior, and to determine the allocation of growth resources, such as education and leisure time, to each group. The best training that society can afford should, of course, go to the superior group—in order to assure equality of opportunity for the development of their talents. It would seem more generous for us to take some responsibility for the matter, perhaps by devising a system of handicaps to counteract the injustices of nature.[1]

Two lines of defense might be raised against these criticisms of the equality of opportunity principle.

First, the defender might argue that the principle need not, or should not, be expounded and applied, as it has been in my treatment, in a context of social competitiveness. The principle could be construed as one which encourages the individual to compete against himself, as it were, to compare what he is with what he might become. The contest is not between oneself and others, but between one's actual and potential selves, and with the individual, rather than society, judging the outcome. This is a very interesting, and, in my opinion, hopeful revision of the principle. It would shift the criteria of judgment from guilt and utility over to shame and nobility, and it would shift the locus of judgment from society to the individual. This shift is possible, but it would require a reformation in our present ways of thinking about equality of opportunity, for those ways are in fact socially oriented and utilitarian. In sum, this defense against the criticisms is in the strict sense no defense at all. It is irrelevant in the strict sense that instead of meeting the specific charges, it shifts the whole question to a different battleground. It is an alternative to the existing, operative theory, and not a defense of it.

The second defense is a defense, though not a strong one. It consists in pointing out that the metaphor of the footrace oversimplifies the reality which is relevant in a discussion of the equality of opportunity principle. What actually goes on in a society is not just one kind of contest, but many kinds, so that those who are not so good at one thing may find a different contest where they have a better chance of winning. Furthermore, there is not just one prize in a given contest, but many. Indeed, in our affluent society we might be able to arrange affairs so that everyone gets at least something: there need be no losers.

This defense has much to recommend it, but it does not reach to the basic points. As was suggested before, although there can be many contests, many avenues of opportunity, in our society, their number is not unlimited. The basic point is that the whole theory of equality of opportunity must be implemented within a set of conventions which defines the potentialities which are favored and encouraged and distinguishes them from others which are discouraged. One who strives to develop potentialities which are discouraged in a given society quickly finds his efforts tagged silly, or dangerous, or dysfunctional. This is inherent in any society, and it stands as an insuperable barrier to the full devlopment of a principle of equality of opportunity. In sum, we discourage some talents and virtues and contests, and encourage others. Furthermore, even among those which are encouraged there is a hierarchy of merit: we reward the winners in some contests more handsomely than in other contests. It remains only to add, that even in a complex society where many contests go on, and even in an affluent society where it would seem that no one had to be the loser, we know full well that some prizes are only consolation prizes, not the real thing, perhaps even demeaning to their winners. When the fat man who finishes last in the footrace is given a prize for "best try," we know, even while we smile, that he has lost more than he has won.

The formula of equality of opportunity, then, is by no means the warm and generous principle it seems to be on first view. In addition, it provides no escape from the theoretical embarrassment produced by the discrepancy between the facts of inequality and the moral-political commitment to equality. It is necessary to seek another path out of the difficulties, and this time we shall try the way around which the largest body of serious writing has centered.

III

This way consists essentially in saying that the discrepancy is not really so great as it seems to be. Beneath all the surface differences and inequalities there are still some things common to us all, some things, or perhaps just one thing, we all share in equal measure. From this juncture, the formulation can move in either of two directions, depending upon whether the writer stresses one thing we share in common, or a number of things.

The one thing we all share in common is membership in the same species: all are equally human; all, by virtue of their membership in humanity, stand on the same step or rank in the order of being. This fact that we are all born into the same species is then said to require that all men be regarded as equals in certain important respects. Jefferson's formula in an early draft of the Declaration expresses this idea perfectly: "We hold these truths to be sacred and undeniable: that all men are created equal and independent, that from that *equal creation* they derive rights inherent and inalienable."[2]

The fact of a common species-membership is held to have moral and political significance. This fact was the very foundation of the political and moral philosophy of such Enlightenment thinkers as Jefferson and Paine. For them, once man's species characteristics were identified, a long train of consequences followed concerning how states should be constructed.

Our anthropology today is greatly advanced over that lamentable mixture of faith, hope, charity, and crude observation which passed for the science of man in Jefferson's day, and our understanding of the protean connections between "fact" and "value" is immensely richer than his. On the other hand, though our knowledge is broader than his and our logic keener, our vision is poorer. Our age has been unable to construct a philosophical anthropology, a general answer to the question, what is man? So the theorist of today, lacking the verities of Jefferson's simpler age, and entangled in a hopeless thicket of facts, finds it hard to follow Jefferson. The theorist of today may be able to see that the reminder that a man is a man offers something for the construction of political theory, but he cannot see that it offers very much. The reminder seems so general as to be nebulous, entailing no specific directives, and therefore uninteresting.

Even the catastrophic political events of this century have not provoked theorists to a reexamination of Jefferson's "equal creation." Naziism, with its denial of a common humanity, its assignment of some men to the category of subhumans, produced very little rethinking of the problem. What it did produce was a frantic effort to refute, by scientific methods, the Nazi theories of racial inequality. But that was never the issue, and the fact that so many thinkers in the West thought it was is itself a telling measure of how widely this aspect of our heritage has been forgotten or misunderstood.[3]

For Jefferson, the proposition of human equality was meant to be a strict scientific proposition. He worked mightily to persuade himself that all the races of mankind did in fact stand on the same level in the order of created being. Then, under the impact of Darwinian ideas, the Jeffersonian view faded, and the idea of the hierarchy of the races became popular among Western thinkers. The riot of irrationality and obscenity which passed for Nazi race science put an end to this style of thought, and the respectable scientific community bent its efforts towards showing that there were no inherent genetic inferiorities or superiorities among the races.

This whole "scientific" discussion, from the Enlightenment forward, represents a grievous misunderstanding of what the claim to equality based upon the idea of a common humanity was all about. That idea was never meant to be a scientific proposition, a universal statement based upon the observation of empirical phenomena. In fact, it was meant to deny precisely what observation confirmed: that there were great differences among men, and that these differences were what mattered in deciding how men should be treated. The older, pre-eighteenth century idea of a common humanity, often denied but never forgotten, was a moral assertion based not upon a generalization of experience but upon a postulate of reason and an exercise of faith. The assertion was often expressed in religious terms: we are all children of the same God and of equal worth in His eyes. Here the writer might emphasize our common natality (we are all born equal under the same creator) or he might emphasize our common mortality (we all live under the same sentence of death). The assertion was also often cast in more strictly philosophical terms as, for example, by the Stoics. Here too the idea was meant to express not an empirical equality, but an equality of existing under the same ultimate conditions. The assertion could also be made in a specifically political forum, as in that magnificent reply to Ireton, affirming that "the poorest he that is in England hath a life to live as well as the richest he." There is the heart of the matter: each one has a life to live, not a role to perform; that life must be lived, not acted out according to some prefixed pattern; and one must live it, not give over the responsibility for it to someone else. It is this common and ultimate responsibility that each has for the living of his own life, this understanding that in the end each is responsible to the self and before all others for making his life a worthy one, that has always stood at the heart of the idea of a common humanity as the ground of a claim for a minimal equality of treatment.

This is why the Jeffersonian attempt to ground equality on a scientific proposition about nature (that is, about the place of the human species within the order of nature) so easily produces such frightful consequences. It is the first and basic step in the reduction of a moral to a "natural" idea. The last easy step is taken when men are regarded as material, or resources, on a plane with the other resources which we take from nature for our own uses. For the point is, resources are means to ends, not ends themselves; and the main criteria applicable in the use of resources are the criteria of relevance and efficiency. Once the claim to equal treatment was based upon nature, the actual content of that treatment became contingent, entirely dependent upon the ends a given state or authority had in view. In one state under one set of conditions this treatment might consist in a code of fair play and respect; in another state under another set of conditions, the treatment could just as "validly" consist in the destruction of millions of people as substandard or superfluous material.

The idea that matters here might emerge more clearly if it is framed in different terms. The word "nature" has many meanings and uses, some of which bear directly on our topic. That which is natural is generally distinguished from that which is artificial. In the vocabulary of political philosophy the natural is distinguished from the civil, as in the many discussions of the differences between the natural and the civil state. In theology it is used as the opposite of the terms spiritual and supernatural. In all these contexts the natural designates a realm not made by man but subject to such uses as we can and wish to make of it. Scientifically considered, nature is that which we have divested of mystery, stripped of autonomy, and subjected to our ends. It is that over which we have gained knowledge and manipulative power. This is the meaning concealed in the platitudinous expression that science "conquers nature" and pushes back the boundaries of ignorance and superstition.

An object is somehow reduced, diminished, when it is scientifically examined and manipulated: astronomy strips Helios and Selene of their divinity, and we are left only with the sun and the moon; the god of the grape is banished by the science of viticulture; Darwin in his old age remorsefully said that his knowledge of nature's workings had deprived him of the joy he had taken as a young man in its beauties and mysteries.

To see what is at stake here, remember how reluctant we are to treat some objects objectively. Concerning some objects, the mind resists the intellectual and imaginative movement necessary to thrust them into mere nature and treat them as mere objects. Many of us still have this feeling about the human body, for example. Even though all of the great religions tell their believers that after death the physical remains of the person are of no significance, most of us are quite squeamish about irreverent or objective handling of dead bodies. We cannot overcome the lingering feeling that the body is more than mere nature, the feeling that it still retains something of the spiritual about it. I understand that even the medical student has some bad moments before he can methodically cut up the human corpse assigned to him.

I have argued that the decisive step in this process of the "naturalization" of man took place in the Enlightenment.[4] The whole structure of high Western culture had for nearly two thousand years rested on a moral conception of man—on the idea, in the Christian formulation, that we are created in the image of God. This way of defining man overlooked the material, tangible realities of the human animal, and stressed the spiritual and intangible. Man was the creature who was formed after a certain model of perfection, and to be a man meant to aspire to a certain mode of ethical conduct. The Enlightenment took the decisive step toward overthrowing this idea and replacing it by a conception of man standing on exclusively naturalistic premises. At first this naturalism retained a content which it had inherited from the older theisms, but it quickly became apparent that this content was without any solid intellectual foundation. The specifically humanistic content disappeared, and man came to be seen as no more than a very highly developed animal—the animal with a prodigious brain and with the power to make tools. Soon came the inevitable next step of stressing in the definition of man those of our characteristics which are most purely animal: physical vigor, will, the predatory virtues. What had begun as a metaphysical conception ended as an entirely naturalistic one. Science and reason had taken the last step in the "conquest of nature" and had finally conquered man, reducing him to mere nature. All that had changed was the meaning of a word, but that change had left the creature which the word denoted without any claim to such things as dignity, freedom, and rights. All men might still have a claim to equal treatment (though, if natural criteria prevail, why should they? Why shouldn't the strong have greater rights than the weak?) but that claim no longer had a specific ethical content, a content which prescribed the treatment fitting to men as men. All might still be given equal treatment, but there was no reason why the content of that equal treatment might not be the treatment accorded to pigs or cabbages. This was the terrible secret at the heart of modern Western civilization which was exposed by the Nazis. Benjamin Constant prophetically mapped the whole journey: "De la divinité par l'humanité a la bestialité."[5]

Although the destination of the journey has been shown to all who have eyes, political theorists have been only slightly impressed by the view. Contemporary writers continue to attempt a justification for equality based on a naturalistic definition of man. A recent essay offers an example of the general type.[6]

Williams holds that a significant claim to equality of treatment for certain purposes can be made on the basis that those who belong to the same species share certain things in common. He sees three respects in which all men are alike: the capacity to feel pain; the capacity to feel affection for others; and the desire for self-respect, by which he means "a certain human desire to be identified with what one is doing, to be able to realize purposes of one's own, and not to be the instrument of another's will unless one has willingly accepted such a role."[7] That men are alike in the possession of these characteristics Williams thinks is "indisputable." Furthermore, he thinks this alikeness is not trivial, because it provides the basis for a criticism of "political and social arrangements that systematically neglect these characteristics in the case of some groups of men, while being fully aware of them in the case of others. . . ."[8]

The assertion is not indisputable. It is not even entirely clear. And if it were both indisputable and clear, it might still be a useless way to approach the problem.

It seems to me, first of all, that Williams glosses over many things that matter here by making the word "alike" do the work of the word "equal." Perhaps all men are alike in having the capacity to feel pain, but surely all do not have this capacity in equal degree. Similarly, even if all men do in fact have the capacity to feel affection for others (which is doubtful), they plainly have the capacity in varying degrees. Furthermore, even if all of us have these two capacities, we are not all equally pained by the same things, or equally capable of feeling affection for the same objects. In sum, men are unequal in their capacities for pain and affection, and they differ in their objects of pain and affection. Granted these points, one could make as reasonable a case for treating men differently, in accordance with their unequal capacities for and different objects of pain and affection, as one could for treating them alike, on the ground that all have the capacity for pain and affection, regardless of differences in degree of capacity and objects of attachment.

It is doubtful that the third capacity, the "desire for self-respect," is a universal characteristic of man. I only say doubtful, and not more or less than that, because the formulation in Williams' essay is imprecise. As it stands, the formulation sounds more like an echo of Westen bourgeois individualism than like the voice of science announcing a universal empirical discovery. As it stands, part of the formulation needs to be clarified: is it likely that a student who cheats on examinations, say, has "a certain human desire to be identified with what [he] is doing"? A persuasive affirmative answer to that question would require a richer and more intricate knowledge of psychology than we yet have.

Even if it were established as a matter of fact that all men are equal (not alike) in certain empirical respects, it is not clear that this alone would validate a claim for equal treatment. Let us assume that all people do possess in equal degree the three characteristics specified by Williams—or, for that matter, any others. (The kind of argument which Williams tries to construct would rest on firmer empirical support if he had chosen different characteristics; e.g., certain needs, such as the need for food, sleep, water.) That would still not take us far toward the conclusion of equal treatment. While all the members of a group may be equal in some respects they will be unequal in others. All the members may have the capacity to feel pain, but only some will have very high intelligence, for example, or white skins, or the qualities needed to make excellent soldiers. It might then be argued that those who possess these special characteristics should be treated differently from those who lack them, regardless of the fact that all share certain characteristics in common.

The question is, what things shall be accepted as constituting the foundation for a claim to equal (or to unequal) treatment? It is not clear to me why and how the natural species characteristics set forth by Williams provide a firmer foundation for a claim to equal treatment than other characteristics not shared by all members of the species provide for a claim to unequal treatment. His argument reduces to the idea that since all the members of a species share certain traits in common they should be treated alike. Horses, being horses, should not be treated like cats, which are cats. Each species should be treated by a rule appropriate to itself. But this argument, rooted as it is in exclusively naturalistic premises, will never rise above naturalistic conclusions. Knowing that a creature is a horse and not a cat does tell us that it should be fed hay rather than fish. In sum, the form of the argument permits only minimal, naturalistic conclusions. The human claim to equal treatment has always demanded much more than that, because, until modern times, it was a claim rooted in a philosophical and metaphysical, not a naturalistic, conception of man.

IV

During the last ten or fifteen years there has come to the forefront a new argument for equality of treatment. Measured by volume and frequency of expression, and by the high offices of those who so loudly and frequently proclaim it, it is one of the two leading ways of thought in the current dialogue. I refer to the argument from utility, the argument which consists fundamentally in saying that if we treat all our citizens equally that will advance us toward other goals we desire. Specifically, it is claimed that equal treatment of Negroes, for example, will strengthen our domestic economy and our international position. The details of the argument have been so widely broadcast that there is no need to repeat them here. This is probably the argument which, in the end, will do the most toward achieving an approximate equality of treatment in certain areas. Even Professor Gunnar Myrdal, who perfectly understands that the dilemma of equality is a moral one, believes that the solution of the dilemma will come on the economic front and by economic means. This progress will be accelerated by our growing awareness that our political security requires the votes of the emergent nations, most of whose populations are nonwhite.

There is little to be said about this way of thinking about the problem. One can only repeat what is obvious: a utilitarian solution of a moral and philosophical problem is exactly that—utilitarian. Even while we take satisfaction in the progress toward the solution, we cannot escape a certain sadness and discomfort in the realization that the victory comes on the wrong front and is gained by the wrong weapons. Something very precious, albeit very obvious, seems to be disappearing from men's minds in the present struggle. That is the simple fact that the utilitarian argument and solution makes of men a means. If we "grant" the Negroes equality not out of a profound and unequivocal sense that we should, but out of a calculation that it is in our interest to do so, the Negro remains exactly what he has been for three centuries—a useful tool for the purposes of white America. Only a very few of those now involved in the struggle (for example, James Baldwin) seem thoroughly aware of this elemental point. Baldwin's conviction that the struggle for Negro equality offers the possibility for the moral regeneration of white America is profoundly right. There is every evidence that this possibility is being drowned in the language of utility—the language of jobs, housing, education, and political influence.

The other most popular argument today for equality of treatment (which, in this argument, means mainly equality of access to public facilities) is the sociological-legal argument. We should treat all persons equally in certain respects because the Constitution, as implemented in particular laws and interpreted by the courts, says we should. The fundamental law demands equality under the law.

If we explore this answer a bit further, we soon discover that the Constitution and the laws have not always said this; or, at least, if they have, only recently have men listened. The Framers did prescribe equal treatment under the law for all persons; but Chief Justice Taney concluded that they did not consider Negroes persons. Even after the Fourteenth Amendment settled the question against Taney, Justice Brown was still able to argue that while "the object of the amendment was undoubtedly to enforce the absolute equality of the two races before the law,"[9] that object did not demand the abolition of all distinctions based upon color. Laws might permit or require the separation of the races in such places as schools, theatres, or railroad cars without implying the inferiority of either race to the other, and without violating the commandment of equality. Not until 1954 did the full Court discover that the Constitution really meant equality, and that separation implied inequality, even if the physical facilities supplied to the two races were equal. Separation by itself deprived the children of the minority group of equal educational opportunities.

It is not quite accurate, however, to say that the Court made this discovery in the Constitution. It actually found it in "modern authority," which had learned, since 1896, that segregation alone produced in the child a sense of inferiority, which in turn reduced motivation to learn, and this in its turn retarded the child's educational and mental development. In other words, if you ask why the law demands equal treatment in all respects, the answer, according to Chief Justice Warren, is that sociologists and psychologists have discovered the fact that inequality jeopardizes the individual's prospects for development. Justice Warren hardly found it necessary to go beneath that argument, and the modern discussion has stayed pretty largely on the same level. In a real sense, this is a misfortune, for the Court, and following it, the public, let escape a splendid opportunity to refresh its memory of some of the components of the basic liberal democratic theory of constitutional government. That theory provides one of the most interesting of all approaches to the topic of equality, and to it we now turn.

The great liberal and constitutional theorists of the modern era (Locke, Kant, Madison, Bentham) all rested their political theories on conceptions of human nature. Their commentators never tire of pointing out that all of these conceptions are grossly oversimplified. Such criticism, however, is beside the point: it misses their intention.

These writers did not try to develop an exhaustive psychology. Rather, they devised a political psychology. They abstracted from the infinite diversity of human actuality the traits or factors that mattered most in the building of a political order along constitutionalist lines. When a political order is deliberately contrived, when the builder deliberately sets out to build a structure that will hold political forces in certain predetermined shapes, then it is important that he have uniform and standard materials to work with. The need for a uniform building material is inherent in the very idea of building a constitutional edifice. The constitutional architect requires men of a standard size and shape, just as the "real" architect requires building materials of specified and uniform properties. In sum, the first reason for the assumption of human equality and uniformity made by these writers is simply that such an assumption is inherent in the constitutionalist way or style of thinking about politics.

If the first reason is inherent in the style of constitutionalist thought, the second is central to its basic substantive intention. All of these writers shared the view that the chief purpose of the constitutional edifice was to provide a secure framework within which men might pursue their private ends. The basic distinction in constitutionalist thought is the distinction between public and private, and the main purpose of the public institutions is the protection of private rights (typically conceived as property and liberty). Now, the most distinctive proposition of the constitutionalists is the idea, which all of them expressed with one or another degree of clarity and comprehensiveness, that the most efficient way to preserve variety and difference—individuality—in the private sphere is by treating men uniformly in the public sphere. In a phrase, these theorists postulated public equality in order to preserve private inequalities. This is the point of their "oversimplified" conceptions of human nature, which are all really conceptions of human equality.

This is why criticisms of their theories of human nature on empirical grounds are largely beside the point. These writers were constructing a psychology for political purposes, not scientific ones. It is obvious that their conceptions of human nature owe little to observation. The man of whom they write is a creature of the theoretical reason, not a flesh and blood resident of the world. This theoretical everyman is conceived as having but one, or, at most, a few attributes which are relevant to the construction of a political order. He is a generalized and diminished man, reduced to fear (Hobbes) or will (Kant) or interest (Madison) or the passion for distinction (John Adams) or pleasure-pain (Bentham). He is an elementary stimulus-response mechanism, a quantum of energy which is set into motion under specifiable conditions and directed toward specifiable ends. All that matters for political purposes is that his external behavior be regular, predictable, and subject to the general laws of political motion. These laws are as precise and comprehensive in the political realm as the general laws of motion are in the physical realm.

Provided with these uniform materials, the political architect can build states of great size and admirable symmetry. He need hardly bother with real men at all. Real people—the complex, variable, disorderly creatures who move about in the world—are not needed in the political order erected by the constitutionalists. Conversely, these real men do not need the political order except as a shelter within which they may safely pursue their important (private) interests. Put differently, every one of the great constitutional theorists tried to invent a self-regulating mechanism, a system which would run by its own laws and require the least possible amount of deliberate human care and guidance. Machinery would replace character and fortune as the governing principle of states. James Madison's "new science of politics" was new in the exact sense that it showed political architects how to design institutions which would work in certain ways and produce certain results regardless of the qualities and intentions of the persons who occupied them.

Everything about people except the thing which the theorist held as the basic component of the stimulus-response mechanism is ignored in the construction of the polity and excluded from the meaning of citizenship. This state of being ignored is exactly what the constitutionalists meant by freedom. Freedom rests on being left alone by the public authority, and consists in the unhampered pursuit of one's private interests. As Hobbes put it, liberty exists where the laws are silent. And when the laws speak, they say the same thing to everyone. Constitutionalist theory first asserts that, for political purposes, all subjects shall be regarded as equal in certain respects. It then says that when the state deals with these equal men it shall deal with them equally. Hence, the state specifies that all men shall, within a prescribed area, behave in the same way. It then defines or constitutes this area in which behavior must be uniform as the public realm: the public realm is the area of uniform and equal behavior. This space is kept as small as possible, so that the private space can be as large as possible. Liberty, which expresses our inequalities and diversities, resides within the zone of privacy. The fundamental convention, then, is that all men shall be treated as equals in the public realm, in order that they will be able to express their inequalities in the private realm. By assigning the principle of equality to one territory and the principle of inequality to another, the constitutionalists thought that both could be preserved without conflict. It is an ingenious idea, and one with many ramifications.

The radical separation of public and private has some important consequences for the theory of moral personality—the conception of the good man, and the understanding of how natural man develops into moral man. The most important of these consequences is the idea that no one's real worth shall be judged in the public forum and by public criteria. The inner self is entirely private, invisible to the public gaze, shielded from public judgment. This means that the public realm is without authority either to validate or to invalidate a man. Conversely, no one can achieve validation in the public realm. The concept of equal citizenship requires that each be treated in public as if he were as good—or as bad—as any other man, and it forbids a public judgment as to whether he really is. That judgment may be made only in the private sphere.

The constitutionalists' everyman has often been criticized on esthetic and moral grounds. Such criticism misses the point as much as the empirical criticism does. Everyman was never meant to be an attractive figure, but only a useful one, and in that he succeeds.

First of all, the construct of public equality serves as a mask behind which one's inner self can hide from the probing, judging eyes of anonymous others. In the huge and heterogeneous polities of today that is a very important protection, for the fact is that each of us must today live much of our life among virtual strangers, and no one can safely endure or morally accept judgments of his worth made by strangers. No man can turn himself over for moral judgment to others who do not share his hopes and fears, his code of righteousness, his loves and hates. In the constitutional polity, with its postulate of equality, each of us in effect is under a contract of strictly limited public liability. This is probably the only technique which can protect any meaningful liberty and personal integrity in the giant states of today. Despite the Biblical injunction to the contrary, one cannot love the public as oneself. The very division between familiars and strangers makes it necessary in the huge political societies of today to find a means to ensure familiars that they will not be compelled to treat strangers as though they were intimates, and, at the same time, to guarantee the strangers that they will not suffer by reason of being outside the pale. When an aggregation of men exceeds the (very small) number that can be included within the circle of familiars, it seems both necessary and reasonable that the ties that bind them should be affectively neutral, and that they should benefit no individual at the expense of others.

Secondly, the postulate of equality spares us the risk and trouble of actually looking at the crowds of anonymous others among whom we must live. The postulate requires (and therefore permits) us to treat everyone alike. Hence, we have a ready justification for callous behavior when efficiency or necessity requires us to deal with large numbers of people or when we are in charge of apportioning a scarce resource. It is not necessary to examine and judge individual claims: all fall under an equal rule; so first come, first served. The rule of equality, in case after case, relieves us of the obligation of really looking at the actual person before us and treating him in the one way uniquely appropriate to his own individuality. We need not attend to and make a judgment on that person, and we need not accept the responsibility for acting on our judgment. We need only apply the rule. This too is a real utility, for it reduces the personal risk of living in a complex world, and it saves energy for the task of building a private estate in a busy and complex world. So useful is this rule of equality, and so wide its application in our society, that about the only time one can count on being treated as an individual is when one is sick.

The construct, then, has very real utilities. But it also has some consequences which we may not be so eager to accept. I shall point to a few of the more obvious ones.

First of all, the sharp distinction between public and private, and the subordination of the former to the latter, narrows the stage of public action are greatly reduced—and this was a major aim of the constitutionalists—but so too are the possibilities. Citizenship is not a moral adventure or an educational experience. It is merely a legally defined bundle of rights and powers which the individual may use to defend and advance his interests. The public stage is not regarded as a place where people gather to seek self-understanding and self-enlargement by presenting themselves to others in an open dialogue of thought and action. The citizen is expected to disclose but a fraction of the self to the public gaze, and that will be the same fraction which others expose. The citizen even performs his most obviously public act, the act of voting, in the privacy of the voting booth; and that institution perfectly symbolizes the idea that the citizen need account to no one for his choices. We expect and regard it as entirely legitimate that people will seek to translate private will into public policy through whatever political instruments are available to them, and we assume the right to keep our political opinions and conclusions to ourselves. Politics quickly comes to be thought of as a distinctly second-order and instrumental activity and occupation, subordinate to the primary concerns of the private life. John Adams showed a firm grasp of the point when he wrote that he had to give himself to politics in order that his son might pursue the useful sciences, such as engineering, in order that his son might devote himself to the graceful arts, such as music and literature. This movement from the necessary through the useful to the pleasurable is simultaneously a movement from the public toward the private, and it accurately expresses what happens to the conception of politics in the equalitarian and constitutional regime.

A second troublesome consequence of this way of thinking about politics appears when we reflect on the obvious fact that what is "political" is in large part what we think is political. The "political" is not a category or object of nature, like the stars or sun, which, no matter how our ways of thinking about them change, are not themselves changed by our ways of thinking about them. We may think of the sun as a god, or as the home of a god, or as a huge mass of very hot particles of matter, and none of those conceptions alters in any way what the sun is. The political, on the other hand, is what we think it is, and it changes as our ways of thinking about it change. Hence, when the political realm is defined as the constitutionalists defined it, it tends in fact to become this way: the conception realizes itself. The most important concrete consequence of this way of thinking about politics is that men come to regard the public arena as a place where ordinary men will appear as naturally and act as capably as extraordinary men. The public realm is not seen as the place where great men most naturally gather and where great actions most naturally take place. Rather, the political arena, being itself a place of second-rate action is the place where second-rate people gather to pursue their second-rate ends. This process unfolded in all its major phases during the first century of our independent political life. Thus, at the time of the founding, the public stage held a virtual monopoly of men of the highest excellence. Then, during the time of Jackson the doctrine was officially proclaimed that excellence was not needed even in the highest places of state. That doctrine achieved its practical fulfillment in the "hard cider" election of 1840. And finally, during post-Civil War America the field of grand action and large enterprise manifestly became the realm of the economic, not of the political.

Finally, the narrowing of the political stage and the downgrading of the political vocation means that many of those (always relatively few) whose natures demand political expression are condemned to frustration for want of a noble and spacious place in which to act. And many others, who find joy in watching political action, are deprived of a commodious theater and noble plays to attend. When the political stage is narrowed at the rear by the rule of bureaucracy (which is the very model of the regime which acts by the rule of equality) and shortened at the front by the noisy and unedifying private performances of factions, hopeful political actors and spectators are left with little that is worth doing or seeing. Henry Adams would have spared himself much lugubrious whining and regret had he accepted his ancestor's forecast of the progress of the constitutional machine. The earlier Adams had labored precisely to build a machine which would not need future Adamses to tend it, but Henry never quite understood this, and felt abandoned in the cold of private life while his nature yearned for the warmth of public life.

So, there are gains and losses here, a price paid for every advantage obtained.

The intent of the constitutionalists was generous, even noble. They worked to build a political order which would acknowledge that common men had as much claim to dignity and importance in their lives as uncommon men had in theirs. They accomplished this by sharply distinguishing the public and the private, and by insisting that all men be treated in public as if they were equals.

On the other hand, the everyman of the constitutionalists is not a generous or noble, not even an interesting figure. The man hypothesized (and even created) by Locke or Madison, say, cannot matter much to us. We cannot love him, and we cannot hate him either. Surely we cannot see him as a friend.[10] Such men will to live together out of a recognition of mutual convenience, and on the understanding that they won't have to live together very closely. Each must respect the privacy of the others.

None of the great constitutional theorists argued that his everyman was admirable and ought to be accepted for himself. They argued, rather, that equality of public treatment would secure private diversity and inequality. Formal public equality sets the framework within which a multiplicity of private differences and inequalities can flourish. Constitutionalism accepts a formal unity—a unity of rules and procedures—on the public level in order to protect a diversity of substantive unities—unities of sentiment, value, and interest—in the private sphere. The rules of the road tell us how we must drive, but they do not tell us where we must go. The basic assumption of the whole system is very clear: no partial community may impose its substantive vision of the good life on the whole community. On the level of the whole, our unity is formal, not substantive.

The whole point of the postulate of equality in constitutional theory, then, is that it provides the basis for a public order and unity. Now, it is of course true that real people, not hypothetical equals, act in that public order. However, two qualifications are set on this action; and these qualifications are so important that they greatly shape the tone and content of action in the public realm.

In the first place, the laws and institutions of the constitutional system encourage some kinds of actions and discourage others. Specifically, they encourage actions which are in conformity with the nature of the hypothesized everyman, and they discourage actions which deviate greatly from that norm. In other words, the laws and institutions produce an expectation that certain actions will take place in public and that others will not. I am suggesting that if you institutionalize a conception of man as the pursuer of interest, for example, that in itself tends to produce the kind of behavior it predicts: the hypothesis creates the facts that confirm itself. The workings of this process in American politics are very plain. With us, all political action is assumed to be action in pursuit of interest: that is what politics is; anything else is virtually illegitimate.

In the second place, although action in the public realm is action undertaken by real men, the rules of the game require us to treat those actions as if they were the actions not of real men, but of the hypothetical creature posited by the laws and institutions. We look at action in the public realm through a special lens which filters out much of what is really going on and admits only selected aspects of the whole. Everything that we see and do in the public realm is constrained by deliberate rules. We agree to see only certain things, and to call those things the whole. We agree not to "pierce the veil," not to probe beneath the surface of rule and convention to the realities within. To see how thoroughgoing this distinction is between public and private, consider again the radical difference we have established between criminal and moral guilt. In the perfectly realized constitutional state, all relations between men would be governed by rules, not by feelings. Above all, every manifestation of public authority would be impartial, general, and anonymous, for the constitutionalist regards personal judgment and authority as dangerous in practice and as illegitimate in principle. The ideal is "a government of laws, not of men."

V

In this essay I have tried to characterize and briefly analyze some important ways of thinking about equality. Five ways were examined: (1) equality as equality of opportunity, (2) equality as an ethical claim based on membership in the same natural species, (3) the argument for equal treatment based on utility, (4) claims to legal equality based on certain modern psychological and sociological pictures of man which purportedly reveal that inequality cripples individual development, and (5) the constitutionalist approach. No summary of the main points seems necessary. Nor are there any overall conclusions to be drawn. Manifestly, I have offered no final answer to the question of equality. There is not even such a thing as the "question of equality" in any very tight sense: there is, rather, a bundle of events, ideas, and feelings about which we can think, worry, agitate, and act in more or less incoherent ways.

The form of this essay, and especially of the section just above, might give rise to a certain misunderstanding, and before closing I shall try to obviate it. One can discuss only one thing at a time, a grammatical necessity which has a way of making the things one is talking about seem more independent of each other than may actually be the case. One approach to equality does not necessarily exclude others. It should be especially emphasized that the constitutionalist approach, being formal, actually demands to be filled in by one of the other approaches, such as the equality of opportunity or utilitarian theories discussed above. The great virtue of the constitutionalist approach is precisely that of permissiveness: within the (flexible) boundaries flowing from the postulated everyman and defined as the public sector, the content of public policy may be whatever men wish it to be. No policy within these boundaries is illegitimate in principle; any policy accepted becomes, by the fact of its acceptance, legitimate.

It is important, however, if one would keep one's thinking clear, not to equate "legitimate" with "justified." To say that a given public policy is legitimate is only to say that it does not conflict with the terms of the constitution. The justification for the policy rests on other grounds: religious, empirical, utilitarian, ethical, or some combination of these. The grounds themselves are neither supplied nor supported by the constitution.

The constitutionalists, in other words, have offered a specifically political way of thinking about equality, a way which owes little to observation or to the moral sense. Their everyman is a construct, not an empirical portrait, and it is a construct drawn specifically for political ends, the most important of which are the maintenance of public peace and the preservation of private diversity. We can try to understand that construct, discuss its logic, and trace out its consequences in political reality. We cannot, without vast intellectual confusion and surprising practical consequences, deal with the construct either as an empirical generalization, or as a full guide to the making of public policy, or as an ethical justification for equal treatment.

It seems to me that very much of the public discussion of equality in America today has failed to remember these distinctions, with curious and possibly perilous results. Those who are "against equality" in the current political debate and struggle are really against other things. Specifically, they are against losing the liberty to treat Negroes as inferiors; and they are against the claim of Negroes to be subject in the public realm only to the rules and standards applicable to everyone—a claim solidly based on our whole constitutionalist theory of equality. On the other hand, those who are "for equality" also really sometimes seem to be for other things. Specifically, they seem to be for the conversion of a highly complex political and ethical struggle into a crudely drawn ideological struggle, a battle between victims and oppressors in which no one has the right not to be militant. Those whose sense of the complexity of the situation makes it hard for them to act vigorously, or who cannot see that their own interests are involved in the struggle, or who simply cannot see that a given situation is any of their business are brought under the general indictment that in a democratic community everyone is responsible for everything, so that those who do not energetically help to destroy evil share the responsibility for its existence. Some of those who are currently "for equality" sometimes seem also to be not just for equality of public treatment, but really for the exclusion of consideration of differences in race and cultural style even from our private judgments.[11]

Under these conditions, a victory for either side may bring regrets to everybody. I tried to suggest above that no matter which side wins (surely the Negroes will) the moderates or neutrals will continue to bear both their own guilts and the curses of the contestants. What the white anti-equalitarians have to lose is plain. It may not be so obvious that the Negroes will have to pay a price for their victory, but they will. At a mimimum, that price will be loneliness and anonymity. Negroes will be required to forget that they are a natural community. They will be expected to see each other only as individuals, as private persons with private destinies, rather than as members of a community of experience and destiny. They will be asked to take up membership in the lonely crowd along with the rest of us. The price of equality is the loss of fraternity.

There may be a higher price to pay, one whose possible dimensions are just beginning to appear. I can suggest only the barest outlines of what matters here.

It was argued above that the constitutionalist idea of equality of status (rights, duties, obligations) in the political sphere does provide the necessary external foundations for both political and personal liberty under modern conditions. But that is only the surface. Disturbing things are happening in the interior. If we ask, what is the nature of the liberty which is actually being pursued in the private sphere, I think we have to answer that at least the main meaning of that liberty for most men today is the meaning foreseen by Dostoyevsky: the right of the endless multiplication and ready gratification of material and sensual desires. In the fulfillment of this liberty we shall come to look as alike in the private as in the public sphere. This liberty diminishes private men, just as the constitutionalist theory of equality diminishes public man. In effect, equality is being extended from the political sphere to the sphere of character, so that, increasingly, we share not only an equality of rights, obligations, and duties, but also an equality of opinions, attitudes, values, and manners.

This is a consummation which the great theorists of political equality devoutly did not wish. By establishing public equality, they hoped to encourage and protect a great variety of private inequalities. But we have developed a concept of private liberty which stresses those aspects in which we are alike, thereby moving us toward a condition in which the constitutionalist everyman in construct becomes the everyman in fact. There is something imperialistic in the equalitarian temper: it refuses to stay within the borders originally set for it. Tocqueville wrote a sentence on this topic which might provide the starting point for our own serious rethinking of the problem: "To conceive of men remaining forever unequal upon a single point, yet equal on all others, is impossible; they must come in the end to be equal upon all."[12]

Notes

1. Under some circumstances, generosity and guilt, rather than the cool and efficient principle of fair play, might require that we devise a system of handicaps to counteract the injustices not of nature but of society. Negroes, for example, are currently struggling for equal opportunity. Why should they not (I expect they will) claim more than that—superior opportunities

for education; preferential treatment in employment—as compensation for the injustices of the past? Could this claim be morally resisted?
2. Quoted from Julian P. Boyd, *The Declaration of Independence: The Evolution of the Text* (Princeton, N.J.: Princeton University Press, 1945), p. 19. Italics added.
3. Hannah Arendt's *Origins of Totalitarianism* is a notable exception to these remarks.
4. It might be said that the naturalization of man was only a specific application or concomitant of the general modern notion that nature can serve as an autonomous standard for human life, divorced from religion or philosophy. Once we treat ourselves as part of nature, subject to laws which we can only discover and not create or will, analytic knowledge supplants philosophical knowledge and manipulative activity is loosened from purposive activity.
5. Quoted here from Emil Brunner, *Christianity and Civilization* (New York, N.Y.: Scribner's, 1948), p. 3.
6. Bernard Williams, "The Idea of Equality," in Peter Laslett and W. G. Runciman, eds., *Philosophy, Politics and Society,* Second Series (Oxford: Blackwell, 1962), pp. 100-32.
7. *Ibid.,* p. 114. See also p. 112.
8. *Ibid.,* p. 112.
9. *Plessy v. Ferguson,* 163 U.S. 537 (1896).
10. One can understand much of the spirit and intention of modern constitutionalist theory if he remembers that it has neither need nor place for friendship in the polity, whereas in Aristotle's time, "those who frame the constitutions of states set more store by this feeling than by justice itself." *Ethics,* Book 8. In the modern view, friendship has no place in public life because it corrupts the rule of law. The political machines of an earlier America were hated by the liberal reformers precisely for this reason. As Tim Campbell, the boss of one of those machines said, "What's the Constitution among friends?"
11. An example is provided by certain maneuvers in Congress over the recent civil rights bill. The Administration proposed a bill which, among other things, barred discrimination in restaurants, lunch counters, hotels, retail stores, movie theaters, and other places of public entertainment. When the bill went to the House Judiciary Committee, a group of liberal democrats, aiming for a "tough bill," tried to broaden this list to include every activity licensed by the state. Among other things, this would include private schools and many private clubs with liquor or gaming licenses.
12. *Democracy in America* (New York, N.Y.: Vintage, 1954), Vol. I, p. 55.

Equality of Opportunity, and Beyond

I

Equality is a protean word. It is one of those political symbols—liberty and fraternity are others—into which men have poured the deepest urgings of their hearts. Every strongly held theory or conception of equality is at once a psychology, an ethic, a theory of social relations, and a vision of the good society.

Of the many conceptions of equality that have emerged over time, the one that today enjoys the most popularity is equality of opportunity. The formula has few enemies—politicians, businessmen, social theorists, and freedom marchers all approve it—and it is rarely subjected to intellectual challenge. It is as though all parties have agreed that certain other conceptions of equality, and notably the radical democratic conception, are just too troublesome to deal with because they have too many complex implications, too broad a scope perhaps, and a long history resonant of violence and revolutionary fervor. Equal opportunity, on the other hand, seems a more modest proposal. It promises that the doors to success and prosperity will be opened to all yet does not imply that all are equally valuable or that all men are really created equal. In short, this popular and relatively new concept escapes many of the problems and pitfalls of democratic equality and emphasizes that all should have equal opportunity to develop and be paid for their talents, which are of course far from being equal.

The doctrine itself is attractively simple. It asserts that each should have equal rights and opportunities to develop his own talents and virtues and that there should be equal rewards for equal performances. The formula does not assume the empirical equality of men. It recognizes that inequalities among men on virtually every trait or characteristic are obvious and ineradicable, and it does not oppose differential evaluations of those differences. Nor is the formula much concerned with complex chains of normative reasoning: It is practical and policy-oriented. In addition, equal opportunity is not, in principle, confined to any particular sector of life. It is held to be as applicable to politics as to law, as suitable for education as for economics. The principle is widely accepted as just and generous, and the claim is often made that application of the principle unlocks the energies necessary for social and economic progress.

Whereas this conception of equality answers or evades some questions, it raises others. Who is to decide the value of a man's talents? Are we to be measured by the commercial demand for our various abilities? And if so, what happens to those whose special gifts are not recognized as valuable by the buying public? And most important, is the resulting inequality, based partly on natural inequalities and partly on the whims of consumers, going to bury the ideal of democratic equality, based on a philosophy of equal human worth transcending both nature and economics?

These are serious questions, and it is my intention in this essay to probe their deeper meanings, as well as to clarify some major assumptions, disclose the inner spirit, and explore some of the moral and political implications of the principle of equal opportunity.

II

The first thing to notice is that the usual formulation of the doctrine—equality of opportunity for all to develop their capacities—is rather misleading, for the fact always is that not all talents can be developed equally in any given society. Out of the great variety of human resources available to it, a given society will admire and reward some abilities more than others. Every society has a set of values, and these are arranged in a more or less tidy hierarchy. These systems of evaluation vary from society to society: Soldierly qualities and virtues were highly admired and rewarded in Sparta, while poets languished. Hence, to be accurate, the equality of opportunity formula must be revised to read: equality of opportunity for all to develop those talents which are highly valued by a given people at a given time.

When put in this way, it becomes clear that commitment to the formula implies prior acceptance of an already established social-moral order. Thus, the doctrine is, indirectly, very conservative. It enlists support for the established pattern of values. It also encourages change and growth, to be sure, but mainly along the lines of tendency already apparent and approved in a given society. The doctrine is "progressive" only in the special sense that it encourages and hastens progress within a going pattern of institutions, activities, and values. It does not advance alternatives to the

Equality of Opportunity, and Beyond   195

existing pattern. Perhaps we have here an example of those policies that Dwight D. Eisenhower and the theorists of the Republican Party characterized as the method of "dynamic conservatism."

If this argument is correct, then the present-day "radicals" who demand the fullest extension of the equal-opportunity principle to all groups within the society, and especially to Negroes and the lower classes, are really more conservative than the "conservatives" who oppose them. No policy formula is better designed to fortify the dominant institutions, values, and ends of the American social order than the formula of equality of opportunity, for it offers everyone a fair and equal chance to find a place within that order. In principle, it excludes no one from the system if his abilities can be put to use within the system. We have here another example of the repeated tendency of American radicals to buttress the existing framework of order even while they think they are undermining it, another example of the inability of those who see themselves as radical critics of the established system to fashion a rhetoric and to formulate ends and values that offer a genuine alternative to the system. Time after time, never more loyally than at the present, our radicals have been our best conservatives.

Before one subscribes to the equality-of-opportunity formula, then, one should be certain that the dominant values, institutions, and goals of the society are the ones he really wants. The tone and content of much of our recent serious literature and social thought—thought that escapes the confines of the conservative-radical framework—warn that we are well on the way toward building a culture our best minds will not honor. The facile formula of equal opportunity quickens that trend. It opens more and more opportunities for more and more people to contribute more and more energies toward the realization of a mass, bureaucratic, technological, privatized, materialistic, bored and thrill-seeking, consumption-oriented society—a society of well-fed, congenial, and sybaritic monkeys surrounded by gadgets and pleasure-toys.

Secondly, it is clear that the equal-opportunity policy will increase the inequalities among classes. In previous ages, when opportunities were restricted to those of the right birth and station, it is highly probable, given the fact that nature seems to delight in distributing many traits in the pattern of a normal distribution, and given the phenomenon of regression toward the mean, that many of those who enjoyed abundant opportunities to develop their talents actually lacked the native ability to benefit from their advantages. It is reasonable to suppose that many members of ascribed elites, while appearing far superior to the ruck, really were not that superior in actual ability. Under the regime of equal opportunity, however, only those who genuinely are superior in the desired attributes will enjoy rich opportunities to develop their qualities. This would produce, within a few generations, a social system where the members of the elites really were immensely superior in ability and attainment to the masses. We should then have a condition where the natural and social aristocracies would be identical—a meritocracy, as Michael Young has called it.[1]

Furthermore, the more closely a society approaches meritocracy, the wider grows the gap in ability and achievement between the highest and the lowest social orders. This will happen because in so many fields there are such huge quantities of things to be learned before one can become certified as competent that only the keenest talents, refined and enlarged by years of devoted study and work, can make the grade.[2] We call our age scientific, and describe it further as characterized by a knowledge explosion. What these labels mean from the perspective of equalitarianism is that a handful of people possess a tremendous fund of scientific knowledge, while the rest of us are about as innocent of science as we have always been. So the gap widens: The disparity between the scientific knowledge of an Einstein and the scientific knowledge of the ordinary man of our day is greater than the disparity between a Newton and the ordinary man of his day.

Another force helps widen the gap. Ours is an age of huge, complex, and powerful organizations. Those who occupy positions of command in these structures wield enormous power over their underlings, who, in the main, have become so accustomed to their servitude that they hardly feel it for what it is. The least efficient of the liberal social welfare states of our day, for example, enjoys a degree of easy control over the ordinary lives of its subjects far beyond the wildest ambitions of the traditional "absolute" rulers. As the commanding positions in these giant organizations come to be occupied increasingly by people who have been generously endowed by nature and, under the equal-opportunity principle, highly favored by society, the power gap between the well- and the poorly-endowed widens. The doctrine of equality of opportunity, which in its origins was a rather nervous attempt to forestall moral criticisms of a competitive and inequalitarian society while retaining the fiction of moral equality, now ironically magnifies natural differences by policies based on an ostensibly equalitarian rationale. The doctrine of equal opportunity, social policies and institutions based on it, and advances in knowledge all conspire with nature to produce more and more inequality.

This opens a larger theme. We untiringly tell ourselves that the principle of equality of opportunity is a generous one. It makes no distinctions of worth among people on any of the factitious grounds, such as race, religion, sex, or nationality, that are usually offered for such distinctions. Nor does it set artificial limits on the individual. On the contrary, it so arranges social conditions that each of us can go as high as our natural abilities will permit. Surely, nothing could be fairer or more generous.

The generosity dissolves under analysis. The doctrine of equal opportunity, followed seriously, removes the question of how people should be treated from the realm of human responsibility and returns it to "nature." What is so generous about telling persons they can go as far as their talents will take them when their talents are meager? Imagine a footrace of one mile in which ten men compete, with the rules being the same for all. Three of the competitors are forty years old, five are overweight, one has weak ankles, and the tenth is Roger Bannister. What sense does it make to say that all ten have an equal opportunity to win the race? The outcome is predetermined by nature, and nine of the competitors will call it a mockery when they are told that all have the same opportunity to win.

The cruelty of the jest, incidentally, is intensified with each increase in our ability to measure traits and talents at an early age. Someday our measuring instruments may be so keen that we will be able to predict, with high accuracy, how well a child of six or eight will do in the social race. Efficiency would dictate that we use these tools to separate the superior from the inferior, assigning the proper kinds and quantities of growth resources, such as education, to each group. The very best training and equipment that society can afford would, of course, go to those in the superior group—in order to assure equality of opportunity for the development of their talents. It would seem more generous for us to take responsibility for the matter, perhaps by devising a system of handicaps to correct for the accidents of birth, or even by abandoning the competitive ethic altogether.

Three lines of defense might be raised against these criticisms of the equality-of-opportunity principle.

It might be replied, first, that I have misstated the principle of equal opportunity. Correctly stated, the principle only guarantees equal opportunity for all to enter the race, not to win it. That is certainly correct: Whereas the equal-opportunity principle lets each individual go as high as his natural abilities will permit, it does not guarantee that all will reach the same height. Thus, the metaphor of the footrace twists the case in that it shows fools, presumably deluded by the equal-opportunity doctrine, trying to stretch hopelessly beyond their natural reach. But there is no reason to think that fat men who foolishly compete against Roger Bannister are deluded by a doctrine. They are deluded because they are fools.

These reservations are entirely proper. The metaphor of the footrace does misrepresent the case. But it was chosen because it also expresses some features of the case which are often overlooked. The equal-opportunity principle probably does excite a great many people to dreams of glory far beyond their real capabilities. Many observers have pointed to the frequency of grand, bold, noble "first acts" in the drama of American life, and the scarcity of any "second acts" at all. The equal-opportunity principle, with its emphasis on success, probably does stir many men to excesses of hope for winning and despair at losing. It certainly leaves the losers with no external justification for their failures, and no amount of trying can erase the large element of cruelty from any social doctrine which does that. Cases like that of the footrace, and our growing ability to measure human abilities, make it clear that the equal-opportunity principle really is not very helpful to many people. Under its regime, a man with, say, an Intelligence Quotient of eighty, is given equal opportunity to go as far as his native ability will take him. That is to say, it lets him go as far as he could have gone without the aid of the doctrine—to the bottom rung of the social ladder—while it simultaneously stimulates him to want to go farther.

Secondly, it might be argued that the equality-of-opportunity principle need not be interpreted and applied, as it has been in this treatment, within a setting and under the assumptions of social competitiveness. The principle could be construed as one that encourages individuals to compete against themselves, to compare what one is with what one might become. The contest takes place between one's actual and potential selves, rather than between oneself and others.

This is an interesting, and hopeful, revision of the principle. It would shift the focus of judgment from society to the individual, and it would change the criteria of judgment from social utility to personal nobility. This shift is possible, but it would require a revolution in our present ways of thinking about equality, for those ways are in fact socially oriented and utilitarian. Hence, this defense against the criticisms is really no defense at all. It is irrelevant in the strict sense that instead of meeting the specific charges it shifts the question to a different battleground. It is an alternative to the existing, operative theory, not a defense of it. In fact, the operative doctrine, with its stress on overcoming others as the path of self-validation, is one of the toughest obstacles in the way of an ethic of personal validation through self-transcendence. The operative doctrine specifies success as the test of personal worth, and by success is meant victory in the struggle against others for the prizes of wealth and status. The person who enters wholeheartedly into this contest comes to look upon himself as an object or commodity whose value is set, not by his own internal standards of worth but by the valuations others place on the position he occupies. Thus, when the dogma of equal opportunity is effectively internalized by the individual members of a society, the result is as humanly disastrous for the winners as for the losers. The winners easily come to think of themselves as beings superior to common humanity, while the losers are almost forced to think of themselves as something less than human.

The third defense is a defense, though not a strong one. It consists in explaining that the metaphor of the footrace oversimplifies the reality that is relevant to an appraisal of the equal-opportunity principle. What actually occurs in a society is not just one kind of contest but many kinds, so that those who are not good at one thing need only look around for a different contest where they have a better chance of winning. Furthermore, there is not just one prize in a given contest but several. Indeed in our complex and affluent society, affairs might even be so arranged that everyone would win something. There need be no losers.

This reply has some strength, but not enough to touch the basic points. Although there are many avenues of opportunity in our society, their number is not unlimited. The theory of equal opportunity must always be implemented within a set of conventions which favors some potentialities and discourages others. Persons who strive to develop potentialities that are not admired in a given society soon find their efforts tagged silly, or wrong-headed, or dangerous, or dysfunctional. This is inherent in any society, and it forms an insurmountable barrier to the full development of the principle of equal opportunity. Every society encourages some talents and contests, and discourages others. Under the equal opportunity doctrine, the only people who can fulfill themselves and develop their abilities to the fullest are those who are able and eager to do what society demands they do.

There is, furthermore, a hierarchy of value even among those talents, virtues, and contests that are encouraged: The winners in some contests are rewarded more handsomely than the winners in other contests. Even in a complex society, where many contests take place, and even in an affluent society, where it might seem that there had to be no losers, we know full well that some awards are only consolation prizes, not the real thing, and a bit demeaning to their winners. When the fat boy who finishes last in the footrace gets the prize for "best try," he has lost more than he has won.

The formula of equality of opportunity, then, is by no means the warm and generous thing it seems to be on first view. Let us now examine the doctrine from another perspective.

III

The equal-opportunity principle is widely praised as an authentic expression of the democratic ideal and temper. I shall argue, to the contrary, that it is a cruel debasement of a genuinely democratic understanding of equality. To argue that is also to imply, of course, that a genuinely democratic conception of equality is not widely held in the United States.

The origins and development of the principle are enough to throw some doubt on its democratic credentials. Plato gave the principle its first great statement, and he was no democrat. Nor was Napoleon, who was the first to understand that the doctrine could be made the animating principle of the power state. In the United States, the Jacksonian demand for equal rights was assimilated by the Whigs and quickly converted into the slogan of equal opportunity. It soon won a secure place in popular political rhetoric. Whig politicians used the slogan to blunt popular demands for equality—interpreted as "leveling equality"—while defending the advantages of the wealthy.

This argument from origins is, of course, merely cautionary, not conclusive, but other, more systematic considerations, lead toward the same conclusion.

The doctrine of equality of opportunity is the product of a competitive and fragmented society, a divided society, a society in which individualism, in Tocqueville's sense of the word,[3] is the reigning ethical principle. It is a precise symbolic expression of the liberal-bourgeois model of society, for it extends the marketplace mentality to all the spheres of life. It views the whole of human relations as a contest in which each competes against all others for scarce goods, a contest in which there is never enough for everybody and where one man's gain is usually another's loss. Resting upon the attractive conviction that all should be allowed to improve their conditions as far as their abilities permit, the equal-opportunity principle insists that each individual do this by and for himself. Thus, it is the perfect embodiment of the Liberal conception of reform. It breaks up solidaristic opposition to existing conditions of inequality by holding out to the ablest and most ambitious members of the disadvantaged groups the enticing prospect of rising from their lowly state into a more prosperous condition. The rules of the game remain the same. The fundamental character of the social-economic system is unaltered. All that happens is that individuals are given the chance to struggle up the social ladder, change their position on it, and step on the fingers of those beneath them.

A great many individuals do, in fact, avail themselves of the chance to change sides as offered by the principle of equality of opportunity.[4] More than that, the desire to change sides is probably typical of the lower and middle classes, and is widely accepted as a legitimate ethical outlook. In other words, much of the demand for equality, and virtually all of the demand for the kind of equality expressed in the equal-opportunity principle, is really a demand for an equal right and opportunity to become unequal. Very much of what goes by the name of democratic sentiment—as that sentiment is molded within the framework of an individualistic, competitive society and expressed in the vocabulary of such a society—is really envy of those who enjoy superior positions, combined with a desire to join them.[5]

This whole way of thinking leads effortlessly to the conclusion that the existence of hierarchy, even of oligarchy, is not the antithesis of democracy but its natural and necessary fulfillment. The idea of equality of opportunity assumes the presence of a mass of people of average talents and attainments. The talents and attainments of the superior few can be measured by comparison with this average, mass background. The best emerge from the democracy, the average, and set themselves over it, resting their position securely on the argument from merit and ability. Those on top are automatically justified because they owe their positions to their natural superiority of merit, not to any artificial claim derived from birth, or wealth, or any other such basis. Hence, the argument concludes, the workings of the equal-opportunity principle help the democracy discover its own most capable masters in the fairest and most efficient way. Everybody gains: the average many because they are led by the superior few; the superior few because they can legitimately enjoy rewards commensurate with their abilities and contributions.

So pervasive and habitual is this way of thinking today that it is virtually impossible to criticize it with any hope of persuading others of its weaknesses. One is not dealing with a set of specific propositons logically arrayed, but with an atmospheric condition, a climate of opinion that unconsciously governs articulate thought in a variety of fields. Something like this cluster of opinions and sentiments provides the framework for popular discussion of the origins and legitimacy of economic inequality. We are easily inclined to think that one gets what one deserves, that rewards are primarily products of one's talents and industry, secondarily the consequences of luck, and only in small part the function of properties of the social-cultural structure. Somewhere around three-fourths of all personal wealth in the United States belongs to the richest fifth of our families.[6] There is no evidence, in the form of major political movements or public policies, that this distribution shocks the American democratic conscience—a fact suggesting that the American conscience on this matter simply is not democratic but is, rather, formed by the rhetoric of equal opportunity. Similarly, the giant public and private bureaucracies of our day could not justify for a minute their powers over the lives of people if the people so used did not themselves believe in the justness of hierarchy based on merit—merit always defined as tested competence in a special subject matter, tested mastery of a special skill or craft. Most modern writers on the theory of democracy accept this argument for elitism and point out happily that no serious moral or political problems arise so long as avenues for the movement of members into and out of the hierarchies are freely provided. The principle of equal opportunity, of course, does just that.

The basic argument is not new. What is new is the failure to appreciate the profoundly antidemocratic spirit of the argument. This failure is the specific novelty of the "democratic" thought and sentiment of our day, and it makes today's democrats as amenable to domination as any men have ever been. It is only necessary to persuade the masses (usually an easy task) that the hierarchs possess superior merit and that anyone (one naturally thinks of oneself at this point) with the requisite ability can join them.

All that can be said against this orientation is that a genuinely democratic ethic and vision rejects oligarchy as such. The democrat rejects in principle the thesis that oligarchy of merit (special competence) is in some way different in kind from oligarchy of any other sort, and that this difference makes it nobler, more reasonable, more agreeable to democracy, than oligarchies built on other grounds. The democrat who understands his commitment holds oligarchy itself to be obnoxious, not merely oligarchy of this or that kind.

The argument for hierarchy based on merit and accomplished by the method of equal opportunity is so widespread in our culture that there seems no way to find a reasonable alternative to it. We automatically think that the choice is either-or: either hierarchy and orderly progress or anarchy and disorderly stalemate. But that is not so. It is hardly even relevant. The fact that it is thought to be so is a reflection of the crippling assumptions from which modern thought on these matters proceeds. It is thought that there must be hierarchies and masses, elites and nonelites, and that there can be no more democratic way of selecting elites than by the method of equal opportunity. The complexity of affairs demands elites; and democracy and justice require selection of those elites by merit and equal opportunity.

Of course there must be hierarchy, but that does not imply a hierarchical and bureaucratic mode of thinking and acting. It need imply no more than specialization of function. Similarly, the fact that complexity demands specialization of function does not imply the unique merit and authority of those who perform the special functions. On the contrary. A full appreciation of complexity implies the need for the widest possible diffusion of knowledge, sharing of views, and mutual acceptance of responsibility by all members of the affected community.

Of course there must be organization, and organization implies hierarchy. Selection of the hierarchs by the criterion of merit and the mechanism of equal opportunity seems to reassure the worried democrat that his values are not being violated. But hierarchy may or may not be consonant with the democratic spirit. Most of today's democratic thinkers soothe themselves on this question of democracy and organization with the assertion that everything that can be done is being done when organizations permit factions, provide channels of consultation, and protect individual rights by establishing quasi-judicial bodies for hearing and arbitrating disputes. Certainly these guarantees are valuable, but they have little to do with making organizations democratic. They are constitutionalist devices, not democratic ones.

Before there can be a democratic organization, there must first be a democratic mentality—a way of thinking about the relations among people which stresses equality of being and which strives incessantly toward the widest possible sharing of responsibility and participation in the common life. A democratic orientation does not grow from and cannot coexist with the present bureaucratic and "meritorian" ethic. It is an alternative to the present ethic, not an expansion or outgrowth of it. When the democratic mentality prevails, it will not be too hard to find the mechanisms for implementing it.

IV

I hope my argument will not be interpreted as some sort of mindless demand for the abolition of distinctions or as a defense of the ethic of competition. The argument was mainly negative in intention, attempting to show that the idea of equality of opportunity is a poor tool for understanding even those sectors of life to which the notion of equality is applicable. It is a poor tool in that, whereas it seems to defend equality, it really only defends the equal right to become unequal by competing against one's fellows. Hence, far from bringing us together, the equal-opportunity doctrine sets us against each other. The doctrine rests on a narrow theory of motivation and a meager conception of man and society. It reduces man to a bundle of abilities, an instrument valued according to its capacity for performing socially valued functions with more or less efficiency. Also, the doctrine leads inevitably to hierarchy and oligarchy, and tries to soften that hard outcome by a new form of the ancient argument that the best should rule. In all these ways, the idea of equality of opportunity constitutes a thorough misunderstanding of a democractic conception of equality.

It is not the primary task of this essay to set forth a genuinely democratic conception of equality: that is a work for another time. Still, enough should be done in the second part of this essay to arrest the most obvious and most likely objections to the first part.

The equal-opportunity principle is certainly not without value. Stripped of its antagonistic and inequalitarian overtones, the formula can be used to express the fundamental proposition that no member of the community should be denied the basic conditions necessary for the fullest possible participation in the common life, insofar as those conditions can be provided for by public action and through the use of public resources. This formulation will take one some distance toward a democratic conception of equality, but it must be interpreted carefully, for it can easily turn into just another defense of the equal right to become unequal.

Still, the formulation does provide some useful guidelines. It obviously implies equality in and before the law. It also implies a far greater measure of economic equality than is the case today. The issue here is not material comfort. Nor does it have anything to do with the notion that justice is served when economic goods are allocated according to the actual work (in the customary definition) each one does. That is impossible. We may urge that each should contribute according to ability; we must surely insist that each be provided for according to need.

What the criterion of a substantial degree of economic equalization requires is the establishment of the material conditions necessary for a generous measure of freedom of choice for all members of the community, and the establishment of the conditions necessary for relations of mutual respect and honesty among the various economic and social groups within a society. This is not some kind of levelling demand for equality of condition. It is no more than a recognition of the obvious fact that the great material inequality that prevails in America today produces too much brutishness, impotence, and rage among the lower classes, and too much nervous vulgarity among the middle classes. There is no assertion here that economic equalization is the sufficient condition for the democratic New Jerusalem. Rather, the assertion is negative. As Arnold put it, "equality will never of itself alone give us a perfect civilisation. But, with such inequality as ours, a perfect civilisation is impossible."[7]

The equality-of-opportunity principle, as formulated above, also implies the equal right of each member to share in the political life of the community to the fullest extent of his interest and ability. But this is the point at which the principle, no matter how carefully formulated, easily leads one away from a democratic view. The equal-opportunity principle as employed today in, for example, discussions of representation and voting rights, really does nothing more than fortify the prevailing conception of political action as just another of the various steps individuals and groups take to secure and advance their own interests and advantages. In this view, politics is but another aspect of the struggle for competitive advantage, and we need political power in order to protect and advance our private powers. This conception of politics is drawn from the economic sphere, and never rises above the ethical and psychological possibilities of that sphere.

When it is understood that the principle of equal opportunity is in our time an expression of the competitive, capitalistic spirit, and not of the democratic spirit, then the boundaries of its applicability begin to emerge. To the extent that competition is inescapable, or socially useful, all competitors should have the same advantages, and this the equal-opportunity principle guarantees. In any competitive situation, some will do better than others, and it seems just that those who do well should be rewarded more generously than those who do poorly. This too the principle guarantees.

The basic question, however, is not whether competition should be praised or condemned, but where and under what conditions competition is a desirable principle of action and judgment, and where and under what conditions it is not. Some kinds of competition actually draw people more closely together whereas others produce antagonism and isolation. The problem is to distinguish between these kinds, encouraging the former and discouraging the latter. Peace is but a euphemism for slavery unless our competitive energies are given adequate outlet. Most people probably have some need for both inward and outward striving. Perhaps the struggles against other people and the struggles within the self can be brought to some kind of balance in each individual and in society as a whole. Ideally, we might strive toward a truly pluralistic society in which nearly everybody could find a specialty he could do fairly well and where he would enjoy friendly competition with others. Judged by this imaginative possibility, our present social order is a mean thing. It is a kind of institutionalized war game, or sporting contest, in which the prizes are far too limited in kind, the referees and timekeepers far too numerous, and the number of reluctant and ill-adjusted players far too high. We need a social order that permits a much greater variety of games. Such a social order could, I think, be based on an effort to find a place for the greatest possible range of natural abilities among people. The variety of available natural abilities is enormous and worth much more exploration than any of the currently dominant conceptions of social order is willing to undertake. In the United States today, the fundamental justification of the equal-opportunity principle is that it is an efficient means for achieving an indefinite expansion of wealth and power. Many people are unsuited by nature for that competition, so that nature itself comes to seem unjust. But many of the injustices we regard nature as having perpetrated on individuals are actually no more than artifacts of the narrow view we take of nature's possibilities and a consequent distortion of the methods and ideals by which we attempt to transcend nature. For example, in defining intelligence as what I.Q. tests measure, we constrict the meanings of intelligence, for there are many modes of intelligence that the tests do not capture—nature is more protean than our conception of it. Furthermore, having defined intelligence in a certain way, we then proceed to reward the people who have just that kind of intelligence and encourage them to use it in the pursuit of knowledge, which they are likely to do by building computers, which in turn give only certain kinds of knowledge. Thus our constricted definition of nature is confirmed by the methods we use to study nature. In this special sense, there might still be something to say for the eighteenth-century idea that society should imitate nature.

We must learn to ask questions like these about the method of competition and the principle of equal opportunity. The task is to define their proper spheres of action, not to treat them as blocks to be totally accepted or rejected. At the outer limit, it seems clear that whereas every society is to some extent competitive and competition in some sphere is socially and individually valuable, no society ought to exalt the competitive spirit as such, and the equal-opportunity principle that implements it. Both conceptions tend naturally toward selfishness unless carefully controlled.

V

In addition to equality of opportunity, there is another kind of equality that is blind to all questions of success or failure. This is the equality that obtains in the relations among the members of any genuine community. It is the feeling held by each member that all other members, regardless of their many differences of function and rank, belong to the community "as fully as he does himself."[8] Equal opportunity, far from strengthening this kind of equality, weakens it.

When this point is reached, when the discussion turns to the meanings of equality involved in a democratic conception of membership and a democratic conception of ruling and being ruled, the equal-opportunity principle — no matter how carefully formulated—begins to mislead. A fuller conception of equality is needed, one stripped of the antagonistic and privatistic overtones of the equal-opportunity principle. That fuller conception, in turn, requires a broader view of politics than is afforded by the "who gets what, when, how" perspective.

Political life occupies a middle ground between the sheer givens of nature and society on the one side, and the transcendental "kingdom of ends" on the other. Through political action we strive publicly to order and transform the givens of nature and society by the light of values drawn from a realm above or outside the order of the givens. People, acting together, define the ideal aims of the common life and try to bend realities toward them. Through acting with others to define and achieve what can be called good for all, each realizes part of his own meaning and destiny. Insofar as we are beings who want not merely to live but to live well, we are political beings. And insofar as any man does not participate in forming the common definition of the good life, to that degree he falls short of the fullest possibilities of the human vocation. No one can assign to another dominion over his life without becoming something less than a man. This way of thinking about political action leads to an idea of equality whose tone and implications are very different from those of the equal-opportunity formulation.

Other features of political action lead in the same direction, and, specifically, require a rejection of all claims to rulership based on the ancient analogies between the art of ruling and other arts. When you contract with a carpenter to build a house, you may assume that the carpenter's skills are sufficient to the work that is to be done. But when citizens elevate some among them to places of political authority the case is different. Politics has so few givens and so many contingencies and complexities, contains so many dangerous possibilities and so few perfect solutions, and is such a baffling mixture of empirical, prudential, and ethical considerations that no individual or group has knowledge and skill sufficient for all situations. As John Winthrop said, no man can "profess nor undertake to have sufficient skill for that office."[9]

Winthrop's comment, grounded as it is on a solid understanding of the political vocation, is a just rebuke to all claims for political authority based on technical competence. Relations between politician and citizen are very different from those between craftsman and employer. Politicans cannot be said to serve or to execute the will of citizens in the way that craftsmen can be said to serve their employers. Nor can politicians claim authority over their work and over other persons engaged in that work on the grounds of technical competence. The relations between politicians and citizens, in sum, are relations among equals in a number of important senses. Above all, their relations are built on premises that, when properly understood, encourage genuine conversation among the participants, not merely the transmission of information and commands up and down a line. This way of thinking about the matter presumes equality among citizens in the sense most basic to a democratic understanding of the relations among the members of a political community—in the sense of equality of being—and hence presumes the widest possible participation in and sharing of responsibility for the policies that govern the whole community.

Just as political authorities may not lay claim to superior rights on the ground of special merit, neither may ordinary citizens absolve themselves from partial responsibility for public policies on the ground that their task is done when they have selected those who will take active charge of the affairs of the polity. The democratic idea offers no such easy absolution from shared responsibility and guilt.

This sharing of responsibility and guilt may be one of the reasons why a genuinely democratic conception of equality is not easy to accept even by those who call themselves democrats. It is comforting to think that someone else is competently in charge of the large and dangerous affairs of politics: Somebody else rules; I just live here. Hierarchy and oligarchy provide subjects with that comfort and with easy escapes from shared responsibility and guilt. This freedom from political responsibility is very valuable to people who would much rather devote themselves to their private interests anyway, than share the burden of caring for the public good. The doctrine of equality of opportunity, tied as it is to the principle of hierarchy, easily leads to moral arrogance on the part of the winners and to the taking of moral holidays by the losers.

A proper view of equality still leaves wide scope for the existence of necessary and just superiorities and differences, but it brings a different mentality to their appraisal. Certainly, some things are better than others, and more to be preferred. Some vocations and talents are more valuable than others, and more to be rewarded. The implication here is only that the more highly skilled, trained, or talented man has no ground either for thinking himself a better man than his less-favored fellows, or for regarding his superiorities as providing any but the most temporary and limited justification for authority over others. The paradigmatic case is that of the relation between teacher and student. The teacher's superior knowledge provides a just claim to authority over the students. But central to the ethic of teaching is the conviction that the teacher must impart to students not only substantive knowledge but also the critical skills and habits necessary for judging and contributing to that knowledge. The teacher justifies his authority and fulfills his duty by making himself unnecessary to the student.

Perhaps this at least suggests the outlines of a democratic conception of equality and draws the boundaries of its applicability. The heart of such a view of equality is its affirmation of equality of being and belonging. That affirmation helps identify those sectors of life in which we should all be treated in a common or average way, so that the minimal conditions of a common life are made available to all: legal equality, equal rights of participation in political life, equal right to those average material provisions necessary for living together decently at all. It also stresses the greatest possible participation in and sharing of the common life and culture while striving to assure that no person shall determine or define the being of any other.

This is what equality is all about, and it is a great deal.[10] But it is far from everything. Beyond the realm of the average and the comparable lies another realm of human relations where notions of equality have no relevance. Hence, a fair understanding of equality requires a sense of the boundaries of that realm in which equalitarian categories do not apply.

Those boundaries begin where we try to define man himself. Every attempted formulation of equality stumbles on the mystery and the indefinability of the creature for and about whom the formulation is made. In the end, it makes no sense to say that all men are equal, or that any two men are, because it is impossible to say what man is. It is easy to abstract a part from the whole, and define that part in terms that make it commensurable with the same parts abstracted from other whole persons. Thus, one can define an American citizen in terms that impart perfect sense to the proposition that all American citizens are equal. But when it comes to talking about whole men and about man, the concept of equality is mute. Then there is only the mystery of being, the recognition of self and others.

Lawrence has expressed the idea perfectly, and he should be permitted the last word:

> One man is neither equal nor unequal to another man. When I stand in the presence of another man, and I am my own pure self, am I aware of the presence of an equal, or of an inferior, or of a superior? I am not. When I stand with another man, who is himself, and when I am truly myself, then I am only aware of a Presence, and of the strange reality of Otherness. There is me, and there is *another being*. ... There is no comparing or estimating. ... Comparison enters only when one of us departs from his own integral being, and enters the material mechanical world. Then equality and inequality starts at once.[11]

Notes

1. Michael Young, *The Rise of the Meritocracy* (London: Thames and Hudson, 1958). Young's book imaginatively explores the conditions under which Jefferson's lovely dream of rule by the natural aristocracy turns into a nightmare of banality and outrage. The main condition, of course, is the dedication of virtually all creative energies to the goal of material abundance.
2. Success is a function of both inborn talent and the urge to do well, and it is often impossible to tell which is the more important in a particular case. It is certain that the urge to do well can be stimulated by social institutions. How else can we account for Athens or Florence, or the United States?
3. *Democracy in America* (New York, N.Y.: Vintage, 1945), Vol. 2, pp. 104-05.
4. Some civil rights leaders are suspicious of open enrollment plans to combat *de facto* segregation for precisely this reason.
5. "The greatest obstacle which equality has to overcome is not the aristocratic pride of the rich, but rather the undisciplined egoism of the poor." Proudhon, as quoted in James Joll, *The Anarchists* (Boston, Mass.: Little, Brown, 1964), p. 67.
6. Oscar Goss, "The Political Economy of the Great Society," *Commentary* (October, 1965), pp. 31-37, p. 37.
7. Matthew Arnold, essay on "Equality" (1878), in *Matthew Arnold: Prose and Poetry*, ed. by A. L. Bouton (New York, N.Y.: Scribner's, 1927) p. 362.
8. John Plamenatz, *Man and Society* (New York, N.Y.: McGraw-Hill, 1963), Vol. II, p. 120.
9. John Winthrop, "Speech to the General Court," July 3, 1645, in Perry Miller, ed., *The American Puritans: Their Prose and Poetry* (Garden City, New York: Doubleday Anchor, 1956), pp. 91-92.
10. As Paine said, with permissible exaggeration, "inequality of rights has been the cause of all the disturbances, insurrections, and civil wars, that ever happened...." Thomas Paine, *Works*, ed. by J. P. Mendum (Boston, Mass.: 1878, 3 vols.), Vol. I, pp. 454-55.
11. D. H. Lawrence, "Democracy," as quoted in Raymond Williams, *Culture and Society, 1780-1950* (New York, N.Y.: Columbia University Press, 1958), p. 211.

Equality of Opportunity and the Just Society

"All social values . . . are to be distributed equally unless an unequal distribution . . . is to everyone's advantage. Injustice, then, is simply inequalities that are not to the benefit of all" (62, all parenthetical references are to John Rawls' *A Theory of Justice* [Cambridge, Mass.: Harvard University Press, 1971]). With that thesis, powerfully argued, John Rawls calls us forward to a vision of the future which captures the deepest yearnings and highest aspirations of the democratic ideal. "Justice is the first virtue of social institutions, as truth is of systems of thought" (3). With that assertion, Rawls recalls us to the very origins of political philosophy, reminding errant political theorists and citizens alike that justice is their first concern. Not power, or the GNP, or efficiency, or the endless pursuit of private interest but justice is the proper subject of political thought and action as it is the defining characteristic of the good state.

The reminder and the call come to a people as short of memory as they are of vision. We are sleepwalkers approaching a precipice, and our judgments of our prospects are clouded by fear, by cynicism, and by the habit of living with the knowledge that at least two governments, swollen and stupid with power, can virtually destroy civilization in an hour. The end may be near. There may not be enough time or energy left for the peoples to call up their powers of social invention and devise the means of rescue. Nor do I think for a minute that a book alone can do much to wake us up. Perhaps the most it can do is to remind us of what we have already lost. Still, it is certain that if we do not look upon ourselves as creatures worth saving we shall go down.

John Rawls' book does honor and address us as such creatures, and reminds us that we honor ourselves most when we strive to build social arrangements that encourage self-respect, intelligence, and reciprocity. Only to the extent that a society is just does it provide such encouragement, and the just society is profoundly equalitarian in its basic arrangements. So Rawls argues, and as the argument joins hands with Aristotle in its assertion of the primacy of justice, so does it join hands with Marx and Rousseau in its assertion of the primacy of equality within justice.

The social welfare, or corporate capitalist and state socialist regimes of our day have exhausted their moral resources. We see all around us persons haunted by intimations of the end of the human experiment, whether in war, or in the despoilation of the earth, or in the wasteland of bureaucratic and technological regimentation. The emancipation of the race from political, economic, and social servitude has been the common aim of revolutionaries from 1776 to the present. While accomplishing much, all these vast efforts have lost momentum. We have no widely held conceptions of feasible future alternatives where democracy and human dignity might prevail. The forces of the Left, which once offered hope, nearly all have fallen victim to the theory that the big state and the hierarchical party are the proper instruments for building the good society. Their efforts and achievements, while no doubt more noble than anything offered by the Right, are badly flawed monuments to that bad theory. On the Right, work, thrift, enterprise, and profit are defended as moral values by only a few fanatics. Rather, corporate capitalism is said to be an effective method for raising the GNP and assuring a high level of consumption. No honest writer even pretends that the huge states of the West are in any significant sense democracies. At best, those regimes are praised as reasonably good guarantors of private liberties and reasonably satisfactory reconcilers of conflicting group interests. We hardly even pretend any longer that the whole system is admirable, worthy in its own right of loyalty and devotion. Probably the only real focal value offered us by our societies today is the satisfaction of private desires, largely through consumption. Beyond that, the system is pointless, able to make no defense for itself, not admired much even by those who live in the rooms at the top.

I paint this familiar picture (once again) to set the context for what follows. John Rawls' book appeared at a time when serious ideas were in short supply, and it has provided the raw materials for a still-booming academic industry. Most of this commentary has been narrow and technical, precisionist and professional. While *A Theory of Justice* perhaps invites responses of that sort, being itself in parts quite technical and professional, the main source of that impulse is found in the Alexandrian tone of social theory in the universities today. We are masters of method, heirs of the Baconian conviction that great and difficult ends can be reached by standard and common means. I think that in the end one has not responded adequately to a *A Theory of Justice* until one has appreciated the vision of the good society which is at its center. That vision is profoundly equalitarian: As Rawls puts it, in his characteristically moderate and modest tone, the two basic principles arrived at in the original position "express an equalitarian conception of justice" (100). I shall try to have a conversation with Rawls on the subject of equality—its place in the theory of justice; its place in the institutions and policies of the just society.

The subject is of the greatest practical importance. It is plain that the underlying question of all major domestic political debates in the advanced societies with social welfare regimes is the question of equality. What is the desirable degree of inequality? Which inequalities are acceptable and which are not? By what criteria shall we weigh claims to varying shares of the primary social goods? These are the profoundest, underlying questions of political life in the social welfare states, and increasingly it is recognized that we have no coherent answers to them. In the presence of that (growing) incoherency, policy wobbles and public opinion grows querulous. You will search the literature long to find a serious thinker or large body of political opinion which supports and respects the present methods and policies of distribution as just and efficient. Modern economies with welfare structures continue to deal out, with fine and seemingly inevitable impartiality, a consistent portion of want and waste to some and abundance and uneasy privilege to others. The social welfare regimes themselves, while huge and entrenched, seem increasingly fragile. Buffeted by organized groups pressing for incompatible relative shares, legislatures everywhere are numbed in stasis and confusion, unable to contribute a genuinely intelligent and independent voice to the formation of major policies. Everywhere there is a huge increase of centralized power, located in unstable political executives and unwieldy bureaucracies. The fear grows that the whole system could collapse, due to its own complexity on the one side, and to the excessive expectations and demands of various groups and interests on the other. The welfare state has aroused in many the expectation that government ought to be doing something for them, and as this expectation spreads to more groups in the population, so too spreads the mentality either of parasitical dependence on government handouts or of cynical rooting in the government trough. Policies are made by coalitions of self-interested minorities, with little attention to anything that can be called the public good. Furthermore, more and more people experience and accept the system as being this way, and in that acceptance, of course, reveal their own self-contempt while expressing contempt for others.

To put this in more neutral language, we might call on the standard distinction between genuinely public or collective goods, goods which must be available to all if they are to be available to any (national defense, or public parks, say, are the usual examples), and particular goods which can be made available to some and denied to others. The social welfare states are increasingly in the business of providing private goods, and the well-being of a great many groups depends on active and extensive government support. These supports are usually made in the form of income transfers and subsidies of many kinds, and it is these, not the provision of public goods, which excite the most passionate interest and provoke the most intense feelings of envy, resentment, and greed. Besides, there is also the issue of who will pay (privately, often indirectly) for public goods: a steel producer, forced to install expensive equipment to reduce air pollution, passes the charges on to consumers. Our methods of making decisions lead to increasing tension among all sorts of groups, and to pervasive dissatisfaction with a government which tries to do more and more for more and more groups. Even as governmental efforts and agencies expand, gratitude for those efforts and respect for those agencies decline.

Behind these manifest confusions lies a deeper confusion about the meaning of justice and the just society. That, in turn, translates into the question of what inequalities are acceptable and justifiable, and what are not. The present stalemate and confusion cannot last, for the system is inherently dynamic (the chief indicator of this is inflation, which leads to demoralization, increasing hostility among groups, and the erosion of moral limits). Seen in this perspective, then, John Rawls' book, although it is in the nature of an academic treatise in political philosophy, addresses the most important practical political questions of our time. At stake in the question of justice is the question of democracy itself.[1]

Equality of Opportunity

In *A Theory of Justice* John Rawls proposes a basic shift in our operative definition of equality. He wants to move us away from our present understanding of equality of opportunity over to a new meaning which he calls fair equality of opportunity modified by the difference principle and the principle of redress. The former, he says, suffers from a number of serious defects which the latter avoids. The remainder of my discussion centers on this topic. The best place to begin is with Rawls' criticism of the idea of equality of opportunity.

That notion is one of the brightest stars in the liberal firmament, and one of the chief aims of liberal reform. Let every individual be assured an equal opportunity with every other individual to gain the goods and achieve the benefits which society affords. No one must enter the contest under socially imposed handicaps. It is society's duty to see that all have an equal position at the starting gate. Then the race goes to the swiftest, the prize to the most deserving. That way we not only achieve justice among groups but also assure social progress. Each can rise as far as his talents and ambition will take him, so none can justifiably look with envy at those above. Equal opportunity releases energy, assures progress and innovation, and treats everyone with equal justice.

The principle of equality of opportunity sharpens to a cutting edge the primary liberal tenet that the individual is the basic unit of society and that all social arrangements are to be judged by reference to how they aid or hinder the fulfillment of individuals' needs, purposes, and abilities. Thus, the equal opportunity principle was one of the most effective weapons in the assault against the institutions of fixed hierarchy, rigid classes, and ascribed status. All places were to be equally open to all contenders under conditions of fair competition. Birth, patronage, tradition had no claims. Individual merit and ambition alone were to be the criteria for the allocation of places, and the race was to be open to all on equal terms. The implementation of equal opportunity meant nothing less than "a complete social revolution: a change in the social base of status and power, and a new mode of access to place and privilege in the society."[2]

Modern bourgeois society is based on this principle and is inconceivable without it. Equality of opportunity is taken as a rule of justice, and deviations from it bear the taint of illegitimacy and unfairness. Group after group has employed the principle in its struggle to overcome one or another kind of handicap and disadvantage. In its formulation as "careers open to talent" the equal opportunity principle is in theory, if not always in practice, at the very heart of the meritocratic society. That society awards the places of honor and high reward to trained or educated technical ability. Hence, equal opportunity requires equal access to the institutions which provide that training, and to the jobs which follow from it. If individuals or groups have been handicapped by prior social disadvantages, then it is a public duty to take affirmative action to overcome those disadvantages. By a logical extension, then, equal opportunity has grown to include a great variety of measures designed, as former President Johnson put it, to remove the "shackles" previously imposed by social attitudes and conditions on some of the contestants, such as blacks, various ethnic minorities, women, and others who have been weighed down by the burdens of poverty and prejudice.

Up until just a few years ago, this understanding of equality as equality of opportunity reigned virtually unchallenged. It is still by far and away the dominant conception of equality in the public mind and the dominant conception employed in the making of public policy. Today, however, in some quarters the principle has come under attack. Far from being a remedy for inequality, and thus a move toward justice, the principle is held to be the fountain of new kinds of inequality, and thus a move toward injustice. Some writers are arguing that equality of opportunity should be replaced by equality of expectations, or even equality of results. John Rawls agrees with much of this criticism, and proposes that the liberal principle of equal opportunity must, as a requirement of justice, be replaced by a new understanding of "fair equality of opportunity." Let us look at his critique.

The Equal Right to Become Unequal

It is not my purpose to discuss the logic by which Rawls derives the principles of justice from the "original position." Rather, I shall cut into *A Theory of Justice* two or three levels above its foundation, in order to move quickly toward the topic of equal opportunity. However, for the sake of easy reference, let me set down once again the familiar two principles (302-03):

First Principle:

> Each person is to have an equal right to the most extensive total system of equal basic liberties compatible with a similar system of liberty for all.

Second Principle:

> Social and economic inequalities are to be arranged so that they are both: (a) to the greatest benefit of the least advantaged, consistent with the just savings principle, and (b) attached to offices and positions open to all under conditions of fair equality of opportunity.

The first of these principles applies mainly to the equal liberties of citizenship—freedom of speech, association, the vote, and so forth. It will not much concern us here, although it should be noted that claims for equality increasingly take the form of expanding the concept and logic of equal citizenship into the areas of economic and social rights and benefits.[3] In a very important way, the notion of equality that is based on the equal status of citizens pervades Rawls's discussion of all other aspects of equality.

The second principle concerns the distribution of what Rawls usefully calls the primary social goods: rights and liberties, opportunities and powers, income and wealth, and a sense of self-worth (92). This is the principle which will concern us most. It proposes that persons in the original position would agree that justice requires an equal distribution of the social primary goods in all cases except where it can be shown that an unequal distribution is to the greatest advantage of the least advantaged group in the society. Rawls is here adopting an idea which was at the heart of primitive Christianity and which was powerfully reaffirmed by Marx: if you want to know whether a society is just, you must examine that society from the point of view of its lowliest members. The eyes of the poor and lowly—the least advantaged, as Rawls calls them—are the eyes that matter when it comes to looking at justice.

Armed with this principle, and standing at the vantage point, Rawls examines two other formulas for distributing the social primary goods. The first is the "system of natural liberty " (72). It requires formal equality of opportunity so that all have "the same legal rights of access to all advantaged social positions " (72). Thus, all careers are, in principle, thrown open to talent. But no effort is made to preserve an equality or even similarity of social conditions among the competitors. Hence, distributive shares are improperly influenced by both natural (e.g., native or genetic strengths and weaknesses) and social (e.g., poverty) factors that are utterly arbitrary from a moral point of view. The "system of natural liberty," then, is radically defective as a principle of just distribution.

The liberal interpretation recognizes this, and improves upon it by trying to "mitigate the influence of social contingencies and natural fortune on distributive shares" (73). This view insists on fair equality of opportunity, which means, for example, that such factors as social class should not unduly affect either the conditions of entry or the outcomes of the contest for distributive shares. Society must take affirmative measures to assure that "those who are at the same level of talent and ability, and have the same willingness to use them, should have the same prospects of success regardless of their initial place in the social system. . . ." (73).

The liberal interpretation of equal opportunity is a great improvement over the system of a merely formal right to compete for positions. It insists that careers must genuinely and substantively, and not just formally and legally, be open to talents. Still, it too is defective as an interpretation of equality and as a principle for distributing the primary social goods. At this point in the argument, Rawls finds two major defects in the liberal interpretation. First, although this interpretation tries to reduce the effect of social contingencies, it still "permits the distribution of wealth and income to be determined by the natural distribution of abilities and talents" (73-74). Such an outcome is of course arbitrary from a moral point of view. "There is no more reason to permit the distribution of income and wealth to be settled by the distribution of natural assets than by historical and social fortune" (74). Secondly, the principle of fair opportunity can be implemented only imperfectly, at least so long as the family exists. It is simply impossible in practice to secure similar chances of achievement for those similarly endowed, because the extent to which natural powers and faculties develop is affected by an enormous number and variety of social conditions. Some of these factors are unknown to us, others could be equalized only at enormous cost, and still others could never be equalized at all.[4]

Democratic Equality

So, if we are genuinely to treat all people equally as moral persons, and not allow shares in the benefits of social life to be determined by the natural lottery or social fortune, then we need a different interpretation of equality. That needed interpretation is reached "by combining the principle of fair equality of opportunity with the difference principle" (75).

The difference principle asserts that inequalities are justifiable only if they are to the advantage of the worst-off representative man or group. We are to agree to consider the unequal distribution of talents and abilities among a population as a general social resource which can be arranged to work to the advantage of all, rather than as a source of strength for some and weakness for others. No one is to benefit from the contingencies of nature or social position "except in ways that redound to the well-being of others" (100). In the conception of justice as fairness, people in effect agree to share one another's fate. Reciprocity and mutual benefit must prevail over considerations of social efficiency and technocratic values (see 106-07).

It is important to appreciate here that Rawls is distinguishing between two senses of "desert" which are often confused. On the one side, we say a person "deserves" superior social rewards if he has done what the social system requires or expects of persons. On the other side, we sometimes think that persons with greater natural talents, say, deserve those talents or at least deserve the great advantages that come from exercising them. But this is surely wrong. From a moral point of view no one deserves his place in the distribution of native abilities any more than he deserves the place in society into which he was born. Hence, the more advantaged have no basis for claiming benefits unless those benefits contribute to the welfare of others, and especially to the welfare of those least advantaged by nature or social position.

Finally, the democratic interpretation of equality (fair equality of opportunity modified by the difference principle) is completed by adding still one more dimension, the principle of redress. Just as undeserved advantages must be minimized, so must undeserved disadvantages be compensated for. "Thus . . . in order to treat all persons equally, to provide genuine equality of opportunity, society must give more attention to those with fewer native assets and to those born into the less favorable social positions. The idea is to redress the bias of contingencies in the direction of equality" (100-01).

Now, Rawls does not forward the principle of redress as the sole criterion of justice. It must be weighed in the balance along with others. Still, some examples will show that he goes quite far along the road of redress—certainly farther than anything met in present social policy. He suggests, for example, that greater resources might be spent on the early education of the less rather than the more intelligent (101). Or, as another example, he proposes that the social minimum (the level of primary social goods below which no one must fall) should be set at the point which maximizes the expectations of the least advantaged group over the long term (285). Obviously, such suggestions travel farther along the equalitarian road than anything contemplated in such established compensatory efforts as "headstart" or skill development or curriculum enrichment programs. It is not excessive to say that by the time Rawls is done, the last are put first; and this is said to be required by the democratic understanding of equality, and by the conception of justice as fairness. Persons must receive not according to their abilities but according to their needs.

A Theory of Justice is the most comprehensive and sophisticated effort in recent social theory to formulate what can properly be called a democratic and even socialist ethic. Rawls is far more consistent and coherent on this subject than Marx—let alone Engels—ever was. He sets nothing like the restrictions on substantive social and economic equality that the early liberals (e.g., Locke) did. Indeed, he goes far beyond even such great democratic thinkers as Jefferson, for whom equality under the law of nature implied nothing about equality of condition in society. Indeed, Jefferson comes close to being a "meritocrat," as can be seen in his plan for education, for example, or in his view that the "natural aristocracy" was the most precious asset of mankind, and that the best society was that which brought the natural aristocracy to the fore. In some of his writings (e.g., *Agrarian Justice*) Tom Paine went as far toward equality as Rawls, but in others he pulled back (e.g., his defense of chartered corporations and unequal incomes in *Dissertations on Government; The Affairs of the Bank; and Paper Money*).

Edward Bellamy (*Equality*) went farther toward "equal shares" than Rawls has, but he encumbered his case with such a heavy scheme for the regimentation of labor and the hierarchical, antidemocratic organization of government that few readers have found it palatable. Among recent writers, only George Bernard Shaw, so far as I know, made an argument for equal shares of the social product anywhere near as far-reaching as the one made by Rawls.[5] Shaw defined socialism as complete equality of income, and proceeded to make a lively, even brilliant, defense of socialism so defined. Unlike Rawls, however, Shaw's case for equality is largely a case against the absurdities and irrationalities of the wage system as a method for measuring and rewarding individual contributions to the social good. Shaw offers little in the way of philosophical and moral argument for equality.

It should be apparent that in making these comparative assessments of "how equalitarian" Rawls is, I am leaving out of the comparison primitive societies, equalitarian utopian literature (such as More's *Utopia*), and the many—usually short-lived—efforts to establish equalitarian communities. This leaves out a lot, but the exclusion is justified because Rawls himself does not draw on these literatures and experiences. There is no doubt, for example, that the earliest communities of primitive Christians were radically equalitarian. Thus: "And all that believed were together, and had all things common; and sold their possessions and goods, and parted them to all men, as every man had need" (*Acts* 2:44-45). Again: "And the multitude of them that believed were of one heart and of one soul; neither said any of them that ought of the things which he possessed were his own, but they had all things common. . . . Neither was there any among them that lacked: for as many as were possessors of lands or houses sold them, and brought the prices of the things that were sold, and laid them at the apostles' feet: and distribution was made unto every man according to his need" (*Acts* 4:32-35).

Rawls does not consider such materials for perfectly understandable reasons. He is a man of reason, not of faith; a philosopher, not a true believer. Justice may be the first virtue of society, but the theory of justice is only part of the whole theory of the good society. Besides, such experiences and ideas as those described in *Acts,* or those propounded in say, Babeuf's *Conspiracy of Equals,* were entirely and even fiercely "perfectionist" in nature, while Rawls' logic, as we shall see, precludes perfectionism.

Justice as fairness sets the claim for equality above all other claims save that of liberty; and, as we have seen, "equal liberty," while formally prior to the difference principle, in the end requires for its implementation a far greater measure of social and economic equality than is presently the case. Rawls does not discuss liberty and equality within the familiar liberal framework which promptly sets them against each other as clashing and nearly incompatible principles. He sees the two as mutually enabling, and he stands as far as possible from the view which sees the moral life as, to use Weber's expression, the battlefield of "warring gods." Moreover, he is utterly unwilling to see equality as just one among many values, none of which has priority over the others.[6]

For Rawls, then, equality comes first. Goods are to be distributed equally unless it can be shown that an unequal distribution is to the advantage of the least advantaged. Furthermore, redress for the disadvantaged has a prior claim on the social conscience and on social policy over any considerations of efficiency or progress. That too is entailed in justice as fairness.

The Ambiguities of Equality

No ethical principle is without its ambiguities and uncertainties. No single principle can provide a guide in all cases of judgment and decision, for the complexity and heterogeneity of real situations and events inevitably outstrip the simplicity of abstract principles. And it is doubtful, regardless of the quality of the logic employed, whether all persons will ever agree on a definition of the good society, or even of the primary feature(s) of the good society.[7] Hence, it is no surprise that a number of difficulties can be found in Rawls' democratic interpretation of equality and equal opportunity. I shall discuss a few which I think troublesome, but readers must of course decide for themselves whether they think them so.

To begin, there are some complexities implicit in the principle of redress. On the whole, it is not too far off the mark to say that for Rawls the just society is the society of equals. In pursuit of this society, he proposes that persons or groups disadvantaged by the "natural lottery" or by their social position are to be compensated for these undeserved disadvantages. In general, the claims of the less fortunate take priority over all other claims. Thus, as mentioned earlier, Rawls suggests that "greater resources might be spent on the education of the less rather than the more intelligent. . . ." (101).

Apart from the question of return on investment—trying to make silk purses out of sows' ears—this surely raises the questions of justice. Perhaps the least fortunate should come first, but in putting them first, Rawls comes pretty close to penalizing or handicapping the more fortunate. If the greater social resources go to the least naturally endowed and least socially favored persons, that in effect puts a handicap on the better endowed and more favored. One might agree with Rawls (104) that the better endowed cannot claim that they deserve social arrangements that do not contribute to the welfare of others. But by the same token, how can the less fortunate claim that they do deserve such arrangements? Or, to put the question differently, by what arguments would one persuade the better endowed that they should be penalized for the sake of the lesser endowed? At a certain point, and I expect that point would be reached quite quickly, such persons would find it hard to see such a society as "a collective venture for mutual advantage" as Rawls puts it. Denied the resources needed to develop their high potentialities, seeing those resources diverted to persons of lower potential, such persons would probably find other and harsher words than "mutual advantage" and "cooperative venture" to describe their society.

It is difficult to find the right words here. One feels some shame in questioning that the least fortunate should have priority on the social conscience and in the making of social policy. And today very few wish to return to the cruelties and stupidities of a Social Darwinist rationale for ignoring the needs of the poor and the poorly endowed as necessary for progress and the improvement of the race.

Still, it is not easy to see that justice requires the full reversal (the last shall be first) that Rawls says it does. We do sometimes feel it right to "handicap" the most favored, but rarely do we make such arguments in the name of justice. Rather, we bring other considerations to bear. For example, race horses are handicapped according to their track records, but that is done not in the name of justice, but in order to make the race interesting to bettors. Or, a party of backpackers might agree that the strongest members should carry the heaviest loads, not in order to serve justice, but because all the members want to reach the same destination at about the same time. Furthermore, a hiking party has nothing like the complexity of a social order, with its multiplicity of persons, groups, interests, needs, and values. Under actual social conditions it is enormously difficult to explain, justify, and implement the kind of handicapping or redress which Rawls proposes.

Add to these considerations the fact that those who occupy the least favored social positions might occupy them out of choice—or, if not out of choice strictly speaking, out of a combination of personal and social factors so complex that no one really knows how to sort out and untangle them. In the United States today, for example, public education through high school is fairly easily available to all, and yet one-fifth of the students drop out before graduation. I do not think it has been shown that those persons quit mainly out of economic necessity. The reasons are many and heterogeneous, but in the end, the person chooses to drop out. How do the difference principle and the principle of redress apply here? Society may have strong obligations to compensate those who are kept down or held back for faults not their own, but if persons do not avail themselves of socially provided opportunities, then does society have still further and continuing obligations to compensate them for the losses that accumulate over life as a consequence of the early failure to take advantage of offered opportunities?

Suppose we were still to answer "yes"; that regardless of the reasons or factors that put persons among the least fortunate, those persons' needs and claims still take first priority in the distribution of social resources. Now comes an additional problem. Very often, we simply do not know how to help such persons. We do not know what resources provided in what ways would be genuinely helpful. The "problems" of some groups and individuals can seem intractable. Our wisdom is limited; our knowledge uncertain; our means and methods coarse and haphazard. Enormous expenditures can produce very small results, despite the best will and intention in the world.[8] Much experience seems to indicate that probably the only method that genuinely restores the unrestoreable, provides opportunities and liberties to the derelict and destructive, is the "method" of political and social revolution. *A Theory of Justice* moves entirely within what might be called an administrative and technical framework, and never comes close to talking about social revolution.[9]

I make this point because much experience with the efforts of the welfare-oriented regimes shows that it matters. Despite considerable effort, those regimes have been able to do rather little to stop the dynamic which continues to produce and reproduce very unfortunate disadvantaged groups. We have begun to read about families in their second and third generation of dependence on public subsidy. The War on Poverty ended in a decisive victory for poverty. Helping the unfortunate has produced a huge, unwieldy, and expensive bureaucratic establishment, but nobody is very satisfied with the substantive results. Furthermore, in the United States at least, most welfare efforts are aimed only at establishing a social minimum, a level below which no one can fall, and that is a much simpler task than the one set by Rawls' difference principle complemented by the principle of redress. When even this much simpler task has produced administrative, political, and moral problems that are far from solution, we must expect the task proposed by Rawls to strain to the breaking point our resources of social judgment, knowledge, and skill.

So, then, the difference principle appears simple and practical enough until it comes to the point of application, where, I think, it shows less utility as a guide to policy than one would wish. There are social conditions under which the difference principle is easily applied. We might imagine a band of Eskimo, say, who are facing starvation. They decide that the hunters among them should get the largest share of the band's food supplies because if the hunters grow too weak to hunt the whole group will perish. Under such conditions, it is not hard to understand and to apply the principle that goods should be distributed equally unless it can be shown that an unequal distribution is to the advantage of the least advantaged groups. There, something very like what Rawls calls "chain-connectedness" (80 ff.) really does obtain. But that is rarely the case (and even more rarely can it be seen to be the case) in large and highly complex societies. In such societies, it is not easy to say what would be required in the way of a showing, a proof, that an unequal distribution is to the advantage of the least advantaged. What would qualify as an argument? Rawls rejects efficiency and progress as criteria, just as he rejects the argument put forward by Keynes that the disproportionate share of wealth and income appropriated by the new rich of nineteenth-century capitalist society was justified because this unequal distribution "made possible the rapid build-up of capital and the more or less steady improvement in the general standard of living of everyone" (299).[10]

It might be possible in fairly simple cases, then, to persuade the members of disadvantaged groups that an unequal distribution is in their interest, whether right now, or at some future time. For example, it might be possible to persuade the disadvantaged that all the expensive resources society devotes to the training of highly skilled surgeons, as well as the rewards of income and status which society lavishes upon such persons, are in the interest of themselves as well, for anyone might at some time urgently require the services of a skilled surgeon. But there won't be all that many cases so clear cut. Society devotes large resources and lavishes great rewards on many kinds of persons and activities where the question of "advantage to the least advantaged" admits of no answer at all, let alone a clear and simple answer. What about lawyers, or musicians, or psychoanalysts, or professors of classics, or dancers? Try to apply the difference principle to decide whether elementary school teachers or university professors should have the higher salary. And yet, of course, such questions are the very stuff of social policy. I am not sure that the difference principle offers much guidance in dealing with them.

This leads to another question, which properly belongs mainly to other writers but which I must at least mention. Certainly one of the basic propositions—even the keystone—of *A Theory of Justice* is the thesis of the priority of the right over the good (31 ff.). Closely connected with this is the argument that while indeed some view of the good or of goodness is necessary in defending justice as fairness against other conceptions, something less than a full theory of the good will suffice. As Rawls puts it, what is needed is "the thin theory of the good" (See Secs. 15, 29, and 60, and esp. 395-97, 433-34). The basic idea of the thin theory of the good is that "rational individuals . . . desire certain things as prerequisites for carrying out their plans of life. Other things equal, they prefer a wider to a narrower liberty and opportunity, and a greater rather than a smaller share of wealth and income (396). These four things, of course, are what Rawls calls the social primary goods, which, according to the difference principle, are to be distributed equally unless it can be shown that an unequal distribution is to the advantage of the least advantaged group in the society.

Now, this is clear enough until one adds to the list of primary goods the one which Rawls calls "perhaps the most important," namely, self-respect

(440). We respect ourselves when we have a secure conviction that our plan of life is worthwhile, and when we are confident of our ability to carry out our intentions. Now, Rawls has already argued that persons in the original position would not adopt the principle of perfectionism: no single plan of life, or conception of the best life, would be accepted. Hence, "for the purposes of justice [we] avoid any assessment of the relative value of one another's way of life" (442; see whole of Sec. 50). "Democracy in judging each other's aims is the foundation of self-respect in a well-ordered society" (442).

Rawls says that the social bases of self-respect are sufficiently assured if "for each person there is some association . . . to which he belongs and within which the activities that are rational for him are publicly affirmed by others" (441). In a different vocabulary, we gain our sense of self-esteem largely from our standing in our reference groups.

Now this is certainly correct. But it raises questions for the theory of justice as fairness which, I think, Rawls treats too lightly. Can one even imagine a society whose members are truly neutral ("avoid any assessment of the relative value") among all ways of life and all associations formed around the many particular ways or plans of life? In a very real sense, a society is a collectivity whose members agree that some ways of life, some values and activities and characters, are better than others and more to be preferred. Indeed, the decisive feature of real and healthy politics is collective decision-making about the best collective life. No social order is as indifferent toward the variety of plans of life as Rawls suggests, nor as tolerant as he argues the theory of justice requires them to be. Even the most devoted pluralist draws the line somewhere. And I am pretty sure, as an empirical matter, that no actual society regards all associations and activities as equally valuable so long as they "fulfill the Aristotelian Principle (and are compatible with the principle of justice)" (442). Perhaps we are not all "perfectionists," and perhaps most societies are not perfectionist either in the full sense of the term; but each of us has a streak of perfectionism in him, and every society has a tendency that way. Society may be, as Rawls puts it, a "social union of social unions" (520 ff.), but society is also a (whole) social union in which some (partial) social unions are preferred to others.[11]

These considerations matter a great deal when it comes to the question of the distribution of the social product, or of the social primary goods. Let us for a moment imagine ourselves as active citizens and policy-makers, considering society from a legislative point of view. Many inidividuals and groups with different aims and memberships will press their claims for one or another kind of subsidy. Many social needs and possibilities will come to our attention and we shall have to decide which ones we shall encourage and which not. We need criteria to help us decide where and how to allocate the scarce resources at our disposal.

Now, is it likely that we would choose the difference principle as our criterion, and treat all claimants equally unless we could be convinced that an unequal distribution is to the advantage of the least advantaged? As soon as one puts the question this way, one sees the impossibility, even the ludicrousness, of the answer which, as I understand him, Rawls would give. We might employ a variety of criteria, some no doubt more respectable than others, but I doubt whether the difference principle would—or even could—be important among them. We must decide what we want our society to look like, which means that we must decide to encourage some activities, groups, and ways of life and to discourage others. Or, to put this in another vocabulary, we must establish priorities among the many possible needs and purposes which call for assistance. The difference principle, I think, is of virtually no help in doing this. It is indeed, difficult even to imagine how it has any bearing on the problem. Probably one or another, more-or-less coherent version of perfectionism is needed. The legislator, or the citizen, who treated all groups and ways of life equally unless to treat them unequally would be to the advantage of the least advantaged would be regarded, I think, not as a just person but as a fool or a shirker—one who either did not understand the very nature of social choice, or one who evaded the burdens of choosing.

If this is approximately correct, it follows, I think, that justice as fairness fails to achieve one of its most important goals—"to establish an enduring basis of self-respect throughout society" (441). Society (the legislator, the citizen) cannot treat all groups and ways of life as equally deserving of respect. To do so is, I think, flatly impossible. Since self-respect does, as Rawls says, come in important part from social approval of one's way of life, and since societies must approve some ways more than others, some groups and persons must find their plans of life socially disapproved relative to others. And insofar as self-respect derives from social approbation, such disapproved groups and persons will partly lack the social basis of self-respect. Just as the difference principle in particular fails to offer a guide to the allocation of social resources among the various ways of life, so does justice as fairness in general fail to provide the social basis for self-respect for all persons pursuing different paths of life within the social order.

Meritocracy and Equality

The idea of meritocracy has come in for some hard criticism lately.[12] John Rawls seems to align himself with the main thrust of the criticism. In fact, his very "description" of meritocratic society comes closer to denunciation than any other passage in *A Theory of Justice:*

> This form of social order follows the principle of careers open to talents and uses equality of opportunity as a way of releasing men's energies in the pursuit of economic prosperity and political dominion. There exists a marked disparity between the upper and lower classes in both means of life and the rights and privileges of organizational authority. The culture of the poorer strata is impoverished while that of the governing and technocratic elite is securely based on the services of the national ends of power and wealth. Equality of opportunity means an equal chance to leave the less fortunate behind in the personal quest for influence and social position. (106-07)

That is a remarkable formulation. It appears to confuse some of the worst features of the civilization of the United States with some of the best features of the basic concept of meritocracy. Materialism, competitiveness, a wide gap between upper and lower strata, individualism, the passion for political dominion—these are indeed prominent characteristics of our civilization, but they are certainly not the defining properties of the idea of meritocracy. The basic idea of meritocracy is that those who hold the positions of authority and prestige should have earned them through the exercise of some skill, knowledge, or talent that the society desires and honors. The main idea is simply that the best should lead the rest, and that social institutions and processes should be arranged so that the places of authority and prestige will be genuinely open to all who have, or who can develop, the virtues, skills, and knowledge required to perform ably in those positions. It confuses thought to identify meritocracy as such with the substantive values and goals of a materialist and power-oriented society.[13]

The question of what ends and aims a society should set itself, and of what values, experiences, and types of human beings it should honor—these are political questions of the greatest importance. But they are not as such questions of justice. Nor do they as such have any bearing on the principle of meritocracy, which is simply that the top positions in the social order should be genuinely open to all who have the appropriate talent, knowledge, or virtue. It certainly makes sense to want those who are competent and worthy of praise to occupy the positions of authority and prestige. The big political job is to decide what is worthy of praise and honor, and then to arrange social institutions so that the best persons do get to the places of authority. This, it seems to me, is hardly a question of justice at all. It is a political question. And furthermore, no elaborate theory is needed to explain or to justify the point. The society which does not know what it means by the best way(s) of life, or which does not care, or which chooses the wrong ways, or which does not know how to honor and reward those who are most competent to hold authority might be just or unjust, or neither. What it would certainly be is foolish, contemptible, or vicious, and likely to endure more by lucky accident than by prudence.

Let me put this point sharply. Justice may indeed be as basic to the good society (may be "the first virtue of social institutions") as Rawls says it is, but equality of distribution may not be as basic to justice as he says it is—or, at least, not as basic in the ways he says it is. The question of justice really arises when those in the positions of authority either get there by methods which violate other persons, or when, once on top, they exploit their positions and take advantage of those beneath them. Great disparities of wealth, power, and status between the higher and the lower strata are certainly unjust, and *A Theory of Justice* offers us one cogent explanation of why this is the case. Similarly, when the top positions are not genuinely open to all on the basis of merit, that too is unjust, and here again Rawls' book helps us understand why. In these ways and areas, the difference principle and the principle of redress make genuine contributions to our understanding both of equality and of the just society and offer useful guidance in the formation of social policy. These are valuable contributions and *A Theory of Justice* merits much praise for making them.

But, as I have suggested above, when the principles are extended to some of the other areas where Rawls takes them, they offer as much confusion as clarity, and perhaps endanger things worth holding dear. *A Theory of Justice* does, I think, show some traces of the "levelling" spirit which aristocratic temperaments have always feared in democracy—though I do not mean to suggest that there is even the faintest whiff of envy or resentment anywhere in Rawls' book. What I mean, rather, is something different. I think Rawls is persuasive in his general argument for the priority of the claims of the disadvantaged and unfortunate. But I do not think he has found the right way both to acknowledge that priority and to open the widest possible avenues for the best to rise to positions of eminence and authority through work and talent. And surely, keeping those avenues open is not a matter merely, or even mainly, of favoring the private advantage of the best and most talented, but a matter of advancing the public good. There is a kind of bias in the book against differences of status and reward. He develops a powerful argument for the equal respect due to each of us as human beings and as citizens of a state that claims to be a democracy. But, I think, he does not find the way to combine this equal respect for all with the greater praise and rewards which are owed to some.

When we think of "the best" we should not restrict ourselves to what is rewarded in this time and among us. The concept is, practically speaking, a universal. That is, there has probably never been a social order without a ranking system, a table of values, a pattern of awarding honor and prestige. This is as basic and as widespread a concept and practice as equality, and at least as important as equality is in any theory of social justice. We might want and deserve to be treated in some respects as equals, but we also want to honor and reward the best. Furthermore, there is probably no labelling or classifying term used by human beings about human beings that does not carry a connotation of high and low, superior and inferior. In the human realm, every comparison or distinction is invidious. We want to be treated alike, but we also want to stand out and be treated as different.

A Theory of Justice understands wholeheartedly the urge toward equality, but it does not appreciate fully, I think, the passion for distinction and the place that passion occupies both in the lives of individuals and social orders, and in the formulation of patterns of distributive justice.

Notes

1. John Rawls himself never loses sight of this—one-third of his book concerns quite practical questions—but many of his critics have.
2. Daniel Bell, "On Meritocracy and Equality, "*The Public Interest*, No. 29 (Fall, 1972), p. 41.
3. On this extension of the logic of the equal status of citizenship to include social and economic equalities, see T. H. Marshall, *Citizenship and Social Class* (Cambridge, England: 1950), esp. p. 9 ff.
4. More and more criticism of the liberal concept of equal opportunity centers on the argument, accepted by Rawls, that the principle cannot be implemented in practice. See, e.g., my "Equality of Opportunity, and Beyond," reprinted in this volume; and Christopher Jencks, et al., *Inequality: A Reassessment of the Effect of Family and Schooling in America* (New York, N.Y.: Basic Books, 1972). The Jencks book is especially important, for it casts into doubt both the efficacy of all efforts to equalize educational opportunity, and the belief that excellent educational background and high achievement in later life are directly and strongly correlated. This, of course, brings into question the very foundations of the meritocratic society.
5. Louis Crompton, ed., *The Road to Equality: Ten Unpublished Lectures and Essays by Bernard Shaw* (Boston, Mass.: Beacon Press, 1971). See especially the essays "Redistribution of Wealth" and "The Simple Truth About Socialism." Both were apparently written around 1910, but not published during Shaw's lifetime.
6. This is of course where positivist and relativist theories leave the matter. For an example, see Isaiah Berlin, "Equality as an Ideal," in Frederick A. Olafson, ed., *Justice and Social Policy: A Collection of Essays* (Englewood Cliffs, New Jersey: Prentice-Hall, 1961) pp. 128-50.
7. It is important to note that the proposition that "justice is the first virtue of social institutions. . . . " is more in the nature of an assertion than of a rationally justified claim. Rawls does offer a number of strong considerations for the proposition, but they in no way add up to a "proof." Others have brought forward equally strong considerations in favor of say, stability, or the protection and encouragement of religion, or the development of an esthetic, moral, or military elite as the first virtue of social institutions. Rawls lumps all such efforts together as "perfectionist" theories, and tries to show that men in the original position would not choose them. Other writers on

Rawls have dealt with these and related problems. I mention them only to show that it is possible to disagree with Rawls at the most fundamental level.

8. Most public programs designed to help the unemployed and unskilled gain employable skills show this very inefficient ratio between cost and benefit.

9. To see what I mean here, examine Rawls' discussion of the institutions required to implement the theory of justice (esp. pp. 195-201). The approach is that of the gadgeteer. For a political understanding of how justice is to be achieved, see, e.g., William Hinton, *Fanshen: A Documentary of Revolution in a Chinese Village* (New York, N.Y.: Random House, 1966).

10. Perhaps Keynes' argument is shoddy when judged by the theoretical requirements of justice as fairness, but there is much to be said for it in a rough-and-ready way. The great economic improvements in the condition of the poorer classes during the nineteenth and twentieth centuries were in fact made possible by the cornucopia of goods produced by the technological revolution and the capitalist spirit of enterprise. These forces, and not any theory of justice, have been the mainsprings of improvement in the conditions of the poor. Similarly, it is easier to mount social welfare programs in times of great economic growth than in times of recession. Compare the enormous expansion of redistributive programs in the United States between 1960-65 and today.

11. Of course, The Aristotelian Principle (for definition, see 426) itself contains or provides a standard of judgment among ways of life. And I am not sure Rawls is right in saying that the application of this Principle "is always relative to the individual. . ." (441). That is certainly not so in Aristotle himself, who argued that one way of life was superior to all others, that the persons who followed this way were superior to others, and that societies which encouraged and rewarded the superior way were superior to those which did not. This raises questions which are central to Rawls' whole theory, but not central to the portion of it which most concerns me. Hence I pursue those questions no farther.

12. In many ways, the finest criticism still remains that of Michael D. Young's fiction *The Rise of the Meritocracy, 1870-2033: The New Elite of Our Social Revolution* (London: Thames and Hudson, 1958).

13. It also confuses thought to identify completely the actual persons and institutions who hold power and authority in the United States with the meritocratic ideal—presenting the actual situation as though it embodied the ideal. This confusion is often made by anxious academic persons who leap to defend their esteemed institutions and privileged positions against the invasion of imagined hordes of the unqualified marching under such banners as "affirmative action" or "equal opportunity." I once overheard a conversation between the Chairman of the Political Science Department of a major university and a black publicist and politician which went to the heart of the matter. The politician observed that he saw very, very few blacks among the faculty. The Chairman earnestly responded that if only qualified minority persons could be found, his Department would jump to hire them. The politician replied, in effect: "No, no, you don't get my point. I know a lot about this campus, and I know there are plenty of dumb white sons-of-bitches on the faculty. What I *don't* see here are dumb black sons-of-bitches."

... And The Pursuit of Happiness

> "Our object, like that of all sentient beings, is happiness."
> Constitution of the New Harmony
> Community of Equality, 1825

> "I fear we are not born to be happy."
> Nietzsche

I

New Harmony, unhappily, lasted but two years; and that may be all there is to say finally about happiness. Perhaps the last word on every fundamental human subject is a platitude, something everybody knew all along. Even so, that is no argument against discussing the basic matters, but only against pushing the discussion too far. There may be useful things to say right up to the final point.

The premise that superficiality is wisdom may seem unpromising, but the realities of the case demand it. Happiness is a peculiarly difficult subject to frame and to analyze. Certainly I am not qualified to discuss it by virtue of deep personal knowledge. Lack of personal experience, however, never stopped an academic man from writing. He consults other writers, more learned than himself, and grows professionally wise on his reading. So I searched the authorities, hoping to find an end to my own ignorance. A little reading produced two disappointing conclusions.

When writers turn to the subject of happiness, their tone becomes grave, even mournful. It seems that happy men do not write about happiness; or, at least, writing about happiness makes men sad. Happiness, as Archbishop Whately said, is no laughing matter.

As if that were not puzzling enough, the search also uncovered a great variety of conceptions of happiness, no one of which has ever held indisputable sovereignty over the rest. Webster's big dictionary defines the term as "a state of well-being characterized by relative permanence, by dominantly agreeable emotion ranging in value from mere content to positive felicity, and by natural desire for its continuation." One's first response to such a string of serious words on such a common topic is the suspicion that their author was unsure of himself. That suspicion grows with reflection, for the phrase "relative permanence" reminds one that the root of the word happy is hap, which also lies at the root of happening and happenstance, and branches into accident, fortune, and fate. Happiness originates in a thing of the moment and reaches to the lot that befalls one in life—a sardonic etymology, suggesting that our happiness owes less to our deliberate efforts than to accident and fortune.

That reflection gains strength from another feature of the case. Happiness as a goal of action is unlike the other goals that men pursue in one important way. Ordinarily, if you want to reach a goal you must take steps deliberately directed toward it. If you want to become an eminent scholar or an excellent billiard player, you will have to give many years to your books or your billiards. Happiness is different. It is a target which can be hit only by aiming at something else. The thought must have struck Hawthorne, who likened happiness to a butterfly, which flits away when chased, but which may come and light on your hand if you will only sit quietly, occupied with something else. Enough Webster.

A ponderous encyclopedia of law defines happiness as "that enjoyment of life which attends upon, and is almost identical with, welfare." That definition is a triumph of professional ignorance over nature, for daily observation teaches that welfare and happiness are often not synonymous. Your child is not made happy when you deny him that extra cookie for his own good. Men still usually prefer the moment's happiness to the long future's welfare, despite four hundred years of Protestantism and two hundred years of Utilitarianism, despite even old age.

Moving from the law to the poets and the sages, one meets only variety. Aristotle thought the happiest life to be the life of study and contemplative activity, a view similar to that of Augustine, who held that of all the goods, only wisdom and knowledge of God could make a man happy. But when the great scholar Max Weber was asked why he studied and thought so much, he replied that he wanted to see how much he could bear—not the words of a happy man. Leaving the few aside, perhaps John Adams was right when he said that the happiness of the common man consists first in his dinner and then in his girl. Hume thought it impossible to establish qualitative distinctions among kinds of happiness—as did Bentham, with his notorious "pushpin is as good as poetry"—and held that all who are happy are equally happy, regardless of the ground or content of their happiness. Boswell reports that when this argument was mentioned to Johnson, that gentleman gravely made a distinction: "Sir, that all who are happy are equally happy is not true. A peasant and a philosopher may be equally *satisfied* but not equally happy." For centuries the philosophers agreed that happiness is the highest good, though they disagreed about what constitutes happiness. Kant ended the agreement even on the formal proposition when he argued that "nothing can possibly be conceived in the world, or even out of it, which can be called good without qualification, except a Good Will." In effect, Kant argued that being worthy of happiness is higher than happiness.

Many men have supposed that we are made for happiness, or that the search for happiness is the prime force of human action, but others have doubted this. Some have believed that our greatest happiness lies in giving happiness to others, but Shakespeare knew "how bitter a thing it is to look into happiness through another man's eyes." La Rochefoucauld made the same thought sting when he said you can always endure the unhappiness of your friends. Some have thought that happiness consists in the possession of a solid estate, while as many others have said that it is granted only to those who have no anchors in the things of this world. Power, virtue, love, solitude, friendship, the pleasures of the senses—each has been recommended by some, and rejected by others, as constituting true happiness.

I mention these endless and irritable arguments among the authorities in order to make a few basic points. First of all, it is clear that logic and learning are impotent in this matter, incapable of adjudicating among the many claimants. Furthermore, this babel teaches that there are as many conceptions of happiness as there are powerful human desires. Finally, one ought to have sense enough not to presume that he can unsnarl the tangle by advancing his own conception as correct and definitive. Dr. Johnson's pronouncement was the wisest ever made on the meaning of happiness: if you look up the word in his *Dictionary* you will find it defined as felicity; look up felicity and you will find it defined as happiness. So I shall not field a personal conception of happiness and advance it against all opponents. Rather, I shall discuss some of the notions and theories of happiness proposed by some influential American writers. My intention is modest: to make clear what a dazzling and motley thing the "right to pursue happiness" is.

II

It is proper to begin with Jefferson, for it was he who taught us that the pursuit of happiness was our birthright. But it is helpful to remember that the notion was not original with him. Jefferson himself said, in reply to a rather ungracious charge by John Adams, that when he composed the "Declaration" he aimed not for originality but for vigorous expression of the common opinion. As applied to the term that matters here, Jefferson's appraisal is accurate. The notion that men had a right to pursue happiness was well on its way toward becoming a major premise of libertarian political argument by the middle of the eighteenth century. By the Republican period, the idea had become a rallying cry for the most varied political groups. Indeed, a phrase very like Jefferson's was used by George Mason in the Virginia Declaration of Rights of May, 1776. Mason there wrote that men had certain inherent, natural rights, "among which are the enjoyment of life and liberty, . . . and pursuing and obtaining happiness and safety." Furthermore, Jefferson's affirmation that the people had the right to lay the foundations of government on such principles "as to them shall seem most likely to effect their Safety and Happiness" was much older in America than either his or Mason's expression of happiness as a natural right. In his *Vindication of the Government of New-England Churches,* written in 1717, John Wise held that the main business of the state is to attend to "the happiness of the people." James Otis, in his *Rights of the British Colonies,* of 1764, said that the end of government is to "provide for the happy enjoyment of life, liberty, and property," and ten years later, in his treatise on *The Legislative Authority of the British Parliament,* James Wilson argued that the whole purpose of the political compact was "to ensure and to increase the happiness of the governed. . . . The consequence is, that the happiness of the society is the *first* law of every government." In the same year, Josiah Quincy, Jr., stated that the purpose of government was to advance "the greatest happiness of the greatest number." So these ideas were in the air, and Jefferson was in fact voicing the common view of the matter. Whatever happiness itself might be, men in America had the right to pursue it.

The question that matters, then, is, in what does happiness consist? In early America, four main answers were given to this question. I shall first briefly state these answers, and then offer some fuller comments on two of the more interesting writers on the subject.

1. The notion of happiness, strictly speaking, does not enter Puritan writing to any extent until early in the eighteenth century. John Cotton employs the word in his discourse on "Christian Calling," and it appears in the title, though not in the text, of a sermon delivered by William Hubbard in 1676. Even though the word was not used, however, the things for which it stood were sought. There were two such things, and the progress by which the one came to crowd out the other epitomizes the course by which Massachusetts-Israel became Massachusetts-U.S.A.

The first is suggested in John Smith's *Description of New England*, a pamphlet written in 1616 to encourage settlers to come to the New World. Smith straightforwardly appealed to material motives, to the promise of prosperity.

> Who can desire more content, that hath small meanes; or but only his merit to advance his fortune, than to tread and plant that ground hee hath purchased by the hazard of his life?
>
> For I am not so simple to thinke, that ever any other motive than wealth will ever errect there a commonweale, or draw companie from their ease and humours at home to stay in *New England* to effect my purposes.

The other was expounded in John Winthrop's masterly address on "Christian Charity," delivered while the colonists were still on board ship. His elevated sentiments express a different conception of the purpose of the settlement, and open New England's dialogue between piety and prosperity.

> The end is to improve our lives to do more service to the Lord, the comfort and increase of the body of Christ whereof we are members, that ourselves and posterity may be the better preserved from the common corruptions of this evil world, to serve the Lord and work out our salvation under the power and purity of His holy ordinances.

Winthrop's view was the official one. The felicity of a Christian consisted partly in doing good works in this world, though still moving through daily life as a pilgrim, living amidst the comforts and pleasures of the world with "weaned affection," as John Cotton put it, and partly in enjoying the "happy state of reconciliation to God." In doctrine, at least, happiness had nothing to do with the pleasures of prosperity. It was an austere sort of happiness, the sort found through righteous service and obedience here, and through concentration on the hoped-for bliss to follow hereafter.

H.L. Mencken's caustic remark, that Puritanism was the gnawing worry that someone somewhere might be happy, was about as right and as wrong as such deft comments usually are. The early years were a time of severe trials in which the very life of the Puritans was under peril. The pursuit of happiness is irrelevant when the pursuit of mere life is the pressing business. Very soon, however, perhaps around the third quarter of the seventeenth century, life itself became secure, and there was energy to spare for other things. The Puritans then did not respond simply with the fear that the pursuit of happiness would corrupt their kingdom. They sanctioned the pursuit, provided that the goals sought were of a certain kind: the happiness of grace, and the happiness of humble and righteous service to others in one's daily occupation.

But the two ends soon became confused, and then the second consumed the first. The Puritans could never quite disabuse themselves of the notion that godliness, which was to be pursued for its own sake as the only true good, brought prosperity to all it touched. It was easy, given the full theory of general and special providences, to slide from the notion that prosperity is a sign of divine favor to the notion that prosperity itself should be pursued as part of a godly way of life. With that easy step, the fall from gratitude for grace received to self-congratulation for virtue achieved was inevitable. By the time of Cotton Mather the cycle was complete. In one sentence he admonishes the faithful to serve loyally to do good for the pure sake of good, even to "monsters of ingratitude," while in the very next sentence he gleefully assures do-gooders that they shall receive "bountiful and seasonable recompences." The seed was there from the beginning, planted by Calvin, who had written that "riches should be the portion of the godly rather than the wicked, for godliness hath the promise in this life as well as the life to come."

At any rate, the fall from Puritanism to Yankeeism was rapid and complete. The Puritan stood erect, his backbone stiffened by virtue and piety, head high and eyes fixed on heaven, only so long as his feet were planted in the thin and grudging earth. When the wilderness was transformed into firm and comfortable estates, the spine softened, and vision lowered from the higher realm to this one, with the necessary result that he could no longer enjoy the goodness of either without guilt. The real difficulty was there from the beginning in that too-sharp contrast between eternal felicity or horror on the one side and worldly joy or gain on the other. To choose either exclusively is to lose the best of both. A noble culture and religion must find a view of life profound enough to understand both the joys and the burdens which attend a regard for our responsibilities, and to achieve a repose in the face of both joy and sorrow. That repose is simultaneously less and more than what most men have meant by happiness.

2. The second answer given to the question of happiness in early America was a straightforward materialism, often phrased in a Lockean vocabulary. In this view, happiness consists in the satisfaction of material desires, especially the security of substantial property and a comfortable station in society. A great number of solid Americans expressed this view, and a few must speak for the rest.

John Dickinson, in his *Letters from a Farmer in Pennsylvania,* 1767, forged a chain out of happiness, freedom, and property, with property as the anchor, and used the chain thus made to bind the British Parliament. "Let these truths be indelibly impressed on our minds—that we cannot be Happy without being Free—that we cannot be free without being secure in our property—that we cannot be secure in our property, if, without our consent, others . . . may take it away—that taxes imposed on us by Parliament, thus do take it away." Noah Webster's *Examination into the Leading Principles of the Federal Constitution,* 1778, announced the fundamental Whig proposition that happiness for the individual lay in property securely held, and that happiness for society lay in property widely distributed.

> Virtue, patriotism, or love of country, never was and never will be . . . a fixed, permanent principle and support of government. But . . . a general possession of land in fee simple . . . is the very *soul* of a *republic.* While this continues, the people will inevitably possess both *power* and *freedom;* when this is lost, power departs, liberty expires, and a commonwealth will inevitably assume some other form.

Chancellor Kent, speaking in the New York Constitutional Convention of 1821, provides the last example. Throughout that memorable debate, Kent spoke in defense of sound Whig principles. He saw abundance already all about him, and he held that those who did not yet enjoy it need only work for it. Instead, the rabble seemed bent on improving their own lot by action aimed not at advancing themselves through honest industry, but at plundering their betters. The results could only be disastrous all around, for it was evident to Kent that American prosperity was the mark of divine favor, and sufficient for the achievement of happiness.

> Discontent in the midst of so much prosperity, and with such abundant means of happiness, looks like ingratitude, and as if we were disposed to arraign the goodness of Providence. Do we not expose ourselves to the danger of being deprived of the blessings we have enjoyed? When the husbandman . . . has filled his barns and his graneries . . . if he should then become discontented and unthankful, would he not have reason to apprehend that the Lord of the harvest might come in his wrath, and with his lightning destroy them?

The idea that property is the foundation and means of happiness is a very old one, and it gained new impetus from many English and American publicists of the seventeenth and eighteenth centuries. In the thought of Locke, for example, one's property was regarded as the objectification or extension of one's personality, so that the condition of the latter could be appraised by examination of the former. In time, the possession of a decent competence came to be regarded by the middle classes as the very substance of goodness and happiness. The property had to be solid and tangible, something one could set foot upon and survey with proprietary eye. It is an idea still widely held in our own day, but with a shift of accent that makes all the difference. In the earlier periods, no writer stressed the joys of property as the means of pleasant consumption. The emphasis was always on possession. Today material goods are seen as the means to happiness only if the goods can be used up. Happiness lies not in acquisition but in consumption.

3. An answer which had some advocates in early America was that happiness consists in the fulfillment of man's communal and fraternal needs. This was perhaps the happiness that Tom Paine had in mind. It was surely what was meant by Paine's friend Joel Barlow, and by Walt Whitman, who often wrote as though the whole American destiny lay in "amativeness," and for whom democracy was a synonym for "adhesive love." But the strongest and most lyrical affirmation of the fraternal conception of happiness came from Thoreau, whose essay on friendship in "A Week on the Concord and Merrimack Rivers," is the noblest ever written by an American, and among the noblest written by any man.

This view of happiness was very much in the minority; as Thoreau put it, "You may tread the town, you may wander the country, and none shall ever speak of it. . . ." Most Americans were convinced that happiness was prosperity, and for this what was needed was individual enterprise, not friendship: getting ahead required leaving others behind. Tocqueville detected a strange melancholy and sense of loss pervading American life despite its energy and comfort, and surely the missing element was the element identified by Thoreau. Tocqueville thought the root lay in the inherent tendency of democracy to set each man apart from his fellows, causing him to forget both ancestors and successors, and leading him to believe that he alone was responsible for his destiny.

Driven out of American life by the pursuit of prosperity, and purged from political discourse by the language of contract and natural rights, the conception of friendship as the substance of a happy life found a fugitive haven in the classic literature of the nineteenth century. Innocently loving male pairs occupy the ethical and thematic centers of our greatest early novels: the chaste affection of Natty Bumppo and Chingachgook; the "cosy, loving pairs" of Ishmael and Queequeg; the dream journey of Huck and Nigger Jim; Dana's discovery of the comradeship of sailors. These pairs must always meet and move in nature, the forest and the river, for they sense that society would misinterpret and corrupt their natural union. It is as though the novelists had reached by a different route the liberal conclusion that interest and antagonism, not affection and harmony, are the motive forces behind society and state. Friendship has no need for institutions, builds none, and is jeopardized by those that others build.

One member of each pair is white, the other dark. This is an oblique way of saying that these unions are natural in another meaning of the term, that is, illegitimate. Banished from society, fraternity can survive only in the shaded regions, and among the children of those regions. The American sense of loneliness in the midst of crowds and hunger in the midst of abundance reaches mythical expression in the fraternal pairs of these great books. Driven out of our conscious lives, the conception of happiness as the fulfillment of the fraternal sentiment haunts us ever more insistently in the dreamwork of our literature.

4. The last main answer to the question was that which equated happiness with the living of a socially virtuous and useful life. This was probably the dominant view among the men of the founding. The author of the "Declaration" thought along these lines, and so did Benjamin Franklin—in his later years. Since those men and that moment hold authority in American political life, the views of Franklin and Jefferson merit careful attention.

III

The young Franklin, he who was to become the characteristic American, gave an answer to the question of happiness which was so radically un-American that both he and America agreed to forget it. The answer was presented in what Franklin called "a little metaphysical piece" entitled *A Dissertation on Liberty and Necessity, Pleasure and Pain,* published in 1725 when he was nineteen. The piece was provoked by Franklin's reading of Wollaston's *Religion of Nature.* Franklin thought some of Wollaston's reasonings were murky, and in the *Dissertation,* he set out to shed a truer light on the subject.

Section II of the essay opens with the proposition that to suffer is to live. Creatures do nothing until they are excited by some uneasiness or pain: men do not pursue happiness; they flee pain. "We are first mov'd by *Pain,* and the whole succeeding Course of our Lives is but one continu'd Series of Actions with a View to be freed from it."

Pain produces a desire for relief, and this desire will be exactly as strong as the pain which produced it. The satisfaction of this desire is what men call happiness, or pleasure, and no happiness can be greater than the pain which gave rise to the desire to escape. "*Pleasure* is wholly caus'd by *Pain,*" and "the Sensation of Pleasure is equal, or in exact proportion to the Sensation of Pain."

These axioms established, Franklin's argument marches toward its conclusion with geometrical rigor. Every living creature has as much pain in its life as it has pleasure, and "no Condition of Life or Being is in itself better or preferable to another: The Monarch is not more happy than the Slave, nor the *Beggar* more miserable than *Croesus*." Since "the *highest Pleasure* is only Consciousness of Freedom from the deepest *Pain*," all attempts to show that some kinds of pleasure are qualitatively superior to others are idle. Furthermore, just as no given condition or station of life is preferable to any other, life itself is not preferable to death. Pleasure and pain cancel out, so that if some living being has enjoyed during its life ten units of pleasure, it must also have suffered ten units of pain. The overall result is zero, which is exactly what it would have been had the creature never lived at all. Finally, Franklin concludes, since pleasure and pain are equal and inseparable, "*No state of Life can be happier than the present* . . . ." So much for the prospects of progress in this world, and for the joys of paradise in the next.

It is hard to know what construction to put on this "little metaphysical piece." Read seriously and straightforwardly, it emerges as a mocking repudiation of the American dream almost at the moment of its conception. But that may be too heavy; perhaps it is enough to see Ben's prank as just another young man's slaying of his Sunday school teacher. Franklin himself thought of the essay as a youthful "erratum" in a generally sound and upstanding life. At first he considered it quite a clever piece, but as time went on he began to suspect that although the argument might be true the conclusions were not useful. Later still he began to suspect that it might not even be true. Discussing the essay in his *Autobiography*, he "doubted whether some error had not insinuated itself unperceived into my argument so as to infect all that followed, as is common with metaphysical reasonings." Prudence dictated retreat: "There were only a hundred copies printed, of which I gave a few to friends, and afterwards disliking the piece, as conceiving it might have an ill tendency, I burnt the rest, except one copy. . . ." It is worth adding that Franklin does not specify the insidious error.

We do not really know if Franklin still held in 1776 the views he had declared in 1725. Prudence censored them from his expression, but vanity and reason may have kept for them a place in his private mind. If he did retain any part of them, he must have enjoyed a deliciously subversive chuckle when he read his friend Jefferson's "Declaration," for if "no state of life can be happier than the present," what could be more futile than a revolution fought for the right to pursue happiness? There is a work for Sisyphus.

As if this political heresy were not enough, Franklin moved on to strike at the utilitarian theory of the relations between virtue and happiness. He summarized the argument of the first part of the *Dissertation* in the statement that "nothing could possibly be wrong in the world and that vice and virtue were empty distinctions, no such things existing. . . ." This implies that anything called virtuous action, resting as it does on "empty distinctions," cannot be justified or supported on the ground that it produces happiness, because happiness is produced specifically by the successful flight from pain.

This is a keen comment, one that goes to the heart of the American inability to escape utility—the belief that virtuous action is useful action and that the virtuous man is the happy man. Yet Franklin respected it so little, or feared it so much, that he burned it. If we ask why he did that, the answer is, perhaps, that he simply could not take his subversive idea in any hopeful direction. So, he first strode resolutely up to the edge, looked over, and then drew back. To see where he retreated after his view over the edge, one need only read the section of his *Autobiography* where he describes his earlier intention to publish a small book on "The Art of Virtue."

> In this piece it was my design to explain and enforce this doctrine: That vicious actions are not hurtful because they are forbidden, but forbidden because they are hurtful . . .; that it was therefore everyone's interest to be virtuous who wished to be happy even in this world.

In the manuscript of the *Autobiography* there appears at this point a marginal note which perfectly summarizes Franklin's chastened vision after the view over the edge: "Nothing so likely to make a man's fortune as virtue."

IV

Thomas Jefferson called himself an Epicurean, and that seems to me an accurate self-appraisal. Most of his many scattered comments on the nature of happiness and virtue, and on the relation between the two, do have an Epicurean ring.

In his "Syllabus of the Doctrines of Epicurus," Jefferson summarized his theory in one definition and three short propositions: Happiness is the aim of life; Virtue is the foundation of happiness; Utility is the test of virtue. He defined happiness as "to be not pained in body, nor troubled in mind, i.e., In-do-lence of body, tranquility of mind." Virtue consisted in prudence, temperance, fortitude, and justice. Utility meant for Jefferson what it means commonly: that which is useful or beneficial to oneself or others.

What is considered useful varies from society to society. In summary, as he wrote to John Adams in October of 1816, if an act "effect[s] the happiness of him to whom it is directed, it is virtuous. . . . The essence of virtue is in doing good to others, while what is good may be one thing in one society, and its contrary in another."

There, briefly, is the theory, and it immediately raises a question. What is the connection between this theory of happiness and political action? For Epicurus, happiness was found in the garden, not in the assembly. It required withdrawal from politics. (Montesquieu thought that Epicurean doctrines had contributed much toward the corruption of Roman political virtue.) For Jefferson, too, happiness was to be found at Monticello, not Washington. The pursuit of happiness in this Epicurean sense, then, is obviously not even a political pursuit, let alone a revolutionary one. Yet Jefferson used the phrase in a political and revolutionary document. There seems to be an incompatibility between the action and the theory.

The problem can be solved in a certain way. For Epicurus in particular, and for Epicureans as a type, withdrawal from political life was necessary for the achievement of happiness. But for Jefferson that withdrawal was not possible: there were just too many political problems and possibilities. Hence, the pursuit of happiness had to be postponed until the political world was set aright. Jefferson nowhere indicates that happiness is to be sought or found in political action. The whole thrust of his thought leads, to the conclusion not that men pursue happiness in the political realm, but that political action is unfortunately necessary from time to time in order to arrange the public affairs so that it will be possible for individuals to pursue happiness in the private realm. It is possible to justify political involvement in Epicurean terms, as Jefferson did, but only at the expense of making public life entirely secondary and instrumental to private life.

If this is accepted as a solution to the political problem raised by Jefferson's theory of happiness, then the way is cleared for an approach to a different order of problems. What are the prospects of success in the quest? Granted the right to pursue private happiness, what hope have we of overtaking it? Is nature so constituted that the pursuit can succeed, or is there something in the constitution of things that dooms the quest to failure? Jefferson apparently feared that there were two such factors, one in the general constitution of nature, the other specifically in human nature.

The factor in nature is pain, or grief. In effect, Jefferson was faced here with his own form of the problem of theodicy. Although he wanted to see nature as perfect in every part, and a model for all human actions, he had to confess that he detected a flaw in nature's beneficent design. In wondering about this, Jefferson risked blasphemy against the only god that really mattered to him. How deeply this troubled him can be measured in a passage from a letter to Adams of April 8, 1816:

> My temperament is sanguine. I steer my bark with Hope in the head. My hopes, indeed, sometimes fail . . . There are, . . . even in the happiest life, some terrible convulsions, heavy set-offs against the opposite page of the account. I have often wondered for what good end the sensations of grief could be intended. All our other passions, with proper bounds, have a useful object . . . I wish the pathologists then would tell us what is the use of grief in the economy, and of what good it is the cause, proximate or remote.

The element in human nature which stood as an obstacle—perhaps an immovable one—to the achievement of happiness is self-love, or selfishness. As he wrote to Thomas Law in June of 1814, Jefferson wished it could be abolished:

> To ourselves . . . we can owe no duties, obligation requiring . . . two parties. Self-love, therefore, is no part of morality. Indeed it is exactly its counterpart. It is the sole antagonist of virtue, leading us constantly by our propensities to self-gratification in violation of our moral duties to others . . . Take from man his selfish propensities, and he can have nothing to seduce him from the practice of virtue. Or subdue those propensities by education, instruction or restraint, and virtue remains without a competitor.

In one sense Jefferson should not have wondered about the "use of grief in the economy," for in his own thought it was only through the opposition of pleasure and pain, or grief, that one could distinguish what was virtuous from what was vicious. Yet in another sense he had a very real problem. Having defined happiness as "not to be pained in body nor troubled in mind," he obviously had to be concerned about the value of pain and suffering. One way to solve this problem is to hold that pain is a necessary condition for the very possibility of leading a virtuous life. One could argue that it is our egoism, our propensity to self-gratification even at the expense of giving pain to others, which makes the struggle toward virtue or nobility meaningful. If the noble or virtuous life is easy, then it is lacking in that very thing which makes it noble, namely the effort to rise above self-gratification and impose a law on the self in obedience to a higher imperative.

But Jefferson did not follow this path. He believed, on the contrary, that life could be virtuous without pain and without the existence of selfishness, temptation, and shortage. As he put it, virtue can exist "without a competitor." Indeed, it would be best if all its competitors were simply eradicated from the human heart.

The conclusion of the matter, it seems to me, is that the Jeffersonian pursuit of happiness guided men in an endless circle: to be happy, be virtuous; to be virtuous, be useful; to be useful, make men happy; to make men happy, be virtuous; and around again and again. Furthermore, the whole process seems thoroughly subjective—each rolling around his own circle—until we remember the final element of the theory, the element that specifies utility as the test of virtue. If we ask who is to judge whether happiness (virtue) is happiness, the answer is, the others around you. What they regard as useful is what you shall regard as virtuous, as that which produces happiness.

Jefferson in effect first assimilated private to social virtue, and then reduced both to utility. Virtue in this usage is mainly negative and conservative. It means remaining innocent, not paining oneself or others. It also means that one should do what others deem useful. Bringers of new values thus become immoralists, in Nietzsche's sense; and Jefferson's doctrine logically condemns both Jesus and Socrates. The reward of happiness naturally follows such "virtuous" behavior because that behavior is shaped precisely to please others, the givers of all rewards.

With this, the theory completes its circle. When actions must be deemed useful in the eyes of others before they can be deemed virtuous in one's own eyes, then there is laid the ethical foundation for what Tocqueville called the tyranny of the majority, and the psychological foundation for what Riesman has called the other-directed personality. The theory escapes both subjectivism and the confrontation with pain—with the possibility that individual virtue may not bring happiness—but it does so only through a total flight to society. The pursuit of happiness, a phrase which Jefferson used to justify a revolution for freedom, and by which he sought to license the individual for a private quest, turns out to be a race which one can enter only by giving up private judgment and individual freedom.

It is but a step from this to the bleak paradox of our own day. Today we tell ourselves, in an endless stream of books and essays and addresses, that true happiness consists in self-expression. And yet, when one tries to realize this happiness, he discovers, to his despair, either that he has no self to express, or, to his embarassment, that he seems to express himself about the same way everyone else does. I have tried to suggest that the seed of this sad discovery was already there in Jefferson's theory. The seed is the enduring American inability to escape utility as the test of virtue and the insistence that virtue must have a social reward.

V

Very little of this seems relevant today. We have come far from the Puritan conception of happiness as piety or the Jeffersonian conception of happiness as virtue. Even Franklin's notion that happiness consists in doing useful things for others—with the understanding that such action will also bring prosperity to oneself—is not widely shared today. The Whiggish theory of happiness as possession of property has undergone a shift of emphasis toward consumption which amounts to a virtual recasting of the original idea. Even the notion of happiness as a fulfillment of fraternal affections has been recast into something like social acceptance. We have produced a three-sided conception of happiness of our own, with little help from history or philosophy.

1. Happiness consists in bountiful consumption. It is impossible to document this idea with precision because we are dealing here, not with a specific concept or theory, but with an atmospheric condition. The mass media daily bombard and entice us with jazzy visions of the delights of consumption: the Bower of Bliss plus the hygienic conveniences of technology. One has to assume that these visions, to a significant extent, describe our folkways and articulate our dreamways. If you could open the head of the typical American and dump his thought patterns out on a table for examination, what you would see there would be, not deep grooves cut by religion, ritual, and custom, through which all the forces of life flow, but snatches of advertising jingles and a network of S-R arcs leaping from forces in the Id to objects in the world of consumption. We perhaps forget how telling an indicator of our outlook is provided by the fact that we accept a statistic called the Gross National Product as the main official measure of the public well-being. No politician today would dare suggest that the nation is swollen with luxury, even though a long and powerful tradition teaches that luxury is the death of republics.

2. Happiness consists in having fun. Happiness is thrill and novelty, romance, speed, and games. And it is all very expensive and very energetic. We have made happiness hum.

And yet, if you watch the members of the lonely crowd busy having fun, you will see a curious thing. The bright laugh darkens suddenly to doubt and puzzlement, even sadness, as though the person was not sure he was enjoying himself. There are certain features of the situation which might well produce doubt.

The fun culture is highly commercialized and lacking in spontaneity, powered by an engine outside the person rather than within. The fun morality is very vulnerable to peer group judgment, not self-directed and sure of itself, but needing confirmation in the noisy approval of others. It has none of the attributes of the serious play of children. At its margin, it shades off into the search for oblivion, whether in alcohol, sex, gadgets, or drugs. All this suggests that much of our fun activity is undertaken not in and for itself, but as a means to other purposes.

Perhaps one of those purposes is the achievement of status and social approval. In large and growing sectors of our society—not alone in youth culture—a person who does not have much fun is looked upon as some sort of unfortunate fellow, a little disagreeable, and not a very desirable "friend." On the other hand, a person who has lots of fun therby raises both his own prestige and the prestige of those around him. He has a high "Happiness Quotient," which a contemporary psychologist of some notoriety is able to measure on a useful instrument of his own devising called a Euphorimeter. It is advantageous to know such a person because the acquaintance enhances your social standing. Besides, with any luck at all, some of his happiness will rub off on you.

There might be still another purpose, drearier than the first. Perhaps a large part of our feverish pursuit of fun has as its real function the filling of the empty hours which technology has brought to millions of people who lack both the inherited culture and the personal resources to know what to do with their time. We seek fun in order to kill time—as though we were not thereby killing eternity too. Ours in an age which, although it has achieved great physical successes, has lost psychological and moral meaning for the individual. People are adrift, their customs hollowed, their religions desiccated, their futures threatened by the very technological powers that once promised happiness. In such a time, we must keep frantically busy in order to fill the emptiness, and having fun is increasingly the recommended way of keeping busy.

The fun theory of happiness nearly excludes the very dimensions of life which make genuine delight and joy possible: activity which is undertaken not for self-gratification, but out of disinterested care and appreciation for the activity itself; admiration for esthetic elaboration of impulse, which requires discipline and knowledge; belief in the reality of intangible and unmeasurable values. For these the fun theory substitutes the criteria of display, motion, and instant reward.

3. Happiness as self-actualization or self-realization. On one level, this conception is mainly ludicrous, and a trifle pathetic. On another level, it appears as the most important contemporary theory of the good life.

We are flooded with books and articles telling us that happiness consists in being liked by others so that they can be manipulated to one's own ends. There is an equally large how-to-do-it literature telling how one can, at home, in just a few minutes a day, overcome shyness, guilt, and pessimism, thereby retooling his personality from a negative, drab, unpopular model, into a positive, bouncy, popular model. In this view, happiness is an internal state, a psychological condition. Still, we are assured that the psychological bounce resulting from faithful performance of the happiness exercises will provide the energy needed for success in the external world. Adler, slightly vulgarized, has replaced Franklin, greatly vulgarized, as the true prophet of happiness.

On another level, the conception of happiness as self-realization or self-actualization has more intellectual merit. It is, in fact, the chief contribution of our time to the perennial discussion.

The new conception is mainly the contribution of psychologists: Kurt Goldstein, Erich Fromm, Carl Rogers, Gordon Allport, and Abraham Maslow are among the more important. There are of course differences among these writers concerning both the nature of the forces or potentials in the self that are to be actualized, and the process by which these potentials become actualized, but all of them agree on the main point, which, in Maslow's phrasing, is "the necessity for the postulation of some sort of positive growth or self-actualization tendency within the organism, which is different from its conserving, equilibrating, or homeostatic tendency, as well as from the tendency to respond to impulses from the outside world" (*Motivation and Personality*, p. 341). In this view, then, there is a natural tendency, an entelechy, for the organism to become whole, for one to become oneself. And to become oneself is to be happy, for happiness is the feeling-tone which accompanies self-actualization. It is a by-product of successful self-realization. "Happiness is an achievement brought about by man's inner productiveness . . . the accompaniment of all productive activity, in thought, feeling, and action" (Fromm, *Man for Himself*, p. 189).

There is much to be said about this theory, but space permits only a few comments.

John Dewey has persuasively argued that the notion that men aim at self-actualization or happiness rests on a confusion between ends-in-view and standards of judgment. Our aims or ends are objects of desire, and are always concrete and specific: the love of this woman, the defeat of that rival. Desires are specific, but self-actualization as an object of desire is so vague as to offer the actor no counsel. Not all desires, however, are approved, whether by the individual's own moral sense, or by the moral sentiments of the community. Hence, there must be a standard for adjudicating between desires, and the self-actualization-happiness principle offers one such possible standard. Happiness, then, really seems to be not an end men can aim for, but a possible standard by which to judge the worth of the ends they do aim for.

It follows that we must forget self-actualization in order to get it. Furthermore, observation suggests that the man who does aim consciously at self-actualization runs the risk of becoming a psychological athlete, forever flexing his psychological muscles. He easily becomes very self-centered, even priggish in a curious sort of way, and, given the vagueness of the goal, a waffler in the intellectual and moral life.

Even when the concept is taken to be a standard of judgment rather than an end-in-view, it easily leads to an extreme subjectivity of doctrine and expression, if not always of action. For most men, most objects of desire are culturally set. One accepts the group's valuations as one's own, even while pretending that one has chosen. Self-actualization is today operationally translated as "do your own thing"—something that has never happened on a large scale among any populace outside the nursery and Bedlam, where it can be permitted because there is a keeper who holds ultimate power over all the inmates. These new doctrines, then, given the climate of opinion of our day, are peculiarly likely to lead their believers into delusions of autonomy, while delivering real power to the custodians—the Hobbesian sovereign who bases his claim to obedience on the need for order in the best interests of the subjects themselves.

Another aspect of the self-actualization theory stresses, as Lawrence Kubie has written, "freedom and flexibility to learn through experience, to change and to adapt to changing circumstance." This is rapidly becoming one of the leitmotif notions of our day. In a large body of literature, the ability to adapt becomes the measure of health and happiness.

Moden life surely does demand that ability, but what if modern life is mad? The very malleability of human nature can be the ruin of man. We can adapt to almost any circumstances, can become almost anything. But the notion of man, the idea of what it means to be human, is a work of art, a highly artificial and restrictive set of distinctions valuing some things and scorning others. In short, given the malleability of our species, our ability to become almost anything, the question of what is worth becoming remains basic and inescapable. The canon of adaptability, while it might enhance happiness under modern conditions, offers no counsel on that question.

These are the ideas which now have us in their grip, and it is a melancholy thing to see how few resources they leave us when the pursuit of the theory does not achieve the promised reality. Perhaps we have lost sight of, or have lost the courage to confront, the knowledge that it is our lot to be always a beggar at the gates of the kingdom of happiness, and that we are in the greatest danger when we think we have found the key to the gate. Perhaps the counsel of sanity here is that the attainment of limited goals, and the achievement of a temporary and qualified unhappiness, is the highest felicity which men and nations can realize in an indifferent universe. We cannot take the "hap" out of happiness, and much of our present unease may lie in the attempt to do exactly that.

I have only one other suggestion to make, surely an imprudent one, perhaps even an un-American one. It may be that the pursuit of happiness is a goal unworthy of a great nation or a great individual. Certainly the individuals and nations we admire the most have not been the happiest ones. Admirable people have sought nobility, or beauty, or magnanimity, or purity of heart—all treasures of the spirit, and not conditions of the external world. The pursuit of happiness, as defined in America, may be a pursuit peculiarly congenial to the genius of democracy in that it does, in the end, mean the sovereignty of desire. Desires are something we all have, and if we take desire as the norm, there is no way to establish the superiority of any one of them over any of the others. And while this is an orientation congenial to a mass democracy, it is not one which points the way toward excellence.

It may even be that in announcing our goal as happiness we are selling ourselves short, and denying something that runs very deep in human life. The history of so many human ideals, institutions, customs, and beliefs makes sense only on the supposition that we do many of the things we do in order to make our lives, not happy, but worthwhile, demanding, difficult, challenging, even painful. Willingness to sacrifice happiness and pleasure for other things seems at least as basic to human life as does the pursuit of happiness. And if that willingness is the source of much that is terrible and cruel in the human record, it is also the source of nearly everything that is beautiful and noble.

Does that mean we must give up all talk and hope of happiness, manfully consigning it to the trashbin of youthful dreams? Of course not. In *The First Circle*, Solzhenitsyn tells a fable which states the whole matter. Two prisoners are having a conversation about happiness. One of them, a professor, tells how, building on Goethe's line from *Faust* ("Oh, moment, stay! You are so fair!") he had once demolished the notion of happiness:

> "At one of my prewar lectures... on the basis of that quotation from *Faust* I developed the melancholy notion that there is no such thing as happiness, that it is either unattainable or illusory. And then a student handed up a note written on a piece of graph paper torn from a tiny notebook: 'But I am in love—and I am *happy*! How do you answer that?'"
>
> "What did you answer?"
>
> "What can you answer?"

Insiders and Outsiders

In this land where by law and doctrine some 100 million persons are eligible to participate in political life, a scarce sixty percent bother themselves even to the extent of casting a vote regularly in presidential elections. By any of a number of more substantial criteria of participation, such as attending political meetings, giving time or money to political causes, engaging others in political argument, reading books or articles on public affairs, or running for office in party or government, the 40 million who do not vote would be joined by millions more. Taking the 40 million as the working fact, it is clear that our democracy has somehow created a huge minority who are not citizens in Aristotle's sense at all. They are ruled, but they do not rule.

Why worry about the forty? The system works, after all. More than that, it works benignly and efficiently. Compared to the dark chronicles of most polities, America is a shining thing—or, if not shining, at least decent and becoming. Or perhaps the classical Conservative and Liberal position is enough: to incorporate the forty is to admit ignorance and passion into the community. John Adams might have been right when he said that the first desire of the vulgar man is for his dinner-pail and the second is for his girl. Let him have both, of course, but for the sake of us who are cut of finer stuff, silence all talk of bringing him into the system.

Much might be said for these theses, but the American liberal-democrat dare not let himself say it. He cannot accept the consolations of the argument from history for he has rejected history as the guide and standard. As Tocqueville said, the American appeals not to history but to prophecy. Neither can arguments about the brutishness of the mass be comfortably employed. So, the forty percent is a scandal which the liberal-democrat must think about. He has to say that we must think about the forty because we no longer hold the hateful belief that some men are slaves by nature. Or he says that we must think about the forty because they are our shame and our burden: the system has crippled them and made them what they are. Or he says (and this is frequently heard today) that we must think about the forty because in these grave times we must make the fullest utilization of our human resources. The liberal-democrat then, must regard the forty as a "problem" for biological, moral and military reasons.

Set aside the liberal-democratic blinders and just look at the sixty and the forty as players and nonplayers in a game. Take as the first assumption the simple statement that when forty out of 100 eligible players do not play in a game, it might be because they do not like that game. They might not care for the game's prizes or participants, its rhythm or its rules. And perhaps some nonplayers do not care for any social game whatever. As a first step in the exploration of this assumption, start with the obvious assertion that when only sixty of a possible 100 players play the political game, that will greatly affect the nature of the game itself.

One question runs across the whole terrain of American history: who may play the political game? The question was first raised in Winthrop's Massachusetts when those not among the visible saints presumed to assert that that should not disqualify them from full participation in civil affairs, and it is raised still in our own day as public and private agencies compile their dreary accounts of denial of political rights in Mississippi. From 1630 to 1967, from Massachusetts to Mississippi, the question has been asked; and over this whole scene only one answer has really been acceptable—everybody. The history of the American political game is the history of enlarging the number of players. Furthermore, every basic change in the game itself, in its rules and rewards, has been brought about in large part through an expansion of the roster of eligible players. Every large shift of public mood and every great turning point of public policy has been associated with an enlargement of the electorate (Jefferson, Jackson, Lincoln, the enormous implications of Populism, the second Roosevelt). Each of these periods of expansion was followed by a period during which new elements were absorbed (various ethnic groups after the New Deal), or perhaps cast off (Southern Negroes after Reconstruction), and the system sank back into a kind of slumber (Monroe and the era of good feeling, Van Buren and the triumph of a kind of internal Whiggery within the Jacksonian party, Grantism and the triumphant capitalism of the post-Civil War era, the lethargy of Eisenhowerism). The important point is that the energy for each great change has come from groups which had previously been outside the system, and every great changer has understood that his grand strategy of change must be that of enlarging the effective electorate.

That strategy has been pursued so vigorously that now virtually everybody has the right to play. But the forty seem not to want to. They are not even much interested in watching. This suggests that for the foreseeable future we will lack the energy to undertake really large and novel political enterprises, for those who play a game are committed to its rules and eager for its prizes. They do not wish to change things.

All this comes down to one point. Just about all the talk today among political analysts concerning "the tensions that divide the community," the "conflicts between classes and interests," the "issues in the political struggle," is superficial. This talk deals with the divisions between Democrats and Republicans, liberals and conservatives, Northerners and Southerners, farmers and city people, businessmen and workers, and so forth. These distinctions, although real, are superficial, for all of these people play the game. They disagree about who shall get how much, but they all agree on what is worth getting. They are all Insiders.

The fundamental, though blurred, distinction is that between Insiders and Outsiders, the sixty and the forty. And the fundamental, though muted, struggle is not over such questions as, shall labor get higher wages or business higher prices, or shall farmers get higher subsidies, or shall tariffs be reduced? The struggle is over the question, for what shall people be given the right to play politics? For what things shall political energy be used?

My argument clearly assumes that the Outsiders want things which cannot be gained within the political game as it is now constituted. Later I shall suggest what some of those things are.

For the moment, consider another question. Why, in an officially democratic polity, has so little been done to muster the forty? I assume that the "get out and vote" campaigns are not serious, except in the case of the Negroes. The nonvoters just are not stimulated by such appeals. They do not really even "hear" them, and they have slight interest in choosing between the available alternatives. If we were really serious about getting out the vote, we could simplify registration requirements and pass compulsory voting laws. Then the Outsiders would vote. Furthermore, they would probably vote quite "responsibly," if a bit resentfully, simply because they were not brought into the system on their own terms. If compelled to choose, most Outsiders would prefer the Democrats and social welfare over the Republicans and private enterprise. But they would vote for neither with great enthusiasm. The chief objections to this proposal, one might anticipate, would be that the method of compulsory voting runs against the American grain, and that compulsory voting violates the true spirit of democracy, which rests on the principle of voluntary participation.

I see little merit in the argument that compulsory voting violates the spirit of democracy: at least, such democracies as Australia and Belgium have not thought so. There is more weight in the argument that it would run against the American grain, but the rhetoric which would be employed in defending this position would, if penetrated, show some rather different reasons for rejection from those explicitly offered. One of the two main reasons why we shall not pass a compulsory voting law is that the Republicans know that the new voters would vote Democratic. The other is that the Insiders fear that the introduction of the Outsiders would endanger the system because ambitious or unscrupulous politicians, hoping to enhance their own electoral fortunes, would find dangerous ways to appeal to the Outsiders. I think this fear is exaggerated, as suggested above, but there is little doubt that the Insiders do in fact have the fear. That is no surprise, for if there is anything the American liberal-democrat fears it is democracy. What the liberal-democrat really wants in politics is procedural due process and an orientation toward conflict which stresses negotiation, compromise, and balancing—all within a framework of limited, basically material goals. Even the commitment to majority rule is of doubtful sincerity for the liberal-democrat is quite willing to accept decisions taken by a rather small minority of the eligible electorate: Rosseau is impractical and dangerous.

So, the real answer to the question of why so little has been done to involve the forty is that the issue is too hot to be handled, too heavy with fearful potentialities. If the forty entered the game on their own terms they might blow it apart. If they were dragged into it by compulsory voting laws, renegade politicians would find a way to appeal to them (as happened with the new Negro vote during Reconstruction). Insiders do not want these things to happen. They feel, and fear, that a serious attack on the problem of involving the forty requires the development of a political agenda and style which would interest the forty. The forty do not care much for what the sixty are fighting about, and they care even less for the rules and style of the fight itself. They want new issues and cleavages, new programs and goals, new heroes and villains—in short, a new agenda and a new game. He who discovers this agenda and carries it to the forty will rule the nation. So the Insiders fear, and they are right.

The argument might be recast. So far, I have argued that support for large change always come from outside a system, that the Insiders understand this, and that they tell it to themselves in a language that conceals their fear and ennobles their selfishness. Now, it is suggestive that the sixty nearly always attribute the indifference of the forty to ignorance, low economic and social status (SES), irresponsibility, shiftlessness, and the like.[1] What is so telling about this rationale is that it is exactly as old as the argument between Insiders and Outsiders itself. And that argument had already found its frank and explicit answer in the ancient institution of ostracism and the ancient spirit of exclusiveness. For centuries the rationale has been advanced by Insiders to justify the exclusion of the lower classes from the system. Cloaked in euphemism, the argument is still used today. Sometimes the argument is clothed in the dispassionate language of social science: low political participation is a function of low SES; to raise participation you must raise SES. Sometimes it is dressed in an older language: the citizen has a duty to participate, so he must be "educated" and shamed into performing his duty.

But this is the old argument incompletely stated. Stated fully, the sentence would read that the Outsider must be educated and shamed into acknowledging this duty as the Insider sees that duty. In political action, one makes his fate dependent upon the wills of others. They judge his case and decide his destiny. And no one willingly turns himself over to strangers: those who judge him must be similar to him. Hence, the Insiders' argument always contains the implicit proviso that if only the excluded ones were like us—if only they shared our tastes, respected our values, and accepted our burdens—then we would admit them into the community. This point merits elaboration.

We know that as education rises so does participation, not only in quantity but, we presume, also in quality. So there goes abroad the call for "education for responsible citizenship." We discuss the "vast task," the "great challenge" of arousing the apathetic to a recognition of the duties and an appreciation of the joys of responsible participation in the community's political life. This always and necessarily means responsibility as defined by the Insiders, participation as understood by the Insiders, and therefore education designed by them too.

In the United States, the institution of popular education has from the start been one of the mightiest weapons in the war against the Outsiders. It has been the great hammer for blunting their sharp edges, pounding down their rough differences, smoothing them into the bland community of the Insiders. This has been true from the earliest pronouncements of Benjamin Rush and Horace Mann, through the prodigious campaign to Americanize the foreign born, on to the current doctrine of developing the spirit of cooperation and teaching the skills of harmonious social living.

There are no limits to the capacity for collective self-delusion. We proudly tell ourselves that our system of universal public education is the noblest expression of our whole democratic way of life. The public school is at once democracy's seedbed and loveliest flower. But is it? Plato satirically painted democracy as "a charming form of government, full of variety and disorder, and dispensing a sort of equality to equals and unequals alike." In a democracy "all things are just ready to burst with liberty." All are treated generously there, and even "the horses and asses have a way of marching along with the rights and dignities of freemen; and they will run at anybody who comes in their way if he does not leave the road clear for them." Plato of course despised democracy, but his contempt did not blind him to some of its basic features. If I were to attempt a formula to capture the essence of the democratic ethos, it would go something like this: democracy is the creed which takes a man as he is, and says—that is good enough.

Some do manage to escape, either by psychic migration or by physically checking out. It is my impression that few of the dropouts are "average" or "well adjusted" students. The dropouts tend to be the "losers" in terms of intelligence and social background, and the "winners," usually the highly intelligent or gifted. For both, Babbittism is a transparent mythology that offers no place for misfits and strangers. The educators are now giving earnest attention to the dropouts, and we may expect the dropout rate to increase.

The same antidemocratic meanings could be found in the prescriptions of the social scientists, but it is unnecessary to explore them in any depth here. Low participation is undeniably associated with low SES, but is it demonstrably a function of SES? Is it possible that men are not apathetic because they have low SES, but that they have low SES because they are apathetic? I suspect that neither is wholly correct. My case requires only the possibility that both may be partially correct. Similarly, when the social scientist advises, "raise SES and you will raise participation," he is quite right. But he is also talking in the same language as the schoolmaster. The secret is contained in that deceptive technical word, socialization. Of course participation will rise, because the original man has disappeared under the socialized man. He has been converted into a new man, an Insider, with Insider rules and rewards. We are confronted by a strange type: the social scientist as schoolmaster. The social scientist actually helps make his objects of study what they are. Then he studies this manufactured material and finds, redundantly, that its behavior confirms his science.

Consider the public school in that light and it looks like an antidemocratic agency. The public school is dedicated to the proposition that every man should be made over in the image of the hearty, gregarious, and materialistic Insiders; for it is largely true that in its ethos the public school has never risen much above the level of George F. Babbitt. Lacking Plato's courage to be contemptuous of democracy, but fearing its implications very much, the American educator teaches Babbittry and calls it democracy, not even understanding that to do so is to violate the very spirit of democracy. It seems clear again that the American liberal-democrat fears democracy above all. So deeply does he fear it that to an institutional system which was brilliantly designed to obstruct deomcratic action, he has added an educational system whose main task is that of erasing the differences among individuals and turning them all into Insiders.

Students of voting behavior have found that level of formal education is positively associated with level of political participation. Education is the great discriminator between the actives and the indifferents. Given this finding, liberal-democrats go on to argue as though freedom, vital citizenship, and human dignity will all flower when everybody is adequately educated. The argument clearly rests on the cheerful assumption that education reveals the truth of liberal-democratic values.

But the reasoning is curiously beside the point, and more subtle than the case demands. Obviously, it is not education as such, but the *kind* of education one receives, its actual content, that largely conditions the values and opinions one holds. Our social theorists rarely reflect on that fact when they interpret the education-participation finding. Furthermore, there is an important question of the time context within which the education-participation relationship holds. While differentials in the level of education among various groups certainly contribute to group differentials in political participation, it is a fact that the late nineteenth-century American political universe was characterized by a higher degree of political participation than has prevailed during recent decades—decades during which the general level of formal education has risen far above its nineteenth-century level.[2] From the point of view of social science, we are becoming a nation of deviant cases.

To sum it up, there is a better explanation for the abstention of the forty than the standard (Inside) one of low SES, low education, low achievement need (shiftlessness), and the like. The forty abstain because the present system will not entertain the alternatives that meet their needs. As soon as one says this he encounters another doctrine popular among both liberal-democrats and social scientists, the doctrine that persons with the greatest needs participate most actively in politics. Most present explanations of nonvoting assume this, and some very authoritative explanations explicitly announce it as a basic proposition.[3] I think the thesis has not been proven. It rests upon a mechanistic, stimulus-response theory of personality and a rigid structural-functionalist theory of social order, both of which reflect an Insider bias. When one sees social scientists fall victim to that blindness, he almost despairs of the possibility of Mannheim's freefloating intelligentsia. It is quite obvious, contrary to the "need produces involvement" theory, that those whose needs for the goods of the Great Society are greatest, participate in it the least.

The explanation that the forty abstain because the present system does not formulate and will not admit the policy alternatives that meet their needs seems more convincing. It is at least plausible when examined in the light of something we all know, namely, that in order to understand a political system, it is as important to know what may not and does not go on within it as it is to know what may and does go on within it. For some purposes it is useful to think of a community as a number of persons among whom certain beliefs may not be held and certain acts may not be done. An ideology and a system of institutions are as much barriers against certain beliefs and actions as they are embodiments of other beliefs and actions. You will not understand much about the Soviet Union until you understand that it is a community where men may not profess belief in capitalism and where they dare not form political associations hostile to the Communist Party. Similarly, you will not understand much about the United States until you understand that certain things are forbidden in it, and that these forbidden things contribute greatly toward the abstention of the forty from politics.

Holding the explanation as at least plausible, then, recall one other obvious fact. One cannot enter a game without the permission of those who are already playing. This is as true of the political game as it is of a sandlot baseball game. Furthermore, when one wants to enter a game, he must agree to enter that game. He must accept the going rules, authorities, and prizes as the only legitimate ones, for those who are already playing will admit no others. The nonplayers may or may not want those rules, authorities, and prizes, but if they want to become players they must want them.

When there are 100 legally eligible players, but only sixty actual players, we can safely say that the rules, authorities, and prizes of the game do not interest the nonplayers. Perhaps some of the nonplayers just do not care for organized activities at all, while others do not care for the only game actually open to them. The forty may have very deep needs, but a given game can satisfy only some needs, not needs in general. Hence, it is misleading to say that those with the greatest needs participate most actively in politics. It is more accurate to say that some have deep needs but do not care for organized games, that others may like organized games but find that the available games will not admit, and that still others find their needs satisfied in the only game offered. Persons of the last class are much more likely to participate in the present game than are those whose needs require a different game. It is unusual to find a man who likes football as much as he likes chess. The present political game apparently does little to satisfy the needs of the forty.

With this the argument is almost complete. Let me repeat that it revolves around the thesis that the real division in our polity is not between Democrats and Republicans, or liberals and conservatives, or haves and have nots, but between Insiders and Outsiders. Virtually all political behavioralists hold that the basic division is that between those who have more worldly goods and those who have less. It is quite true that this is a dominant division—among Insiders. It is what their arguments are mainly about. But it is not the basic division between Insiders and Outsiders.

What is that division? The answer is already implicit in the answer to the question concerning the nature of the divisions among the Insiders. The Insiders, virtually all of them, share one orientation, which I shall call gregariousness or sociability. For them, being means being-a-part-of. They cannot conceive of an existence which is not oriented to the tribe and governed by its rules. They also share one dominant value: they are deeply committed to material goods. They want more worldly goods, and their divisions are based on the fear that what one gets another might lose, and on different beliefs concerning how such goods can best be produced and distributed. The Outsiders do not share this overriding commitment to sociability and materialism.[4] Hence the division between the sixty and the forty is a division between those who are predominantly devoted to sociability and materialism, and those who are not. This is the split which gives America the astonishing aspect of a swarming plutocracy (in spirit) which calls itself a democracy but which literally does not hear the voices of an enormous minority. That minority, when it attends to politics at all, must see the whole enterprise as a kind of silly or cynical game in which a lot of fools make a lot of noise and waste a prodigious amount of energy in the pursuit of unimportant goals.

What do the forty want? At the risk of bringing down on myself the wrath of all ethnic protective associations and all good liberal-democrats, I shall present a few stereotypes which might suggest what the main groups which compose the forty admire and desire, what prizes the political game would have to offer in order to attract their interest and energy. I commit the sin of stereotyping with some casualness here because later on I shall retract much of what I am about to say. Besides, I like the Outsiders better anyway, so what's a little stereotyping among friends?

Negroes: history and identity; pride of person and race; revenge against the oppressor; reputation; recognition of one's passional and sensual powers; a chance to stand tall and be seen; decent jobs.

Casual and migratory workers: space to move in; intimacy with a glorious and uncluttered nature; a certain periodicity in life (work-debauch-lassitude-work, all within the encompassing rhythms of nature); freedom; personal pride and independence; masculine affection and comradeship; irresponsible sex; broad humor; and behind it all the feeling that somewhere there is a home to go back to.

Mexican-Americans: that stirring complex of prides called *macho*; a composure which can suddenly hurl itself into total action; smoldering resentments and grudges; chiefs and heroes; pronounced differences between the sexes; much indolent time; and a religion that is at once mysterious, embracing, and authoritarian.

Puerto Ricans: most of what applies to the Mexican-Americans also applies to them.

Youth including Beats, Hippies, Angries, and delinquents, but excluding the old young men of the organization and the career): identity; space and freedom for testing, seeking, and growing; comradeship; spontaneity and sincerity; a zone of irresponsibility for personal adventures; some privacy from the adult world; opportunity to challenge authority; a chance to lose (gain) oneself in a knightly quest; unselfish causes worthy of devotion; honest work and honorable vocation.

Old People: sense of being part of things; some useful work to do; the confidence that their past achievements are respected; opportunity to counsel and help the young; enough novelty to permit them to feel that important things can still happen to them; a social and physical landscape which retains some of its familiar features.

As one scans the list a fairly clear pattern emerges. The Outsiders prize a variety of things, but promiscuous sociability and material goods are not prominent among them. Call the Outsiders Personalists, with values that directly enhance the self and its vocation. The Insiders are Materialists, alienated from and fearful of the self, busy greeting their associates with one hand while they pile up worldly goods with the other.[5]

When we remind ourselves that politics is only one expression of a people's total life style and experience, it becomes clear that the politics of the Insiders can have little appeal to the Outsiders., Nothing in it for them to win or lose. Just not their game.

Now I want to retract much of what I have said. All that went before was deliberately oversimplified so that detail would not get in the way of the main purpose, which was to establish the division between the sixty and the forty, and so that complexity would not obscure my secondary intention, which was to question certain of the standard ways of looking at political participation. Now I want to reshape the model closer to reality and add some of the relevant detail.

I have suggested that the unity of the political system is composed of three parts: the rules of the game, the stakes of the game and the needs of the players. To be an Insider is to be committed to all three of these things as they appear within the present system. There are two difficulties with this formulation: (1) the unity of the political system is in actuality more complex than the game analogy suggests; (2) the division between Insiders and Outsiders is not as simple as I have made it out to be; in reality, it is not always easy to tell which is which, and there are many types of each.

Although the political system does have a unity, its unity is not the simple unity of most games. The system's parts are widely dispersed. The American political game has been going on for nearly 180 years, and large portions of the past exist in the present and help shape the future. The rules, customs, and prizes are numerous, complex and changing. The players come and to with great rapidity, and have a diverity of styles. No one is entirely sure what leads to success and what to failure. In sum, although the system has a unity, that unity can be formulated only at a level of abstraction so remote that it cannot tell us much about political realities at a given moment. The unity of the abstracted system, while necessary for an overall comprehension of our political life, will not tell us much of what we need to know in order to understand political affairs at one point in time and space. For that understanding, we must go to the historians and journalists, and we must master a host of particular facts and ideas. I do not intend to abandon the analogy of the game, but I want to make it clear that I am aware of its limitations. Those limitations are central to the next point, which is the difficulty of distinguishing Insiders and Outsiders.

The trouble is that Insiders and Outsiders are not dichotomous types. The dichotomy fails in two ways. First, given the complexity of the political system, and especially the multiplicity of its parts, the same man can be simultaneously inside some parts of it and outside others: he may accept some aspects and conform to some expectations but reject others. Secondly, he may accept or reject with varying degrees of intensity.

Instead of thinking in the language of dichotomies, then, it is necessary to think in terms of a continuum running from complete acceptance of all parts of the system to complete rejection of the whole system. For convenience, this continuum can be called the Inside-Outside scale. We might also outline some regions along the scale and give them descriptive labels: enthusiastic commitment and participation; active participation; moderate participation; ritualistic performance of expected duties; indifference; alienation; hostility; treason. Conceptualized in this way, it becomes clear that the point at which a person should be called an Insider must be arbitrarily set.[6] It is always a matter of degree. With this understood, we can discuss the problem in terms that admit more of the complexity of the real world.

It will be helpful at the start to define the Real Insiders rather strictly. There are no solid figures or definitions in this area, but the following data will suggest their approximate number. About .25 percent of the eligible electorate are precinct leaders or regular precinct workers. The top political elite of party and public officials amounts roughly to another .25 percent. In 1952, about 2 percent of the electorate belonged to a political club. In

1954, about 5 percent did some volunteer campaign work. In 1955, about 2.5 percent of the eligible electorate said they had made a financial contribution to a political cause during the preceding twelve months. The Michigan Survey Research Center classifies about 3 percent of the electorate as having an orientation toward political events which is coherent, articulate, and systematic enough to be called—quite loosely—an ideology.[7] These figures total 13 percent of the electorate. Recognizing that the categories overlap, we might cut this about in half and describe 7 percent as being Real Insiders.[8]

A great many people pay some attention to politics. They watch the game on television, and they will go to some trouble to learn what is going on. But their interest is not keen, and their knowledge of the rules and players is thin. They do make some investment in the system, however, and give it some kinds of support. Should these people be called Insiders? In some senses, yes; in others, no. Start by calling all fifty-three of them Spectators.

Most of the fifty-three are materialists and sociabilists in the senses indicated before. These are the main reasons why they watch the game, but they are not the only ones. Perhaps twenty-five to thirty-five percent of the Spectators are quite deeply interested in the game. These involved ones can be divided into three groups. First, the handful of journalists, scholars, men of letters, and a few laymen who take politics seriously, either as a sector of human life which they wish to understand for its own sake, or as a field of such vast importance that they think they cannot safely ignore it. These we can call Students, for their interest in politics is mainly moral and intellectual. Next, there are a small number who rather think they might themselves like to become players. Thirdly, there is a larger group of alert Spectators who watch the game closely because they think their interests can be damaged or aided by the outcome. Groups two and three, then, watch the game because they have something to win or lose in it. They are Gamesters.

For the rest of the Spectators, the game is no more than a sometime thing, remote from their main interests. They attend to the game for any of a number of reasons, most of which can ultimately be referred back to sociability: habit; vague sense of duty; because everyone else does; the prestige of being well-informed; a source of material for small conversation. Most studies of voting behavior are about these people, but we really know little about them. This is so, I have suggested, because the social scientists have brought certain ideological predispositions to the task of studying them, and because the data about them have been poured into inappropriate analytic containers.

We might understand more about the Spectators by applying to their behavior the ideas which strike anyone who watches a large crowd at any spectator event. There are many and varied notions among the spectators as to just what the game is all about, and many of them have only the faintest idea of what is going on. The crowd is quick to choose heroes and villains from among the players, and many people will remember little more about the game than that number twelve was really mean, while twenty was great. The underdog will win the affection of many just because he is the underdog. Others support one of the contestants out of ethnic loyalty, or because their friends do, or because their family has always done so. As the game proceeds, small groups of spectators here and there will become bored with what is happening on the field and start little games of their own. Many people will have their attention diverted from the game by any of a great number of adventitious factors: the weather, a pretty girl, some annoying person sitting near them, worry about personal or family problems. Some go to the game because other people do, some because they love the crowds and color, others because they just felt like an outing, and still others because they know one of the players, or because it is good for their reputation to be seen there. Large sections of the crowd will become momentarily very upset about apparent violations of the rules. The crowd's mood will undergo large and sudden shifts. And so forth.

Still, what holds them together is that they are all at the game. And here we approach the cutting point between Insiders and Outsiders. As in any other game, the cheers and boos of the Spectators will have some (possibly quite large) effect on the players. What is more important in understanding the political game, however, is the fact that the players know fairly accurately what actions of theirs will evoke cheers and boos from the Spectators. The players control the game, not the Spectators. This, I think, establishes the basic sense in which the Spectators are Insiders: their responses can be predicted by the professionals. The Outsiders, in contrast, are unknown quantities. Their behavior cannot be predicted with much accuracy or confidence.[9]

In summary, although there are many differences among the Spectators, they share two things: they accept and support to one or another degree the prevailing game; and their responses are fairly predictable. These attributes distinguish them from the Outsiders.

It is time for a closer look at the Outsiders. The same two qualifications which conditioned the discussion of the Insiders apply here: the idea of the complexity of the system, and the idea of the continuum. From this perspective, it becomes clear that the Outsiders are not a people apart. They are just more Outside than the Spectators. There are many types of Outsiders, and many degrees of outsideness. In general, three features characterize the Outsiders as a type: (1) their responses are not predictable by the experts; (2) they see little connection between their own needs and interests and what can be achieved through political action; (3) they share a sense of the small importance of what is won and lost in American politics.[10] These three things the Outsiders share. But that is about all. There are many differences among them.

Look again at the six groups I caricatured some pages back. Those groups do make up a substantial portion of the Outsiders, perhaps seventy-five to eighty percent, and they do share the three attributes just mentioned. But they share few substantive interests upon which a political program might be built. Sex, revenge, pride, space, comradeship, adventure, noble causes, stability, and the rest, do not fit together very well—though it would be dangerous to forget that now and then a demagogue comes along who for a while can make them seem to.

More importantly, the central concerns of these groups are in conflict with the only concerns that have a legitimate place in the political system. This strikes a prodigious theme, which I shall only open here. The theme is fear, fear of the return of the repressed.

The American liberal-democrat long ago made a choice, and that choice is now the inarticulate major premise of the political system. The liberal has elected prudence (postponement, restraint, regularity) over both the ideal and the elemental as the energy and rationale of the polity. He has put down both the transcendental and the subterranean, both Plato and Freud, and has enthroned comfort and common sense. Many aspects of the tone of our political life become understandable when this is understood. The great stress on status, for example, comes in part from this. In a society which values status, one can relate to others according to the badges of rank. He avoids personal involvement, keeps the other at arm's length, and thus avoids risking the self. The idea of equality performs the same function. Employed as a useful ideology, the doctrine of equality means that you do not have to look at, measure, and treat another person according to his unique personal qualities. You can treat all alike, under the convenient doctrine that all deserve to be treated equally. Social relations can be conducted by rule, in a bureaucratic style. The self need not be risked.

The Outsiders, on the other hand, prefer the personal and the intimate over the remote and aloof. They stress the passional depths and the ideal heights of life, and they want closeness, commitment, personal judgment in the relations among men. They risk the self, and do not hide behind impersonal rules and abstract standards. The liberal-democrat has repressed these dimensions of life, substituting for them interpersonal relations governed by rule, fairness, and ritual equality. This may be the deepest issue between Insiders and Outsiders. This is the issue which shows the fear at the heart of the established order, and it is this fear which helps explain the difficulty of finding a program to unite the Outsiders. The stakes are so great that the smallest apperance of any such movement or program must be implacably opposed by all Insiders.

The last, and obvious reason why it is difficult to combine the substantive needs and values of the Outsiders into a program and movement is that many of those needs and values do not go unfulfilled. They are satisfied outside the political realm, and they enter the public concern only as they present problems of public order and propriety for the rest of us. That is, they are political problems in the sense that they often become police problems.[11]

It appears, then, that a political agenda which would unite the Outsiders into one movement probably could not be built. The Outsiders are defeated by diversity, by their unwillingness to share the orientations of the Insiders, and by the anxieties which their desires arouse among the Insiders. Hence, there is not one minority of forty, but a minority of many minorities which total to forty; and, for certain purposes, these divided minorities must face a solid phalanx of the sixty. As long as they remain divided, they cannot act effectively against the Insiders. As long as they hold the values they do, the Insiders must fear them and cannot admit them into the system on a plane of equality. Individual members of Outsider groups will be admitted, but only at the price of casting off most of what makes them Outsiders. The typical case is that of the "good" Negro who is apparently accepted by his white neighbors, and who, out of that heartening experience of success and acceptance, comes to think that all the members of his race can be accepted if only they will become like him. The good Negro who thinks this way is wrong because those who gain acceptance on such terms are not really accepted at all, but enjoyed as curiosities, and because they are no longer really Negroes at all, but white men of the middle classes with unfortunately dark skins. The error consists in failing to understand that every minority problem is fundamentally a majority problem. The same error was made by many Jews who thought that if only the Jews would correct their own faults they would be accepted by the Germans. Thousands of Jews individually tried that, as thousands of Negroes do. It was a failure to understand that from the point of view of the German, the Jew's crime was that he was a Jew. It was a failure to understand that the problem was basically a majority and not a minority problem, and a social problem rather than an individual one. The same is true of our Outsiders. Their failure to grasp the nature of the problem produces two main consequences: an enormous amount of self-hatred among the Outsider groups for not being "better" than they are; and an inability to cope with the realistic situation in ways that enhance the chances for group survival.

So it is unlikely that an agenda could be devised which would unite the forty into the Party of the Outsiders. In the absence of that, the politicians will continue to seek safe and limited ways of catering to at least some of the desires of the Outsiders. Those desires will typically be the materialistic ones, for they are the ones which the system can most easily formulate and fulfill: security for the aged; fair employment practices for Negroes; minimum wages for the poorest workers; school assistance for the young; and so forth. In an abundant society, responding to these demands requires only a small redistribution of wealth and space. It does not require fundamental expropriations or reorientations. The opposition to even such modest programs comes from those Insiders who still are not sure that things work this way. Theirs is still the psychology of scarcity. They fear that what others get they lose. But this fear only provides the energy of a conventional interest politics, not the dynamite of a radical politics of identity and mission. The politicians can continue to cater to some of the material desires of the forty and the system will remain basically intact. It will remain a politics of rulebound sociability and the distribution of material goods. The system would be threatened only if the forty began to demand not a liberal-democratic politics of sociability and distribution, but a democratic politics of personality and passion. But their own divisions and indifference, plus the skill of the professionals, plus the fears of the Insiders stand glacially against that possibility.

Let me now make amends for the stereotypes and pay some respect to the complexities of reality by offering a somewhat fuller description of the Outsiders. Forget the previous stereotyping and labeling of actual groups as Outsiders. Substitute the following classification of styles of being Outside. From stereotype to typology:

Indifferents: these are the ones for whom the political world hardly exists. They are neither much for nor much against, but basically inattentive. They cannot be called Retreatists because they had never occupied a forward or involved position from which they have subsequently withdrawn. More women than men will be found here. Fairly large numbers of young people are Indifferent, because the young are deeply engaged in their personal worlds, seeking a mate, vocation, and identity. The bulk of the Indifferents come from the lower SES groups, because they have not been fully socialized into the middle class political culture, because their life spaces are small, because the demands of job and family take most of their energy, and because they are unable to forge intellectual and practical links between their private condition and the public realm. There is also a cool style of Indifference, assumed by those who have seen through the system and found it tawdry. This will include some of the highly educated, a few creative artists, and a few Beats and Hippies.

Retreatists: these people were once Inside but have been driven out by fear, despair, or fatigue. Their mood is dominated by nostalgia for an earlier day when all things were fair, and by a Henry Adamsish impotence and displacement in the present. Two types make up most of the cases. The first are those who once engaged intensely, and who either got burned or saw their hopes defeated. Examples would be the innocents of the Independent Progressive Party of 1948, who watched untoward things happen to their hero and their program; and the variety of reformers and men of good will who fell victim to McCarthyism. Having been burned once, they are leery of the political world. Those who have retreated out of despair include reformers who saw their good intentions smashed, and the lower class groups who for a time followed a hero who shook them out of their lethargy but who was then himself brought down by a variety of forces. Many of these despairing ones were left in the wake of Populism. In recent times, the two defeats of Adlai Stevenson convinced many well-intentioned men that American politics had no place for nobility. The second main type of Retreatists consists of those who have withdrawn from the stream of public life not primarily out of fear or despair, but out of fatigue. The old folks are the largest group here. Their resignation from politics is just one aspect of their general resignation from life.

Suppliants: this category embraces those who would like to be Spectators, or even Activists, but to whom the system says "No Admittance." These unlucky ones have the proper goals, attitudes, and orientations, but something about them is "wrong"—their color, accent, religion, place of origin, personality, or abilities—and they are excluded. The Suppliants make up the largest pool of recruits for moderate changes in the rules of the game and the distribution of prizes. They have great energy because they have justice on their side: they can rightfully appeal to the ideology of fair play and equal opportunity, and they can feel a legitimate resentment when equal access to the good things is denied them. In the past, members of this group came largely from the immigrant groups, especially the Irish and Italians. Today the people and the goals represented by such groups as CORE and the NAACP best represent the category. The number of Suppliants is declining, for the system eventually admits those who accept it, who show themselves willing to play for the conventional stakes, and who push persistently for admittance: not so long ago, "Irish Need Not Apply"; in 1960 an Irishman won the first job in the land. Once admitted, the Suppliants have a way of becoming more Inside than the Insiders.

The Negroes and the Mexican-Americans are the last of the great blocs of ethnic Suppliants. When they are admitted into the system, or pacified, America will have reached the end of an era. For some fifty years the fundamental dynamic of American domestic politics has come from the demands of the minorities for admission. But the Era of the Minorities is now coming to an end; and as it ends there also must end the very meaning of "reform" and the entire pattern and process which political intellectuals and radicals have used to measure "progress" in American political life—the process of bringing more and more of the goods of materialism and sociability to more and more people. The old house is indeed burning down, as Baldwin has said, and no one knows what the new house will look like.

Castoffs: this category is occupied by the pathetic ones who were once Inside, and who according to the official myths still are, but who in fact have been thrown aside by social change. Their sadness is that they once had a place but no longer have it. Their shame and anger are that while the official rhetoric proclaims them Inside, they are Outside. Farmers and old people constitute most of the Castoffs, and these same two groups contribute disproportionately to the anomic population. The response of the Castoff to his hurt is a combination of bewilderment, resentment, suspicion, and readiness for extreme action. The farmers present an interesting example of this mood. They are among the most erratic and unpredictable of all social groups, largely because for them ideology and reality are quite out of step. The farmer has a hard time honestly believing in his professed ideology of individualism and the rural virtues because his everyday experience is so very different from his ceremonial doctrine. When the farmer succeeds, he succeeds through organization, technology, regulation, and subsidy. And the greater the success, the greater the regulation and subsidy. As his subsidy grows, so grows his irritation when reminded of the gap between his slogan of individualism and his reality of public dependency. The fact is, the farmer knows as well as the rest of us that there is agricultural overproduction (within the present framework of economic doctrines and relations) so his very legitimacy is challenged. We have come a long way from the time when a Bryan might seriously say, "burn down your cities and leave our farms, and your cities will spring up again as if by magic; but destroy our farms and the grass will grow in the streets of every city in the country." It is hard for the farmer to believe that we need more of what we already have too much of, so even while he wins the battle of subsidy, he loses the battle of self-justification. When farmers lose the economic battle—and many small farmers have—they typically join the ranks of the urban wage earners, but they continue to live in the past, indulging themselves in a politics of nostalgia and resentment. The old folks, in this respect like the farmers, have been passed by.

They are tired and sad. They withdraw. Occasionally they show themselves capable of vigorous collective action, as in California, and they stand ready for moral revenge against the present system in the name of its purer past. These last will be found in the ranks of the Goldwater Republicans and the Birchers.

Ritualists: these are the ones who go through all the motions of supporting the system, but without really knowing why, and without much genuine satisfaction in the exercise. There are a great many Ritualists among us, but it is not easy to identify them by the methods of empirical social research. They give all the proper "good citizen" responses to questions concerning political interest and participation, so they turn up high on scales of citizen duty, responsibility, political efficacy, and the like. But what matters here is intangible; the feel of an experience. They do the proper things, but something is lacking. There is a hollowness and a vague yearning about their performances, a sense that although they do the right things, they do not have the right feelings. It is as though one had left half his heart somewhere, and cannot remember where. These people have been thoroughly socialized, however, so they cannot imaginatively remove themselves to a point outside the system from which they might look back and locate the sources of their malaise. Most of the Ritualists will be found among the middle and upper classes. They have a lot of what they system offers, and they anxiously assure themselves that that is what they really want, but they cannot help wondering why they are not more serene. As said before, these people are hard to locate, but a proper search might turn up a lot of them in suburbia and in the managerial-manipulative positions of the white collar world.

Idealists: these are the ones who take the system's democratic and humanitarian myths very seriously and who, therefore, see the reality of politics as a disgrace. For them, politics is the pursuit of noble ends and they cannot accept a system where the reality falls so short of the ideal. These persons are utopians and moralizers. The highest concentration of Idealists will be found among young people and among the well-educated adults of the liberal professions and the academic and intellectual worlds. Very few appear among the lower classes. Almost to a man, they have never met a payroll. Many of the Idealists are Spectators who are torn between closer involvement and greater separation. But they remain Spectators in the sense that the professionals can nearly always predict their responses (liberal); and they remain Outsiders in the sense that they cannot decide whether to embrace or to reject the system.

Realists: like the Idealists, the Realists see the gulf between the myth and the reality, but they accept the gulf as necessary, and even take pleasure in it. They see the whole of life as tarnished anyway, so why should politics be any different? They are scathing critics of the Idealists. Realists take pride in their toughmindedness, and they have a sneaking love for the arts of manipulation. They have seen through the political game and can't be taken in. Their real heroes are the shrewd operators, the Nixons of American politics. Probably a good many Spectators can be classified here. Most of the Realists are self-made men in the worlds of business, journalism, public relations, and organized labor. Not a few of them will be found in the academy, where they find sport in scoffing at their tender-minded colleagues, who believe that ideal ends matter. They are Outsiders in the important sense that they have rejected the ideal premises and promises of the system as no more than a political formula, but they are Inside in the sense that they believe no alternative would be much better.

Aliens: these people reject the standard prizes and feel no duty to give the system aid and comfort. Their attitude toward the Insiders is one of hostility and contempt, which may be expressed in active or passive forms. They typically abstain from politics, but if they do enter they are inclined to raise extreme demands and employ illegitimate modes of action. Beats and Hippies are the best examples of the Aliens who remain aloof from the system. Some alienated persons confront the system aggressively in order to transform it: Communists, Black Muslims. Most of the alienated ones lack an articulate ideology, but just pervasively feel that the system presses heavily and corruptly upon them and asks tawdry things of them. Here the largest contingent is made up of the young, who have not yet put away their faith in the ideal, and some members of certain ethnic and racial minorities, who resist the stultifying sociability of the system and resent its repressive treatment of their claims. A few Aliens do have a fairly coherent ideology, and they seek to transform the system by the light of nobler alternatives to present practices and goals: SNCC and the Mississippi Freedom Democratic Party might be examples.

This classification does not cover all the Outsiders, but it catches most of them. It should now be made explicit that not all who fit into the categories behave in ways that are manifestly outside of or hostile to the system. The American polity is able to accommodate a good many Outsiders working within itself. It is also part of its genius to muffle the voices of the Outsiders and make it hard for malcontents to admit that they are Outside or to understand and express why and how they feel Outside. Discontent is dissipated by the woolly myths of democracy, humanitarianism, and progress. The burden is thrown on the discontented ones. The suspicion is always that their discontent is the symptom of personal failure or sickness. In addition, many who are physically Outside are psychically Inside. This is the case, for example, with most Suppliants.

The hidden genius of the American system is that it can tolerate as many Outsiders as, and perhaps more than, say, France, and yet proceed as though they hardly existed. This is due in part to the nature of the party and electoral systems, in part to the non-ideological character of our politics, and in part to the content of that atmospheric opinion which Louis Hartz has called the Lockean consensus. The American system thrives upon anomy. It offers sufficient promise to keep alive the hopes of Idealists and reformers. By incessant rhetoric and judicious subsidy it blunts the wrath and salves the pain and guilt of the Castoffs. Enough Suppliants gain admission to keep the rest hopeful. The Realists find vocations in the system as manipulators, and they can always enjoy the sport of laughing at the Idealists. The professionals are adept at playing off the fears and hopes of the different groups.

The openly and aggressively alienated ones with a doctrine constitute no threat because they are so few. I am inclined to think that only the Ritualists as a type and young people as a group can offer any real challenge. Both of these classes might silently withdraw, thereby depriving the system of present support and future recruits. Both the Ritualists and the young are at least potentially alienated. Should their potential alienation become actual, their very alienation would drive them into conflict with the system, simply because great numbers of people cannot be harnessed uncomplainingly into roles that sicken them with the sense of emptiness and the guilt of personal sellout. Under such conditions, these two groups might contemplate playing the game in order to change it.

But as soon as one says that, one is brought back to the sustaining root of the present system, its nonideological character. For if you enter a game in order to change it, you must know what game you want to play in place of the old one. The America of today is barren of such visions. Our spiritual malaise is our political health.

Notes

1. A special form of the charge of irresponsibility is frequently brought against certain Outsider groups, such as artists and scientists. They are charged with a certain cold, intellectual arrogance and aloofness.
2. See Walter Dean Burnham, "The Changing Shape of the American Political Universe," *American Political Science Review*, Vol. 59 (March, 1965), pp. 7-29, esp. p. 22.

3. See, e.g., S.M. Lipset et al., "The Psychology of Voting: An Analysis of Political Behavior," in G. Lindzey, ed. *Handbook of Social Psychology* (New York: Addison-Wesley, 1954), Vol. II, pp. 1124-75.
4. I am inclined to think that sociability is the decisive quality which defines the Insiders, and that materialism is but one aspect of the meaning of sociability in the United States. But it is hard to say for sure where the one begins and the other ends.
5. This does not imply that the Outsiders do not care for material things: it is plain that many of them do. But it is equally plain that they do not care for them above all else. In America, very few people who really want material success, regardless of how much it might cost in terms of other values, can't get it.
6. Could the dividing line be drawn at the point where a person honestly, willingly, and out of a sense of duty answers a single question about himself asked by a social science investigator?
7. Data drawn from Angus Campbell et al., *The American Voter* (New York, N.Y.: Wiley, 1960), passim.
8. In absolute numbers, this amounts to about as many people as are members of the Communist Party in the Soviet Union.
9. In one sense, of course, the behavior of the Outsiders can be predicted: the Outsider will not play the game, and will not watch it. Therefore, for most purposes, the Outsider can be ignored. It is only when the Outsiders show some signs of interest in the game that the professionals (and the social scientists) become worried, for then their responses cannot be predicted. Consider how anxiously we are always trying to figure out what "they" (e.g. ghetto dwellers, youth) want. The whole modern theory of mass society in its political dimensions rests squarely on this quality of unpredictability characteristic of the Outsiders.
10. A fourth feature applies to a few Outsiders, but is not generally characteristic of the class. A few Outsiders do have a sense that what is won and lost in American politics is important, but they shun involvement because they believe that such games almost inevitably become corrupted so that the right things can never even be articulated.
11. The successful, resented Insider envies the Outsider—for his greater personal liberty and passional satisfaction.

Violence in Juvenile Gangs: Some Notes and a Few Analogies

The scope of this essay is much narrower than its title may suggest. I shall first offer a small hypothesis, or idea, and then elaborate it by calling upon certain concepts and metaphors drawn from the stock vocabulary of political analysis. Little attention will be given to details either of argument or of data.

Deprivation, Rage and Violence

The core of the idea is contained in a passage from Hannah Arendt: "The vehement yearning for violence is a natural reaction of those whom society has tried to cheat of their strength."[1] Stated fully, the hypothesis runs as follows:

1. Juvenile violence is the physical manifestation of the emotional condition called rage.
2. Rage, in turn, is the product of deep deprivation, of not getting something that is intensely wanted, and perhaps needed.
3. The common expression "blind rage" calls attention to the fact that, when deprivation covers large and important sectors of life and its pain penetrates to the very core of one's being, then its causes become blurred in the mind of the sufferer. Unable to blame the pain on anyone or anything in particular, he blames everything and everyone in general. Hence, he cares little where his violence strikes. It falls, as it were, upon targets of opportunity. Those targets are frequently the members of other gangs, but they may also be nameless and blameless members of society at large.
4. The deprivations that produce the rage of juvenile gang members may be divided into two kinds, for purposes of analysis. The first is the lack

of decent living conditions. It alone will not produce the rage that leads to violence, especially if the culture offers self-justifications and nonmaterial satisfactions to those of poor estate. However, a culture that emphasizes material comfort and progress and enjoins all to get ahead imposes a heavy burden of guilt, despair, and envy upon those who, for one or another reason, are not successful. The second kind of deprivation, somewhat harder to formulate and to measure, can be called the deprivation of authority and of the future. That recalls the passage from Arendt, for to deny a person authority and the future is indeed to strike at the source of his strength.

Let me now call attention to one of the most striking and apparently paradoxical features of the rage of juvenile gang members: It is simultaneously blind and furious, yet subject to systematic control. Their rage is cultivated and hoarded as a resource that may be thrown at any object. That the object is usually another gang or the members of other gangs is easily understandable, because typical fighting gangs must compete with each other for scarce goods: territory, deference, reputation, girls. There is enough energy left over from these combats, however, so that the violence may sometimes be unleashed against nameless and innocent bystanders.

But, regardless of its object, the rage itself is structured and directed. Some fighting gangs in our large cities have an organization for combat which closely resembles that of a well-developed political entity. They have specialists in strategy and tactics, intelligence officers, supply personnel and armorers. The channels of communication for military information are highly developed and closely guarded. The techniques and tools of violence reveal a remarkable inventiveness; the boys easily transform some of the most harmless artifacts of everyday life into deadly weapons. So carefully is their rage organized that even the proper mental state is achieved before the commitment to violence is made. Gang leaders have been known to subject their followers to periods of close and chafing discipline in preparation for a fight. Or they will launch an attack after a particularly long and weary period of boredom. The gangs engage in war games within their own membership. Gang legends and memories are chiefly legends of warfare and warriors. The members frequently use intoxicants of various kinds just before a rumble, to work themselves into the proper frame of mind.

This dire combination of blindness and structure, which gives gang violence its specifically terrifying quality, is strikingly similar to the qualities of modern political rage. It was the combination of blind fury and systematic control which made Hitlerism the appalling thing it was.

The reason for this fearsome combination of qualities is to be found in the profound alienation of the juvenile gang from society, an alienation so penetrating that it calls upon violence not merely as a way of hitting back. Rather, their violence undergoes aesthetic elaboration and is suffused with moral and ritualistic meanings.

Juvenile gangs must be recognized as tribes at war with each other and with the world. Not only their style of violence, but also their dress, language, mores and emotional state, all express this sense of combat. So does their internal government, which is typically authoritarian or tyrannical in structure. So does their code of justice, in which the worst crime is treason against the gang and the worst personal fault is the lack of "heart," by which the gang members mean, not courage, but something more like abandon of the self to action, without regard for consequences.

One national figure who seems to recognize this condition of total war is J. Edgar Hoover of the Federal Bureau of Investigation. In his view of the world, our two most virulent enemies are the "Commies" and the "Young Hoodlums." Although I rarely see the world as Hoover does, on this question I think he is half right. Now, if we are in such a state of war, then society has several alternatives for dealing with the situation. It can, for example, follow a get-tough policy and attempt to crush the enemy. This is what Hoover and a great many law enforcement officers propose. Here my agreement with Hoover ends. In addition to its moral obtuseness, a large body of evidence persuades me that a get-tough policy is stupid and inefficient.

Again, a society faced by an enemy within or without can ignore the whole condition. This policy entails great peril, unless there are the strongest reasons for believing that one's enemy is well on the way toward natural extinction. Juvenile gang violence shows no signs of that. On the contrary, the evidence indicates a large and steady rise during the past fifteen years.

One might also try to rehabilitate the enemy. Much might be done here, and we have hardly even begun to do it. Furthermore, I am inclined to believe that most of our present programs of rehabilitation are based on false assumptions; the main one is that young persons who turn to organized violence are inadequately socialized. Hence, it is said, the remedy is to socialize them, imparting to them our values, goals and burdens. If they can be made to understand us, they will join us; or, at least, they will stop hating us. To gain their understanding, so the argument concludes, we must first give them ours.

This entire approach seems to me distorted, in two ways. First, as the poetical theorist of violence Georges Sorel pointed out, the attempt to impose "pure" understanding and compassion on a situation of deep hostility often leads, especially during the opening stage of relations, to an intensification and expansion of the violence. The objects of such attitudes come to think they are not being taken seriously—not really being seen, but merely looked through toward some abstract consideration. Their violence in the first place was their tortured way of saying they had grave claims to make, and of demanding that those claims be heard and honored. Offering pure understanding and compassion seems a way of failing to hear and act on their claims. This approach is also misleading because it fails to ask the question, "Socialization to what?" Unless we ourselves are so hopelessly oversocialized as to be unable to imagine any society more perfect than the present one, we must acknowledge that some aspects of the present order are unworthy of acceptance. Paul Goodman, in *Growing Up Absurd,* has made this case with vigor and intelligence.

It should be noted that certain enlightened agencies, especially in New York City, have understood this. The street workers who go directly among the gangs have scored some commendable victories. There are many reasons for this, but surely a primary one is the fact that the street worker takes both his own position and that of the gang member seriously. These workers virtually serve as ambassadors from society to the gang. As such, they accept a certain code of ethics. They do not, for example, attempt to remake the entire structure of the gang. Rather, they recognize it as a real entity with its own distinct way and right of existence. They simultaneously engage in spying activities, attempt to maintain a generally stable and peaceful relationship between the gang and society, and try to convert certain vulnerable individual gang members to loyalty to their own regime. The very ambivalence of the street workers' role, I think, lies behind their relative success. The gang members understand, for example, that although they can say almost anything to the street worker without fear of its being used against them, he is duty bound to report to his superior certain information, such as the heavy use of narcotics or the possession of guns. On the other hand, the street worker is unlike ambassadors of state in that he need not espouse, either in public or in private, all the policies and goals of the regime he represents.

The last and most promising policy for a society dealing with an enemy is that of negotiation. Negotiation with the gang is possible, for each side has something to give and to gain. Society wants peace; the juveniles can give it. In return, society can give the gang members some things they deeply want and need. More than that, the initiative for negotiation can come from society, because society is in the position of power, from which it can take large steps toward ending the state of war by striking at the causes of the rage. Those steps are so obvious and the resources committed thus far so few, that one is almost compelled to conclude that society is not serious about wanting to end the conflict.

Certain themes in our culture make it difficult for us either to recognize the existence of hostile bands in our own midst or to treat them as groups having a real claim on us. Proudly and in doctrinaire fashion we remind ourselves that ours is the land of opportunity where all doors are open to talent and enterprise. So pervasive is this ideology, and so many are the doors which are in fact open to energy and talent, that we cannot understand why anyone should feel left out. We promptly assume that those who do are looking for excuses to cover their own shortcomings. Furthermore, we assume that people who will not walk through those doors already open, but insist on butting their heads against the wall, are either stupid, or naturally vicious, or crazy. It rarely occurs to us that many doors are in fact closed to many people. Above all, it rarely occurs to us that any man in his right mind might not want those good things on the other side of the door called success.

Here we approach the heart of the matter. As has been pointed out, society can open negotiations from its position of power, and it can direct some of its vast resources toward the causes of juvenile rage. This would mean a serious effort toward improving juveniles' economic and social environment: better housing, decent recreational facilities, better schools, improved and enlarged psychological counseling services, better vocational training and opportunities, and the like. Although these things would not abolish the problem, they would surely alleviate it; attempting them would serve mainly as a token that society takes its juveniles seriously enough to come to terms with them. Much more is needed, and that much more will be far harder to provide.

The greater need is suggested by this formula: Although society holds the position of superior power, it by no means holds the position of superior authority.

Authority and Power

Following Bertrand de Jouvenel, authority can be defined simply as "the faculty of gaining another man's assent."[2] This means that a person has authority when he is able to persuade others to accept his proposals. The very word's rich origins and associations suggest the place of authority in human life. An authority is one whose word or counsel we trust, whose advice we follow; he is one who creates or builds some work, who instigates a work, although others may actually complete the job. He is one to whom the actions of others must be traced back. Hence, he is the "father" of their actions. The one term "authority" richly combines in itself this dual meaning of father and creator. To quote Jouvenel again, the authority is "the father of actions freely undertaken whose source is in him though their seat is in others."[3]

A person or an institution becomes such a source of actions freely undertaken by others in two ways. First, by example—one shows others the way by going there oneself; and second, by being able to assure others that the actions he wishes them to take are rightful, and will succeed. Here are authority's two profoundest functions: It provides justification and it increases the confidence and sense of power of those under it by assuring them that they themselves will be enlarged by the actions they undertake at authority's request. Authority, far from confining and depleting individuals, liberates and enriches them.

If authority is to vouch for the rightness and success of actions, it must have a rationale that backs its claim to assent. This must include an account of reality, an explanation of why some acts are preferable to others and a vision of a future toward which the followers of authority may aspire. Put differently, this rationale consists of a more or less coherent body of shared images, ideas and ideals that gives to those who share it a systematic, simplified and comprehensive orientation in time and space. It links the past, the present and the future into a meaningful whole. It has a compelling and energizing power, for those who share it understand that it demands certain actions of them. It is serious and fundamental. It links means to ends in a continuum that goes beyond mere expediency or the pragmatic. Authority at once personifies this rationale and is justified by it. Without such a rationale, authority dissipates, leaving a vacuum that will soon be filled by power.

Only one term properly fits the phenomenon I am trying to describe, ideology. The word is in bad repute today, and I hesitate to introduce it. ("Authority" is also a word in bad favor today. That the two should fall together is not accidental, for they lean on each other.) It is my argument, however, that no matter what we do with the word, we cannot do without the reality. All of us at times need the strength ideology gives, but never more so than during adolescence. Young people steer themselves through that dangerous passage only by the light of a future they can deem worth growing up to. That future is provided by ideologies of one or another kind.

Holding this as an argument, I must offer authority for it. In a recent essay, Erik H. Erikson offers a few tantalizing hints concerning the role of ideology in identity formation. "Youth,", he writes, "needs to base its rejections and acceptances on ideological alternatives vitally related to the existing range of alternatives for identity formation."[4] Youth needs an ideological polarization, a "breakdown of the multiplicity of values into a few which coerce commitment."[5] Young people need a clear and intelligible comprehension of life to guide their earnestness, their seeking, their asceticism and their indignation. Finally, Erikson argues, identity and ideology become two aspects of the one process of achieving a higher form of identification, namely "the solidarity linking common identities."[6]

If the larger community does not provide out of its own resources of ideas and experiences the material for the fabrication of such identity-forming ideologies, young people will find those materials elsewhere. Many, perhaps especially the gifted ones, will escape into a private utopia. It is as if, since the objective and external community has failed him, the young person becomes his own community of one. Another substitute for a community-derived ideology is found in those fads that are so much a part—often the most vital part—of adolescent life in America. We should not forget that those spontaneous, intense and transitory commitments and aversions we derisively call fads are, in fact, a debauched form of ideology. Finally, some young people—especially those on the economic, ethnic and cultural margins—will develop negative and hostile ideologies leading to negative and violent group identifications. This, of course, is the heart of my argument concerning the origins and meanings of violence among juvenile gangs.

It seems to me that virtually the only, or at least the main, values that the United States today offers its young people are the endless production and consumption of material goods and the joys of conforming to a certain hearty, gregarious code of behavior which has never risen far above the standards of George Babbitt. As we face the outside world, we are held together by hatred of a common enemy. Materialism, Babbittry, and anticommunism—these are the central meanings of our community. So decisively have they failed to provide meaning and a future for the young, that some, driven in addition by outrageous conditions of daily life, take to violence. Having been given no future, they wish to destroy the present. Having been given no meaning, they rage against all surface meanings. But I think we shall never come to terms with them until we understand that their rage and violence are tortured ways of reaching for meaning, for authority and for the future. The tragedy is that the clenched fist can only smash, it cannot grasp.

Although our society can negotiate from strength it cannot negotiate from secure authority. It was the loss of authority that got society into trouble in the first place. Those who observe the weakening or breakdown of the family as a cohesive unit—one which could introduce the young to both the trustworthiness and the responsibility of mature life—rarely, it seems to me, confront the full implications of their observation. Two points matter most here. First, the breakdown of the family is increasingly a cross-class and transnational phenomenon; it is limited to no one class, section, or country, though of course it is more pronounced in some places than others. Second, the loss of the family—more accurately, the loss of the parents as prime authorities in the lives of children—is probably an irreversible trend of modern life. All children today more or less suffer the loss of authority, and this trend will in all likelihood continue. Consequently, if the burdens of authority and ideology are to be shouldered at all, they must be shouldered increasingly by the formal institutions of public government: the school, various local and state welfare and recreational agencies, the police, the army and possibly organized youth corps. It is depressing that these organizations themselves increasingly seem to lack direction, vision and a meaningful sense of their function and vocation. Lacking the rationale of authority, they are reluctant to shoulder the very burdens and responsibilities their work demands. I believe, indeed, that they are increasingly reluctant even to acknowledge these burdens and responsibilities, concealing their evasion under a pervasive doctrine of permissiveness and acceptance. Hence, the breakdown of parental authority is coupled with reluctance and inability to supplant that authority by governing institutions which are themselves adrift. If this is correct, violence on the part of the young is not the consequence of an authority that misunderstands youth, but, rather, the result of no authority whatsoever. No orientation toward the juvenile problem is more pathetically blind and blindly dangerous than the slogan "What those kids need is to be taught some respect for authority." What those kids need is to find authority. They will learn respect for it by themselves.

Power Without Authority

When authority leaves, power, often specifically physical, enters. When power is challenged, violence follows. To the juveniles, society presents and asserts itself mainly through the police, who have power, but no authority. When challenged, they quickly resort to violence. An old, and under certain conditions correct, definition of the state sees it as the agency in society which holds a monopoly on the means of violence. That dreary definition comes close to the reality of the state for juveniles. Small wonder that they emulate the state, challenge its monopoly, and try to convert it into an oligopoly.

Under these conditions, violence becomes for the gang both a value in itself and a valued means to other ends. So estranged are the juveniles from society that they can only rage at it and copy its own men of violence. And yet, they do not quite understand their hate, nor are they altogether sure of its legitimacy. This ambivalence is easily explained, for the young, tough, cool gang member wants and needs society even while he rages at it. He needs both its love and its authority. His transgressions must grow ever more extreme until he gets what he needs, for they are his way of reaching for both love and authority.

Nor will negotiation succeed so long as society presents itself as power without authority. Authority must simultaneously punish, accept and instruct. The police can only punish. Attempts at rehabilitation based on either "pure" compassion or the technique of co-opting the vicious ones into the system will not work either, because delinquents seek a love that is bound to authority: They want to be men, not children. Co-optation will not work because a hollowness in the system itself produces their frustration and thus their rage. If this were not so, the lower classes alone would become alienated and delinquent, whereas these phenomena are on the increase among middle-class youth. They are appearing, not only in the United States, but in the other prosperous and increasingly prosperous countries of western and northern Europe, as well as in such countries as the Soviet Union, in which standards of living have risen rapidly in the last few years. On February 11, 1962, *The New York Times* reported that Polish officials were dismayed to discover, and at a loss to understand, a fifty percent increase in juvenile delinquency during the past three years, when economic conditions had improved handsomely. Mere prosperity or comfort is not the answer. Society must offer the young an authority and a meaning worth growing up to. Otherwise, they will refuse to grow up, and will continue to strike out.

A New Ethic

The broad relations I have been trying to chart did not begin yesterday. They are, in fact, among the defining characteristics of what we loosely refer to as "the modern era," which was born in the Renaissance and the Reformation.

The Renaissance opened with the rebirth of ancient learning and ended with the death of the ancients. Consequently, the modern era begins with an attack on authority and age, and with a commitment to youth and the new. So successful was the Renaissance attack that, today, being young is considered good in and of itself, and being old is at best a misfortune, at worst an embarrassment. When even the adults long to be young, the young have nothing to grow up to. They can never become elders; they can only grow old.

The Reformation produced a somewhat different, though closely related, result.[7] From that era we have inherited a legacy called the Protestant Ethic. Received opinion today holds that the Protestant Ethic is dead, but I am not convinced. Value systems die hard, and they have a way of shaping judgments and behavior long after they have disappeared as explicit and consciously held doctrines. So it is here. The Protestant Ethic may be in its grave, but its spirit still roams abroad to haunt us.

The Protestant Ethic gave us a moral vocabulary celebrating individual achievement and responsibility. It taught us to believe that we could rightfully expect moral satisfaction from our work and from our sacrifices of the present for the future. Today those virtues and expectations do not seem appropriate to our social situation, yet we have found no substitutes and we are uneasy. We experience a large and growing discrepancy between what our value system and moral rhetoric prescribe and the typical behavior that modern social organization demands. Our moral vocabulary honors individual exploit, whereas our social system needs and produces organization men. Modern sociology tells us we are all status seekers, whereas our inherited social ethic condemns status seeking. Our inherited work ethic honors the labor that produces life's basic necessities, emphasizing individual skill and enterprise; yet, today more and more men are engaged in the routines of making, say, Yo-yos, and more and more others in creating a market for them.

In sum, our value system and our social system are out of joint. The former does not give us a moral vocabulary which justifies what the latter requires. The result, I think, is a pervasive malaise, a vague sense of betrayal, and the feeling that somehow a great deal of our social system is not admirable. At the very least, a culture that does not honor much of what its members must actually do produces a very uneasy population. That uneasiness falls differently on persons differently located in the social structure, and I believe its impact is relevant both to the origins and nature of juvenile violence and to the ways in which society at large perceives and copes with that violence.

The Task

If my argument has any merit, it indicates that our fundamental task is to provide a meaningful society and culture, one worth growing up to. This task is so difficult that any comments about it here must necessarily be inadequate. Still, there is one most significant point that I wish to make.

Our task is, above all, intellectual. It is a task for thought. We need constructive and sympathetic efforts toward understanding our situation and discovering whatever better alternatives it offers. In this sense, our task is that of reviving positive utopian, ideological and mythological thought on the widest scale. By utopian thought, I mean attempts to "make the possibilities of the future imaginatively concrete."[8] Given this definition, our age is not lacking in utopian thought; on the contrary, we are rich in such thought, but our riches consist largely of utopias that are destructive, baneful, even satanic. I am asking for positive utopian thought, which projects visions of a noble future worth growing up to.

This will not be easy, since so many powerful tendencies of our time are against it. For one, our grim experience with attempts to realize Marxism, the grand utopia of the nineteenth century, has almost led us to conclude that every effort to translate ideals into reality must end in defeat at best, terror at worst. Still, it should also have taught us the more hopeful lesson that means and ends are inextricably related, requiring equal care. For another, our critical and scientific age regards the debunker more highly than the dreamer, which makes it almost illegitimate to dream. The dreamer needs faith, hope and courage to withstand contempt and ridicule, or—worse—amused indifference. Hence, the very forces that destroyed the old dreams also stand in the way of making new dreams. Nevertheless, only the dreamers can save us from the realists.

Notes

1. Hannah Arendt, *The Human Condition* (Chicago, Ill.: University of Chicago Press, 1958), pp. 203–04.
2. Bertrand de Jouvenel, *Sovereignty: An Inquiry into the Political Good,* tr. by J. F. Huntington (Chicago, Ill.: University of Chicago Press, 1957), pp. 203–04.
3. Ibid., p. 30.
4. Erik H. Erikson, "The Problem of Ego Identity," *Journal of the American Psychoanalytic Association,* Vol. 4, No. 1 (1956), pp. 58–121.
5. Ibid., p. 80.
6. Ibid., p. 81.
7. This and the next two paragraphs owe much to B.M. Berger, "The Sociology of Leisure: Some Suggestions," *Industrial Relations,* Vol. I. No. 2 (1962), pp. 31–45.
8. Kenneth Keniston, "Alienation and the Decline of Utopia," *American Scholar,* Vol. 29, No. 2 (1960), p. 182.

The Case for Patriotism

I intend to write something of a plea for patriotism. That intention is so uncongenial to almost eveybody who is likely to read the essay that I want to spell it out with some care. In doing this, I wish not to disarm the critics, but to help them find the right target.

Consider first the state of opinion and sentiment on the subject.

Patriotism is unwelcome in many quarters of the land today, and unknown in many others. There is virtually no thoughtful discussion of the subject, for the word has settled, in most people's minds, deep into a brackish pond of sentiment where thought cannot reach. Politicians and members of patriotic associations praise it, of course, but official and professional patriotism too often sounds like nationalism, patriotism's bloody brother. On the other hand, patriotism has a bad name among many thoughtful people, who see it as a horror at worst, a vestigial passion largely confined to the thoughtless at best: as enlightenment advances, patriotism recedes. The intellectuals are virtually required to repudiate it as a condition of class membership. The radical and dropout young loathe it. Most troublesome of all, for one who would make the argument I intend to make, is the fact that both the groups that hate and those that glorify patriotism largely agree that it and nationalism are the same thing. I hope to show that they are different things—related, but separable.

Opponents of patriotism might agree that if the two could be separated then patriotism would look fairly attractive. But the opinion is widespread, almost atmospheric, that the separation is impossible, that with the triumph of the nation-state, nationalism has indelibly stained patriotism: the two are warp and woof. The argument against patriotism goes on to say that, psychologically considered, patriot and nationalist are the same: both are characterized by exaggerated love for one's own collectivity combined with more or less contempt and hostility toward outsiders. In addition, advanced political opinion holds that positive, new ideas and forces—e.g., internationalism, universal humanism, economic interdependence, socialist solidarity—are healthier bonds of unity, and more to be encouraged, than the older ties of patriotism. These are genuine objections, and they are held by many thoughtful people. I shall try to respond to them toward the end of the essay.

The obstacles to speaking for patriotism do not end with brackishness of opinion. For if some people favor patriotism, largely for the wrong reasons, and some oppose it, largely for the wrong reasons, others hardly think about it at all. Millions of Americans are simply without patriotism, and this large group includes all classes and kinds of persons. They do not think unpatriotic thoughts, but they do not think patriotic thoughts either. The republic for them is a vague and distant thing, absent from their hearts, lost to their eyes. Reflecting this indifference, our great patriotic holidays, now administratively arranged to provide long weekends, are less occasions for shared remembrance and renewal of the political covenant than boosts to the consumer economy. That modern compendium of man's knowledge of man, the *International Encyclopedia of Social Sciences*, apparently agrees that patriotism is a nonthing, for it is silent on the subject.

There is another obstacle to discussion. The word patriotism is a member of a family of words and largely takes its meanings from its membership. Some other members of the family are legacy, covenant, reverence, loyalty, nurture, roots, citizen, debt, gift and republic. These words, which once clarified the matter, today encounter the same barrier of mystification-distrust-indifference as does patriotism itself. All these words must appear in the discussion: there are no satisfactory alternatives. Furthermore, these words cannot be cut out of our political lives as easily as they have been dropped from our encyclopedia. If we lose them, it will not be easy to find replacements, and we may learn too late that the loss was grievous. Still, many people do not now share this view of the matter, and this sets a difficult obstacle in the path of discussion.

Patriotism has certainly declined in the United States. Nor is this decline the result of recent or transient causes. Most of the widely known patriotic associations were formed in the last decade of the nineteenth century, which suggests that as the natural springs of patriotic sentiment dried up, the land had to be irrigated. By now the land is so parched that even when American participation in the war in Southeast Asia comes to an end, along with all the reports of American corruption and exploitation at home and abroad, I doubt whether we shall love this country any the more, although we might despise it less.

I have little hope that my plea for patriotism will succeed, and much anxiety that it will be heard by many as fatuous or wrong-headed. Citizens would not need the argument, and noncitizens probably cannot hear it. Still, I shall make the argument. I do so partly out of blockheadedness, partly out of a wish to repay a welcome debt to patriotic predecessors and contemporaries, and partly for two reasons that might carry more weight. The first reason stems from my affection and respect for fellow-citizens, and from my wish to see them even more respectable than they are. We have lost patriotism. Although many count the loss small, and many others do not know it has occurred, I believe that the loss is great. The second reason stems from my wish to see a revitalized radical politics in this country, and from my conviction that Susan Sontag is correct when she says that "probably no serious radical movement has any future in America unless it can revalidate the tarnished idea of patriotism."[1] The radicals of the 1960s did not persuade their fellow-Americans, high or low, that they genuinely cared for and shared a country with them. And no one who has contempt for others can hope to teach those others. A revived radicalism must be a patriotic radicalism. It must share and care for the common things, even while it has a "lovers' quarrel" with fellow-citizens.

Natural Patriotism

Since patriotism is a complex and dangerous word, we must give some care to definition. But not too much care, for like all the important political words, it cannot be protected against the vicissitudes of history and passion; and not the wrong kind of care either, for the word comes not from the laboratory but from life. The word will not hold still while we attach a single, universal meaning to it, but we can describe a nucleus of meanings.

At its core, patriotism means love of one's homeplace, and of the familiar things and scenes associated with the homeplace. In this sense, patriotism is one of the basic human sentiments. If not a natural tendency in the species, it is at least a proclivity produced by realities basic to human life, for territoriality, along with family, has always been a primary associative bond. We become devoted to the people, places, and ways that nurture us, and what is familiar and nurturing seems also natural and right. This is the root of patriotism. Furthermore, we are all subject to the immense power of habit, and patriotism has habit in its service. Even if we leave the homeplace for a larger world, finding delight in its variety and novelty, we delight as much in returning to familiar things. The theme of homecoming is the central motif of patriotic discourse, as old and as deep as the return of Odysseus from Troy, and the feeling is always the same:

> When we saw the top of the mountain from Albuquerque we wondered if it was our mountain, and we felt like talking to the ground, we loved it so, and some of the old men and women cried with joy when they reached their homes.[2]

The other side of the case is the melancholy figure of the lone wanderer, or of the Stoic whose "my home is everywhere" meant he had a home nowhere.

To be a patriot is to have a patrimony; or, perhaps more accurately, the patriot is one who is grateful for a legacy and recognizes that the legacy makes him a debtor. There is a whole way of being in the world, captured best by the word reverence, which defines life by its debts: one is what one owes, what one acknowledges as a rightful debt or obligation. The patriot moves within that mentality. The gift of land, people, language, gods, memories, and customs, which is the patrimony of the patriot, defines what he or she is. Patrimony is mixed with person; the two are barely separable. The very tone and rhythm of a life, the shapes of perception, the texture of its hopes and fears come from membership in a territorially rooted group. The conscious patriot is one who feels deeply indebted for those gifts, grateful to the people and places through which they came, and determined to defend the legacy against enemies and pass it unspoiled to those who will come after.

But such primary experiences are nearly inaccessible to us. We are taught to define our lives not by our debts and legacies, but by our rights and opportunities. Robert Frost's stark line, "This land was ours, before we were the land's," condenses the whole story of American patriotism. We do not and cannot love this land the way the Greeks and the Navaho loved theirs. The graves of some of our ancestors are here, to be sure, but most of us would be hard pressed to find them: name and locate the graves of your great-grandparents. The land was not granted to us in trust by a Great Spirit, nor are there in this land a thousand places sacred to lesser deities. Having purged ourselves of pantheism, we do not dwell in a realm alive with sacred groves and fountains.[3] We are all doctrinal monotheists and our only patriotic god is the god of battles. We took the land from others whom we regarded as of no account. The land itself we saw as a resource for comfort and power available to all who had the strength to take it. Among us, only persons (artificial as well as natural) have rights. The homestead has none. We may buy, sell, and use it as we wish. It has no claims we need heed or even hear. Still today, and even in the ecology movement, the same attitude prevails: Save *Our* Coast. Still possession, not union and stewardship.

Perhaps this lack of natural patriotism is some part of the explanation of American restlessness and rootlessness.[4] When Europeans first came to this land they saw nothing but savages in a howling wilderness, both of which had to be conquered. Seeking neither welcome nor permission from those already here, they imposed their alien god and ways on the "new land." That original act of conquest and sacrilege was repeated innumerable times as the wave rolled west, until now the very land accuses the intruders. There can be no experience of homecoming without welcome, and we shall not feel welcome here until we learn how to ask it of those who alone have it to give. That we may be slowly coming to understand this is one of the few hopeful signs for American patriotism.[5]

Perhaps it is impossible to know whether the nature of the conquest helped produce American restlessness and rootlessness, but it is certain that the restlessness and rootlessness in their turn make a natural patriotism nearly possible. The seeds of patriotism can germinate on even the stoniest ground, but they must have time to put down roots. We are a nation on the go, always moving, and always with somewhere left to move to. Many of us now even have mobile homes, with no roots in the earth at all. The purpose of life is to get ahead, and getting ahead means leaving others behind—an outlook which makes us distinctive among the nomadic peoples. There is little piety toward the past and the future is something to be conquered. Ages and generations of care are required for the nurturing of that primary patriotism of place which has been a treasured and defining experience of most of humankind. In recent American letters, perhaps only William Faulkner, Robert Frost, and Edmund Wilson wrote in the language of natural patriotism—and Wilson became querulous toward the end. We are a people to whom the experience of displacement is so natural that we do not know we are displaced, and it is hard for us to appreciate how desolating the experience can be for others. The following words were written by a Laotian poet pleading for a way of life now destroyed by American bombs:

> Pity—our houses, ricefields, inheritance—we must abandon. The ricefields will grow jungles. They will become a wild place filled with tigers. Have pity; the lands, the ponds with fish, everything; pity the bathing hole where no one will come to swim and muddy the cool waters. Pity the crabs, fish, game, bamboo shoots; our kind of food. Sorrow for the fruit trees we planted in the garden and around the village, the clumps of large and small bamboo; have pity! . . . The day does not exist when we will forget.[6]

Can we for whom "relocation" means moving elsewhere in pursuit of income and opportunity understand this? Have we found satisfactory substitutes for it in batting averages, or color televison, or flights to the moon?

In sum, then, that kind of patriotism which Tocqueville called instinctive is not available to us.[7] There is no way to measure the weight of this loss, but if instinctive patriotism is the basic urge I think it is, then the loss is heavy. Surely, human beings can feel the lack of something they need even though they might never have had it. To feel the loss of something, it is not necessary first to have had that thing. (Consider "love," for example, which many psychologists say we all need, even though many of us have never had it.) The trouble is, that when a deprivation is of this sort the victim may not interpret his condition correctly: people attempted all sorts of cures for goiter before they learned about iodine. Not knowing what it is one needs, one mistakes symptoms for cause, and tries to fill the need through harmful substitutes for the real thing. Perhaps this is the case with us.

Just one step removed from land patriotism is patriotism of the city. Both center on the idea and sentiment of home and nurture. Both acknowledge that the foundation of life is debt. Both shape individual life by reference to the common and familiar things. Their only important difference is in the object of attachment. The city is the creation of human beings and is in that obvious sense artificial, the image of an ideal, while the land, even when altered by labor and love, remains fundamentally the work of nature. The supreme expression of city patriotism is to be found in Pericles' eulogy for the Athenian dead, and a study of that discourse will teach one all that can be learned about the subject.

Certainly city patriotism can be as intense as patriotism of the land. Machiavelli cared more for his city than for his own soul. And Fustel de Coulanges' book on *The Ancient City* describes how much of human life could be founded on the city's gods, exhibited in the city's temples and public spaces, and protected by the city's walls. Each family had its private home and hearth, but the city was a second home, made by all and common to all. City patriotism was profoundly "social" in its orientations: Socrates did not like to leave Athens for even a day in the country, because he could not talk with trees.

City patriotism, then, is not profoundly different from land patriotism, though it is a step beyond it in the direction of the artificial and the ideal. Like land patriotism, it too is declining. In the times when cities were few, they were precious to their citizens by reason of their very artificiality. A small man-made thing protected by its walls from the vast wilderness without, the city nourished a life which was distinctively human. As time went on, the works of the human kind appeared everywhere, becoming less valuable as they became more common. That is true the world over. In the United States, in addition, cities have been from the beginning products largely of the impulse of profit and hustle, owing little to the sacred and the traditional. Hence, there is as little of city patriotism among us as there is of the ancient patriotism of place. Furthermore, the people and shapes, as well as the monuments and traditions, of our cities change so rapidly that citizens have no time to form solid and enduring attachments. Even the sports teams, closest modern equivalent to the gods of the ancient city, can be moved by a few million dollars.

Covenanted Patriotism

But if instinctive patriotism and the patriotism of the city cannot be ours, what can be? Is there a type of patriotism peculiarly American; if so, is it anything more than patriotism's violent relative, nationalism?

Abraham Lincoln, the supreme authority on this subject, thought there was a patriotism unique to America. Americans, a motley gathering of various races and cultures, were bonded together not by blood or religion, not by tradition or territory, not by the walls and traditions of a city, but by a political idea. We are a nation formed by a covenant, by dedication to a set of principles and by an exchange of promises to uphold and advance certain commitments among ourselves and throughout the world. Those principles and commitments are the core of American identity, the soul of the body politic. They make the American nation unique, and uniquely valuable, among and to the other nations. But the other side of this conception contains a warning very like the warnings spoken by the prophets to Israel: if we fail in our promises to each other, and lose the principles of the covenant, then we lose everything, for they are we. This makes it quite clear that we are dealing here with a conception very different from Rousseau's advocacy of a civil religion as the bond of political community. For Lincoln, the principles of the covenant set the standard by which the nation must judge itself: the nation is righteous and to be honored only insofar as it honors the covenant. For Rousseau, the civil religion is designed to induce the individual to venerate the nation itself. I shall hope to show that the best way to define the failure of American patriotism is to see it as a decline from the noble example and promise of Lincoln's conception, to the banal performance of Rousseau's.

Lincoln developed and expounded his conception of the national covenant over a number of years and on a number of significant occasions. One of his fullest statements of the idea came when he was about to enter the highest office in the land. On his way to Washington to take up the Presidency, Lincoln was invited to speak in Independence Hall, Philadelphia. Deeply moved by the place, he expressed his understanding of America's meaning and mission in a handful of memorable words—and half-consciously revealed his own and the nation's future. The whole speech should be read. Here are some critical passages:

> I am filled with deep emotion at finding myself standing here in the place where were collected together the wisdom, the patriotism, the devotion to principle, from which sprang the institutions under which we live. . . . I can say . . . that all the political sentiments I entertain have been drawn . . . from the sentiments which originated, and were

given to the world from this hall in which we stand. I have never had a feeling politically that did not spring from the sentiments embodied in the Declaration of Independence. . . . I have often inquired of myself, what great principle or idea it was that kept this confederacy so long together. It was . . . something in that Declaration giving liberty, not alone to the people of this country, but hope to the world for all future time. It was that which gave promise that in due time the weights should be lifted from the shoulders of all men, and that *all* should have an equal chance. . . .

Now, my friends, can this country be saved upon that basis? If it can, I will consider myself one of the happiest men in the world if I can help to save it. If it can't be saved upon that principle, it will be truly awful. But, if this country cannot be saved without giving up that principle—I was about to say I would rather be assassinated on this spot than to surrender it.[8]

In this discourse Lincoln asserted that the articles of the political covenant are both perfectly clear and grounded in the firmest authority. Three years later, on land consecrated by blood, he repeated the same themes. The nation born in 1776 was "conceived in liberty, and dedicated to the proposition that all men are created equal." Continuing in unbroken line, generation was tied to generation by that common birth and promise. In a fragment written early in 1861, but not published, Lincoln stated his understanding of the relation between covenant and people—between the Declaration of Independence on the one side and the Constitution and Union on the other. He expressed the connection by a luminous metaphor drawn from the Book of Proverbs. The principle announced in the Declaration he called an "apple of gold," while "the Union and the Constitution are the pictures of silver, subsequently framed around it. The picture was made, not to conceal, or destroy the apple; but to adorn and preserve it. The picture was made for the apple—not the apple for the picture" (IV, 240).

One more statement, this time from the young Lincoln. Again the occasion is significant. Lincoln had just been elected to the Illinois legislature, and he accepted an invitation to address the Young Men's Lyceum of Springfield: an occasion of beginning, then, like the speech in Independence Hall. Lincoln chose as his theme "the perpetuation of our political institutions" (I, 108-15).

He opened the discourse by reminding his listeners that the men of the Revolution had fought to found a polity dedicated to liberty and self-government. Those principles were safe while the founders lived for they knew the price that had been paid for them. The scenes and memories of the struggle were visible to their eyes and lively to their memories. Many individuals and families treasured and retold the stories of sacrifice and danger. But now those scenes are distant. We who came after the struggle and had no part in it cannot see it in the scars on our bodies, cannot even relive it through the eyes and voices of the actors. Being distant, we easily forget why those others fought and died, and we cannot justly value the gift they gave to us. Our forgetting opens the path to talented persons of great ambition who, if they cannot gain fame by preserving the principles of the founding, will gain fame by wrecking them. Only if the founding principles are kept alive and pure in the minds and hearts of the citizenry shall we be safe from perverted ambition—or, indeed, safe from ourselves. We must, then, see as the chief task of political life the task of political education: inculcate respect for valid laws as a "political religion"; retell on every possible occasion the story of the struggle; teach tirelessly the principles of the founding. The only guardian of the compact is an informed citizenry, and the first task of leadership is the formation of such a citizenry.[9]

This is a conception of patriotic devotion that fits a nation as large and heterogeneous as our own. It sets a mission and provides a standard of judgment. It tells us when we are acting justly and it does not confuse martial fervor with dedication to country. Lincoln also reminded us that the covenant is not a static legacy or a gift outright, but a burden and a promise. The nation exists only in repeated acts of remembrance and renewal of the covenant through changing circumstances. Patriotism here is more than a frame of mind. It is also activity guided by and directed toward the mission established in the founding covenant. This conception of political membership also decisively transcends the parochial and primitive fraternities of blood and race, for it calls kin all who accept the authority of the covenant. And finally, this covenanted patriotism assigns America a teaching mission among the nations, rather than a superiority over or a hostility toward them.[10] This patriotism is compatible with the most generous humanism.[11]

Now, only the willfully blind could fail to see that American patriotism in practice has failed to live up to Lincoln's teaching of the ideal. Most of the reasons are obvious; others are more subtle.

First of all, certain peoples were excluded from the covenant, some from the beginning, some later on: Indians, Negroes, Mexican Americans, Orientals. Then too, from early on, liberty was largely interpreted as private liberty, and equality soon came to mean equal opportunity to compete for the prizes of wealth and power. There was little teaching of liberty as public liberty—the power of acting with others to shape the conditions of the common life. (Henry Adams thought the political age had ended by 1816, supplanted by the economic age.) The activity of politics was seen as but another of the instrumentalities by which self-interested individuals advanced toward private goals. The very notion of a public good dissolved into an aggregate of particular goods, and Lincoln's conception of the patriotic citizen as one who treasures and upholds the basic principles of the political covenant dissolved along with it.[12]

Today our skepticism toward all notions of disinterested, public-regarding behavior is so thoroughgoing that the patriot can hardly appear. We are inclined to regard all professions of public-spirited and altruistic motive as the blandishments of a charlatan or the deceptions of a schemer—and we are largely right, for over time, a people gets the politics it expects and asks for. When these political conceptions were added to the ethic of competition and mastery in the economic sphere, the ground was prepared for the full flowering of that individualism which Tocqueville diagnosed as the deadliest enemy of civic virtue. In sum, liberalism and capitalism corrupted the covenant, while racism denied it to large groups of the population.

Other forces completed the work which liberalism, capitalism, and racism had begun. The idea and experience of a covenanted community have deeper roots in the American past than those exposed by Lincoln. The Puritan Commonwealth of New England was exactly such a community. Individuals became members of the community only upon acceptance of certain articles of religious faith and morals. That acceptance had to be proved in practice, and to the satisfaction of the guardians of the covenant. Social institutions were designed to encourage performance of the covenant. The Puritans discouraged the formation of isolated, private farmsteads and tried to keep all persons in the towns, in sight of each other, and with life centered in the meetinghouse. In sum, membership was not a right of birth. It had to be earned, and was the reward of choice and effort. Institutions were designed to encourage the choice and supervise the effort.

That idea of earned membership still forms the center of American nationality, but time and circumstances have worked strange changes on it.[13] As time went on, America opened its doors to the stranger on easy terms. Only one restriction remained: the strangers had to become republicans. They had to accept the fundamental terms of the founding covenant. The Constitution even specifies that each state shall have a republican form of government. We imposed no religious tests for membership, no tests of cultural or linguistic background, no tests—with well-known exceptions—of blood or race. But we did require a profession of republican faith. In that decisive way, the New England idea of earned membership in a covenanted community persisted. It is a fascinating idea, at once universal and generous and parochial and narrow: universal and generous in that it is willing to embrace as members a great variety of human and cultural types, rejecting neither Turk nor Greek *qua* Turk or Greek, blind to divisions that had for centuries brought the Old World to repression and war; narrow in that it reduced the person to official beliefs, denying the significance of all those other things that go to make up character and style, all those things that human conversation is about.

As time went on, the narrowness prevailed against the generosity. First of all, the social institutions that provided the nursery and school for learning and following the covenant declined. The close New England town gave way to the isolated homestead, or to the city of recent immigrants. No longer was life lived and tested under the eyes of familiars. Then, the forgetting that Lincoln so feared took its toll so that the gift of public liberty seemed a small one. Our teachers began to teach, and we to value, private life and liberty above all. The growth of capitalist enterprise and the spread of the competitive ethic hastened the work of isolation and privatization. And then, during the last third of the nineteenth century, capitalism became equated with America itself. At the very time when the free enterprise system was being swallowed by the corporate system, the ideology of free enterprise became identified with the spirit of Americanism. Finally, with the huge immigrations of 1890-1920, and with the emergence of the United States as a world power, efforts to assimilate the foreign-born and assure their loyalty were greatly accelerated. More and more we turned to propaganda and to one or another form of loyalty test. An American became one who would not profess certain beliefs or who would not do certain things: from belief in anarchism, to the practice of polygamy, to joining the Communist Party, and on to disavowing the use of revolutionary force and violence. A nation of strangers, ignorant of the most important things about the folks next door, we attempted to assure predictable behavior by requiring ritual disavowals of feared beliefs and practices. The quest for consensus in national politics followed almost naturally—as though patriots were persons who did not disagree, as though patriotism were a matter of professing certain doctrines and supporting the party policies of the day, rather than a steadfast devotion to the founding principles and a disinterested search for the good of the whole.

The "apple of gold" tarnished, while we polished the "picture of silver." Rousseau's conception of a civic religion drove out Lincoln's conception of a covenanted citizenry whose patriotism was exercised in active dedication to the promises and goals of the republic.

Even so, Lincoln's idea remains alive as possibly the only saving conception of patriotism possible for us. It is surely the understanding of patriotic duty that inspired the civil rights activity of the 1960s, and that for one glorious moment called more Harvard seniors to the Peace Corps than to the Business School. It is the only idea of civic obligation that can provide a full defense for civilly disobeying laws or orders circumscribing liberty or violating the principle of equal justice for all. The idea was expressed by many of the young men who publicly refused conscription during the late

1960s on the grounds that the Vietnam War violated America's obligations to itself and to the nations—expressed not by those who fled or hid, or who used the labyrinth of the law to avoid the burdens of moral choice and political action, but by those who publicly resisted and publicly paid the penalties of resistance.

Lincoln's conception of covenanted patriotism also offers the noblest rationale for active citizenship (government of, by, and for the people) resident in our tradition. Virtually every other argument for participation familiar to Americans starts from the premise of self-interest and sees political participation in exclusively instrumental and economistic terms. Seen in this light, SDS's "Port Huron Statement" of 1962, with its conviction that the individual should "share in those social decisions determining the quality and direction of his life," is the finest expression of the Lincolnian idea in recent times. The Port Huron Statement offers a vision of an active and cooperative citizenry who see the political system as *their* system, and who understand that if the system is to survive according to its own principles, it will survive only by their efforts, and not by the ministrations of an elected monarch and an elite of managers, no matter how benign and competent. Such an elite might be able to keep order and distribute comfort, and might even be able to defend the populace against external enemies and help it to adjust to the strains of incessant change at home, but it cannot preserve the system on its own principles. It cannot do that because one of those principles is that the system belongs to the citizens. It is theirs; and at the moment an elite "saves" it for them, at that moment it dies.

Finally, Lincoln's idea proposes a strictly political definition of our nationhood, one which liberates us from the parochialisms of race and religion, and one which severs patriotic devotion from the cult of national power. It is, in my estimation, a calamity that this idea of patriotism has been so corrupted and subverted among us. The work of reviving, purifying, and establishing it is the supreme task of American political education.

Nationalism

A covenanted polity might be our finest tradition and best hope. It is not our reality. That reality is nationalism.

Even natural patriotism has a face less attractive than the one drawn above. Our preference for our own home and ways is easily understandable, and on the whole, admirable. Understandable too, but less admirable, is the easy step from preference to pride. Our peculiar characteristics easily come to seem not just the best for us, but the best. And they remain the best because they are ours. The logic may be weak, but the psycho-logic is very strong. Furthermore, the strange ways of others may seem to us not merely inferior to our own, but dangerous and threatening. Fear and distrust of the stranger are the dark force of patriotism, and they are as potent and flammable as the saving force of love for one's own.

The moral thrust of patriotism, then, is inherently ambivalent. It simultaneously unites and divides, encourages both concord and discord. There is no way to eradicate that ambivalence. It is this feature of the sentiment that has brought many to yearn for its disappearance. But that is a mistaken yearning, based on failure to see that not just patriotism but every human devotion both unites and divides. Every devotion draws a magic circle around some people and things, excluding others, and thereby automatically divides the world into those within and those outside the circle. Love does that, and so do faith and loyalty. Division and conflict are built into the dialectic of devotion.

The real trouble enters with the recognition that patriotism is not just a moral devotion but also a political passion, an attachment to political objects. From a group's political history come most of the points of pride, the revered heroes, the memories of sacrifice and courage, and the goals and values which form the ordinary member's sense of shared identity and shape his conception of patriotic duty. Through that history one becomes a participant in the corporate life, sharing its destiny, appropriating its triumphs and defeats, making its will one's own. Socrates called the laws of Athens his parents.

That corporate life is organized. It has a focus and a structure. And when that organization takes the form of the state, patriotism is easily warped to destructive ends. States are in their very nature combat organizations. They claim a monopoly of the legitimate use of force, and they employ propaganda to shape the thoughts and emotions of members. Through propaganda, the state incessantly tries to convince citizens that the support and enlargement of state power is their first duty, even to the point of overriding all other duties, even to the point of excusing lies and murder. The state may be, as Nietzsche called it, the coldest of cold monsters, but it knows well how to heat up the passions of its subjects. That is the elementary and invaluable political knowledge of the statesmen of our day, right or left: Fidel Castro's exploitation of the theme of anti-Americanism has been a more valuable resource in the consolidation of the Cuban state than any amount of material aid the United States could possibly provide; the architects of the Cold War, using anticommunist propaganda, gave the Pentagon a stronger foundation than could ever have been built from tradition and prudence.

In our time the nation-state has successfully claimed itself to be the sole legitimate object of patriotic attachment, with results that have been on the whole disastrous. Many lesser loyalties fell before the surge of nationalism, and patriotism, too, had to be reduced in its objects and meanings. In earlier times, when people were enclosed in narrow circles of experience and devotion, the proper vocation of education was to call them out of the parochial, urging them toward higher and more general loyalties. But now the situation is different, and perhaps the task of education is different too. E. M. Forster spoke the untimely words appropriate to our time when he said that if ever it became necessary to choose between betraying his country or his friend, he hoped he would have the courage to betray his country.

Because nationalism is so pervasive today, it seems to be almost in the order of nature. But that is wrong. It is patriotism of the kind described at the outset of this essay that is natural. Nationalism is artificial. It is the product of specific social, economic, and intellectual forces and just as it was born only yesterday, it could die tomorrow. Nationalism takes sentiments basic to the nurture of human life, welds them to a certain political structure, and warps them in an almost entirely bellicose direction. It appeared in the states of the West at a definite stage of history and it filled definite needs. Nationalsim could triumph only when liberalism had proceeded so far in its work of breaking the bonds among men that new ones were needed to provide at least a minimum of warmth and some measure of connectedness and direction. In all the liberal states, the same two myths were forged to replace the broken links: nationalism was one; the cult of progress the other. Outside the West, nationalism has typically flared up in response to humiliations imposed by Western states on traditional cultures and regimes.

Feelings of nationality existed long before the modern age, to be sure, but they were largely inarticulate and unorganized. They were not shaped and sharpened by propaganda into a unity of emotion, thought and will: Machiavelli's appeal for a prince to unify Italy and liberate it from the foreigners had to wait three hundred and fifty years for an answer. But patriotism and nationalism were not the same, and nationality was not regarded as the foundation of the political order. In the classical age, for example, those who called themselves Greeks had a strong sense of common nationality which distinguished them from non-Greeks. Greeks spoke the same language and had many gods and ceremonies in common, but they gathered themselves politically into a large number of city-states, each autonomous and with its distinctive regime. The Greek treasured his unique city as much as he treasured his common Greekness, and did not think that common nationality required a single political organization encompassing and commanding the loyalty of all Greeks. Similarly, for nearly the whole of recorded history, right up until quite recent times, most wars took place not between different national groups, but either between great empires or between tribes, regions, and cities of kindred nationality. Struggles were either cosmopolitan or local, not nationalistic. Admittedly, the war between the Jews and the Philistines provides an early example of nationalist conflict—complete even to the use of inflammatory propaganda—but the case is anomalous.

We live so fully enclosed in the circle of nationalism that we can hardly see beyond it. Hence, it is useful to emphasize just how recent the phenomenon is. Up until only yesterday in China, family and clan set the horizons of loyalty. What we call Italy and Germany have been unified states for less than a century. When George Washington said "my country," he meant Virginia, a usage which persisted until some time after the revolution of 1776. Our own civil war was the greatest nationalist struggle of the nineteenth century.[14] The South surely had the better of the Constitutional argument, and only arms could clear the way for the definition of the American polity as an "indestructible Union, composed of indestructible States" (Texas v. White, 1869).

Vast changes in the foundations of social life were required for the appearance and triumph of nationalism, changes that in sum amount to a characterization of modernity. The decline of religious faith as the basic bond among people and as the primary source of cultural life prepared the way. So too did the breakdown of cultural isolation consequent upon the development of improved means of travel and communication. These gave persons experience of others who before had hardly been present. Up until very recently, the whole territory inhabited by what we would today call a nationality, a territory often characterized by great variety of climate, landforms, and customs, was practically unknown to ordinary persons. It could become known only through travel or instruction, and these were restricted to a tiny minority. Another force decisive in the production of nationalism was the (still continuing) consolidation and growth of centralized state power. By imposing the same laws and officers on large numbers of people, by subjecting those people to the same historical experiences, the great monarchies of England, France, Sweden, and Prussia, and the huge republic of the United States were instrumental in producing common attitudes and traits among a large population. In time, this formed what is loosely called a national character—a thing real enough, though hard to define, and by no means immutable: the French used to think the English riotous. The centralized state simultaneously molded national character and claimed to be its sole legitimate defender and spokesman.

Another factor in the production of nationalism was the dissolution of the monarchical and dynastic principle of political legitimacy. Modern nationalism is inconceivable without the idea of popular sovereignty as the base of political legitimacy, and without the breakup of the feudal and monarchical orders. Popular sovereignty promised that the ruled would henceforth be the rulers. When the disintegration of the old order was completed, and societies became aggregates of individuals, then nationalism became the cement which held these particles together, and popular sovereignty the myth that told them they were now in charge of their own futures.

In our own day, a number of forces have given nationalism new vitality, and further corrupted the primary meanings of patriotism. One such force is the fiction that blood or race is the biological source of nationality and the basic bond among human groups. Another is the doctrine that sees the *Volksgeist* as the ever-welling fountain of nationality in all of its cultural and political manifestations. Still a third is the conviction on the part of certain nations—a conviction fostered by propaganda always and by terror and repression when necessary—that they are the bearers of precious cultural and biological seeds which must be safeguarded against enemies and planted among the unconvinced and the ignorant. Under the crusading impact of these ideas, nationalism in recent times has been a force almost wholly productive of death and exploitation.

We are still in the middle of the story of nationalism. No one can say where it will end, how long it will last, or whether it is even compatible with the survival of civilization. Two contrary tendencies vie at the moment. On the one hand, the formation of dozens of new states since World War II has meant the spread of nationalism on a world scale. On the other hand, in the older states of Europe and to a lesser degree in the United States, nationalism is ebbing. State centralization continues apace, certainly, but more under the cool logic of technology and rationalization than under the hot ideology of nationalism. But no new cohesive or cementing forces which might take the place of nationalism are yet visible (even such supranationalist ideologies as socialism and race are bent to nationalist ends), and it is doubtful whether nationalist faiths will disappear until other faiths arise to replace them.

The task of the patriot today, I think, at least in the United States, is to work to weaken the principle of nationalism and to cut its connections with the state. Nationality can be severed from nationalism, and nationalism can be depoliticized—just as religion was. No one can say if or when that day will arrive, but the struggle to hasten it is perhaps the most worthy political struggle of our time. Through that struggle, people might begin to rebuild the conditions for patriotism, and to revitalize the life-giving devotion for the things of the homeplace, a devotion whose absence now leaves us all displaced persons—tribeless, homeless, heartless ones bounced between a narrow egotism on the one side and an unsustaining universalism on the other, to be caught by a fierce nationalism in the middle.[15]

Some Objections: Historical, Moral, Psychological

At the outset, I described certain obstacles in the path of an argument for patriotism, acknowledged their severity, and promised to return to them.

1. Some will object to the word itself. It is a fact that the word does not appear in English usage until 1726 (though all the "ism" words are relatively recent; nationalism, for example, does not appear until 1844). Thus, it seems risky to associate the term with primitive emotions and ancient political experiences, as I have done. Furthermore, the banner of patriotism has been waved by at least as many scoundrels as noble men: for every Lincoln there is a Stalin. Hence, it seems risky to recommend a revival of the word and the emotion.

I admit these troubles with the word, but no other will do. Just because the word is new is no evidence that the thing is: there were viruses before there was a word for them. Besides, when Lincoln (and he was not the only one) said "patriotism" he meant something noble and interesting.

It won't do to banish words because we dislike some of their associations. Most rich words are a little rank. Of course language is often confusing, but it is also the most wonderful expression of our humanity. When we banish a word or truncate its meaning, we also truncate ourselves. There is a good bit of evidence that our humanity is today being abbreviated by this process.

It might also be politically dangerous to banish the word, because we may need it someday. Suppose the President were to suspend the writ of *habeas corpus* for persons opposed to his Court appointments. We might consider it our patriotic duty to resist; and if we did, we would probably see ourselves as acting in the tradition set by patriotic forefathers—taking the mantle of Jefferson, for example, who called upon his countrymen to fight for the ancient rights of Englishmen. We would be much weaker politically if that patriotic argument and tradition were not available to us.

Hence, it is right and prudent to keep the word alive, and to recommend the experience. Ben Johnson called patriots "sound lovers of their country." I want to restore that sense of the word.

2. Readers might be willing to let me use the word as I want, but they might still argue that the taint of history cannot be removed from it. Specifically, patriotism has been so tied up with nationalism and all its horrors in the modern age that the two can never be separated. Prussian officers served the Nazi state out of patriotism. General Curtis B. LeMay proposed bombing Vietnam into the Stone Age out of patriotism. In recent American politics, the only man who talks more about patriotism than President Nixon is Governor Wallace. Patriotism and nationalism are

inextricably linked in modern history, and both spell ignorance and hate.

In response, one would say first that it is not satisfactory here to reel off the names of monsters: for every scoundrel who called himself a patriot one could name a good man who also claimed the name. The enemies of nationalism, fighting against the state and for their families, their city, their land, or their conception of a just society—such have called themselves patriots, too.

Certainly some ignorant and cruel people have claimed the name of patriot, but that does not mean that ignorance, cruelty, and patriotism are all the same. We really do use different words for the different phenomena. Few today would call Senator Joseph McCarthy a patriot—vicious perhaps, a fool possibly, but not a patriot. As for ignorance, there are of course ignorant patriots as well as ignorant nationalists. But there are also sophisticated versions of each. It does not help thought to collapse the words or the things.

Moreover, I think that the modes of knowledge and ignorance characteristic of nationalism and patriotism are different. The knowledge of the patriot, especially of the natural patriot, is rich in memory or history and is solid and sensuous in its texture. This kind of knowledge is concrete and conservative. Its emotional tone is made up of reverence mixed with nostalgia. Such knowledge has little of the abstract about it and is not easily packaged for export. Hence, its main military expression is characteristically defense against invaders. It does not claim universality, and patriots do not comfortably support wars of expansion or wars of "principle." Edmund Burke, whose writings embody all these characteristics of patriotic thought, defended one revolution and opposed another, precisely on the grounds that the one was conservative and concrete while the other was abstract and universalist in its claims. What is today called "people's war" can only succeed when the military fish can swim in the sea of the people. That is to say, people's war is defensive and local. I think this is the kind of war characteristic of patriotism. Should it turn out that people's war, rightly conducted, has the capacity to endure and prevail against huge invading forces, that could show the way to tremendous change in world history—a real shift in the balance between nationalism and patriotism.

Nationalism, on the other hand, is rich in the knowledge of instrumental rationality, the knowledge needed to define the properties of the world as resources and to convert those resources into power. The organization of the nation-state is the political expression of the process of technique, as Jacques Ellul calls it, the process of systematically converting the things of the world into resources of power. Consider this passage from Karl Polanyi's discussion of the early stages of the modern nation-state:

> Politically, the centralized state was a new creation . . . which . . . compelled the backward peoples of larger agrarian countries to

organize for commerce and trade. In external politics, the setting up of sovereign power was the need of the day; accordingly, mercantilist statecraft involved the marshaling of the resources of the whole national territory to the purposes of power in foreign affairs. In internal politics, unification of the countries fragmented by feudal and municipal particularism was the necessary by-product of such an endeavor.[16]

That is to say, nationalism was specifically built out of the rubble of patriotism, and the chief tool in the destruction was instrumental rationality systematically employed to convert the world into resources for economic and political power.

Very early in its progress the nation-state added ideology to its armory of weapons for aggression and expansion. Those ideologies have been many, but each claims that it is not partial, so that the expansion of the nation-state can be presented as something other than the victory of the stronger. Ideology lets the nation-state parade its might and cloak its ambition as the embodiment of a universal principle. From G. W. F. Hegel to W. W. Rostow the process has been the same. "Modernization" is our version of Hegel's idealization of the Prussian State. Like very good nationalist ideology, it ranks the U.S. number one on a universal scale of values and is made for export to other countries.

Patriots make no such claims to universality, and, in that way at least, are wise in their ignorance.

Certainly there can be a patriotism more "advanced" than devotion to place alone, more devoted to ideals and principles, which is still not aggressive and expansionist. That kind of patriotism can even believe its own principles superior and yet feel no missionary urge to impose them on others. The New England Puritan intention to build a "city on a hill" is one example; Lincoln's vision of America as a promise and hope to the oppressed everywhere is another; Bourne's idea of a transnational America based on mutual respect and acceptance of variety is a third. This patriotism can have a teaching mission, but the teaching is done by example: others will see the shining city and take from it such light as they need.

We need a principle of political loyalty that can keep alive a noble tension between love for one's own place and respect for the places of others. It is very difficult for either the militant nationalist or the promiscuous universalist to honor that tension. Both of them smash through the complexities of cultural diversity, reducing them to a principle: for the nationalist, the principle is "ours is superior to the others"; for the universalist, the principle is "all are equal." The obscurantism and aggressiveness of the former obviously produce injustice. So does the eclecticism which rejects nothing, though here the injustice is less obvious. If a group within a foreign society which we will not judge protests against an injustice within its own social order, shall we still not judge? Suppose the same injustice should exist among ourselves. Have we any right to oppose it at home if we kept silent when we saw it abroad? The position of critic at home but conformist elsewhere, and the position of conformist at home but critic elsewhere, are equally contradictory and productive of injustice.

I think the patriotic mentality has a fair chance of keeping the noble tension alive. To be a patriot means to live out of a recognition that one is a member of a particular society and culture. But so are all other human beings; and their particular memberships are as important to them as ours are to us. Hence, there is no contradiction—only a tension—between taking up one's particular place and acknowledging one's condition as a member of humanity, for each member of humanity has a local habitation. We may believe that other societies, or some other society, are not as good as our own. But even if we believe that, we have no method for proving it. Recognizing that no society can be judged absolutely good or absolutely evil, it is still possible to treasure our own, even while criticizing it, and to judge others', even while respecting them. Toward all other societies than one's own one may take up a privileged position, as it were, liking them or not, as one wishes. One's own society is the only one in which one must be involved, and from which one must struggle for disengagement: there is no privileged position possible here, only the necessities of social existence. The patriot, I think, easily grasps this lesson, and easily applies it to his thinking about other peoples. Patriots know, for example—and the knowledge is almost instinctive—that only residents, not outsiders, can radically change a society's ways and customs without wrecking the society, for the changes are made from within, and that makes all the difference. This attitude by no means denies, though it admittedly does not indiscriminately encourage, borrowing from other cultures to improve one's own. At the same time, the patriotic orientation is basically conservative. Indeed, the emotion itself seems a throwback to what Rousseau called that "middle ground between the indolence of the primitive state and the questing activity"of the expansionist and technological states. Perhaps that middle condition really was, as Rousseau held, the "best for man." Perhaps too the emotions peculiar to it were healthier than the emotions associated with both the nationalism and the universalism of our day.[17]

So, it is possible and important to distinguish between patriotism and nationalism; or, more specifically, to break the confused connection between patriotism and the modern nation-state. If the whole world were to become American territory (or Russian, or Japanese, etcetera) the conception of the American state as we know it would become unnecessary. But the conception of the community will never be discarded. The word "state" represents (usually) hostile divisions of the earth, and signifies the progressive formation of connections among villages, cities, and regions. This development occurs in response to the need of all men to live together, and in response to the urge of some men to dominate that living together. But if all the boundary lines representing states were erased, and the state as we know it disappeared, the conception of the community would not be threatened. It will exist as long as mankind exists. Patriotism is the emotion and bond characteristic of community. Hence, it too will exist, in more-or-less pure form, as long as humanity exists. Nationalism is an aberration.[18]

3. Why bother to separate patriotism from nationalism, its bloody brother? Why not let both die their historical deaths, while we look and work toward other modes of unity? Today, we are called to be neither patriots nor nationalists, but something more cosmopolitan and more hopeful than both.

The two most frequently recommended alternatives are international (socialist) class consciousness, and internationalism as such. I shall deal with the former only in passing, because I believe it to be a feckless alternative, and that for two reasons. First, World War I showed the weakness of the dream of international class solidarity when confronted by the reality of nationalism. Secondly, there are many kinds of socialists, and there is no inherent incompatibility between being a socialist and being a patriot. Eugene V. Debs was a profound patriot, and so was Ho Chi Minh. Mao Tse-Tung is a patriot, and so is Fidel Castro. I am inclined to judge, on the evidence, that any socialist who thinks his socialism has nothing to do with any special place or special people is either foolish, or dangerous, or both. The examples are legion, beginning with Robert Owen's villages of cooperation, each a tidy parallelogram, relentlessly projected across all the spaces of the New and Old Worlds, even into the backcountry of Bolivia, where they might bump against the *focos* of Che Guevara and Regis Debray. The history of the Comintern provides a particularly instructive chapter.

Internationalism, however, seems more promising. Some varieties of it are very old, e.g., the cosmpolitanism of the ancient Stoics and Epicureans. Others, of greater interest and importance today, are newer. Examples here are the projects of Kant and the Abbe' de Saint-Pierre for world peace achieved through international administrative institutions. There is a direct line of descent from those proposals to the United Nations Organization and the World Federalist movement of our day, with certain contemporary "functionalist" theorists of integration not far off to the side.

These are the responses of humane and enlightened people to the horrors of war and the complexities of living in an ever-shrinking and more crowded world. The great dangers we face if we do not become more international are strong reasons for trying to become so. Obviously, we must have nuclear disarmament. With the threat of annihilation removed, we might then go on to deal with the problems of disease, hunger, crowding, sane and equitable use of world resources, and so forth. Simple patriots, many will say, are not equal to such tasks. They are too narrow in their loyalties, too old-fashioned in their outlooks. We need people of broader views and sharper skills. Patriots, indeed, are part of the problem, rather than part of the solution.

These are serious points. Patriotism obviously costs too much if its price is world peace and justice. I have no arguments that will convert the internationalist—none, even, that satisfy myself. Only a few thoughts that might put the debate on a sounder footing.

First of all, I am not sure that patriots by their nature oppose treaties of disarmament or arms regulations. Nationalists are more likely to do that, if their state is one of the mighty ones. One who rightly loves his country is not eager to see it blown up. Secondly, there are forms of internationalism that are entirely congenial to patriots. An American patriot can enjoy French wine and Russian novels and Greek philosophy as much as anyone else can. More than that, a patriot can have genuine toleration and even respect for other peoples, and an earnest wish that they share equally with him in the blessings of justice and liberty. Thomas Jefferson and Tom Paine, devoted American patriots, were also in this sense devoted internationalists, and saw no clash between the two. They were right, and they might still serve as models of enlightened patriotism.

Those points are worth making, but they do not go to the heart of the matter. That is found in the basic character of the actual internationalizing forces of today, and of the internationalist schemes that are proposed as responses to those forces.

It is a *fact* that the world today is small, crowded, and explosive. But what has produced that fact? Regardless of one's political outlook, the basic answer has to be technology, with some help from imperialism and cupidity. The main expressions and agents of internationalization today are the multinational corporation, propaganda, neocolonialist development and exploitation of weak countries, expansion of the technological mode of production into new territories, highly technologized military systems capable of dealing death at a distance, ruthless destruction of "backward" peoples and cultures, the increasing standardization of life, and meaningless tourism. These are not lovely things. Let's agree to call them, at best, mixed blessings. Surely they have not made the world more peaceful. Nor have they improved the quality of life. On the contrary. The forces that are pushing us toward international uniformity are sterile and life denying. It is not clear to me that we should enlist under this banner.

Patriotism, I have tried to argue, is less a program and a set of forces than a way or style of being in the world. The patriot keeps his eye on the past, on places and things, on traditions. For these reasons, patriotism is often called conservative. It *is* conservative, although it is perfectly possible for a conservative patriot to be a revolutionary. Today, a care for roots is genuinely revolutionary and is connected with freedom: it can slow down the rush toward chaos powered by the innovating, internationalizing forces of our time. I am of course aware that innovations can be rich and human, but it is obvious that most of them today are not. Rather, they partake of the machines whose children they are. Compared to the technological outlook, patriotism is a complexly human and rich idea, connected with life, supportive of liberty and diversity.

In sum, I am suggesting that most internationalism today has utterly confused humanity and its possibilites with technology and its possibilities. No doubt, technology has unified the world in a thousand ways, producing a call on the part of many humane people for world law and the brotherhood of man. But it would be more straightforward for the internationalist to speak less about the brotherhood of man and more about the standardization of the technological order, for it is a brute fact that technology has destroyed and is destroying hundreds of forms of human life. It is a cruel confusion to call that brotherhood, unless one holds that brotherhood can appear only after those who were different are dead.[19]

There are, of course, a few actual tribes and primitive peoples left on the planet, and a handful of older cultures not yet hopelessly debauched. My patriotic recommendation is to leave them alone. No aid; no anthropologists; no tourists.

A Modest Program

I have argued throughout that patriotism is a way of being in the world, rather than a doctrine or program of action. Still, one might suggest a few programmatic steps which, to recall Susan Sontag's words, might help to "revalidate the tarnished idea of patriotism."

The main thing is to strengthen the bonds among ourselves, specifically the bonds of common projects and participation in common situations. Given our reality, that strengthening will require a huge effort to decentralize and to simplify the gigantic structures that now dominate every sector of society—work, education, communications, government. "All Power to the Fragments!"—that, I think, is the right watchword. Everywhere we look today the tendency of power to autonomize itself, to cut itself off from its subjects and become an alien force over them, grows apace.[20] That tendency is always basic to complex social systems and may even be an inevitable law of their nature. We must struggle to devise institutions capable of checking power without canceling it. On the theoretical level, that will require the development of conceptions of authority and community appropriate to our time, and able to supplant the alienating conceptions and practices which now prevail. On the practical level, it will require endless experimentation with and reflection on new ways of living and working together, especially ways that emphasize community, simplicity, and stability.

Education must be approached as a task of preparing persons for freedom and participation. Local and ethnic history should have a large place in the curriculum, and history should be taught not as the flow of some process, but as accounts of decision, action, and conflict, stories of times when people rose above the ordinary and tried to take charge of their lives, thereby doing something memorable in the world. Nothing should be done to encourage on the part of the individual the sense that "someone else is in charge, and I just live here." Everything possible should be done to dismantle the educational bureaucracy and break the stranglehold of officialdom on education. Encourage nonpublic educational ventures: let a hundred flowers bloom.

We must also begin to move toward what must almost be called a revolution of competence in the arts of daily living, so that we no longer stand helpless among our machines and organizations, stupefied by our own productions. This will require a disciplined austerity in material things, the reduction of luxury, and the suppression by moral and educational means of idle consumption and display. We must reduce the intricacies and rigidities of the division of labor, and we must reject the gods of efficiency and comfort. Everything that teaches us to regard the earth as a home, rather than as a mine, must be encouraged. Simplify. Stabilize. Develop personal and small community landscapes. Combat consumerism.

On a more theoretical level, we must formulate new answers to the question, under what conditions does inequality of power and status not pave the way to—or even mean the same as—exploitation and domination? Our slogan of equality of opportunity has shown itself to be a false answer to this question, setting persons against each other as it does, falsifying and obscuring the real grounds of the inequalities among us. But that must not mean throwing out the question with the answer, thereby sinking into the squalid promiscuity that says anything goes and all desires are equal.

Finally, we must rework the swarm of questions around the troubled theme of the relations between vanguard and main army in the struggle for radical change. It is a rock-bottom fact of our condition that if opinions are consulted and votes counted, there will be no radical change. The forces that are transforming the United States today are so basic and pervasive—the chaotic release of energy, the exploitative disruption of all natural and human networks—that they cannot be formulated or mastered in narrowly political terms. What is needed is a new social mind, as Henry Adams called it, a social mind centered on conservation, variety, and balance. That kind of change cannot be deliberately and rapidly introduced and supervised by the few, nor implemented from the top down. A supervised revolution can only enlarge police and administration.

The main activity, then, must be educational. But the education cannot be limited to the writing and speaking of alternative views. The most powerful political-moral teaching combines action and knowledge. Resistance, for example, opens up a space in the political world which would not otherwise have been there. Once open, it remains forever after a possibility, a course which once was taken and which might once again be taken. Action becomes part of history, and is thus available for rediscovery in the future. Nor is the scope of the action the most important factor here: consider the importance in American—even world—history of Thoreau's night in jail. It is enormously important to keep intact the memory of such actions of resistance. One of the greatest weaknesses of the New Left in the 1960s was that the thread had been broken. There really was a silent generation cutting off the 1960s from the 1930s. No matter how thin the thread becomes, it must never be permitted to break. Keeping it intact does not of course assure or constitute success, but it is sufficient reason for acting. Without memory, there is no identity. ("The seat of mind is in memory," as St. Augustine said.) Patriots, I have argued, specialize in that form of knowledge which is memory of action. That is part of their radicalism, especially in an age which grows more and more mindless.

Finally, if political education is to be effective it must grow from a spirit of humility on the part of the teachers, and they must overcome the tendencies toward self-righteousness and self-pity which set the tone of youth and student politics in the 1960s.[21] The teachers must acknowledge common origins and common burdens with the taught, stressing connection and membership, rather than distance and superiority. Only from those roots can trust and hopeful common action grow.

Notes

1. Susan Sontag, *Trip to Hanoi* (New York, N.Y.: Farrar, Straus and Giroux, 1968), p.82.
2. The words are Manuelito's, a chief of the Navaho, describing the return of his people to their ancestral lands. Quoted here from Dee Brown, *Bury My Heart at Wounded Knee* (New York, N.Y.: Holt, Rinehart and Winston, 1971), p. 35.
3. The early Christinas were poor patriots. Their monotheism killed the lesser gods, denuding the land of sacred groves and local shrines. Machiavelli also thought that the Christians were poor patriots.

4. See Chapter I, "The Spirit of Place," in D. H. Lawrence's *Studies in Classic American Literature* for a suggestive development of this theme.
5. These lines were written on Thanksgiving Day, one of the purest of American holidays. And yet, there are complexities to be remembered here as well. The Puritans had not only days of thanksgiving but days of penance too, and they were reluctant to routinize high occasions. They remembered that their plenty was a gift. And what of the Indians? There is not enough whiskey in the land to drown their pain on this day when the conquerors feast.
6. Fred Branfman, *Voices from the Plain of Jars: Life Under an Air War* (New York, N.Y.: Harper and Row, 1972). Quoted here from *New York Review of Books*, Vol. 19, No. 2 (August 10, 1972), p. 20.
7. *Democracy in America* (New York, N.Y.: Schocken, 1961), Vol. I, p. 282.
8. Roy P. Basler, ed., *Collected Works of Abraham Lincoln* (New Brunswick, N.J.: Rutgers University Press, 1953), Vol. IV, p. 240.
9. Lincoln returned time and again to this theme of forgetting, nowhere more powerfully than in his great speech at Peoria (October 16, 1854) where he argued that the Nebraska bill was but one more step along the path whereby "little by little, but steadily as man's march to the grave, we have been giving up the *Old* for the *New* faith." Ibid., Vol. II, p. 275.
10. This mission used to matter to others elsewhere in the world. A report from Russia: "On the morning of the Fourth of July, 1876 . . . hundreds of small, rude American flags or strips of red, white and blue cloth fluttered from the grated windows of the [political prisoners] around the whole quadrangle of the great St. Petersburg prison . . . Reported in Ira Woods Howerth, "Patriotism, Instinctive and Intelligent" (1912); quoted here as reprinted in Maurice G. Fulton, ed., *National Ideals and Problems* (Freeport, New York: Books for Libraries Press, 1968), p. 213.
11. I want to call the reader's attention to Randolph Bourne's essay "Trans-National America" in Bourne, *War and the Intellectuals*, ed. and with introduction by Carl Resek (New York, N.Y.: Harper Torchbooks, 1964), pp. 107-24. It is the only American writing on patriotism known to me that is not shamed by Lincoln's understanding of the matter.
12. For a more sanguine account of the development of American patriotism than the one which follows, see Merle Curti, *The Growth of American Thought*, 3rd ed. (New York, N.Y.: Harper and Row, 1966), ch. 16.
13. The seed of the following analysis comes from G. K. Chesterton's crotchety and brilliant essay in his *What I Saw in America* (London: Hodder and Stoughton, 1922), Ch. 1.
14. See Edmund Wilson's introductory essay in his *Patriotic Gore* (New York, N.Y.: Oxford University Press, 1962).
15. The patriot who needs texts for this work might find them in Abraham Lincoln and Mary Parker Follett: Lincoln for the principles of the covenant; Follett for the practices of organization and action. I shall return to this matter of program at the end of the essay.
16. Karl Polanyi, *The Great Transformation* (Boston, Mass.: Beacon Press, 1957), p. 65.
17. Claude Levi-Strauss, *Tristes Tropiques*, tr. by John Russell (New York, N.Y.: Atheneum, 1967) pp. 381-93, makes a powerfully suggestive argument that Rousseau really was right on this matter. I am indebted to Levi-Strauss for many of the ideas in the foregoing paragraphs.
18. I owe this argument to C. Douglas Lummis, who drew it from Gondo Seikyo, a Japanese agrarian anarchist of the prewar period.

19. R. Buckminster Fuller is a great internationalist and a great prophet of technological unification. Anyone who thinks I have overstated the deadly confusion of technological with human possibilities should read his works. Start with *Operating Manual for Spaceship Earth* (Carbondale, Illinois; Southern Illinois Press, 1969). (Lewis Mumford thinks the place of publication must be an editorial error, for "such a manual could come only from Heaven.")
20. See Maurice Merleau-Ponty, *Signs,* translated by Richard C. McCleary (Evanston, Ill.: Northwestern University Press, 1964), p. 223.
21. "God we were smug and self-righteous," Dotson Rader has recently said of the Freedom Riders, "no wonder the crackers hated us." (*I Ain't Marchin' Anymore*, 1969, p. 16). And no wonder they still do, when the author, professing a new self-knowledge, can still call them crackers. The cracker has little reason for trying to distinguish between highminded and lowminded carpetbaggers. SNCC soon reached the same conclusion. The ecology movement, largely upper-middle-class in composition, has been insufferably highminded and self-righteous, and unwilling even to consider the economic impact of their proposals on the lower classes. The lower classes have lived with pollution for a long time. The upper-middle-classes became aware of it when their playgrounds were threatened.

Power and Purity

For a precious moment in the 1960s, the party of hope and change seemed committed to a serious struggle for the American political future. There were even reports of victories. On the civil rights front, for one, substantial gains were reported. There was talk of a cultural revolution. The universities were tempestuous. Black people spoke in a new voice, and found some new listeners. Lyndon B. Johnson promised a war on poverty at home and an end to war abroad. Beginning with SDS, many groups presented radical critiques of the established order and offered agendas for action looking toward a more just and democratic society. Many thousands of new actors were drawn into political life. Many important things were started; more seemed possible.

All that was an age ago. The questions in the public mind now are the standard ones of costs, corruption, and crime: when will prices go down, the stench of Watergate blow away, and the streets become safe? No fulcrum for radical change there. Some analysts are already proving that nothing happened in the 1960s. Others are saying maybe something did happen, but that the public would rather forget it and return to the 1950s.

But some things really did happen, and among the most important of them was the disappearance of the forces of hope and change. They were not routed; they evaporated. Of course there were too many defeats and too few victories. Leaders fell. Violence undermined trust and prudence. The war continued. The system showed its genius for assimilating some outsiders and frightening others into silence. The love generation was stricken by a plague of bad dope and worse doctrine. But by any standards of struggle that would seem serious to Marx, say, or to McGovern, or to any of a thousand Republican or Democratic county chairmen, or to the workers on the Lordstown assembly lines, or to the hill people of Appalachia, or to most ordinary members of the Mormon Church, the party of hope and change was not defeated in combat. It left the field and faded away.

I am not sure what the right standards are. Many sensible people, looking back over the 1960s, have concluded that we should all have stayed home. On an economistic calculus of costs and benefits that is a sensible conclusion. But perhaps a cost-benefit calculus is not the most appropriate framework for assessing the efficacy of political activity. In politics, there is often a huge disparity between input and output. Sometimes a small effort produces great effects: think of the impact on American history of Lincoln's assassination. Sometimes mighty efforts have puny success: half-a-million soldiers and all the bombs we could drop did not break the spirit of the North Vietnamese and the NLF.

When thinking about this question of the right standards for judging "serious" political commitment, it is also important to measure by the right time scale. John Adams was surely right when he said the American Revolution had taken place in the hearts and minds of the people a generation before 1776, but it still took a war to change the structure of power. Or, look back to the 1950s. America was a glacier then, and no critic could find a foothold on it. That was the era of the cold war, McCarthyism, and the Great American Celebration. Liberals competed to see who could catch the most Communists. The Luce publications heralded the dawn of the American Century, and prominent social scientists announced the end of ideology. There were only two problems of any size: how to control the Communist menace; and how to sell the flood of commodities pouring out of the factories of the affluent society. David Riesman half-seriously proposed that we could solve both problems by dropping Sears Roebuck catalogs and nylon stockings on the Soviet Union. With too few honorable exceptions, social scientists and publicists taught that America was the good society in action.

That was a world ago. The glacier is rotting. New fissures open every day. Every one of the major institutions, from the army to the university, has suffered extensive deauthorization. The society is now held together more by fear and impotence than by hope and civic affection. That condition can, of course, last a long time, but that is not the point. The point is that the country has undergone enormous changes in a very short time. Nor were those changes the natural result of the dialectic, or the inevitable consequences of the dynamics of capitalism, or the logical outgrowth of the technological imperative. They were the results of human activity—the activity of students, blacks, workers, corporation executives, politicians, and Vietnamese, among others. As Machiavelli said, God does not do everything in order not to deprive us of free will and the measure of glory that falls to our lot.

Assessed by the right time scale, then, it is clear that the 1960s were not a time of defeats, but a time of beginnings. Of course most of those beginnings died without fruit, and the few that lived produced more diseased than healthy growths. But this too is a matter of perspective. Beginnings are always pathetically small and most are doomed. We look at a newborn baby and say, "How tiny!" The oak drops 10,000 seeds so that one may grow. And some small beginnings do flourish. Jesus had twelve disciples, and while he may have no more true ones than that now, the movement those first few started has transformed the world.

So everything remains to be done, and the odds against doing much are heavy. But here again it is a question of perspective. What mainly keeps us from the work is not the herculean size of the task as such, but a failure of nerve and will that, if it continues, will be recorded against us by the future as a monumental human failure. What are the right standards of judgment here? Again, I am not sure, but before we excuse ourselves with the soothing thought that "we tried, but nothing can be done; the burden is too heavy and we are too few," we might think first of those few people in that small country in southeast Asia who for a generation now have carried all the weight that two great states could dump on them.

It is at least as much a matter of resolving that the work must be done, as it is a matter of asking whether anything of importance can be done. If we decide to do nothing, things will still be done. The trends are about as clear as they ever are in human affairs. We can reasonably expect a deepening and an acceleration of the forces and tendencies that now dominate the age: rationalization, centralization, technology, militarism, the enforcement of order by police and bureaucracy, destruction of the natural environment, exploitation of the weak both here and abroad, fragmentation of human relations and the social bond.[1]

What is so perplexing about our passivity is that it continues in full sight of those trends and in full hearing of voices pronouncing in the authoritative language of science a sentence of death on this civilization unless a new course is taken. We have built a civilization of great power for a few and much comfort for many. The price is now clear: an unlivable world; a huge population, most of whom are simply superfluous, whose creative and productive capabilities are not needed for the maintenance of the system. The necessary work of this society could be done by perhaps 25 or 30 million people. The old, the young, the black, the poorly trained, and most "ordinary" men and women have been reduced, in social and communal terms, to a nullity—in this society that claims to value human life above all. The order does not need them, and in that most important sense it has wrecked them. They are ciphers in a social process—the wad, as Mailer calls them—of significance to the system mainly as consumers and as actual or potential troublemakers. It is improbable that people will passively accept this condemnation, and it is possible that the end stage of the process we have entered will be an upsurge of nihilism—a wrecked population that can find no way to express its outrage save by striking against the system that has wrecked it.

Fear of such an outcome may move some to constructive action, but not enough. Furthermore, it is ignoble to appeal to fear as a stimulant. The struggle to reassert human agency should be entered because it is a struggle worthwhile in its own right, regardless of the likely outcomes. Human beings really do make their own history, as Marx reminded us. For better or for worse, we can no longer rest in the age-old conviction that what happens in nature and society just happens, just is—"givens" that we must dumbly accept as the results of natural processes, or social laws, or the will of God. The future does not just appear but is created by our own actions and choices; and those actions and choices can be more or less intelligent, more or less benevolent, more or less honorable. This postfatalist consciousness leaves us with fewer excuses and more responsibilities toward our future than previous generations enjoyed, or endured.

Among the obstacles blocking the will to act are certain widely held ideas about the relation between politics on the one side and morality and knowledge on the other. I want to make an argument for political participation, and that means, specifically, that I want to make an argument against those ideas that impede participation. I have little hope that my argument will succeed, and much anxiety that it will be heard as fatuous or wrongheaded. Citizens do not need the argument and noncitizens probably cannot hear it. Ours is a time when citizen life seems all but impossible, and we are a people whose experience of politics is narrow and disheartening, or desperate. Our legacy has predisposed us to despise and to fear politics, and our own experience confirms that predisposition, adding the weight of practice to the already heavy weight of inheritance.

Still, I shall make the argument. I do so partly out of blockheadedness, and partly for a reason that no one has stated better than Kant:

> The only conceivable government for men who are capable of possessing rights . . . is not a *paternal* but a *patriotic* government. . . . A *patriotic* attitude is one where everyone in the state . . . regards the commonwealth as a maternal womb, or the land as the paternal ground from which he himself sprang and which he must leave to his descendants as a treasured pledge. Each regards himself as authorised to protect the rights of the commonwealth by laws of the general will, but not to submit it to his personal use at his own absolute pleasure.[2]

We cannot look long upon political life without seeing an inescapable duality. On the one hand, the state appears as one of the noblest efforts of human rationality to achieve a form of good or happiness unique and indispensable to human life. This aspect of the matter is stated in the incomparable lines with which Aristotle opens the *Politics:*

Every state is an association of persons formed with a view to some good purpose. I say "good" because in their actions all men do in fact aim at what they think good. Clearly then, as all associations aim at some good, that one which is supreme and embraces all others will have also as its aim the supreme good. That is the association which we call the state, and that type of association we call political.

That is the smiling face of the state. Try to keep it before your mind's eye.

Then there is the sinister side, the face of the state made familiar to us by all modern thought and by much practice, ancient and modern. The ancient political philosophers never permitted themselves the indulgence of relinquishing the state to the domain of unreason: it was the creation of man; man is the rational animal; therefore, the state is rational in both origin and aims. The moderns have made that relinquishment. A dozen major and a hundred minor teachers have taught us that politics is the realm of opinion, emotion, and power, with all the evils specific to that realm. "The state is a trick," screeched Emerson, and his voice finds its echoes in the skeptical, unmasking political sociology of our day. "Good men must not obey the laws too well," Emerson added, and again his voice echoes in the popular mood of our day. Behind Emerson's expression stands the whole liberal concept of the state as a regrettable invention of human wit for the taming of human vice. The state is not, as the ancients held, a means for the perfection of human nature. It is, rather, as Paine called it, the badge of our lost innocence. And Marxism agrees with liberalism on the fundamental point, which is that the state is a trick, an instrument springing from class antagonisms and effecting the domination of one class by another. It disappears as freedom appears. "So long as the proletariat still has need of a state," Marx wrote to Bebel, "it is not in order to secure freedom but to put down its adversaries; and the day when it becomes possible to speak of freedom, the state will cease to exist as such." Or take Lenin, the master builder of one of the superstates of today, who wrote in *State and Revolution* that "while the state exists, there is no freedom. When there is freedom, there will be no state."

That is the dilemma, the inescapable dualism of politics: a supreme ideal of reason aiming at a general good that is achievable through no other association than the state; the reality of force, passion, class struggle, and the corruption of public power for private gain. Because both sides are equally real, politics can neither be reduced to the one, as both liberals and Marxists would do, nor elevated to the other, as the Platonists and Hegelians would do. The interweaving of the two makes political life a labyrinth so complex that even Machiavelli was sometimes bewildered, and makes the state a shining castle hiding an abattoir. An ideal of reason, the state also exposes the limits of reason; a tribute to high aspiration, the state also mocks human pretension; an association formed for good, the state also works evil. Given these dilemmas and temptations of political association, citizen life, by which I mean participating in the conduct of the common affairs and sharing alike in ruling and in being ruled, offers simultaneously the noblest expression and the harshest test of the possibilities of being human. When we quit the field of politics, then, we quit the best proving ground for the development of our own humanity. That is what is lost when politics is lost.

The paths of flight from this testing ground are few in number but very attractive to the tired and the self-righteous. The first is the argument from superior knowledge. It is as old as Plato and as new as the Club of Rome. Its expressions range from the sublime mystifications of priesthood and divine kingship to the banal devices of operant conditioning. The basic thesis is always the same: we few know better than the rest of you. Always the same, too, are the main social and political functions of the doctrine.

One characteristic function is that of concealing the true reasons and motives for a course of policy, either out of contempt for the public's ability to understand or out of lack of confidence in one's own case and cause. The *Pentagon Papers* provide many examples. So does Richard M. Nixon's desperate need to crush his political opponents—not just to defeat them, but to destroy them. It is as though one could not be sure of one's own power and rectitude so long as a single dissenting voice remained in the land.[3]

Another main function of the doctrine of superior knowledge is to conceal or to justify inequalities of wealth and power that could not otherwise pass inspection. The process can be observed in any number of places today.

The only social condition under which it is safe for adults to accept the claim of a few to rule by virtue of superior knowledge is where the community is small and there is no economic surplus that is not divided more or less equally among all producers. A very few primitive communities do meet this condition, and in them rule or authority is rarely a means of domination and exploitation. There, the one who has authority is the one who knows best how to do the things that preserve and augment the people. He is the best hunter, the wisest counselor, the steadiest worker, and the most generous giver in times of shortage. Authority rests upon competence and character clearly seen and daily proven. The leader moves others by suggestion and example, not by command and coercion, and he moves them directly, not indirectly through the leverage provided by army, police and bureaucracy. Among the Caribou Eskimo, the headman is "he who thinks." Among the Shoshonis, the headman is called *tekniwuy,* "good talk thrown out to the people." Speaking of his headman, one Comanche said, "I hardly know how to tell about him. He didn't have anything to do, except to hold the band together."[4]

In communities that are too large for each to know the others, and where there is a surplus that is hoarded or divided unequally, claims to rule based on superior knowledge nearly always conceal or justify the unequal division. It is easy to see why. To rule is to choose; to choose well is to choose what is good for self and others; to choose what is good for others requires an ability to take their point of view, to see the world through their eyes. That ability is enhanced by sharing approximately the same living conditions with the others, and it is diminished by large differences of wealth and comfort. Accurate social perception is nearly impossible across a huge and uneven social terrain. That is the wisdom behind the classical republican teaching that the state must be small and the citizens equal, and that luxury is the enemy of liberty.[5]

So far, I have examined the doctrine of superior knowledge from the viewpoint of the rulers. The doctrine also has uses for the subjects. Most of all, it excuses them from caring and taking responsibilty for the common affairs. By saying, "I don't know anything about politics; it's all too complicated for me; let the people who know run things," one exempts oneself from the burdens of public liberty. Furthermore, you can always blame someone else when things go wrong. Sometimes, of course, this know-nothing attitude expresses genuine humility. There are times and subjects where technical, expert knowledge is needed. Far more frequently, however, it expresses a decision not to know, a decision that some things—private things—matter far more than other things—public things. Aristotle called persons who were this way a kind of slave, for they appear to be so bound to their private affairs that you might say they were enslaved by them.[6]

The argument from superior knowledge misunderstands the nature of the knowledge required for the making of good political choices, and out of that misunderstanding exaggerates the importance of the technical and philosophical elements. Steering a state is not, as Plato would have it, much like steering a ship. There are some branches of human activity where skill and knowledge are sufficient to achieve a specified end, but political activity is not one of them. When you contract with a carpenter to build you a house, you may safely assume that his skill is sufficient to the task. But, as John Winthrop said, when you choose magistrates to guide the commonwealth, you must not make that assumption, for no one has sufficient knowledge or skill for ruling. He may not claim it, and we must not grant it. Leaders can only give reasons for their actions, and they must be given, as they must accept, the opportunity to state those reasons. A political leader may never be allowed to conceal his reasons behind the cloak of superior knowledge, saying in effect, I have good reasons and solid evidence but you are incapable of understanding. We, in our turn, must decide the validity of the reasons apart from the outcomes of the action. That is, we may not let our judgment turn exclusively on our appraisal of consequences, for the consequences of action are rarely predictable: fortune has half of the future. There is, then, an element of art in political choice, but it is not that element that can be codified—not, in Michael Oakeshott's figure, that aspect of cookery that is found in the cookbooks.

The argument from superior knowledge also misapprehends the nature of the freedom implicit in action. We have inherited a conception of freedom based largely on mechanistic models. In this view, freedom is understood to be uncoerced choice among alternatives: or, in an equivalent formulation, the quantity of freedom is a negative function of coercion and a positive function of the number of alternatives available to the chooser. As Hobbes put it in *Leviathan,* "Liberty, or Freedom, signifieth, properly, the absence of opposition; by opposition, I mean external impediments of motion."

For a certain range of experience that idea of freedom makes good sense—for example, when a mother tells her child that he is free to choose whatever flavor of ice cream he wishes. It starts to turn into nonsense when we extend the range of experience just a little—for example, when the consumer or citizen is called free or even sovereign because the decision as to what brand of soap he will buy or what party he will vote for is up to him. We begin to reflect that many more factors than physical or psychological constraints and number of alternatives available condition the meaning of freedom. Extend the range a bit more, and the negative concept of liberty breaks down. What can it possibly do with Rousseau's argument that sometimes it is right and necessary to force persons to be free, except to call it an obscurantism or an outrage? And yet, anyone who has ever experienced friendship knows that one of the highest offices of the friend is, through both reproof and encouragement, to require one to live up to one's own highest standard at those times when one would prefer to settle for the second best. Rousseau's expression reminds us that genuine personal freedom, which he formulated as acting in accordance with a law we give to ourselves, often requires the help of others both to formulate and to enforce the "self-given" law. Even the contemporary practitioners of the "do your own thing" conception of freedom quickly discover that most things worth doing cannot be done alone but only with the help of those others whom the theory sees as "impediments." A final example comes from Sartre's frequently quoted formulation in "The Republic of Silence":

> We were never more free than during the Occupation. We had all lost all our rights, beginning with the right to talk. Every day we were insulted to our faces . . . we were deported en masse. Everywhere . . . we encountered the revolting and insipid picture of ourselves that our oppressors wanted us to accept. And because of all this, we were free.

At this point, the Hobbesian conception fails. The free person is not merely a selector among givens, but a creator of new options: between two alternatives, says one of the men in Jean-François Steiner's *Treblinka,* I always take the third. The future is not a result of choices among alternative paths offered by the present, but a place that is created—created first in mind and will, created next in activity. The future is not someplace we are going to, but one we are creating. The paths to it are not found but created, and the activity of creating them changes both the maker and the destination. The place reached is rarely the place intended, and is often unrecognizable to the actor, who is himself altered by the activity. The actor is not a static "I" who arrives unchanged at some predesigned future place.

In sum, liberty and action are virtually the same, and public liberty is acting with others to create a common life. The kind of knowledge appropriate to this conception of liberty bears little resemblance to the knowledge treasured by the modern sons of Hobbes and Bentham, called choice theorists and systems analysts. If we cut ourselves off from public action and fail to develop the kind of knowledge appropriate to it, we risk the loss or atrophy of the distinctively human capacity to join with others in the free and conscious creation of a common life.

There is another variant of the argument from superior knowledge that is especially insidious because it is difficult to detect. It is a certain view of politicians that is built right into the role of spectator.

Most of us watch the game of politics from the sidelines. We are spectators, not players. Although the view from the sidelines enables us to see clearly much that is blurred to the players, it also distorts vision in certain ways. The spectator easily assumes toward the players an attitude of condescension, inclining toward disdain.

This attitude flows easily from the assumption that we have the right to judge. It is fed by the obsequious ways of American politicians, who must ingratiate themselves with a mass electorate. There may be some public men in the United States who think and feel like Coriolanus, or even Richard II, but there are none who talk like them in front of the spectators.

The consdescending eye is not fixed on only the run-of-the-mill players. If it were limited to them, there would be little to worry about, for, after all, the most important thing to say about the ordinary is that it is ordinary. But the spectator is characteristically condescending toward even the best actors, those we might call great. It is precisely against them that we most need to preserve our view of ourselves as being at least as good as anyone else. Excellence indicts us; and it is perfectly "natural," within a democratic ethos, that we should want to evade that indictment. Condescension establishes the distance that makes evasion easy.[7]

To take a condescending attitude toward others is to take a position that is morally dangerous. The others are seen as less rich or full than ourselves.

They come to look rather like big babies: interesting, of course; maybe lovable; perhaps dangerous because they are big babies. But still babies, more or less bumbling, lacking the things we grown-ups have. The condescending view is also morally dangerous because it is easy to be unaware of it. The victims of this form of bad vision characteristically do not know they are victims. Hence, the view from the sidelines is self-justifying and self-perpetuating. Unaware that this view is distorted, the spectator sees no need to correct it.

This is another of the obstacles to participation. Nonparticipation maintains nonparticipation, because the condescending attitude inherent in the role of spectator justifies the role itself. I think this matters a great deal today, not only because most of us are spectators, but also because most writing and teaching about politics is done by persons who are also spectators. Hundreds of thousands of people today study politics in school, and their teachers are not politicians, but spectators of politics: spectators speak to spectators. Condescension is then compounded, for the speaker claims superior knowledge. He is master of the subject matter, and of the students too. This has gone so far that the most authoritative conception of knowledge today is itself a spectator conception: acting and knowing are, and in this view should be, divorced. To gain knowledge we must keep our distance; the knowledge gained justifies us in keeping our distance.

To see how complex the dynamics of condescension are, and how the attitude blocks participation by justifying spectatorship, let us examine some of the ways we distance ourselves from even those actors we call great.[8]

One of the most important differences between great actors—think, say of Gandhi, or Lenin, or Lincoln, or Malcolm X—and most of the rest of us is that they hold their views and ideas in a way we do not. They *are* their views. We *have* views. And most of us, when we think clearly, can acknowledge that we took, or received, most of what we call "our" views from others. We did not create them. Rather, we got them from others, who may have worked very hard for them, and now we call them ours. Great actors of course also take some of their views from others. Some they forge themselves. But once the idea or vision is forged or assimilated, it is held in a certain way. The actor does not have or possess the idea; rather, he is possessed by it. He lives his views. His life is his views, in a way and to a degree unusual among most of the rest of us. Most of the rest of us are many things besides our views or ideas. To an unusual degree great actors are their ideas. More of their lives are contained in, or centered on, their views. In that fascinating way, great actors have a mode or experience of selfhood and identity that is different from ours. That difference makes us uneasy, for we know that at bottom the great actor is demanding of us that we change our lives. We need defenses against that, and the condescension implied in such words as "fanatic," "simplistic," "single-minded" helps provide those defenses. To us, the actor seems too simple, and that simplicity is threatening.

That same identity between the great actor and his views can make him appear ridiculous or foolish to us. Great actors so frequently hold views that appear so simple as to seem silly to us who know the complexities of the world. Consider, as examples, Joan of Arc, or Gandhi, or Martin Luther King. We know the world is too tired and complex to respond to their simple calls. They seem childlike, and our approbation of them often smacks of the approbation we give a "good" child when he behaves nicely, in a manner beyond his years. Most foolish of all, great actors often seem willing to suffer, even to die, for their foolish views. Nothing is sillier than that. They lack common sense and the common restraints of prudence, of family affection, of worries about economic security. There again, they can seem like children, prepared to throw away everything on a chance or a venture that has little hope of success. We would be fools to follow.

Very many great actors think in mythic terms. They are possessed by a myth, they act within it, they see it as more real than the world that others call real. We, of course, think ourselves beyond myth: we are cool, intelligent. We know the difference between myth and reality. We know the facts. It is hard for us to understand how a man such as Malcolm X, say, can passionately believe a myth that we know to be patently false. We are unable to see that the actor's myth can capture essential truths about his condition and the condition of those among whom he acts. Thus, Malcolm's myth taught that the white race is the devil, and to both black and white people that expresses an essential historical truth. But it is a truth too elemental and too ugly for many to accept. We exempt ourselves. We make qualifications. We wish the speaker would have more regard for facts. Is he really so ignorant that he does not know what all the rest of us know? Why won't he listen to reason? Probably his foolish myth is a symptom of neurotic needs and traits in his own character. We smile condescendingly at his myth. When he hits us with it, we want to run.

And so, through condescension, we cut even the great down to ordinary size. We do not appreciate that great actors earn their knowledge the hard way—by asking questions and living the answers—while we earn ours the easy way—by borrowing from others, and by waiting until the case is closed, the action finished, before pronouncing on it. It is easy to be wise after the fact. We do not appreciate the need for "simple" views when emergency demands response. We do not acknowledge that we too have myths. Sometimes, when we look back over our lives, we can see that we acted on a myth, but we cannot see that we are doing that now, for if we could, then our views and beliefs would no longer be mythic. We can only see others' myths, not our own. And, finally, we cannot see that an element of the mythic mentality is probably necessary for action, because we can never know—in the meanings we ordinarily give that term—enough to assure a successful outcome.

In all these ways, the position of the spectator is self-confirming, self-perpetuating. The role produces its own conception of knowledge, and that conception contains a large element of condescension toward even those who act greatly. The role of spectator, and the spectator conception of knowledge, are high obstacles to participation.

The second escape route from the political dilemma is over the high pass of moral purity. Politics are dirty and the state is a fraud, but I am clean, my aims honorable. I have better things to do than politics, and no time to waste on blockheads and schemers. Politics can only distract me from those better things, remove me from the better people who do those better things, and probably splash me with mud and blood in the bargain.

This view is held by many today, and, most importantly, is gaining among the young. The present retreat from politics among the young is not merely the result of too many defeats. It is also the other side of the moralism, the self-righteousness, and the self-pity that set the tone of youth and student politics in the 1960s. The slogan, "the student as nigger," which was once a popular self-characterization among comfortable, ambitious, upwardly mobile, white student liberators, could only seem the height of moral blindness and self-pity to black people, for whom the epithet "nigger" condenses four centuries of inescapable brutality. Such illusory thinking or false consciousness—thought so utterly divorced from the real social conditions of the thinker—cannot possibly provide a base for political alliance and action.

But in saying that political life has no place for moralism, I do not imply that it has no place for morality. The recent examples of, say, Gandhi and Martin Luther King are sufficient to show the foolishness of that assertion. (Gandhi described himself not as a saint who wanted to be a politician but as a "politician who tried to be a saint." He unhesitatingly accepted money from the very man he opposed in the famous strike at Ahmedabad.) Struggle and power are at the heart of politics, but so too are communication and agreement, trust and loyalty. The question of morality in politics is the question of how those communications and agreements can be made so that the power we constitute through them—power among and over ourselves and others—will not mystify and corrupt those who exercise it and those among and over whom it is exercised. I shall suggest in a moment that this formulation is still imperfect—there must be added to it what might be called the institutional dimension—but let it stand for the while.

Decent relationships among human beings are problematic. They do not flow from the spontaneous welling of our essential humanity, our species being. Although they are potential in our nature as human beings, they do not flower naturally but must be cultivated. Nor are they the automatic by-products of liberation from the bondages of ignorance and repression, as such teachers as Erich Fromm, say, or Tom Paine, would have us believe. Nor, finally, can they be realized by moral exhortation. The establishment of a decent common history and just relationships of power among human beings is a work of art, and specifically of the political art.[9]

If this is accepted, then we must leave behind the comforting notion that the problem of political morality is basically solved when good people—our kind of people—with good principles—our kind of principles—take power. Good intentions and good principles do not count for nothing, to be sure, but neither do they necessarily count for all that much in the foundation of an ethical politics. History is replete with the evidence. But, although the case is clear, its elements bear repeating. Take motives and intentions first.

"Know thyself," said the oracle at Delphi, and the goal still eludes us. Indeed, the goal is more distant now than ever, obscured, I think, by the fashionable idea that when we know our appetites, we know ourselves. We are a world we cannot penetrate because we lack the key. And there probably is no key: no matter how deeply we search ourselves, no matter how earnestly we call on great teachers to help us, the essential mystery remains. We, the creatures with consciousness, are the emptiest and the fullest of all the creatures. Compared with the beasts, secure in their instincts and with perfect knowledge of their needs and limits, we are empty. But because we are nothing, we are also everything. We can imagine and create worlds yet unborn. Because we are capable of self-consciousness, we can simultaneously form opinions and attach ourselves to beliefs and objects, and yet stand back from them, incapable of remaining either within the things or within ourselves. There is much in us that is absurd and fortuitous. Everything we are and do could be something else. Where in all this flux is the self? And yet with us it cannot be other than the self that measures all things, for the world is not a cosmos of objects whose laws we know. Rather, we make the laws. Their validity is guaranteed only by us. And yet, our dialogue with self time and again teaches that our most clear and distinct ideas, our most securely held and staunchly defended values and beliefs, may be only veils behind which we hide the truth about ourselves. The pathways from what is private and hidden in us to what is public and revealed to others are labyrinthine. Even more labyrinthine are the paths between what is known to ourselves and what we make public to others. Those who think their own basic motives and intentions are clearly known to themselves have not taken even the first course in that "education in honesty," which Freud called the study of the self.

So then, our true motives and intentions are not only often opaque to ourselves and others, but also are backed by no firmer guarantor than the self. In that sense, they are absurd and contingent, without any claim on others save the claims those others acknowledge. Given these complexities, it is hard enough to be wholly honest or sincere in our dealings even with the few who are close to us. When we move from the small circle of familiars to the large circle of the public, the achievement is impossible. More than that, too strenuous an effort will almost surely produce ruin.

In public life, we are thrown together with many others whom we do not choose and cannot know. Some of those others will be fools and some will be wicked. Only a fool would be honest with a fool; fools must be treated according to their folly. Sincerity, in short, is at most a negative qualification for public life, and not a positive measure of suitability, because when one acts among unchosen others, he must often conceal his real motives and intentions and take on false appearances. But we all are doing that; your fools and my fools are not the same. Hence, the public space is a house of mirrors: all is appearance; and the appearances are caricatures, for each presents not a true self, but the self reflected back to him in the eyes and voices of others. We become lost to ourselves, our genuine thoughts bewildered by the babble of the others.[10]

Machiavelli is right: "... men in general judge more by the eyes than by the hands.... Everybody sees what you appear to be, few feel what you are ... the vulgar is always taken by appearances and the issue of the event." Hence, it is not necessary for a prince to have all the good qualities, but it is necessary to seem to have them. And if the prince in fact has the noble virtues—"mercy, faith, integrity, humanity, religion"—it is equally necessary that he know when not to observe them, when to be moral enough to be immoral, for in action the good or kind way can produce catastrophes, and the faithless or cruel way can turn out the more merciful in the end. Besides, the public usually decides by appearances and outcomes, not by the actor's motives.[11]

But what about good principles? Perhaps our motives are obscure to us, and perhaps they become even more obscure in the flickering light of public life. Perhaps high motives can work evil almost as readily as base ones. Hence, we might acknowledge that good motives and intentions are not enough. But what about good principles? Surely we rightly require them of people in politics, and rightly feel confident in judging between parties and politics on the basis of principles.

I am not sure. If political theory teaches anything, it teaches that in complex societies the first law of politics is getting power, and the second is keeping it. Hence, politics is a relationship among actors, not a morality play of abstract principles. More than that, everyday experience shows that our principles serve our interests at least as often as our interests heed our principles. And, finally, we cannot confidently reason from principles to practice: two persons professing the same principles in the same circumstances may support opposing policies; principles do not necessarily commit us to any specific end and are adaptable to many ends; persons holding the same principles may disagree on their applicability in a given set of circumstances.

In conclusion of the point: in politics, it matters somewhat that one know what principles are professed. But it matters more to know what social forces are behind those principles, and what persons are applying them. When those forces and persons are wrong, then W. H. Auden's lines are right: "All the values in the world won't feed us / Although they give our crimes a certain air."

Part of the problem of morality in politics, then, stems from the fact that the state, while it originates in and aims at an ideal of reason, necessarily employs corrupt—human, all too human—means. I say "necessarily," because the establishment of decent human relations is not natural but a work of art, and the materials of that art are speech and power. How to keep those means from becoming hopelessly corrupt is part of the problem of morality in politics.

Recall that a few pages back I suggested that the problem also has an institutional dimension. Everywhere we look, power shows a tendency to "autonomize" itself, as Merleau-Ponty calls it, to cut itself off from its subjects and become an independent force over them.[12] No sooner does Lenin call for "All power to the Soviets" as the legitimate organs of the revolutionary masses than the Bolsheviks crush the Kronstadt Soviet. That lie begets a swarm of others. Dissent is equated with treason. The growing gap between power and people is filled by the secret police, and truth is put in prison. The revolution produced from within itself the same evils it promised to end. Closer to home, our doctrines and procedures of representation, which were designed to bridge power and people, largely function to widen and justify the gap between them. The very title of Joe McGinnis's book on the 1968 election reminds us that we no longer really elect a president, but sell one. Max Weber studies of the "routinization of charisma" and Roberto Michels analyses of the oligarchic tendencies in organization provide further evidence on the point.[13]

The tendency of power to autonomize itself is basic to large and complex social systems and may even be an inevitable law of their nature. At least, there are no convincing countercases. Must we submit to this law, or can we devise institutions capable of checking power without canceling it? This, I think, is finally the correct way of formulating the problem of the place of morality in politics. I regret that it is more complex and less glamorous than the fashionable formulations.

Now I of course cannot solve the problem. I do know that it is our problem, that it is the basic task facing those who seek a politics that will not mystify and corrupt. The route toward an answer lies in the direction of strengthening among ourselves the bonds that come from sharing common projects and participating in common experiences. The goal to be sought is a situation where those who are affected by a decision make the decision, and where those who decide on a course of policy also implement the policy. Put differently, the desired condition is one where power and authority are virtually indistinguishable. Given our reality, that will require a huge effort to simplify and to decentralize the gigantic hierarchies that now prevail in every sector of society—work, government, education, communications. It will also require a revolution of competence in the arts of daily living, so that we no longer stand helpless among our machines and organizations, stupefied by our own creations. Cast in Marxian language, the world must be reappropriated by the producers. Cast in the language of this essay, the right path is the path of participation.

No one can guarantee that the effort will succeed. But it is clear that the opposite path, the retreat to privatism, offers no favorable prospects. This is so not only because the fate of our times presents itself in political terms, as Thomas Mann said, so that even if you do not go to meet politics it will come to meet you, but also because the despair and contempt for our fellows implied in the retreatist position is morally and intellectually defective. I have argued that humans really do form associations—including political associations—for some good, or according to some conception they have of the good. Hence, even the most hideous vices we see in politics grow not only from what is hideous in man, but as often from what is potentially noble: the desire to advance some good or some truth. That desire meets its firmest test in the political realm by reason of the very nature of that realm—that it is a realm of appearances, a realm where outcomes cannot be anticipated, a realm where imperfect means and sometimes ignoble motives must often be employed in the pursuit of noble ends, a realm where every obstacle or outrage we meet is largely of our own making. Those who shun that test evade both the sternest demands and the highest possibilities of being human. The root meaning of the word "idiot" is a private, ignorant person.

The taking up of this task will require an orientation toward action that is beyond both optimism and pessimism, or hope and despair. Neither attitude is either necessary or justified. We often think that hopefulness is necessary if we are to sustain a struggle over the long run. I am not sure. Hopeful people, when hope is too often defeated, frequently turn spoiled and bitter; or, what is equally debilitating, vacillate between hope and despair. Sustained struggle is more likely to spring from an outlook that catches up both of the opposites and transforms them into something different from each. I have no name for this outlook, but I am pretty sure that its chief ingredients are patience and irony. In any case, hope is as likely to weaken as to strengthen the willingness to act. The right reading of the story of Pandora's box is not that hope was released after all the other evils so that they might be endurable. Rather, hope was the last of the evils.

Despair is not justified, either. Machiavelli's arguments here are convincing. "Fortune," he wrote, "is the ruler of half our actions, but she allows the other half or thereabouts to be governed by us."[14] Hence, even if we come to feel that our situation is refractory, that should not lead us to despair because the final outcome cannot be known until it is complete. "Men may second Fortune, but cannot oppose her; they may develop her designs, but cannot defeat them. But men should never despair on that account; for, not knowing the aims of Fortune . . . men should . . . never yield to despair, whatever troubles or ill-fortune may befall them."[15]

Nor should the movement beyond hope and despair be attempted by a leap upward to some reconciling faith, some conviction that above the disasters and confusions of daily life there rises a realm of harmony whose light will ultimately redeem this earthly realm as well. That haven beckons many today, and takes a variety of forms, ranging from mystical religion, to one or another evolutionist faith, and on to the dream of deliverance through technology. I claim no knowledge of these ultimate possibilities, but I have noticed that many who leap toward them suffer intellectual and moral hernia: contempt for the actual lives they see around them, because those lives are so much less than they could or should or will be. It is one thing to hunger and thirst after righteousness, and another to claim to possess it.

Machiavelli offers good counsel here, too, for while he cautions against both hope and despair, yet still urges involvement and action, he also denies us the haven of final harmony. "Reflecting now upon the course of human affairs, I think that, as a whole, the world remains very much in the same condition, and the good in it always balances the evil; but the good and the evil change from one country to another."[16]

It is sufficient for us to struggle to improve the balance in our own public life. We need not be too scrupulous about where the evil will go then.

Notes

1. Great states and empires can fall from the heights of vigor and competence to the depths of weakness and lassitude in a dreadfully short time: consider Spain. Given the dizzying pace of social change today, America's great day

330 LEGITIMACY IN THE MODERN STATE

may end before we know it. In a troubling work, Andrew Hacker says it has ended. See his *The End of the American Era* (New York, N.Y.: Atheneum, 1970).
2. *Kant's Political Writings*, ed. Hans Reiss, trans. H. B. Nisbet (New York, N.Y.: Cambridge University Press, 1970), p. 74.
3. Tom Wicker has reported that the sight of a lone picket on the sidewalk in front of the White House could drive President Nixon to violent emotion and obscene language.
4. The examples come from E. Adamson Hoebel, "Authority in Primitive Societies," in *Authority*, ed. Carl J. Friedrich (Cambridge, Mass.: Harvard University Press, 1958), p. 226.
5. Along the same lines, see Montaigne's "Observations on Caesar's Methods in War," *Essays*, Book II, No. 34; and Plutarch's *Life of Caesar*.
6. *Politics*, 1254a, 17ff.
7. So, of course, does closeness. Compare Hegel's maxim: a hero is never a hero to his valet—not because the hero is not a hero, but because the valet is a valet.
8. The only validation I can claim for the following paragraphs is that provided by your experience, and mine. Reflect on the occasions when you thought or talked about a "great" politician. Did your thought and talk fall into any of the patterns I describe?
9. The vitality of these myths of natural virtue is astonishing. Already in the *Protagoras* Plato argued, against various conceptions of the "Golden Age," that men were at one time little better than beasts, that they developed higher capacities through social living, that social or city life was possible only through justice and law, and that justice and law were not divine gifts, but products of human intelligence and effort—achievements of artifice, not gifts of nature. Plato's assault against the idea of the naturalness of virtue was logically devastating, but the doctrine is not dead yet: Paine, Marx, and Maslow, to name representative figures, forward versions of it.
10. Hannah Arendt's unqualified argument that we reveal ourselves in public action seems to me to overlook the endless complexity of "appearance." For Arendt's argument, see her *The Human Condition* (Chicago, Ill.: University of Chicago Press, 1959), esp. pp. 175-81.
11. Niccolo Machiavelli, *The Prince*, Ch. 18. I have used the convenient Modern Library edition of *The Prince* and *The Discourses* (New York: Random House, 1949), trans. by Luigi Ricci.
12. Maurice Merleau-Ponty, *Signs*, trans. Richard C. McCleary (Evanston, Ill.: Northwestern University Press, 1964), p. 223ff.
13. See H. H. Gerth and C. Wright Mills, *From Max Weber* (New York, N.Y.: Oxford University Press, 1946) pp. 245-67; and Roberto Michels, *Political Parties* (New York, N.Y.: Free Press, 1962).
14. *The Prince*, Ch. 25.
15. *The Discourses*, Book II, Ch. 29.
16. Ibid., Book II, Introduction.

Decadence and Revitalization: Reflections on the Present Condition

I

Our is said to be a time of crisis, even an Age of Crisis. We have all heard of the multiple crises of our time. Just for starters, call a few to mind. We have the urban crisis, the race crisis, the energy crisis, and the ecological crisis. The family is said to be in crisis; so too are the schools and the church; so too is the system of criminal justice, along with the welfare and health-care systems. Many have described the cultural crisis. Everybody has heard of the crisis of democracy. Indeed, the political world throws up crises of all descriptions, general and particular, at home and abroad. There is a population crisis and a food crisis. Many would add to this list the crisis of authority, along with its Marxist twin brothers, the legitimation crisis and the fiscal crisis of the state. One professor has even descried on the horizon the coming crisis of Western sociology—a sighting that has left most people singularly unmoved.

So, we have no shortage of crises, nor of victims of crises, nor of students and managers of crises. We may be poor in some things, but not in this one. We seem to produce crises as abundantly as the Ford Motor Company produces automobiles, as naturally as rabbits produce other rabbits. It is worth noting, as a sign of the times, that the hottest item on the theory market today is something called Catastrophe Theory.

And yet, there is something awry here; or perhaps a number of things. For one thing, what some will call trouble others will call good news. It is obvious, for example, that there has been an erosion of American power abroad, with a consequent erosion of confidence at home. But many thoughtful people see that not as a crisis but as a hopeful turn toward prudence and modesty. Recent years have also seen a decline in the status and material privileges of the academic classes, especially in the humanistic studies. But it is not clear that academicians may rightly balloon their own distresses into a diagnosis of the sickness of culture and society. And it is clear, after the calamities of recent history, that humanists can no longer have solid faith in the capacity of the humanities to humanize. Not so long ago, Germany, the country which claimed, with much justification, to draw its cultural inspiration equally from the fountains of classical humanism and modern science, turned toward the hell of nihilism. That turning showed that it was as easy for men in our times to read Rilke in the evening and go refreshed to their duties in the death camps as it was for men of an earlier time to worship Christ on Sundays and persecute heretics on the other days. After that discovery, it is difficult for humanists to retain a missionary zeal in their calling, but again, this may be less a crisis in culture than a healthy defrocking of the priests of high culture. Or, for a final example, while some see the unsettlement of family life as a calamity, others see it as a liberation, holding that the nuclear family was always a sweatshop for the wives, a private brothel for the husbands, and an emotional ghetto for the children. No matter where we look, what some will call a crisis others call an awakening, or a liberation, or a step toward dignity and truth.

For another thing, those who are said to be in crisis, or the institutions which are said to be in crisis, do not respond as we might expect them to. They go on largely as they had been going on, though perhaps a little more heavily, a little less joyously, with the announcement of each new crisis. It makes one wonder whether the patient was sick before the doctor diagnosed him, or whether the diagnosis made him feel bad. What is objective and what is subjective here? Or does that distinction make no sense?

In any case, if we are in crisis we seem to be like those whom Nietzsche called the "last man," those who invented happiness—and blinked. We seem to invent or discover one crisis after another, and then blink. Like the last man, we cannot see beyond ourselves, cannot rise above ourselves to the level of vigorous and intelligent response demanded by our task and our condition. Or, perhaps we really cannot tell whether the discoverers and sufferers of crisis—ourselves, the last men—are blinking or not, for so many people these days are wearing shades.

Or, like the child in the nursery tale who cried " Wolf! " when there was no wolf, it may be that we have cried "Crisis! Crisis!" so often when there was none, that now, when there is one, neither those who shout nor those who should listen can take the alarm seriously. It might be better to call ours a needy time, which makes it much like many other times. It might be prudent to think of our time not as a time of crisis, but as a time of transition, or interregnum. Such times can last a long time. They might even be called ordinary times. Many historians say, for example, that the transition from feudalism to capitalism in Europe took three centuries, and is still not complete. Or we might remember that the great and good times in history are few and fleeting: the true classical period in Greece, or the

Renaissance, or the time of the founding of our own republic lasted but a moment, though they still nourish us today. And even in times of decay and disorder something great may be born: the fourteenth century, with its dreadful wars, pestilence, and famine, gave us Petrarch and Chaucer. Despair is always ignorant and never justified. If we could learn to think of our time this way, as neither the best nor the worst of times, we might be able to move from the mentality of crisis and the crash program, with its inevitable cycle of enthusiasm and despair, over to the mentality of patient, disciplined, steady work—not a blitzkrieg, but a long march; not a dash, but a marathon.

There are still other possibilities. Perhaps we really are in crisis, but mistake its true nature. The crisis may be in our whole way of seeing and being in the world. But if that is so, in the very nature of things we would be the last to know it, for we are the crisis. We are the ones who see and are a certain way, and we would have to be other than we are to see differently than we do. Our condition might be like that of the astronomers and natural philosophers who were devoted to the Ptolemaic cosmology. When anomalous observations were reported, observations that could not be fitted into the received system of the celestial bodies and their movements, instead of rethinking their whole framework of thought, those scholars added cycles and epicycles unto the tenth degree, until the system reached such a pitch of tension and complexity—of crisis—that a nudge from Copernicus brought the whole thing crashing. If we are the crisis, like those Ptolemaic cosmologists we can only add cycle after epicycle, specific crisis after specific crisis, but never see the truly radical crisis, which is ourselves.

Something like that is what Henry Adams had in mind when he said that our conditions called for a "new social mind," and added that its creation would require a "jump," a leap out of one frame into another. Something like that is what Martin Heidegger meant, if I understand him, when he said that "What is most thought provoking about our thought-provoking time is that we are still not thinking." That which most truly calls us to thinking has turned away from us as we have from it, so that, blinded by our own knowledge, we do not know that we are ignorant.

Or, still again, something like that seems to have been meant by Nietzsche when he said "the Wasteland grows," adding elsewhere that it must yet grow for a long time. Not for a long time yet will that consummation which has already been reached in Western history be known to have been reached, and we stand ready to take on our task in a way that is essentially right. I suppose that is what Nietzsche was suggesting when he called his *Zarathustra* a book for everybody and for nobody, a book whose message is for all but which none can hear.

Nietzsche thought we stood on the very edge of that consummation. We stand at the moment when humankind is about to complete the journey of mastery which began, according to *Genesis*, with the first man and woman.

We have taken God's powers and are about to assume dominion of the earth as a whole—creating ourselves; transforming matter into energy; annihilating existing matter and perhaps even creating new matter. That is surely a moment of crisis, foretold in the story of the Garden. Writing for that moment, Nietzsche insistently asked: Are we properly prepared to assume dominion? And if we are not, what will be the consequences of our unreadiness? What must happen to us, what must we do to prepare ourselves for making the earth wholly subject to ourselves, thus fulfilling the old prophecy?

Few would answer that we are ready for that task, though many are eager to tell us what we must do to prepare ourselves. R. Buckminster Fuller, in an article called "Cutting the Metabilical Cord," which appeared in a recent number of the *Saturday Review-World*, offers hope, telling us that we are almost ready. "Humanity knew very little when I was young," Mr. Fuller says, but this regrettable ignorance has now been corrected by a "historic information-education explosion and its spontaneous edifying of humans in general." Mr. Fuller says that the skilled craftsmen of his youth "had vocabularies of only about 100 words, many of which were blasphemous or obscene." But now, "the speech pattern of world-around humanity [has changed] from that of an illiterate ignoramous to that of a scholar." And, best of all, youth, "whose metabilical cord of tradition has been cut, now need [but] a few years time to develop competence to take over the world affairs initiative, and that is exactly what universe is apparently about to do next."

Others, recognizing along with Mr. Fuller that we stand at a turning point, but lacking his faith in "universe," counsel us to leave the earth altogether and shoot into space. Governor Jerry Brown has suggested that California mount its own program for building a colony in space, making us earthlings into spacelings. Perhaps the Governor has found in that suggestion the key to the most dynamic potential political alliance of our day—that between the hippies and the aerospace industry. His suggestion also implies that the crisis here on earth is so heavy that the only solution is to hurl ourselves into outer space and become weightless. He may be right. He is surely in the American grain, for it has always been our genius to attempt physical solutions to political and cultural problems.

II

This brief tour of the province of crisis thought should have shown two things: there is widespread agreement that ours is a time of crisis; there is less agreement as to what the crisis is and what the best ways for coping with it are. I, too, admit uncertainty. I think our culture is in trouble but I am not sure what the trouble is. Given that, prudence dictates retreat to safer ground—specifically, to the ground of definition, which academicians love to occupy. I want to ask, what might be meant by a cultural crisis? What can we mean when we say a culture is in crisis?

A search for an answer goes quickly to the root of the word. Culture, both word and concept, is of Roman origin. The word derives from *colere,* which means to tend and care for, to cultivate and preserve. Its original uses referred to the human interaction with nature, the activity of tending and cultivating natural things and processes, thereby improving them, turning the natural world into a place fit for human habitation. The word implies an attitude of devotion, care, aiding and serving, and stands in sharpest contrast to the attitude of dominating nature and subjecting it to our purposes. This is worth remembering in a time when what we call agriculture is less cultivation than assault—operations of ripping, tearing, gouging, and hacking performed by a mechanized army supported by an arsenal of chemical weapons. No wonder our farms are dangerous and disagreeable places to live on, and their products increasingly unfit to eat. One way to suggest the derangement of our thinking is to say that just about every time we use the expressions "natural" and "naturally" and "cultural" and "culturally" we are wrong. An instrumentalist orientation, always straining toward forcing and exploiting, and away from nurturing and caring, pervades our thinking in both areas.

Because the word contained this seed of tending and caring for, it easily grew to include taking care of that which belongs to the gods, their cult. It could refer also the cultivation of our own distinctive human nature, tending to and developing the capacities of mind and spirit. This is the basic meaning we have in mind when we speak of a cultured or cultivated person.

So, beginning with what are in a sense the lowest things, the things of nature, the word ascends to the highest things, the things belonging to god or the gods. Culture is always, as Nietzsche put it, "second nature"—a process of nurturing and developing the highest potentials inherent in and properly belonging to a thing or being. Thus, by taming and shaping through culture our natural impulses, needs, and desires, we give ourselves back to ourselves in a higher or sublime-ated form. It is like the journey Socrates describes in the *Symposium*, where he traces the ascent of love from its origins in carnal desire to its culmination in love of the good, from the desire for sexual possession to the desire for the regeneration and birth of beauty.

Following this lead, there comes into view an idea of what a sound culture might look like. The healthy culture is one which weaves the lowest and the highest things together into a shapely whole, with balance, proportion, and good fit among the parts, and which does this not at the cost of denaturing or devitalizing natural energies, but by transmuting them into purer and more intense form. This is the kind of culture Pericles praised in the "Funeral Oration": "For we also give ourselves to bravery, and yet with thrift; and to philosophy, and yet without mollification of the mind." And: "In sum it may be said both that the city is in general a school of the Grecians, and that the men here have everyone in particular his person disposed to most diversity of actions, and yet all with grace and decency."[1]

This opens another path for thought. If the healthy culture is one which ties together low and high, giving meaning and shape to the passions and impulses, then the sick culture is one where these connections have been broken, and the design of the whole shattered into bits and fragments— where proportion is gone; where cadence gives way to de-cadence; where some pieces of ourselves are torn off and put on their own, to develop as they will, to clash when they do; and where other pieces of a whole life are removed and confined to a reservation or put in a museum, kept in sterile conditions which inhibit growth and movement.

This can be said another way around. We, the humans, are not governed by our instincts and sheer animal needs. Rather, we must govern ourselves, must choose what we shall do and become. Our humanity is not given by nature but must be achieved through culture. We must decide what we shall mean by being human. The vital culture, thus, is one which aids those choices, gives direction, tells us in ways we can believe what is worthy and what is not, gives us self-respect when we choose what is worthy, and supplies consolations for our inevitable losses and defeats.

Now, of course, we set a direction for life and choose among alternative routes by reference to what we have recently come to call values. Values, in their turn, are normally presented to us by our culture. And thus, by a necessary path, we reach the conclusion that the vital culture is one whose values are clear and consistent, and sufficient unto our needs for meaning and direction, for consolation, and for respect or standing in our own estimate and in the estimates of important others.

III

With that, we reach one of the big slogans of our day: the Crisis of Values. The crisis in culture, or the crisis of authority, is at bottom a crisis of values. In turn, the crisis of values is taken to mean a shortage of values. We tell ourselves that our values are hollowed out, drained of vitality, lacking in vigor. Or we tell ourselves that values are in such short supply that few of us, despite great need, can get our hands on enough of them.

Many moralists and critics of culture, following—albeit unconsciously— this economistic metaphor, propose that the way to cope with the shortage of values is to decree new ones and restore old ones. Their policy is something like that of the Democratic Party in 1896, with its call for the free coinage of silver at the ratio of sixteen units of silver to one of gold.

Only by putting more money into circulation could the burdened debtors be relieved. We too are advised by our moral economists to overcome the shortage of values by coining new ones and re-minting old ones until there are enough in circulation for everybody.

I think this gets the case wrong. Our trouble may be not too few values, but too many; not a shortage, but a glut. It is not so much that people in our time lack values, or that modern cultures have meager resources of faith, as that people lack the capacity for faith in anything great, steady, and demanding. Even our devotions have become disposable commodities, more nearly part of the mass entertainment industry than part of culture as I have been using the term.[2] The age abounds in small and easy faiths. Millions go in for mind-cures, and thousands get rich off them. People seek salvation in everything from Deep Mulch to Transcendental Meditation. Religious life in Rome of the second century A.D. was steady and even thin by comparison.

What is characteristic of these faiths is that they are so trivial, privatistic, disposable. It is not that the age lacks values, then. Rather, it teems with so many that all become cheap. It is as though there were a Gresham's Law at work here too, whereby the cheap coin drives out the good. We have plenty of values, but they are of little value. As W. H. Auden put it:

All the values in the world won't feed us,
Although they give our crimes a certain air.

Let me illustrate this point. I have come across a list in a recent *Manchester Guardian* of the top twenty sellers in the self-actualization and culture revitalization business in California. In alphabetical order, the list runs: Actualism, Analytical Tracking, EST, Feldenkrais Functional Integration, Fischer-Hoffman Process, Gurdjieff, Human Life Styling, Integral Massage, Neo-Reichian Bodywork, Orgonomy, Polarity Balancing, Manipulation, Postural Integration, Primal Therapy, Scientology, Silva Mind Control, Synanon, Tai Chi, Theta, Yoga (hatha and raja), and Zen. Just outside the top twenty are such familiar standbys as the Maharaj ji, Krishna consciousness, Born-Again Christianity, and Scouting. After that there's not much left except, say, Punk Rock and Recreational Vehicles.[3]

It is a gorgeous list; lush, tropical. And yet, of a depressing sameness. These are the frantic searchings of those who have reached the pot of gold at the end of the American rainbow, filled up on everything the American Dream promised, and yet feel empty. And so they search for still more commodities, spiritual ones now, and offered at a cheap price. To put it differently, the more the development of late capitalist and technological society makes unlikely or unfashionable the real possibilities of self-respect and self-development, the more these possibilities are offered on the market as commodities—presented as though real experiences could spring to life through an act of will and an exchange of formulas alone. Most of the recent flowerings of the "human development" and "cultural revitalization" movements are less the expression of a victory over dehumanization than the latest and very insidious victory of dehumanization over us. They represent a late stage of what Norman O. Brown has called the *causa sui* project.

I offer this characterization of the currently fashionable search for values less in the spirit of rebuke than of sympathy. I claim no special ability to discriminate hopeful from feckless beginnings. Furthermore, and despite all superficiality and faddishness, these searchers are on to something important and correct in their recognition that what is needed today is a reconstruction of the meaning of personhood. And, finally, I suppose it possible that somewhere in the deserts of the present there has already been planted that new seed or cult which in time will body forth into a new and vital culture. Only the future can decide what is madness and what is great genius in the present. No doubt, that vital beginning, if it is already among us, is very small. Beginnings always are, and that is no argument against them. When we look at a newborn baby, our first spontaneous word is "How tiny it is!," but we don't think less of the baby for that. We know the tiny infant can grow into a strong adult, but it will have to struggle to do so, and it will need a lot of care if it is to prevail against a threatening environment. All big things, in both nature and culture, were once tiny and vulnerable, pathetic and ridiculous. The Chinese Communist Party began among a handful of young men meeting secretly to discuss the distresses of their country. Or, it is reported in the Book of *Acts* (16:9-11) that a man appeared to Paul in a vision and asked him to come over to Macedonia, where many were in need of help. Heeding that call, Paul turned the Christian impulse, then so tiny, westward rather than eastward—with such prodigious consequences as we know. But again, those evangelists too had to struggle and sacrifice to make their vision grow.

In any case, the point that matters here is simple enough, but basic. It is impossible to fabricate solutions to the crisis of values and the breakdown of authority. We cannot deliberately devise, by recourse to expert knowledge and proven methods, specific therapies or solutions for cultural disorders. That is so because a cultural crisis is in no important way like an economic or a military crisis, say, where deliberate, rational, technical calculations are appropriate, where we know what we need and what we must know and do in order to cope with the crisis. Cultures just are not that way. Our knowledge and methods may not be adequate for coping with an economic crisis, but they are *appropriate*. We know *what* we need to know and do, even though we may not know or be able to do it. But we do not know waht an appropriate "solution" to a cultural crisis might be. Nor can we know what we would need to know in order to devise such a solution. About all that can be said on this matter is that whatever comes to supply the foundation of a new table of values will be an emergence, not a fabrication, and will be some combination of old and new elements—though I caution that it is impossible to say with real clarity what "combination" means in this context, or what "old and new" elements may be useful. And finally, there is no way to guarantee that what emerges as a solution and recombination will be benign and vital. It is as likely to be a Cargo Cult, a Ghost Dance, a Jonestown, or Naziism, as it is to be a Renaissance or an Enlightenment. Nor can any of us be sure he can distinguish a healthy from a vicious "solution": even Nietzsche, the subtlest of all physicians of culture, was taken in by Wagner. That is the way cultures are.

IV

Our own case—the case of the large, rich, technologically advanced, rationalistic, and constitutional-individualist societies of the West—has peculiar features which make revitalization among us especially difficult for any foreseeable future.[4] Put it this way. The great moral discoveries and dedications of the West, which might be condensed into the formula reason, freedom, and the individual, have run down in our time, or have turned in perverse and destructive directions, leaving us adrift and uncertain, presenting us with a crisis of values and authority. At the same time, the distinctive method, revolution, which the West invented for reshaping and renewing its large cultural commitments is no longer useful. That leaves us with a twofold crisis: a crisis of substantive values; and a crisis of method for the formation of new and the revitalization of old cultural commitments.

Revolution as it is understood today is a Western invention. The product, like many another, has been exported into other regions, but the idea, methods, and processes of revolution are distinctly Western creations. Moreover, the invention is relatively new: we might date its origin in the English revolutions of 1648 and 1688. Aristotle and Plato wrote about "revolution," of course, but they were writing about something only vaguely similar to the modern phenomenon. It was Tocqueville who first formulated the distinctive characteristics and properties of modern revolution. He defined revolution as theory-guided action to change the fundamental organizing principle and institutions of a social order, and to effect that change quickly and comprehensively.

Every social order has a basic principle from which almost everything else depends, a nucleus around which everything else revolves. Thus, the germinal principle of the old regime was hierarchy, which the democratic revolution replaced with equality. Revolution is an effort to change the constitutive principle of a social order. Furthermore, the change must be consummated suddenly: remember that remarkable night when the revolutionary French Assembly "abolished" feudalism. So, revolution runs swiftly and cuts deeply into the social body. Also, revolution runs broadly, for the revolutionaries try to implement the new principle in all areas of life—political forms, economic processes, religion, education, family life. Nothing is left untouched; all must be remade in the image of the new principle. Also, revolutionary action is theory-guided. The actors have a comprehensive and in their view scientific critique of the old society and a model of the new society. And finally, given that, political intellectuals are an extraordinarily important force in the making of revolutions, both as producers of theory, and as leading members of the organizations of professional revolutionaries whose work is the preparation and implementation of the revolution.

Today, for a variety of reasons, revolution is no longer capable of achieving anything like a renewed world, or even a fair measure of good results. There will continue to be rebellions, probably more and more of them, but true revolution can no longer spring from rebellion as was the case in earlier and simpler times.

This development has gone through a number of stages. In the seventeenth and eighteenth centuries, the sources and targets of the great revolutionary efforts, English, American, and French, were political ideas and institutions which had become ossified and corrupted to the point where they were experienced as alien and constricting forces which had to be removed if people were to accomplish their purposes. Political power had grown enormously and was becoming increasingly centralized. Local freedoms were curtailed, as decrees from the center regulated more and more activities. The aristocratic classes continued to guard their privileges while shirking their ancient duties. Altogether, political power was, and was felt as, arbitrary and despotic. This was the political situation which produced the great revolutions of the seventeenth and eighteenth centuries. And those revolutions made perfect sense; that is, specific changes in political ideas and institutions really could reach to the root causes of felt distress.

Still, even those revolutions confused one problem with another; or, perhaps more accurately, mistook a part for the whole. They confused king and aristocracy, survivals from an earlier age, with the emerging state, which was already large, remote, centralized, and inherently oppressive. The revolutionaries struck down the despot and swept away the gaudy paraphernalia and irksome residues of aristocratic power, but they left the state intact. Indeed, they cleared the path for it, and saw only gain in doing so, because they believed that the new doctrine of popular sovereignty assured that government would henceforth be responsible to the people.

No need to fear power so long as it was based in the people, rather than in a king and aristocracy.

It was Tocqueville again who saw this confusion most clearly, and who foresaw the ambiguous legacy it left for the future. He came to understand that at the time of the Revolution, there were three modes and levels of government in France: a monarch and an aristocracy which had been stripped of real power and function while retaining many of their insulting privileges; remnants of autonomous provincial and local institutions; and the newly emerging state, with its entrenched officialdom and its passion for central regulation. Of the three, the Revolution struck down the two which were old and feeble, with little power to do either harm or good, and elevated the third, with its enormous potential for oppression. The doctrine of popular sovereignty and the practices of representation did more to conceal and strengthen than to control the power of the state, for they dissolved all moral and institutional impediments to the growth of bureaucratic institutions and central power. In their rage to destroy personal and visible rulers, the revolutionaries were blind to the bitter possibilities hidden within the benign formula of a "government of laws, not of men."

So the revolutions of the seventeenth and eighteenth centuries left an ambiguous legacy. Still, they made good sense: the remedy was appropriate to the disease. The revolutions achieved genuine advances for reason, freedom, and the individual. Locke and Voltaire were good teachers.

Moving forward into the nineteenth century, the sources of oppression and alienation became increasingly economic. They were rooted in the systemic need of the capitalist mode of production to extract surplus value—regardless of the cost to workers; regardless of the destruction of older forms of belief and human relationships worked by the unleashing of the profit motive. Here Marx is of course the master teacher, and he understood that capitalism was something different from the older and simpler forms of economic oppression (e.g., lender and borrower, master and slave). Rather, it was a whole new system, in which the exploitative impulse was freed from its embedment in the whole structure of society, replacing ancient religious, customary, and traditional relations with the naked "cash nexus."

Marx gave us brilliant and still illuminating accounts of how abstract this new kind of dispossession could be, and of how bewildered people became when they tried to apprehend their own experiences in this alienated world. The official accounts, and most critical accounts as well, were less understandings than symptoms of the disorder: alienated minds giving alienated accounts of their condition. And when it came to changing this oppressive order by way of revolution, the perplexities multiplied. First, the revolutionaries of 1848 were hypnotized by the image of 1789. They attempted a reenactment of the earlier drama, with the result that 1848 was a farce. The proletarians, Marx said, must draw their poetry from the future, not the past—but how is that to be done? Secondly, the revolutionaries of the nineteenth century found it impossible to develop a long-range strategy and program for changing the fundamental character of the economic order. Such a program must necessarily be highly abstract and complex, since the economic forces and processes which were producing the distress were themselves abstract and complex. In the face of that need, all programs and particular demands seemed simplistic. To get a sense of what matters here, reread the list of Communist demands presented in the *Manifesto* of 1848. Most of them have been substantially realized in the industrial countries of Western Europe and North America, and yet we are no closer now than we were then to the goal of a society "in which the free development of each is the condition for the free development of all." Or, consider the situation of the official Left in the industrialized countries of Western Europe. The Left now finds it impossible to envision a genuine alternative to the established order of corporate capitalism *cum* state socialism, even though that order is felt by many to provide little of the goods of a rich human life other than material comfort and consumer rewards. And finally, given the scope and complexity of the advanced social orders, the means necessary to effect radical change can easily reproduce in themselves the very evils they are meant to abolish. Basically, the revolution cannot be made save by a party organized along Leninist lines, and once such a party is formed, it becomes impossible to keep it under popular control and make it geuninely responsive to democratic impulses. The people becomes the party; the party becomes the central committee; the central committee becomes a cabal, the cabal is mastered by a tyrant; and the people are victims as they were before.

In our own day, the experience of estrangement and dispossession is as broad and deep as it ever has been, but the alienation takes new forms and has new sources. It is no longer so much a matter of people being excluded by law and custom from the places where decisions are made, but a matter of the very ways those decisions are made, and of what kinds of questions are decided. It is no longer mainly a matter of workers being harshly exploited and dispossessed of the values produced by their labor, but a matter of the very ways we have organized work, and a matter of the goods we produce and the goals for which we work. It is no longer a matter of arrogant lords having their way with underlings, but a matter of no visible, personal authority at all: just a system; millions of anonymous technicians, managers, and bureaucrats entangling life in webs of regulation. Alienation today is sweeping and systemic. It is rooted in our very values and embodied in our characteristic ways of doing things. Political and economic alienation and estrangement still persist, of course, but now their forms are much more abstract and their sources harder to identify than when Locke, Montesquieu, Rousseau, and Marx analyzed them. Political and economic alienation are both now absorbed in, assimilated to, an encompassing system of technical alienation. Process is in command. State, economy, and society are remote, huge, and thoroughly technicized and bureaucratized. Hence, the sources and mechanisms of alienation are abstract, almost atmospheric, and we have little direct, specific apprehension of them. We "experience" them only at several removes of reflection.

Dispossession today is best described as dispossession of the self. By this I mean a number of things. One is a reduction, in the sociological sense, of what it means to be a person, of the very content of personhood. Place, family, tradition, religion, vocation—the stuff of personhood—are losing meaning and vitality. The result is a thinning out of the substance of selfhood, of what it means to be a self. Accompanying this thinning out are a dispersal of goals and human capacities, and the drying up of autonomous centers of decision, both in individuals and in local associations. For millions of people politics, work, religion and even family are wastelands and shadowlands, unsubstantial and unrewarding, yet annoying and confining. In addition, what we have long thought of as adult life and experience is losing its power to call and command. We are in the midst of a confused and noisy retreat from the ideals of dignity, self-restraint, vocation, and responsibility. These ideals are being replaced by others which are either infantile or adolescent. There is the childish world of television with its minimal demands on attention and intelligence, its simple moral formulas and trivialization of experience, its call to fulfillment through consumption. The mass media teach that the best world is that of the nursery, with feeding on demand. There is the adolescent ideal, which defines as the "real" experiences exploration and expression, being lonely and misunderstood, absorption in private pains, having vast inner potential which others do not appreciate and which can find no worthy test in the world. The adolescent sees being a star as the only significant life; and that is not because starhood is an adult vision of life but because it is the supreme adolescent fantasy of life.

Alienation and dispossession, then, now touch us at the deepest levels, and if remedial action is to be effective it must be directed there. But it is hard to know what such action might look like. Unable to experience the causes of our distresses directly, most efforts at remedy—our rebellions, liberation movements, and antiestablishment attitudes—are confused and misdirected, more likely to exacerbate than to ameliorate the real problems. The recent rise of terrorism in the advanced countries is one expression of this. Convinced of their own moral purity, the terrorists propose to purge the system by a violent assertion of will. The Jarvis-Gann Amendment is another. Sick of the burdens of big government, and outraged that a lot of cheats and malingerers seemed to be getting something for nothing, the little people of California voted themselves a small tax cut and voted the real estate corporations a big one, and also assured the firing of some thousands of workers on the bottom and at the margins of public employment. Still another (though I know the story is mixed and not yet finished) is the reduction of the women's movement into demands for sexual freedom on the one side, and for equal treatment in the job market on the other. The first side is a perfect example of what Herbert Marcuse meant by repressive desublimation. The ultimate effect of the second probably will be a great expansion of what Marx called the industrial reserve army of capitalism, while its more immediate effect is to increase competition for jobs most of which are harmful or not worth doing. Both sides feed the ethos of privatism and self-indulgence, and extend relations of contract and the cash nexus into more and more areas of life. The chief beneficiary of most recent efforts at reconstruction is the established system.

Meanwhile, those who consider themselves the guardians of the true revolutionary doctrine and tradition of the Left, when not engaged in sectarian hair-splitting, still point the finger of blame at specific groups of men and specific peak institutions. The publications of the Trilateral Commission now enjoy the same celebrity on the Left that the Protocols of the Elders of Zion once enjoyed on the right.

Now, of course, there are great disparities of wealth, income, and power in the capitalist and state-socialist societies. And of course some groups benefit more, or suffer less, from the system than do others. Some entrenched groups can make part of the system work to their own advantage, assuring themselves a cushion against all but the hardest blows. And, certainly, these inequalities are hard to justify by any doctrine of justice or any theory of social efficiency.

But anyone who still supposes that a juster distribution of social costs and benefits constitutes a radical approach to the problem of alienation is closer to 1848 than to 1980. It helps little to attack the ruling class when the values, methods, and attitudes of the managers are shared widely across all regions of the social landscape, and when the system of production, distribution, control, and communication is pervaded by a technological and consumerist orientation with its own built-in logic which crosses all classes and involves all strata. When Marx wrote, the farmers and working classes still had integral and distinctive cultures with their own authority and identity, and could thus offer genuine alternatives to the culture of capitalism. Under those conditions, it made much sense to talk about replacing one class with another, or defending the integrity of one culture against another. But that is not the case today when the classes and strata have been homogenized to a degree inconceivable to the early socialists. Such cultural differences as remain are largely vestigial, or they are puffed up for the profits that can be taken from them, or they are indulged in for the pleasures that can be derived from the narcissism of small differences.

In summary, the great invention of revolution no longer works as a method of renewal. Technical methods and the technical outlook pervade virtually all social formations and processes. More and more people flee from adult visions of life. The consumerist mentality has no strong rival. The populations of the Western countries have accepted the state as the legitimate Grand Inquisitor. Its task is to feed and comfort them, assuring their security and happiness. What is called politics today is largely the administration of the feeding system, and that system has grown so swollen and complex that no general program for changing it on the broad political level and by political means has much chance of producing good results. All programs are simplistic. Besides, any social formation designed to effect basic change at the level of the whole system reproduces in itself the very characteristics of the system it is designed to change— huge scale, hierarchical organization, intricate division of labor and specialization of function, use of the methods of propaganda and mass manipulation. We shall probably see more and more rebellions, but revolution can no longer spring from the fountain of rebellion. The two no longer have the connection they had in earlier days, when the causes of oppression and alienation were tangible and identifiable, so that the rebellious spirit could fix the right target and strike accurately against the agencies which were directly experienced as the obstacles to fulfillment. Under our conditions, rebellion usually misses the mark, hitting what is near and obvious—mere pasteboard masks of the complex and remote causes of our distress.

We do indeed need, as Tocqueville said, a new political science for this new age. It is not likely that those who develop this new science will want to lead revolutions, or that masses will want to follow them.

V

So, by a circuitous path, I reach the familiar conclusion. Yes, there is a crisis of values and authority among us. That crisis takes the dual form of the hollowing out of the great cultural commitments of the West, along with the incapacity of large-scale political movements to produce genuine transformations. The crisis has been brought on by devotion to the religion of technology with its passion for profits and power on the one side, and its craving for limitless consumption on the other—as though living the good life meant making lots of trash and having big bowel movements.

Seen from another angle of vision, the crisis takes the form of a societal growth that is so rapid and complex as to be cancerous. The growth consumes the very energies and destroys the processes that keep social life in a shifting balance and able to correct its own disorders. Growth has been so rapid that it destroys our collective capacities for self-determination and outruns the processes, institutions, and interests that reweave and repair the fabric of social life. We are also, of course, destroying the self-controlling and self-restoring processes and capacities of the nonhuman biosphere.

Our lives, then, are moving in directions and at a pace that we ourselves would not choose, if we *could* choose. Among the few hopeful signs of the times is that more and more people are becoming aware that this is the case. We are becoming aware that our distresses in large part result from the fact that we have outrun our collective ability to cope with our situation. There is increasing recognition that our institutions are so unwieldy, gigantic, complex, and centralized that they are beyond our powers of control. Furthermore, the religion of progress and growth through technology comes increasingly under challenge. There is now a doubter for every believer, even though the believers are still in charge, and even though the doubters are not united in doctrine and purpose.

These are truly hopeful signs, indicating that we might be ready to seek remedies for the deepest disorder of our age, which is Faustianism. We might be shaking off the mad dream of escaping mortality and even dependence on other human beings through total knowledge and control, the dream whose daytime form is the technological project, the dream whose nightmare end was already foretold in Plato's rendering in the *Protagoras* of the Prometheus myth. Giving up the Faustian dream will also require giving up schemes to change the whole system at the level of the system. Here again we must recognize our limitations, and see in them our strength. When Ho Chi Minh was asked how the NLF could perservere knowing the crushing weight of the "objective" forces arrayed against them, he responded that as good Marxists the NLF emphasized the "subjective" factors, which were all in their favor. To try to take charge of the whole system would require such gigantic effort that the social formations capable of producing the required energy would be themselves too huge to be comprehended and governed intelligently by the persons who comprise them. The means required to effect change at the level of the whole would inevitably reproduce within themselves the worst features of the system itself.

Most of the organizations and thinkers on the established Marxist left—those who claim to be today's radicals and legitimate heirs of yesterday's radicals—have wound up setting themselves against most of the hopeful directions of cultural renewal in our time. Most such organizations and thinkers still propose to change the whole system at the level of the system. They still believe that the basic task is to replace one ruling group with another. They still focus on the fact that some groups can make parts of the system work to their own advantage, while others, with less leverage, get less than a just share of the good things. This leads to a politics of redistribution, which, far from breaking the dynamic of exploitation and consumption, far from limiting the technological imperative, far from reducing organizations to a scale of human control and intelligibility, only adds fuel to the fire. That is surely the case with the large Marxist parties of Western Europe, which are as bureaucratic in their practices and as technocratic in their policies as the social systems they would transform. And insofar as those parties have a vision of a better society, it is a vision of a kind of utilitarianism perfected, with benevolent experts managing the factories and distributing the product according to scientific formulas assuring fair shares for all.

Now, I do not mean to bring a blanket indictment against the whole Left. And if I single out the Left for criticism that is because the Right has for many decades had nothing to offer that even merits critical attention. Almost everything that is noble and generous in the struggle for emancipation from political, social, and religious servitude since 1776 has come from the Left. Rather, I mean only to say that the efforts and achievements of the Marxist and semi-Marxist Left are flawed monuments to the flawed theory of the centralized party and state as the proper instruments for effecting social change, and that those same parties and movements have worshipped the gods of technology and development as uncritically as have the forces of the Center and Right.

Furthermore, Marx's own thought contained a large measure of the Faustian urge. Marx saw the driving force of history as the endless production and reproduction of human needs. But his conception of human "needs" and human "necessity" was naive and superficial. Or, to put it differently, the desires that impel us to the endless pursuit of more and more are something other than the mastery over nature, the elimination of scarcity, the achievement of material well-being, and the freedom from necessity which he stressed. Such "needs" are, I think, surface expressions, disguised symptoms, of the truly basic human need of finding a way to bear the emotional burdens of mortality and the inescapable weaknesses of the flesh. What Marx thought of as needs are really attempted consolations and evasions of our inescapable condition of being creatures who know we must die. They are efforts, projected onto the societal level, to "forget" our early and very real total dependence on others, and efforts to find material substitutes for our earliest fantasies of total power.

Marx, then, was one of those who recommended the Faustian path. In order to explain the insatiable urge for progress, which, he argued, sustained the dialectic of labor in history, Marx postulated a "law" of human nature to the effect that the satisfaction of human "needs" always generates new needs. Such a law obviously means that radical discontent is incurable. Hence, we must see as our fate an endless spiral of discontent and attempted mastery accelerating into the future. That future already announced itself in the mushroom cloud over Hiroshima, and we need not renew the invitation to it. Marx was among those who could not face the emotional tasks required of the animal that knows it must die. Instead, he invites us to an endless evasion of that task, in the form of the war against shortage, failing to recognize that we can never escape the ultimate shortage. Rather than talk about the endless production and reproduction of new human "needs," what we need are counsels, institutions, and consolations which can discipline and limit our narcotic gratifications, while helping us find the courage to face the emotional terrors of vulnerability, separation, and final helplessness.

It should be obvious that I do not think there is any way we can Faust ourselves out of the present. It should also be obvious that I think that the only way to make the system governable by intelligence and embraceable by healthy feeling is to break it into smaller social units whose scale is calibrated to our own senses and emotions, and which change at a pace which does not require us to forget all old attachments and abandon all old ways. Finally, I do not think the organization of a new mass party on national—let alone international—lines is the vehicle which will take us into a better future.

Furthermore, even if a new party were the solution, it would not be available to us. There is no large, nascent "we," whether radical or conservative, ready to be galvanized into life by the right issues and leaders. There is a widespread sharing of mood, but that mood is privatistic and defeatist. There are many who share a common condition, but that condition teaches apathy and retreat. Neither the old parties nor any of the recent efforts to build new kinds of organizations (New American Movement, Common Cause, the Black Panther Party, Tom Hayden's CED, the women's movement) has any solid base in popular sentiment. The old parties still have much power, of course, because they are tied into the system of privilege and law at a thousand points, and because there is no visible alternative to them. But they are buildings whose foundations are sagging and whose roofs leak. Their tenants are fleeing by the millions. Jimmy Carter was elected to the Presidency by about one-quarter of the eligible electorate, and that single fact says everything important about the houses of the Democrats and Republicans.

The question, then, is not what direction "the movement" or "the party" should take, for there is no party or movement. It is, rather, toward what broad and largely unsurveyed region should we look for resources that might just possibly, with much skill and effort, and some luck, be made suitable for new foundations? If I am right, if alienation does now touch us at the deepest levels, threatening to decompose the person, it is there that the work must begin. It would be better to forget parties as such. We do not need a new party with a new set of slogans, and even if we did we could not build one, for the resources are not there. We do need new attitudes and experiences which stress and teach human limits and interdependence, and we also need new social forms scaled to our capacities for direct apprehension and designed to help us endure the necessary burdens and relish the possible joys of our shared condition as creatures aware of their own mortality and their dependence on each other. Beyond that, not very much can be said; or, at least, I have no program. I have only a few suggestions as to where we might look for the beginnings of a new political orientation.

VI

When it comes to politics today, most of us are children—albeit rather greedy children, albeit children who have some voice in selecting their parents. Most of what we call politics at the popular level is the selection of those who will govern us, and who in return for the privileges of office promise to protect us from our own weaknesses, from each other, and from our enemies. This is called Liberal Democracy, and it does provide freedom from public concerns for those who want both to be left alone and to be taken care of. It lets nearly all of us, when we wish, disclaim responsibility for whatever the government does that we do not like, while still accepting every advantage we are offered or can extract from that government.

This system has many advantages, but the encouragement of moral maturity among the subjects is not one of them. Nor does the system augment the human capacity for action, or encourage our capacity for joining with others to take care for the general quality of the common life. Nor can the political system as such be seen as the defender of liberty. We have escaped tyranny not because we love liberty, and not by reason of the good design of our institutions, but because the eyes of the politicians and their masters have been fixed on money. They have not been ambitious. Nor can the system even be said to provide security against enemy states. Despite—or, rather, because of—its vast weaponry and huge military establishment; despite—or, rather because of—our continued willingness to pay for this weaponry and establishment, the modern state simply cannot defend the lives and property of its subjects against attack by any other modern state. All it can do is exact revenge: if you kill a hundred million of us, we will kill a hundred million of you, even if that should wreck the planet for all.[5]

So, it must be said that the chief obstacle in the way of starting the work of reconstituting authority and creating values and institutions fit for human beings is that institution which presently claims authority—the state, the present structure of political power. But it will not do to attack that structure frontally, or to try to "take it over" and shape it to new purposes. The state also exists in the minds of the subjects, and that is where it is best attacked. It exists in the minds of the subjects in the form of a few attitudes, and these can be changed. In shorthand expression, these attitudes are privatism, materialiam, moral absenteeism, and the passion for security. These are the attitudes which hold us in moral bondage and make us moral children. Children of course require supervisors lest their exuberance get out of hand and they harm each other. The state gladly serves as nursery attendant—albeit at considerable cost, and despite its inability to defend the nursery against attack—but on the condition that the children do not try to grow up and join with others to take charge of their lives together.

Put differently, we must overcome the attitude that "someone else is in charge and I just work here, getting what I can, doing what I must." In political terms, we must learn to stop thinking of politics as government, as the regulation of affairs by elected and appointed custodians. Properly understood, politics is all those activities concerned with the shaping and the sharing of the common life, and those activities are for everybody. The basic political question is what shall we do, and that is a question for everybody.

The goal of any revitalization movement, then, must be the formation of a free and acting citizenry. The goal is best approached neither by trying to capture the state nor by trying to extract benefits and privileges from it, but by ignoring it as far as possible. We must liberate ourselves from the myth that government "programs" can solve our problems. Every time we turn toward Sacramento or Washington we turn away from the places where people can take care of themselves and each other—the places where they live and work.

Develop alternative institutions. Proceed as though the state were not there. It will come to you soon enough, with both kindly and threatening offers, but if you have done your work well you will be prepared to resist both the blandishments and the threats. In the design of these alternative institutions, there should be the least possible division of labor and specialization of function, the fewest possible fixed and rigid roles. Above all, struggle against a sharp division between those who command and those who obey. The model should be that of an association in which those who decide are as nearly as possible identical with those who implement the decision.

What I am mainly recommending is the launching of thousands of small, local experiments in community living, each trying to find its own path to the development of many-sided persons, each exploring its own vision of life. These experiments would have much power as examples, both good and bad, and at least some of them would develop richer ways to live a life than those currently dominant. The experiments would also develop new connections and networks of association among their participants, thereby acting against the atomization and bureaucratization of modern societies, thereby doing something to strengthen the social bond and restore depth and stability to human relationships. Persons who are fully associated in the shaping and sharing of a common life do not need administrators to supervise their affairs.[6]

Perhaps the single most important subject for experimentation is work, because work is the single most important way persons touch and shape reality, develop their own identities and abilities, and contribute to the lives of others. The notion that people should be liberated from work is mad: Faulkner's statement that we must work because there is nothing else we can do for hour after hour—not eat, or play, or make love—is simple and inescapable good sense. But that need not mean that to work is to suffer. There is nothing better than good work, and nothing more ruinous than spending forty hours a week doing something that is no good. For most people a job, or working, is something someone else will pay them for doing, regardless of its effect on the worker, the employer, or the larger community. Under that definition, many people are unemployed, and most are underemployed or badly employed. We need new definitions of work, and new criteria of good work, for the present ones are cruel and stupid. We might begin by trying as far as possible to separate work from wages, and look on work as those productive activities which the worker and the community, after rational and humane consideration, find worth doing. Let the activity be done with as much grace and dignity as possible, and let the workers develop their own distinctions between tools that genuinely save labor and enhance skill, and those that serve primarily to increase profit and productivity—with productivity defined simply as the largest output at the least cost.

Most recent thought on how to deal with the degradation of work follows one of two paths. The first, exemplified by, say, Murray Bookchin in his *Post-Scarcity Anarchism,* or by Herbert Marcuse in some of his phases, in effect writes off work, holding that since we cannot much raise its quality we should lower its quantity. Let the machines do the work, freeing people for better things.

There is something to be said for this view, since if working is bad the less of it the better. Still, this strategy gives up too much. Suppose that, having turned over to the machines as much as we can, we are still left with twenty or thirty hours of bad work a week. That is too much life to waste. For another thing, this approach also gives up on the whole question of quality—of what work is done, what goods made, at what cost. Shoddy, wasteful, and superfluous goods are what they are, and it is no tribute to intelligence to make them by machine rather than by human power. Furthermore, this strategy also gives up on the question of what people will do with their new free hours. Leaving everything else as it is, and merely reducing the time wasted in bad work, might only expand the time wasted in bad "leisure": more time for TV and hobbies. Finally, the "liberation through technology" policy feeds one of the most dehumanizing tendencies of our time--turning people into personnel, making humans appendages of machines. In *The Machine Stops,* written over fifty years ago, E. M. Forster already foretold the destination of this route.

The second main approach to the question of the quality of work is that of worker control or self-management of the workplace, along with various schemes for placing representatives of workers and the public on the governing bodies of economic organizations. E. F. Schumacher, in his *Small is Beautiful*, has made some interesting suggestions for public representation in corporations. Advocates of worker self-management cite favorably the (short-lived) experiments in Yugoslavia. Some attention has been given to schemes of job-rotation, and to the replacing of isolated, specialized assembly line workers by self-directing teams which set their own rhythms and make a whole product. Practices followed in a few Swedish and West German factories are often cited as examples of the possibilities here.

This route offers more promise than the first one because it does understand that the main problem is to change the character of work itself. Still, it is not without tough obstacles, many of which result from the fact that thinking in this area is characteristically constricted by an outmoded image of reality. The writers write as though the "real" work situation today were much the same as that of the factory workers described by Marx in the nineteenth century. The blue-collar worker, and specifically the "man on the assembly line," is taken as the standard case.

But that is inaccurate. In the advanced technological economies, assembly-line workers make up a small (and declining) fraction of the total labor force. More importantly, the problem of stupid and shameful work runs far beyond the blue-collar classes. It affects the white-collar classes as well, ranging from the lowest clerk to the highest executive, and including the professions. The degradation may be even deeper when the collar is white. Or, at least, today all collars are gray. It is not easy to see how the worker self-management idea deals with this reality.

Even on the factory floor, within the assembly line and mass production setting, the worker control idea has narrow limits. The big decisions, such as those concerning investment policies, will still be made elsewhere, and they will affect everything else. And any scheme of representation, especially within a large and complex setting, has all the familiar shortcomings of the representative device as such: membership apathy; the need for technical knowledge; the dangers of cooptation; use of the methods of propaganda and mass persuasion. Besides, worker self-control, by itself, does nothing to assure justice or even a voice to all the many others who are affected by the activities of a large factory or corporation. And finally, some—myself among them—think there is no way to humanize or democratize, or even make efficient and honest the gigantic and complex organizations which dominate employment and production today. "Giving the workers a voice" at best deals with symptoms, not causes. At worst, it becomes another aspect of managerial control.

So, while such efforts and ideas have some utility, they do not go far enough. Of all the possibilities in this realm, job rotation and exchange perhaps has the greatest potential. It is the easiest to implement. It is the one most likely to give persons real satisfaction and least likely to arouse inflated hopes. It increases knowledge and enlarges the capacity for empathy in the most natural way. It guards against self-deception and deception of others. It can be a lot of fun, and it provides one way to distribute more equitably a lot of jobs which must be done but which are unpleasant or dangerous in the doing. The lives of millions of people would be enriched if they did twelve or fifteen jobs over a lifetime rather than one, or if they did one or two enduring and main jobs punctuated by periods of other kinds of work. The notion has some obvious limitations when it comes to cabinet makers and philologists, say, who need many years to perfect their craft, but I am not so sure it would hurt such people to take an occasional turn at collecting garbage or teaching nursery school.

Of course, a lot of job changing goes on now and it is not clear that it produces all that much more satisfaction among the changers. Most of the job changing does not involve really substantial differences in style of work: the welder does not change places with the chairman of the board; the logger doesn't trade with the nurse. To make much difference in the lives of individuals and in the texture of the social order, the jobs that are changed must be importantly different. And of course, the changes must be largely voluntary; otherwise we shall only create another bureaucratic empire, the Office of Employment Rotation and Exchange, with national, regional, state, and local offices, an army of intricately graded specialists, and a byzantine set of rules.

Despite their deficiencies, job rotation and worker self-management and public representation ideas are still worth exploring and expanding. I think, however, that they should be seen less as practical solutions to the problem of the quality of work than as educational and agitational levers to help pry apart the monolithic idea of "ownership" as exclusive possession and to break up ownership into a heterogeneous assortment of rights, duties, and interests, to be worked out piecemeal and case-by-case. The self-governing workers' groups and the public representatives on corporate governing bodies could gradually, pragmatically, set restrictions on the prerogatives of owners and managers. This path offers more promise than the coarse methods of expropriation and nationalization.

But this still does not reach to the root of the problem of how to make work and the products of work significantly better than they now are. The root is the connection between work and wages. That connection must be loosened. I shall make some suggestions about how to do this toward the end of the essay.

Most effort should go into local experiments mentioned above, and into efforts which simultaneously give workers more control over their work and challenge the monolithic idea of the ownership of productive resources. On a broader but still local level, and working in and through established political jurisdictions, a few pieces of legislation might be suggested. Every effort must be made to destroy the stranglehold of the educational bureaucracy, and to make most education a voluntary and private (as distinguished from what is now meant by "public" in this context) concern. Public education should be reduced to the one basic job of reducing the empire of incompetence in the basic skills and subjects. Local jurisdictions should pass laws requiring any economic enterprise which decides to move elsewhere to first clean up all the trash it leaves behind, and to repair all the damage, human and material, left by its departure. We need a new Homestead Act which would permit individuals or small associations to settle freely on unoccupied public lands, excepting parks and wilderness areas, and to make habitations there, so long as they bring in no building materials, weapons, or power tools. Local jurisdictions should establish financial institutions to buy up abandoned and declining rural properties, selling them on easy terms to energetic and competent persons who would try to turn them back into working farms.

At the state and national level, and in the arenas of electoral politics, electoral blocs should be formed for voting candidates up or down on two issues. Leave theoretical discussion to the theorists. Leave coalition juggling to the inside-dopesters and power brokers. Ask candidates just two questions, and vote for or against them according to how they answer: (l) will the candidate work to make the members of corporate boards of director personally liable for the damages and injuries caused by the activities and products of the corporations? (2) will the candidate work toward the abolition of all forms and uses of nuclear power? Hound candidates on these two questions as single-mindedly as the gun lobby, say, hounds them on "the right to bear arms." Over time, a strong bloc of anticorporation and antinuclear power legislators at both state and national level would be built up by this pressure politics tactic.

The first of these measures would mean trouble for the limited liability corporation, for corporations would not exist in anything like their present form if their directors had to accept personal responsibility for corporate actions. The beauty of the idea is its sledgehammer simplicity and its appeal to the old virtue of personal responsibility. Simplicity is what is needed here, for efforts to "regulate" the corporations have been ineffective. The modern corporate form itself is deadly, and must be destroyed. Obviously, this cannot be done overnight, for although the corporations victimize and stupefy us, we cannot now get along without them. One of the main tasks of the local experiments is that of developing multicompetent persons who are not dependent on huge corporations for their jobs, and who do not need, or who can themselves produce, many of the things that the corporations now provide.

The second measure—ending nuclear power—would undermine the "defense" establishment, and help bring people to the realization that their only real defense is a patriotic citizenry prepared to resist to the end any invasion by a foreign power. It would also bring some urgency to the present half-hearted efforts to conserve energy and to develop alternative forms and sources of energy. And finally, it would make the world a safer and more decent place to live in, both for ourselves and for those who will come after us. As things are going now, the main gifts our generation is giving to those yet unborn are a depleted planet and deposits of lethal radioactive wastes. We shall be cursed for that; and the archeologists of the future who dig around in our dumping grounds are in for some fatal surprises.

Back to the basic question, which is the definition of work and the connection between work and wages, or work and economic survival. I am pretty sure that the path out of the present malaise must take its bearing from this reference point.[7]

Everybody knows the gross facts:

- Millions are unemployed or underemployed; hardest hit are the young, the unskilled, racial and ethnic minority groups, and women;
- Millions work at jobs they hate;
- For a variety of reasons, millions are unemployable and must depend on the dole for subsistence;
- A sizeable number of professional guilds and trade unions hold a near stranglehold over entry into various lines of work, and over wages and the conditions of work in various sectors of the economy. These organizations show little regard for the interests of anyone save themselves;
- Huge and expensive "welfare" bureaucracies manage the poor and the wretched, alleviating some of their worst pains, but unable or unwilling to help them out of the ruts of incapacity and despair;
- More and more people express dissatisfaction with the quality and cost of products and services. The workers, it is said, don't care about doing a good job, and much of what is produced is defective;
- Some substantial portion of crime is rooted in the conditions of poverty and joblessness;
- Managers try wherever possible to replace workers by machines;
- There is an enormous amount of dishonest work, ranging from feather-bedding and make-work through malingering and deception and on to outright lying;
- Nobody really understands all the causes of inflation, but surely some of those causes are to be found in the conditions listed above;
- The gap between the richest and the poorest classes is large. Nor has it appreciably narrowed for twenty-five years.

This is an incomplete picture, composed of the grossest materials. Nobody even knows how to reckon the costs of the wage-work system in terms of lost talent and wasted dreams. We all know those losses are huge, and we seem to accept them. That may be the worst part of the whole picture, for if there were more anger, there would be more hope. Failing that, we can only expect the deadlock to continue. There is a lot of self-contempt in that, almost as though we do not regard ourselves as worth saving.

To break the deadlock we must weaken the connection between work and wages, for that is the master link in the chain that holds the whole irrational and contemptible system together.

Suppose a duplex economy, with one side for those who will work in order to enjoy the things that only a good bit of money can buy, and the other side for those who either do not care much for those things or who want to work in ways and towards ends which bring little monetary reward but which might bring great rewards of other kinds. The simplest way to move toward this dual economy would be to guarantee a subsistence income for all who ask for it. This income would be granted upon request, as a matter of right: no means tests; no eligibility rules; no huge bureaucracy. This subsistence income might be set at, say, six or seven thousand dollars a year for a single adult, with allotments to families or other living units set according to the size of the unit. People could in principle enter and leave the subsistence economy whenever they wished, though it might be sensible to impose a required minimum time, say four or five years, both to avoid frivolity and to give employers some fair sense of the available labor pool. It might also make sense to set a maximum of eight or ten years, mainly in order to insure that everybody who wanted to get into the subsistence economy could do so.

But—keep the rules barebones. The main idea is that there should be a subsistence economy for all who want it, and a wage and money economy for all who want that. No one would have to choose between working and going on welfare or stealing in order to survive at a level of decent subsistence. And do not worry about cheaters. There are so many and so many kinds of them now that the alternative I am proposing would probably reduce their numbers and variety.

This system has many attractive features, not the least of which is that everybody can understand it, while practically nobody understands or is satisfied with the intricate, numerous, and often conflicting provisions of today's welfare systems. The dual economy would at one stroke abolish unemployment, provide a genuinely willing work force, and raise wages and working conditions to a level where hired work would be well-paid indeed, and made as attractive to employees as it could possibly be made. It would also virtually abolish the social welfare industry in all its many branches. It would probably be cheaper in actual dollar terms than the present welfare-unemployment industry. It would certainly cost less in human terms—in the outrages worked on human dignity, and in the degradations of human power caused by the present system of no work for many and bad work for most.

With that, the greatest potential benefit of the scheme comes into view. Remember that the dual economy idea differs not just from the present welfare programs but also from such schemes as the negative income tax or family allotment plans in that no one would be in it who did not want to be. All the other measures currently in force or contemplated include only the losers and the victims, along with, I suppose, a few freeloaders. Under the dual plan, however, most of those in the subsistence economy would be there because they wanted to be, because there was something they wanted to do with their time that seemed more valuable to them than working for money. This means that many, many people of ability, vision, and energy might enter the subsistence side of the economy. We can be pretty sure they would not waste their time. We can be pretty sure that there would appear among us a flowering of creative experimentation with new ways of working, learning, and living. This land would flower as never before. Its future would be in the right hands.

It is of course possible that there may not be enough time for us to call up our powers of social invention and devise the means of rescue. Any call to action today must reach people who are as short of memory as they are of vision. We are sleepwalkers approaching a precipice. Our judgments of our prospects are clouded by fear and cynicism, and by the knowledge that at least two governments, swollen and stupid with power, can virtually destroy civilization in an hour. We see all around us persons haunted by intimations of the end of the human experiment, whether in war, or the despoilation of the earth, or the wasteland of bureaucratic and technological coordination.

So there is no guarantee that my few suggestions will "work," or that there will be time for any suggestions to work. Nothing is assured. Perhaps all we can be sure of is that if we do not look upon ourselves as creatures worth saving, we will go down. But if we do have remnants of virtue as men and women we must begin seeking social arrangements that encourage intelligence, generosity, and honor. I have tried to argue that that search should look toward social forms and relations that are cooperative, localist, and versatile, and away from those that are statist, centralized, and specialist.

Notes

1. Thucydides, *The Peloponnesian War*, the Hobbes translation (Ann Arbor, Mich.: University of Michigan Press, 1959), 2 Vols., Vol. 1, pp. 111-112. The first sentence is a pure distillate of the seventeenth-century style, but easily

misconstrued by a modern reader. The literal rendering of the Greek, according to David Grene, is "We are lovers of beauty, but with cheapness; we are lovers of culture, but without softness."
2. I trust it is clear that I have not been discussing the crisis of culture in the sense of the crisis in the status and function of the high arts. If there is a crisis in the world of art today, it is part of the meaning of mass society. It reflects the demand of the masses for entertainment and the assimilation of the arts to that demand: art as circuses for millions who have bread. Art as entertainment has nothing to do with the enduring functions of art—a mode of experience for the enlargement of human sensibilities and the cultivation of taste and discriminating judgment. Great art legislates, naming and selecting the highest and best out of the jungle of emotions, events, and experiences. In this way, art is like philosophy; or, philosophy, rightly understood, is among the arts. Nietzsche reminded us of this in his wonderful essay on the early Greek philosophers: "The Greek word designating 'sage' is etymologically related to *sapio*, I taste, *sapiens*, he who tastes, *sisyphos*, the man of keenest taste. A sharp savoring and selecting, a meaningful discriminating, in other words, makes out the peculiar art of the philosopher, in the eyes of the people. . . . Philosophy is distinguished from science by its selectivity and its discrimination of the unusual, the astonishing, the difficult and the divine. . . . Science rushes headlong, without selectivity, without 'taste,' . . . in the blind desire to know all at any cost. Philosophical thinking, on the other hand, is ever on the scent of those things which are most worth knowing, the great and the important insights." *Philosophy in the Tragic Age of the Greeks*, tr. by Marianne Cowan (South Bend, Indiana: Gateway, 1962), p. 43.
3. I am aware that California produces more than its fair share of these commodities, with one-half of its people selling one or another spiritual cure and the other half buying. Still, California has often shown the laggard states their future.
4. What follows owes much to Jacques Ellul, *The Betrayal of the West*, tr. by Matthew J. O'Connel (New York, N.Y.: Seabury Press, 1978). For all its spleen this book has more to say about our cultural condition than any other recent work known to me.
5. Working to destroy the illusion that the state is the guarantor of security is the single most important, political-educational task of our time. War is inherent in the system of sovereign states. Locke spoke the elementary truth: "Want of a common judge with authority puts all men in a state of nature." Some people think that nuclear weapons make war unlikely among the great powers, since they recognize that such a war is too horrible to fight. But President Kennedy was ready to go to war with the Soviet Union in the Cuban Missile Crisis. The Soviet Union and China are now turning each other into devils, whipping up more hostility than natural rivalries require. China will surely begin to buy sophisticated weapons from the West, thereby setting off a new spiral in the arms race. There is no international system of crisis management. President Carter has given higher priority to attacking the Soviet Union over human rights than to cooperating with it over disarmament. These facts surely indicate that the great powers do not understand the real danger of war.

Nuclear weapons may have postponed doomsday. On the other hand, those weapons may only shuttle war from the big powers to their proxies and clients, as is now happening in Africa and Asia. Or, as Orwell imagined, nuclear weapons may only provide an outer limit short of which the giants fight with "conventional" weapons. Then, there is nuclear proliferation, which increases the likelihood of war with the addition of each new member to the "nuclear club."

We are farther now from Locke's "common judge" than we were immediately after the destruction of the Tower of Babel.

6. There is some urgency about this. The current economic distresses, and especially the slowing down of growth and the shortage of cheap energy, are already producing angry and panicky reactions. They also raise a strong possibility of a more stringently controlled political economy. We may expect state-corporate arrangements imposing more and tighter controls over many sorts of decisions and goods. There is no reason whatever to expect such arrangements to reduce the size, power, or rewards of the administrative and corporate establishments. Rather, the weakest and most distressed sectors of the population will be pressed even harder. Anger and resentment will grow, and so will the need for police. Only vigorous associations which are dedicated to autonomy and collective development, and whose members are tied together in strong networks of affiliation and mutual help, will have much chance either of standing apart from the vicious race for diminishing resources, or of withstanding the likely state-corporative efforts at coordination.

7. What follows was stimulated by the teachings of Peter Kropotkin, Miles Horton, Paul Goodman, and Wendell Berry. Frithjof Bergmann develops the dual economy idea in his *On Being Free* (Notre Dame, Indiana: University of Notre Dame Press, 1977), esp. pp. 177-231.